Inequality in the Developing World

UNU World Institute for Development Economics Research (UNU-WIDER) was established by the United Nations University as its first research and training centre and started work in Helsinki, Finland, in 1985. The mandate of the institute is to undertake applied research and policy analysis on structural changes affecting developing and transitional economies, to provide a forum for the advocacy of policies leading to robust, equitable, and environmentally sustainable growth, and to promote capacity strengthening and training in the field of economic and social policy-making. Its work is carried out by staff researchers and visiting scholars in Helsinki and via networks of collaborating scholars and institutions around the world.

United Nations University World Institute for
Development Economics Research (UNU-WIDER)
Katajanokanlaituri 6B, 00160 Helsinki, Finland
www.wider.unu.edu

Inequality in the Developing World

Edited by
CARLOS GRADÍN, MURRAY LEIBBRANDT,
AND FINN TARP

A study prepared by the United Nations University World Institute
for Development Economics Research (UNU-WIDER)

OXFORD
UNIVERSITY PRESS

OXFORD
UNIVERSITY PRESS

Great Clarendon Street, Oxford, OX2 6DP,
United Kingdom

Oxford University Press is a department of the University of Oxford.
It furthers the University's objective of excellence in research, scholarship,
and education by publishing worldwide. Oxford is a registered trade mark of
Oxford University Press in the UK and in certain other countries

Published in the United States of America by Oxford University Press
198 Madison Avenue, New York, NY 10016, United States of America

British Library Cataloguing in Publication Data
Data available

Library of Congress Control Number: 2020945720

ISBN 978–0–19–886396–0

DOI: 10.1093/oso/9780198863960.001.0001

Printed and bound by
CPI Group (UK) Ltd, Croydon, CR0 4YY

Links to third party websites are provided by Oxford in good faith and
for information only. Oxford disclaims any responsibility for the materials
contained in any third party website referenced in this work.

Foreword

Inequality is a dominant challenge to development. It influences economic growth and redistribution, and feeds into power asymmetries that can jeopardize democratization and human rights, trigger conflict, and entrench chronic poverty. Inequality is at the core of the United Nations mandate, and is one of the seventeen goals of the 2030 Agenda for Sustainable Goals.

While global inequality fell, by and large, towards the end of the twentieth century, since the start of this century *within*-country inequality has been steadily rising—underpinning intense public and academic debates to the extent that it has become a prevailing policy concern of many countries and in all multilateral agencies.

There has been strong interest for decades in bringing both developed and developing countries together in the analysis of global inequalities and the forces shaping them. Initially the lack of adequate data for such was a fundamental handicap. To address this, UNU-WIDER established the (freely downloadable) World Income Inequality Database (WIID) which compiles income inequality information from primary sources for developed, developing, and transition countries. In turn, the WIID increased the volume of the voice for analytical research on between-country and within-country inequalities. Hence the launch of UNU-WIDER's Inequality in the Giants project—as part of a broad international effort designed to shed light on a set of new questions on such inequalities, by generating integrated datasets and applying a consistent methodology to investigate the determinants of inequality dynamics in ten of the world's largest economies: Brazil, China, France, India, Indonesia, Mexico, Russia, South Africa, the UK, and the US.

Employing advances made in recent decades on the measurement of inequality, as well as in the development of better data to analyse the processes which *generate* inequality, this book is the result of rigorous scientific work by a large team of international experts, each highly qualified within their respective research niches. I sincerely thank the editors—Carlos Gradín, Murray Leibbrandt, and Finn Tarp—for their sharp analytical and editorial skills, which result in giving us a more layered, more nuanced understanding of inequality in developing countries.

UNU-WIDER gratefully acknowledges the support and financial contributions to its research programme by the governments of Finland, Sweden, and the UK. Without this vital funding our research and policy advisory work would be impossible.

Kunal Sen

Director, UNU-WIDER
Helsinki, June 2020

Acknowledgements

This book has roots in discussions in late 2013/early 2014 between Francois Bourguignon, Francisco Ferreira, and Nora Lustig, later adding Murray Leibbrandt, to discuss a project idea put forward by Nora Lustig and referred to as 'Inequality in the Giants'. The team developed the preliminary set of notes from this meeting into a five-page draft research proposal, originally meant to cover nine of the biggest countries in the world (Brazil, China, France, India, Mexico, Russia, South Africa, the UK, and the US. Subsequently, Indonesia was included, so the target number of case countries ended up being ten.

The intention was to mobilize funding from different sources to implement the project with the team of four (above) as principal investigators. Finn Tarp, then director of UNU-WIDER, was invited to join the team, and a large number of potential contributors to the project were invited to a workshop on the sidelines of the UNU-WIDER conference Mapping the Future of Development Economics, held in Helsinki on 17–19 September 2015.

The workshop was productive in terms of ideas. Funding for the 'big' project did not materialize as originally hoped, however. Instead, UNU-WIDER managed to move forward with a subset of countries—namely Mexico, South Africa, and India—coordinated by respectively Nora Lustig, Murray Leibbrandt, and Peter Lanjouw. Subsequently China and Brazil, coordinated by Shi Li and Marcelo Cortes Neri, joined the project, while Carlos Gradín joined the coordination team. The coordinators and their respective teams of authors produced several studies on each country, which were published in the WIDER Working Paper series. Much of this work also reached academic journals.

We felt, however, that a comprehensive book and coherent statement was called for. We therefore put together a proposal that included both the attempt at analysing in-depth inequalities within our group of five large developing countries that jointly account for more than 40 per cent of the world's population and the relationship with global inequality issues. Accordingly, we proposed to frame five country syntheses by broader contributions from development economists who are leaders in the field of inequality measurement, trends, impact, and policies. They agreed and each provided an excellent take on a set of key framework-setting issues that contextualize the country case studies and put them in perspective.

We owe a profound debt to the original team of three for their inspiring stimulus. Their early notes and engagement in the work session organized with UNU-WIDER in September 2015 has been of great value. We would also like to express our most sincere gratitude to the chapter authors in this book for their willingness to participate in the research project and for their many insightful contributions. The same goes for the extensive and excellent group of collaborators on the background papers on each country case, synthesized here in this book.

Warm thanks are also due to UNU-WIDER for institutional support and never failing collaboration. We wish in particular to thank Lorraine Telfer-Taivainen, UNU-WIDER Editorial and Publishing Associate, for sound advice, hard work, and making the collaboration with Oxford University Press run smoothly. Adam Swallow, Economics and Finance Commissioning Editor at Oxford University Press, and his colleagues provided expert guidance with the publication process, and we do wish to acknowledge the anonymous referee reports that helped sharpen our focus and change the organization of the book.

Finally, a word of thanks to the donors of UNU-WIDER—Finland, Sweden, and the UK—for their core support to the work programme of UNU-WIDER, without which this book would not have been possible.

Carlos Gradín, Murray Leibbrandt, and Finn Tarp

Helsinki, Cape Town, and Copenhagen
June 2020

Contents

List of Figures   xi
List of Tables   xiii
List of Abbreviations   xv
Notes on Contributors   xvii

PART I. INTRODUCTION

1. Setting the Scene   3
   Carlos Gradín, Murray Leibbrandt, and Finn Tarp

PART II. GLOBAL INEQUALITY AND
INEQUALITY WITHIN COUNTRIES

2. What Might Explain Today's Conflicting Narratives on Global
   Inequality?   17
   Martin Ravallion

3. Comparing Global Inequality of Income and Wealth   49
   James Davies and Anthony Shorrocks

4. Empirical Challenges Comparing Inequality across Countries:
   The Case of Middle-Income Countries from the LIS Database   74
   Daniele Checchi, Andrej Cupak, and Teresa Munzi

PART III. INEQUALITY IN FIVE
DEVELOPING GIANTS

5. Brazil: What Are the Main Drivers of Income Distribution
   Changes in the New Millennium?   109
   Marcelo Neri

6. China: Structural Change, Transition, Rent-Seeking and
   Corruption, and Government Policy   133
   Shi Li, Terry Sicular, and Finn Tarp

7. India: Inequality Trends and Dynamics: The Bird's-Eye and the
   Granular Perspectives   157
   Hai-Anh H. Dang and Peter Lanjouw

8. Mexico: Labour Markets and Fiscal Redistribution 1989–2014   180
   Raymundo Campos-Vazquez, Nora Lustig, and John Scott

9. South Africa: The Top End, Labour Markets, Fiscal Redistribution,
   and the Persistence of Very High Inequality   205
   Murray Leibbrandt, Vimal Ranchhod, and Pippa Green

PART IV.   INEQUALITY IN A BROADER CONTEXT

10. Economic Inequality and Subjective Well-Being Across the World   233
    Andrew E. Clark and Conchita D'Ambrosio

11. China and the United States: Different Economic Models But
    Similarly Low Levels of Socioeconomic Mobility   257
    Roy van der Weide and Ambar Narayan

12. From Manufacturing-Led Export Growth to a Twenty-First
    Century Inclusive Growth Strategy: Explaining the Demise of a
    Successful Growth Model and What to Do about It   284
    Joseph E. Stiglitz

PART V.   SYNTHESIS AND POLICY IMPLICATIONS

13. Synthesis and Policy Implications   321
    Carlos Gradín, Murray Leibbrandt, and Finn Tarp

Index   339

List of Figures

2.1. Global inequality and its between- and within-country components 19

2.2. Inequality within the developing world 21

2.3. Relative inequality and growth in household income per capita 22

2.4. Global inequality for various weights on (log) national mean income 30

2.5. The elephant graph of Lakner and Milanovic 32

2.6. Lorenz curves for global income 1988 and 2008 33

2.7. Consumption floor for the developing world 36

2.8. Elephant or serpent? 38

2.9. Absolute inequality and growth in household income per capita 39

2.10. Plot of changes in absolute poverty against changes in absolute inequality across developing countries 40

3.1. Income inequality trends 2000–15, selected indices 56

3.2. Trends in wealth inequality vs income inequality, selected indices 57

3.3. Alternative decomposition routes 60

3.4. Between-country and within-country components of income inequality 61

3.5. Between-country and within-country components of wealth inequality 64

3.6. Counterfactual trends in income inequality 67

3.7. Counterfactual trends in wealth inequality 68

4.1. Impact of non-monetary incomes 79

4.2. Labour income availability at the individual level 80

4.3. Taxes and social security contributions as a percentage of total gross income 81

4.4. Extent of missing or zero income 83

4.5. Trends in income inequality (Gini index) in selected middle-income countries (USA as benchmark) 87

4.6. Evolution of income shares held by households with incomes below the 50th, and above the 90th and 95th percentiles 88

4.7. Inequality decomposition in labour incomes 91

4.8. Income inequality (Gini index) versus selected macroeconomic country characteristics 94

6.1. China's Gini coefficient 134

6.2. Growth incidence curves for China 136

6.3. The composition of household income in China 137

6.4. Primary sector employment in China as a share of total employment
       (per cent) 1980–2015   139

6.5. Wage growth of rural–urban migrant workers in China (%)   140

6.6. The shares of fiscal spending on education, medical insurance, social
       security, and agriculture in total budgetary expenditures in China   141

6.7. Growth of exports and imports of China (million US$)   142

7.1. Disparities in human capital outcomes, by social group   160

7.2. Impacts of upward mobility on consumption growth (at different
       percentiles: IV regression 1 (90% confidence bound)   175

8.1. Gini coefficient, 1989–2014   182

8.2. Decomposition of differences in the distribution of earnings: 1989–2014   185

8.3. Relative returns and relative supply of workers by education, college,
       and high school vs rest   187

8.4. Fiscal incidence analysis, core income concepts   194

8.5. Government transfers (% of GDP), 1988–2018   195

8.6. Fiscal policy and inequality, 1996–2015   196

8.7. Fiscal policy and poverty, 2008–15   197

9.1. Difference in estimated mean taxable income between NIDS and PIT
       by income bracket   214

9.2. Total effects of different variables over the distribution of earnings   218

9.3. Concentration curves for direct taxes   221

9.4. Distribution of selected fiscal benefits   222

9.5. The progressivity of each of the three main social cash transfers
       in South Africa   222

9.6. Socioeconomic class sizes, 2008–17   224

10.1. The distribution of the dependent variables   240

11.1. Great Gatsby Curve   263

11.2. Income mobility versus education mobility   264

11.3. Intergenerational mobility in education   266

11.4. Intergenerational mobility versus GDP per capita   268

12.1. Simulated manufacturing output shares   295

12.2. Manufacturing value added (% of GDP) in sub-Saharan Africa   296

12.3. Distribution of active population according to education level   304

List of Tables

3.1. Shorrocks–Shapley decomposition of global income inequality   61

3.2. Shorrocks–Shapley decomposition of global wealth inequality   64

3.3. Shorrocks–Shapley decomposition of changes in global income and wealth inequality   70

4.1. Descriptive statistics of variables used in the empirical analysis   92

4.2. Regression analysis: OLS including all contextual variables   95

4.3. Regression analysis: country fixed effects selecting some contextual variables   98

4.4. Regression analysis: country fixed effects selecting some contextual variables—most recent observations (year > 2000)   100

5.1. Inequality in Brazil by topic, technique, dataset, period of time, and income concept   111

5.2. Income, equality, and social welfare: contribution to growth ordered by disposable income   124

6.1. China's regional and urban/rural income gaps   135

6.2. Gini coefficients of urban wages and income per capita in China, 1988–2013   144

7.1. Inequality trends in real consumption expenditure   159

7.2. Income shares in Palanpur over time (%)   165

7.3. Inequality of individual incomes   166

7.4. Decomposing inequality in India   169

7.5. Welfare transition dynamics based on synthetic panel data, India 1987/88–2011/12 (%)   172

8.1. Bound and Johnson decomposition: 1989–94; 1994–2006; 2006–14 (assuming an elasticity of substitution $\sigma = 2$ and comparing college and high school-educated workers with rest of workers)   188

9.1. Real annual growth rates in South Africa since 1990   206

9.2. Income components in per capita terms (real 2014 prices, rand)   209

9.3. Household composition from 1993 to 2014   210

9.4. Dynamic decompositions including household composition and re-rankings, 1993–2008   211

9.5. Gini coefficients at different thresholds   215

9.6. Labour market summary statistics, 2000, 2011, and 2014   217

10.1. Descriptive statistics: Afrobarometer   241

10.2. Descriptive statistics: Asianbarometer   241

10.3. Descriptive statistics: Latinobarometer   242

10.4. Descriptive statistics: Eurobarometer   242

10.5. Economic conditions and inequality: OLS results in the Afrobarometer   244

10.6. Economic conditions and inequality: OLS results in the Asianbarometer   244

10.7. Economic conditions and inequality: OLS results in the Latinobarometer   245

10.8. Economic conditions and inequality: OLS results in the Eurobarometer   245

10.A1. List of items per dataset   249

10.A2. Number of observations per country per wave: Afrobarometer   250

10.A3. Number of observations per country per wave: Asianbarometer   250

10.A4. Number of observations per country per wave: Latinobarometer   251

10.A5. Number of observations per country per wave: Eurobarometer   252

10.A6. Economic conditions and inequality: OLS results in the
        Afrobarometer—all controls   253

10.A7. Economic conditions and inequality: OLS results in the
        Asianbarometer—all controls   254

10.A8. Economic conditions and inequality: OLS results in the
        Latinobarometer—all controls   255

10.A9. Economic conditions and inequality: OLS results in the
        Eurobarometer—all controls   256

12.1. Manufacturing share of GDP (%)   285

12.2. Deindustrialization in sub-Saharan Africa   296

List of Abbreviations

BRICS	Brazil, Russia, India, China, South Africa group
CCT	conditional cash transfer
CES	constant elasticity of substitution
CFPS	China Family Planning Survey
CHIP	China Household Income Project
DHI	disposable household income
DISE	District Information System for Education
ENIGH	National Survey on Households' Income and Expenditures
FDI	foreign direct investment
GATT	General Agreement on Tariffs and Trade
GCIP	Global Consumption and Income Project
GDIM	Global Database of Intergenerational Mobility
GDP	gross domestic product
GGC	Great Gatsby Curve
GIC	growth incidence curve
GNI	gross national income
HDI	Human Development Index
IBGE	Brazilian Institute of Geography and Statistics
IHDS	India Human Development Surveys
IMF	International Monetary Fund
IPR	intellectual property rights
LIS	Luxembourg Income Study
LIT	learning, industrial, and technology
LSMS	World Bank Living Standard Measurements Surveys (LSMS)
MDGs	Millennium Development Goals
MENA	Middle East and North Africa
MLD	Mean Log Deviation
MRP	mixed recall period
NBS	National Bureau of Statistics
NIDS	National Income Dynamics Study
NSS	National Sample Survey Organization
OECD	Organisation for Economic Co-Operation and Development
PIT	personal income tax
PME	*Pesquisa Mensal de Emprego*
PNAD	*Pesquisa Nacional de Amostras a Domicílio*
PNADC	*Pesquisa Nacional de Amostras a Domicilio Contínua*
PPP	purchasing power parity
PSID	Panel Study of Income Dynamics
QE	quantitative easing

QLFS	Quarterly Labour Force Survey
R&D	research and development
RAIS	*Registro Anual de Informações Sociais*
RIF	re-centred influence function
SARS	South African Revenue Services
SCs	Scheduled Castes
SDGs	Sustainable Development Goals
SIA	scale invariance axiom
SNA	System of National Accounts
SOEs	state-owned enterprises
SSA	sub-Saharan Africa
SWIID	Standardized World Income Inequality Database
TSTSLS	two-sample two-stage least squares
US	United States
WID	World Inequality Database
WIID	UNU-WIDER World Income Inequality Database
WIPO	World International Properties Rights Organization
WTO	World Trade Organization

Notes on Contributors

Raymundo Campos-Vazquez obtained his PhD in economics from the University of Califormia, Berkeley in 2009. Since then, he has worked as a professor in El Colegio de Mexico in Mexico City. He has publications in the *American Economic Review, Oxford Development Studies,* and *American Economic Journal: Economic Policy,* among others. Currently he is on academic leave at the Banco de Mexico.

Daniele Checchi is a professor of economics at the University of Milan. He also serves as a Secretary General of the LIS Cross-National Data Center in Luxembourg. He has published in journals such as *Economic Policy, Journal of Public Economics, European Sociological Review,* and others, and his research interests range from inequalities in educational attainments to educational policies, from wage inequalities to the role of labour market institutions in shaping inequalities of opportunities.

Andrew E. Clark is CNRS research director and a professor of economics at the Paris School of Economics. He pioneered the introduction of subjective well-being in economics in the early 1990s, and its use for the analysis of contextual effects. He has more than 30,000 citations on Google Scholar, and nine papers cited more than 1000 times each. He was among the 'Highly Cited Researchers 2018'—the list that recognizes world-class researchers selected for their performance, demonstrated by production of multiple highly cited papers that rank in the top 1 per cent by citations for field and year in the Web of Science.

Andrej Cupak works as a data expert and research associate at the LIS Cross-National Data Center in Luxembourg. He is also affiliated with the National Bank of Slovakia. His research interests include household consumption and financial behaviour, human capital, income and wealth inequality, survey data, and applied microeconomics more generally.

Conchita D'Ambrosio is a professor of economics at the Department of Behavioural and Cognitive Sciences, University of Luxembourg. Her research interests revolve around the analysis and measurement of individual well-being, both theoretically and empirically. In this respect, she has proposed a number of different axiomatically characterized well-being indices, including measures of social exclusion and of poverty over time, that disentangle the effects of chronic and persistent poverty. She has also worked on the empirical analysis of these indices using data from a variety of different countries. She has published widely in the fields of social-index numbers and income distribution.

Hai-Anh H. Dang is an economist in the Analytics and Tools Unit, Development Data Group, World Bank. His main research is on international development, poverty, inequality, human development topics, and methodology to construct synthetic (pseudo) panel data from cross-sections. He has published in various development journals, including *Economic Development and Cultural Change, Journal of Development Economics, Journal of Development Studies, World Bank Economic Review, World Development,* and has chapters in books published by leading academic publishers. He also serves as a co-editor of *Review of Development Economics*, and on the editorial boards of other journals.

James Davies is a professor of economics in the Department of Economics, University of Western Ontario in London, Canada. His field is public economics and his research has ranged over many topics, from tax policy to inequality measurement. In recent years he has focused on policy to mitigate the economic impacts of climate change and natural disasters, and on the global distribution of personal wealth.

Carlos Gradín is a research fellow at the United Nations University World Institute for Development Economics Research (UNU-WIDER) in Helsinki, and a professor of applied economics at the University of Vigo (on leave of absence). His main research interest is the study of poverty, inequality, and discrimination in both developed and developing countries, especially inequalities between population groups (i.e. by gender, race, or ethnicity). His research deals with enhancing the empirical evidence as well as methodological tools for the measurement and understanding of those issues. His research has been widely published in international journals.

Pippa Green is a South African journalist and writer. She has served as deputy editor for a number of South African newspapers, as head of Radio News at the South African public broadcaster, and as a visiting professor of journalism at Princeton University. She is South Africa's Press Ombudsman and before this worked in SALDRU, editing and writing on employment, inequality, and inclusive growth in South Africa.

Peter Lanjouw is a professor at the School of Business and Economics, VU University Amsterdam. His research focuses on the measurement of poverty and inequality as well as the analysis of rural development, notably via the study of a village economy in rural India and the broader process of rural non-farm diversification. He has co-authored several books and has also published in such leading economics journals as *Econometrica* and the *Economic Journal*, as well as numerous field journals. He is currently editor of the *World Bank Research Observer*.

Murray Leibbrandt holds the National Research Foundation Chair in Poverty and Inequality Research at the University of Cape Town and is a senior research fellow of UNU-WIDER. He is the director of the Southern Africa Labour and Development Research Unit and the African Centre of Excellence for Inequality Research. He has published widely in development economics using survey data and especially panel data to analyse South Africa's poverty, inequality, and labour-market dynamics.

Shi Li is a professor of economics at Zhejiang University, director of the China Institute for Income Distribution at Beijing Normal University, non-resident senior research fellow at UNU-WIDER, and a research fellow at IZA. His research focuses on income and wealth distribution, poverty, labour markets, and rural migration and the labour market in China. He has published in journals such as *Review of Income and Wealth*, *Oxford Bulletin of Economics and Statistics*, *Economic Development and Cultural Change*, and *Journal of Development Economics*. His publications include several edited volumes, including *Rising Inequality in China* (with H. Sato and T. Sicular, Cambridge University Press 2013).

Nora Lustig is Samuel Z. Stone Professor of Latin American Economics and the founding director of the Commitment to Equity Institute (CEQ) at Tulane University. She is also a non-resident senior fellow at the Brookings Institution, the Center for Global Development, and the Inter-American Dialogue. Her research on economic development, inequality, and social policies has been published across more than sixty articles, close to ninety chapters, and twenty-five books and edited volumes. Professor Lustig is a founding member and President Emeritus of the Latin American and Caribbean Economic Association (LACEA) and serves on the editorial board of the *Journal of Economic Inequality*. She received her doctorate in economics from the University of California, Berkeley.

Teresa Munzi is the director of operations at the LIS Cross-National Data Center in Luxembourg, where she is responsible for managing and overseeing all operations in the LIS office. Her research interests include the comparative study of welfare systems and their impact on poverty, inequality, and family wellbeing; and gender differences in employment and earnings.

Ambar Narayan is a lead economist in the Poverty & Equity Global Practice of the World Bank. He leads and advises teams conducting policy analysis, evaluations, and research in development from a microeconomic perspective, and has published research papers and policy briefs on issues that reflect the eclectic mix of topics on which he has worked over the years. He has been a lead author for large World Bank studies, including a recent global report on intergenerational mobility, and regional or country reports on inequality of opportunity, poverty, and the impact of economic shocks. He has a PhD in economics from Brown University in the United States.

Marcelo Neri is director of FGV Social at the Getulio Vargas Foundation (FGV). He holds a PhD in economics, Princeton University. Previously he was the secretary-general of the Council of Economic and Social Development (CDES), president of the Institute for Applied Economic Research (Ipea), and Minister of Strategic Affairs in Brazil. He has evaluated policies in more than a dozen countries and also designed and implemented policies at three government levels in Brazil. Neri's research focuses on social policies, microeconometrics, and well-being. He teaches graduate and undergraduate courses at EPGE/FGV, writes regularly in scientific journals, and has published ten books.

Vimal Ranchhod is a professor at the School of Economics and the Deputy Director of the Southern Africa Labour and Development Research Unit. He is a labour economist who has published widely on labour markets, education, and poverty and inequality.

Martin Ravallion currently holds the inaugural Edmond D. Villani Chair of Economics at Georgetown University. Prior to joining Georgetown in 2013 he was director of the World Bank's research department, the Development Research Group. Martin's main research interests over the past thirty years have concerned poverty and policies for fighting it. He has published extensively on this topic and advised numerous governments and international agencies.

John Scott is a professor-researcher at the Economics Department at the Centro de Investigación y Docencia Económicas (CIDE) in Mexico City, and academic researcher at the Consejo Nacional de Evaluación de la Política de Desarrollo Social (CONEVAL), a public institution responsible for poverty measurement and the evaluation of social programmes in Mexico. He has a BA in philosophy from NYU and an M.Phil in economics from the University of Oxford. His principal research areas include redistributive policies, social and fiscal incidence analysis, poverty and inequality analysis, evaluation of social policy, rural development policies, agricultural and energy subsidies, and health and social security.

Anthony Shorrocks is an honorary professor at Manchester University and director of Global Economic Perspectives Ltd, having previously served as director of UNU-WIDER from 2000 to 2009. He has published extensively on topics concerned with income and wealth distribution, inequality, poverty, and mobility. His recent research on the level and distribution of global household wealth has been published annually in the *Credit Suisse Global Wealth Report and Databook*.

Terry Sicular is a professor of economics at the University of Western Ontario. She has conducted research on China's economy since the 1980s and has published works on topics ranging from China's economic transition to China's rural households and rural economy, and education in China. Her current research focuses on topics related to income distribution and poverty in China. She has edited and contributed to several books, including *Rising Inequality in China* (with S. Li and H. Sato, Cambridge University Press 2013). She has served as a consultant to international organizations such as the World Bank, Asian Development Bank, and UNU-WIDER.

Joseph E. Stiglitz is a professor at Columbia University. He was awarded the Nobel Prize in Economics in 2001 for his work on asymmetric information. He is the co-chair of the High-Level Expert Group on the Measurement of Economic Performance and Social Progress at the OECD. He served as chairman of the Council of Economic Advisors under President Clinton and as chief economist of the World Bank.

Finn Tarp is a professor of development economics at the University of Copenhagen, and was director of UNU-WIDER from 2009 to 2018. His field experience covers more than two decades of in-country work in thirty-five countries across Africa and in the developing world more generally. Professor Tarp's research focus is on issues of development strategy and foreign aid, with an interest in poverty, income distribution and growth, micro- and macroeconomic policy and modelling, agricultural sector policy and planning, and household and enterprise development. He has published widely and is a member of a large number of international committees and advisory bodies.

Roy van der Weide is a senior economist in the Poverty and Inequality Research team within the Development Research Group of the World Bank. He leads the poverty and inequality mapping research within the department. His other research is concerned with the empirics of inequality of opportunity and poverty reduction, and axiomatic approaches to income measurement. His work has been published in a range of academic journals, including the *American Economic Review*, the *Journal of Econometrics*, the *Journal of Applied Econometrics*, and the *World Bank Economic Review*. He holds a PhD from the University of Amsterdam.

PART I
INTRODUCTION

1

Setting the Scene

Carlos Gradín, Murray Leibbrandt, and Finn Tarp

1 Introduction

Inequality has emerged as a key, perhaps *the* key, development challenge of the past decade. It holds implications for economic growth and redistribution, and some of the most influential social science of the first half of the past decade showed that it also translates into power asymmetries that can endanger democratization and human rights, create conflict, and embed social exclusion and chronic poverty (Wilkinson and Pickett 2010; Stiglitz 2012; Deaton 2014; Piketty 2014). As such, inequality is at the core of the United Nations' mandate, and 'reducing inequality within and among countries' is one of the seventeen goals of the 2030 Agenda for Sustainable Goals (SDGs) approved by the UN General Assembly in September 2015. Positioning inequality (SDG 10) as a stand-alone goal confers high visibility upon it. Moreover, the way in which the associated, more specific targets have been formulated links the inequality goal with many of the other SDGs, meaning that 'reducing inequality' is one of the most heavily inter-linked themes of the 2030 SDG agenda.

These concerns also underpin intense public and academic debates, to the extent that inequality has become a dominant policy concern within many countries, in all multilateral agencies, and even for the World Economic Forum (World Bank 2016; Ostry et al. 2019; World Economic Forum 2020). It would be very worrying if the possibility of investigating inequality in the real world in greater depth than was previously the case had not accompanied this intense public concern with inequality. Fortunately, there have been a number of advances in recent decades regarding measurement of inequality, as well as in the development of better data to analyse the processes generating inequality and changes in inequality.

The empirical literature began with a focus on analysing inequality in the industrialized world in detail. The scarcity of in-depth analyses focused on developing countries was associated with a lack of adequate data and research capacity and was not helped by a stubborn and widespread misconception that inequality was not a relevant and pressing issue in poorer countries. This idea, which had its roots in the work of the classical economists of the eighteenth century, generally

Carlos Gradín, Murray Leibbrandt, and Finn Tarp, *Setting the Scene* In: *Inequality in the Developing World*. Edited by: Carlos Gradín, Murray Leibbrandt, and Finn Tarp, Oxford University Press (2021). © United Nations University World Institute for Development Economics Research (UNU-WIDER). DOI: 10.1093/oso/9780198863960.003.0001

held that reducing inequality could conflict with higher priorities such as boosting growth or reducing poverty, by reducing the incentives of the most productive people. Within development economics, a more nuanced version of this view held that there was no need to push for a more equal society because this would be an automatic outcome that would eventually result from higher development, in line with the inverted-U hypothesis proposed by Simon Kuznets. A more textured understanding of inequality in developing countries was facilitated by gradual improvements in the available data. The intense research focus on inequality in both developed and developing countries over the past decade has replaced these ideas with a growing consensus that all highly unequal societies are dysfunctional in many ways, including compromised growth and poverty reduction.

This interest in inequality has also crossed the traditional national borders. There has been much analysis of cross-country comparisons of inequalities, in general. This was complemented by a focus on specific issues such as the middle class or the effects of the great recession (see Gornick and Jäntti 2013; Jenkins et al. 2013; Nolan 2018, among others). The gradual emergence of large databases, such as the Luxembourg Income Study (LIS) discussed in detail in Chapter 4 of this book, facilitated this research, providing researchers with easy access to harmonized microdata for many countries. Initially focused on developed countries, LIS has more recently been successful in incorporating several key middle-income countries.

Increasing interest in analysis of global inequalities and the role of forces like globalization in shaping them has brought developed and developing countries together. Two recent books by Bourguignon (2016) and Milanovic (2016) are prominent examples. Initially, the lack of adequate data for such work was a clear handicap. As reviewed in Ferreira et al. (2015), in response to this there have been many efforts to provide compilations of data from different sources, such as the UNU-WIDER World Income Inequality Database (WIID), which collates information from many primary sources such as LIS, the World Bank (PovCalnet) and other international organizations, Eurostat and National Statistical Authorities, and research studies. Another good example of this new age of inequality analysis with a global perspective is the *2018 World Inequality Report* by the World Inequality Lab at the Paris School of Economics (Facundo et al. 2018). This initiative pursues an ambitious research agenda that includes producing new distributional data combining survey, administrative data, and national accounts, with special attention given to the top of the distribution.

Global inequalities are the result of combining between-country and within-country inequalities. While according to, for example, the widely used Gini measure, global relative income inequality has been falling steadily for more than three decades, this trend reflected convergence in GDP per capita across nations. Relative inequality within countries remained roughly constant in the 1990s and has been rising since 2000. This increase in average within-country relative inequality arose from a very heterogeneous picture among countries and regions, and the same goes for the associated and very sizeable increases in absolute inequality (see Niño-Zarazúa et al. 2017).

Inequalities between countries mostly reflect how successful developing regions have been in accelerating economic growth as compared to richer countries. Asian countries have been quite successful in using their particular export-oriented model and development strategies, as argued in Nayyar (2019). While African countries have experienced robust growth and poverty reduction since 2000 (see Addison et al. 2017), they have struggled to escape from a complex set of initial conditions and have seen more difficulties in finding a pathway to development. However, in these and all other contexts, inequalities within countries are much more heterogeneous. The same forces that can reduce inequality between countries—like globalization—might contribute to higher inequality within both developed and developing countries. Other forces, such as technological progress, have contributed to increased market inequalities everywhere and to increasing profit-shares. Some countries have been more successful in using active policies to curb the market processes that push for higher inequality or, at least, to compensate them using taxes and benefits. In this respect, developing countries—traditionally small states with weak policy capability and generally regressive welfare regimes—face clear disadvantages.

This book aims to contribute to the literature and public debate on inequality by bringing together an analysis of global inequality and a new and comprehensive view of the trends in inequality in five of the world's largest developing countries—Brazil, China, India, Mexico, and South Africa—jointly accounting for more than 40 per cent of the world's population. While this is not a majority population share and omits other important developing country inequality contexts—such as Indonesia, Pakistan, Nigeria, Bangladesh, and Russia—each of these cases are important inequality contexts. Understanding inequalities in these emerging economies is of great value in coming to grips with contemporary inequalities worldwide. This remains difficult due to both data and analytical challenges.

For this reason, UNU-WIDER engaged with a group of highly qualified international researchers to develop the five country case studies within a common framework under its Inequality in the Giants project.[1] These country case leaders, together with their respective country teams, produced a series of in-depth studies for each of these countries. The objective of each country project was to assess

---

[1] The outputs of the project can be accessed at www.wider.unu.edu/project/inequality-giants. The main findings of the project were presented in a special panel during the UNU-WIDER Think Development—Think WIDER development conference held in Helsinki, September 2018. Videos are available on the conference website www.wider.unu.edu/parallel-session/inequality-developing-giants.

the level and trend of income inequality and to understand the processes driving this quantitative picture. Use was made of the best available data and techniques. Most countries have developed a system of household surveys providing rich information to measure inequality as well as to investigate its drivers. The limitations of these household surveys, in terms of underestimation of certain sources of income or consumption and the misrepresentation of certain population groups, are well known. For that reason, other complementary sources such as administrative data, public listings, or big data were used in order to correct for lack of response when this was an issue in underestimation of the top income sources and shares. In some cases, researchers produced new data sets for the research.

Using these rich data sources, different decomposition techniques and the use of regression analyses facilitated identification of the main inequality drivers. Each of these country cases summarize the main findings about long-run trends in income inequality and its driving factors. They contain detailed analyses of three issues: (i) the role of earnings inequality and its determinants; (ii) the role of top incomes (when administrative records or other sources can be combined with household surveys); and (iii) the distributive impact of public policies. Yet, we tailored each country study to its specific needs and authors discuss specific issues that are important to that country, such as spatial inequalities or intergenerational mobility.

The country case studies are summarized in Part III of this book. It is imperative to contextualize this type of fine-grained analysis of within-country inequality within the global context. Therefore, for Part II of this volume, we invited a number of outstanding researchers to provide their take on a set of key framework-setting issues to precede and put them in perspective. Accordingly, Part II focuses on global inequalities in income and wealth, the role of globalization, and challenges in analysing cross-country comparisons. The aim is to provide an overview of the state of the art in our knowledge of inequalities between and within countries, of the main practical and conceptual challenges in undertaking these analyses, and of the necessary steps to move forward in this crucial field of social and economic inquiry. With this as the global context, the five country synthesis studies form Part III. In Part IV, this volume then returns to analysing economic inequality in a broader context. It contains three chapters, which profile, respectively, subjective wellbeing across the world, socioeconomic mobility in China and the United States against the context of seventy-three other countries, and the need for a new growth and development model in developing economies. Collectively, these three substantive parts contain much detail on global and local inequalities and, in Part V, we synthesize key findings and outline policy implications.

Before proceeding, in what follows we provide a synopsis of the eleven individual chapters that make up Parts II–IV of this book to help set the scene and give some up-front guidance on what to expect.

2 Global Inequality and Inequality within Countries

Part II starts with Chapter 2, in which Martin Ravallion clarifies the underlying assumptions behind the conflicting narratives on what has been happening to global income inequality in the past decades. After reviewing the main issues involved, with regard to assessing global trends, he identifies a set of elements that put into perspective the fact that many prominent international scholars produce solid evidence in support of a conventional view according to which global inequality has been declining since the 1990s, while at the same time other prominent scholars produce solid evidence for the opposite view that it has been rising. These elements include people's main reference group—their country or the world—and what type of income growth keeps inequality constant, which depends on the relative versus absolute view. Crucially, and unlike the measurement and analysis of poverty, a focus on inequality requires the inclusion of the full distribution of wellbeing. This is true whether it is explicitly recognized by the analyst or not, and Ravallion shows that opposing empirical pictures of the trends in global inequality can be understood by being explicit about the ethical weight given to the poor or the aversion to inequality from the top of the distribution that is being assumed in each of these analyses. Conclusions drawn about what has happened depend critically on the exact combination of assumptions made.

Understanding the drivers of inequality, even income inequality, requires an analysis of how many dimensions of inequality intersect to produce a given inequality outcome. In Chapter 3, James Davies and Anthony Shorrocks emphasize this important point by analysing the joint distribution of wealth and income and their decomposition into between- and within-country components. This is a particularly insightful approach because both of these metrics feature prominently in the discussions of contemporary inequality, with most contention being about the relationship between them. The authors make this contribution drawing on the *Credit Suisse Global Wealth Report* and *Credit Suisse Global Wealth Databook* which they have produced (Davies et al. 2018a, 2018b). The chapter contrasts the trends in these wealth data, which have featured prominently in international inequality deliberations, with income data from the WIID. For both income and wealth, and for all the inequality indices considered, the degree of inequality attributable to differences in mean income and wealth across countries accounts for much, if not most, of the level of global inequality. As regards changing inequality over time, changes in mean income, mean wealth, and population size have induced a strong downward element in the trend in global inequality, regardless of the inequality index selected.

In Chapter 4, the Luxembourg Income Study (LIS) team (Daniele Checchi, Andrej Cupak, and Teresa Munzi) investigates the development patterns in economic inequality for several low- and middle-income countries, including the five country cases analysed in depth in Part II. They, along with Russia, now form part of the LIS harmonized data, which has so far largely focused on developed economies. Thus, these data are a valuable source of information on inequality within the BRICS and the chapter splices a discussion of Russian inequality into the book. The authors describe the process by which each country data set is prepared for inclusion in the harmonized LIS data. This is invaluable in making clear the many challenges in moving from within-country data and analysis to well-grounded cross-country analyses of inequality for developing countries, and then to analysis to inform strategies to overcome inequality. Without explicit description of what was done to the data in moving from country data sets to a comparable cross-country data set, and even to merged global data sets, one does not have a clear sense of the extent to which the observed inequality levels and trends are driven by differences in the underlying data rather than in the forces driving inequality.

3 Inequality in Five Developing Giants

Part III begins with Chapter 5, in which Marcelo Neri puts forward his synthesis of how, from the dawn of the new millennium, Brazil—one of the world's most prominent high-inequality countries—experienced an unprecedented decline in income inequality that lasted until 2014, with a reversion after that date. Lower earnings inequality was the main driver behind this downward trend. Neri discusses a number of different possible channels that might have helped to reduce earnings inequality. These include heterogeneity among firms and the role of a higher minimum wage. The expansion of education, alongside falling returns, stands out among the driving factors helping to mitigate the particularly high inter-generational inertia. The chapter also addresses the complementary role of tax redistribution and conditional cash transfers in underpinning the reduction in educational and health inequalities among the Brazilian populace.

In Chapter 6, Shi Li, Terry Sicular, and Finn Tarp present China as a country with a classic development trajectory characterized by structural change, increased market integration, and labour absorption, moving along the upward side of the Kuznets inverted-U curve. This process has generated strong economic growth and poverty reduction. However, an incomplete transition from a planned to a market economy has generated increased differentiation of incomes, while creating continued opportunities for rent-seeking, corruption, and hidden income. More recent countervailing factors include expanding government efforts to moderate inequality, especially through social and welfare programmes. Whether the country has already started moving along the downward section of the Kuznets curve will depend on the direction of future reforms.

Hai-Anh Dang and Peter Lanjouw offer in Chapter 7 a comprehensive analysis of inequality trends in India over the past three decades. As with Brazil and

China, the backdrop was one of strong growth and poverty reduction. In the Indian context, this was accompanied by rising inequality in all dimensions, but to differing degrees depending on the dimension considered and the measurement method employed. In order to reconcile these growth, poverty, and inequality levels and changes, the authors interrogate inequality trends across and within the national, state, and microscopic village levels. They show that local-level inequality accounts for the bulk of overall inequality in India. They explore these inequality dynamics further, using synthetic panel data constructed at the household level, to examine intra-generational income mobility over time. This mobility has risen over time, implying that lifetime inequality will be lower than cross-sectional inequality. However, while poverty has fallen, most of the poor who have escaped poverty continue to face high risks of falling back into poverty. Particularly concerning is the fact that intragenerational educational mobility is low and not improving. Moreover, those who remain poor are increasingly chronically poor, and may be particularly difficult to reach via the introduction or expansion of safety nets.

In Chapter 8, Raymundo Campos-Vazquez, Nora Lustig, and John Scott investigate the 'rise–decline–rise again' pattern in income inequality in Mexico. The growth and poverty context for these inequality changes is itself much less positive and more variable in Mexico than in Brazil, China, and India. As in the case of Brazil, the evolution of labour income inequality is key to understanding this inequality pattern, with the skill premium being the key determinant of earnings inequality. The authors highlight two key implications. The first is the need to continue the expansion of access to higher levels of (quality) education and the increase in minimum wages to their 1980 levels. The authors also show that direct cash transfers, including the famous *Progresa* programme, largely targeted the poor in Mexico, but also that their overall redistributive impact remains limited because of their small coverage. Furthermore, the redistributive effect of the entire fiscal system has declined significantly since 2010, as transfers have become less progressive and net indirect taxes have increased.

Murray Leibbrandt, Pippa Green, and Vimal Ranchhod show in Chapter 9 that, in a context of sluggish growth but some reduction in poverty rates, inequality has remained exceptionally high in post-apartheid South Africa. This stubbornly high level of aggregate inequality masks a number of important changes in the texture of this inequality. Again, the dynamics of the labour market are key to understanding this. Education policy has effected a reduction in inequality in years of schooling driven by increases in average education levels. Under the conditions prevailing in the mid-1990s this would have reduced inequality. But over the intervening years the patterns of growth and employment were such that earnings inequality increased as the result of strongly increased returns to tertiary education and to experience, and strongly decreasing returns to levels of education lower than complete secondary. Using tax data, the authors also show that those at the top end of the income distribution have experienced much higher rates of real income growth than the remainder of the population. This is linked to the rising labour market inequality and to strong returns to capital income sources that are only found at the top end of the income distribution. While government grants played an important role in reducing inequality (and poverty) by supporting households at the bottom of the income distribution, these effects have become weaker more recently. The direct tax system is progressive overall, and social benefits are well targeted, but some of the tax benefits are indeed regressive.

4   Inequality in a Broader Context

Part IV of the book moves the analysis from the detail in our country cases back to a broader context of global inequality. Thus far, the chapters in the book have interrogated the measurement and analysis of money-metric inequalities at global and national levels. Full interrogation of these inequalities has required an understanding of their intersection with inequalities in education, gender, race, ethnicity, space, and many other dimensions. These are complicated interactions and they raise the question of how perceptions of wellbeing are correlated with subjective and measured inequalities. In Chapter 10, Andrew E. Clark and Conchita D'Ambrosio empirically explore exactly this question. They explore whether individuals' subjective evaluation of their present and future living conditions is associated with their own current levels of functioning, their subjective assessment of their position relative to other members of the society, and the level of measured economic inequality in their country. Using data from a series of Barometer surveys conducted in 76 countries in Africa, Latin America, Asia, and Europe, combined with money-metric measures contained in the WIID data, the authors are able to look in particular at how these relationships differ across the four world regions. Their results confirm that, across the world, those whose lives are more objectively deprived have lower subjective evaluations of current living standards and, to a lesser extent, lower expectations regarding future living conditions. While they also find evidence about the implications of relative comparisons, these are more heterogenous across world regions. In the developed countries of Europe, those who see themselves as better off relative to others in their country have higher levels of subjective wellbeing. In developing countries this is not a strong relationship. Indeed, Hirschman's famous tunnel effect seems to prevail, especially in Latin America and Africa, in that seeing oneself as worse off relative to others is positively correlated with subjective wellbeing in the present and the future. Finally, the higher the aggregate level of inequality in the country of residence, the higher the expectations of future living conditions globally, with more mixed results on present living conditions also depending on the region.

In Chapter 11, Roy van der Weide and Ambar Narayan examine the trends and patterns in inter-generational mobility for China and the United States. They draw lessons from 'Fair Progress? Economic Mobility Across Generations Around the World', a 2018 World Bank report, which was one of the first attempts to analyse the critical issue of social mobility in the developing world. This allows the chapter not only to focus on China and the United States, but also to compare this detailed analysis to estimates of inter-generational income mobility from seventy-three other countries. Although socioeconomic mobility was relatively high in China before the transition from a planned to a market economy, mobility substantially declined during the period of rapid economic growth. As a result, China converged to the historical low levels of income and education mobility shown by the United States. The study links China's declining mobility to its rising inequality. It finds further support for this 'Great Gatsby Curve' in a negative correlation between income mobility and inequality that is found looking across all seventy-five countries. In showing this, the chapter offers a stark example of a central theme of the book as whole; namely, how high inequality undermines the maximum use of human potential and therefore economic growth and economic development.

Part IV ends with Chapter 12, in which Nobel Laureate Joseph Stiglitz sets out the present-day framework in which development takes place. He begins by discussing the export-led growth strategy. This allowed East Asian countries to reach unprecedented growth rates in the recent past and has been the main factor explaining the decline in between-country inequality. However, it is no longer the reference for developing economies. Stiglitz proceeds to formulate a new and comprehensive development strategy, entailing a combination of policies addressing manufacturing, agriculture, services, and natural resources—for which active and innovative industrial policies will be necessary—as well as a global reserve system that can provide the critical resources. He is boldly making the point that international and national policy communities are obligated to deal with the global and national economic circumstances that actually prevail, rather than those they wished were in place or had been in place three decades ago. Read alongside the detailed interrogations of global and national inequalities in the preceding chapters, this chapter provides a grounded platform for the discussion of the policies needed to address inequality and promote inclusive development in the contemporary world.

In Part V (Chapter 13), which concludes the volume, we synthesize and draw together the multi-faceted lessons that emerge from this volume about data, measurement, and the analysis of inequality and outline the main implications for policy. In sum, and in line with the Stockholm Statement,[2] we point out that

---

[2] See www.wider.unu.edu/news/stockholm-statement-%E2%80%93-towards-new-consensus-principles-policy-making-contemporary-world.

present inequalities of income and wealth and inequality in access to basic services—such as health and education—are ethically indefensible. They undermine social cohesion and economic progress. Policies must be socially and economically inclusive, including initiatives that work through the labour market as well as through redistributive social policies, keeping in mind throughout the long-term goal of promoting social mobility to break inter-generational inequalities.

References

Addison, T., V. Pikkarainen, R. Rönkkö, and F. Tarp (2017). 'Development and poverty in sub-Saharan Africa'. WIDER Working Paper 169. Helsinki: UNU-WIDER.

Bourguignon, F. (2016). *The Globalization of Inequality*. Princeton and Oxford: Princeton University Press.

Davies, J.B., R. Lluberas, and A. Shorrocks (2018a). *Global Wealth Report*. Zurich: Credit Suisse Research Institute.

Davies, J.B., R. Lluberas, and A. Shorrocks (2018b). *Global Wealth Databook*. Zurich: Credit Suisse Research Institute.

Deaton, A. (2014). *The Great Escape: Health, Wealth, and the Origins of Inequality*. Princeton: Princeton University Press.

Facundo, A., L. Chancel, T. Piketty, E. Saez, and G. Zucman (2018). *World Inequality Report 2018*. Paris: World Inequality Lab.

Ferreira, F., N. Lustig, and D. Teles (2015). 'Appraising Cross-National Income Inequality Databases: An Introduction'. *Journal of Economic Inequality*, 13, 497–526.

Gornick, J., and M. Jäntti (eds) (2013). *Income Inequality: Economic Disparities and the Middle Class in Affluent Countries*. Palo Alto: Stanford University Press.

Jenkins, S., A. Brandolini, J. Micklewright, and B. Nolan (2013). *The Great Recession and the Distribution of Household Income*. Oxford: Oxford University Press.

Milanovic, B. (2016). *Global Inequality: A New Approach for the Age of Globalization*. Cambridge: Harvard University Press.

Nayyar, D. (2019). *Resurgent Asia: Diversity in Development*. WIDER Studies in Development Economics. Oxford: Oxford University Press.

Niño-Zarazúa, M., L. Roope, and F. Tarp (2017). 'Global Inequality: Relatively Lower, Absolutely Higher'. *Review of Income and Wealth*, 63(4), 661–84.

Nolan, B. (ed.) (2018). *Inequality and Inclusive Growth in Rich Countries: Shared Challenges and Contrasting Fortunes*. Oxford: Oxford University Press.

Ostry, J., P. Loungani, and A. Berg (2019). *Confronting Inequality: How Societies Can Choose Inclusive Growth*. New York: Colombia University Press.

Piketty, T. (2014). *Capital in the Twenty-First Century*. Cambridge, MA: The Belknap Press of Harvard University Press.

Stiglitz, J. (2012). *The Price of Inequality: How Today's Divided Society Endangers Our Future*. New York: Norton Press.

Wilkinson, R., and K. Pickett (2010). *The Spirit Level: Why Greater Equality Makes Societies Stronger*. New York: Bloomsbury Press.

World Bank (2016). *Poverty and Shared Prosperity 2016: Taking on Inequality*. Washington, DC: World Bank.

World Economic Forum (2020). *Equality, Opportunity and a New Economic Imperative: The Global Social Mobility Report 2020*. Geneva: World Economic Forum.

PART II

GLOBAL INEQUALITY AND INEQUALITY WITHIN COUNTRIES

2

What Might Explain Today's Conflicting Narratives on Global Inequality?

Martin Ravallion

1 Introduction

Public attention to the global distribution of income is probably greater today than at any prior time in history.[1] Yet we hear two very different narratives about global inequality.[2] Many economists claim that inequality has been falling in the world since around 1990.[3] For example, a *New York Times* article by Cowen (2014) carried the headline 'Income Inequality Is Not Rising Globally. It's Falling.'[4] This has been seen as being driven by falling inequality between countries—the disparities in their mean incomes relative to the global mean. Some observers have been led to anticipate a far more equal world ahead. In this vein, Beddoes (2012) writes that: 'The gap between the world's rich and poor will be far narrower in 2050.'

This stands in marked contrast to the claims one often hears about the rising gap between the world's rich and poor. There are many examples. The website of Oxfam International refers to 'A world getting more unequal' and an 'inequality crisis'. Similarly, in a book on global inequality, Hickel (2017: 16) writes that 'inequality has been exploding'. Many observers point to the new 'super-rich'. For example, as evidence of 'today's huge global inequality', Basu (2018) observes that the 'three richest persons have more wealth than all people of three nations—Angola, Burkina, Congo DR'.

---

[1] For their comments the author is grateful to Conchita D'Ambrosio, Marc Fleurbaey, Ravi Kanbur, Max Kasy, Paul Segal, Milan Thomas, Dominique van de Walle and participants at the UNU-WIDER conference, Think Development, Think WIDER, the Normative Ethics and Welfare Economics conference, University of Pennsylvania, and a seminar at the School of Foreign Service, Georgetown University.
[2] Evidence for the claim of high public interest can be found by entering 'global inequality' and 'global poverty' in the Google Ngram Viewer; here you will find the plot of the incidence of these phrases in all digitized text since 1950.
[3] See Bourguignon (2016), Milanovic (2016), Anand and Segal (2017), and Niño-Zarazúa et al. (2017).
[4] Cowen was drawing on the evidence in a working paper subsequently published in Lakner and Milanovic (2016a).

Martin Ravallion, *What Might Explain Today's Conflicting Narratives on Global Inequality?* In: *Inequality in the Developing World.* Edited by: Carlos Gradín, Murray Leibbrandt, and Finn Tarp, Oxford University Press (2021).
© United Nations University World Institute for Development Economics Research (UNU-WIDER).
DOI: 10.1093/oso/9780198863960.003.0002

Deciding which (if either) of these narratives one believes is clearly an important aspect of how one evaluates overall social progress, and the efficacy of existing economic and political institutions. Here too one hears different views. For example, Cowen (2014) argues that falling global inequality is a sign of our success and reduces the need for public redistribution, while Hickel (2017) sees rising global inequality as indicative of a 'development delusion' perpetuated by international financial institutions striving to justify global capitalism.

This chapter tries to make some sense of these differing narratives. One might dismiss one side or the other as poorly informed, or as some ideologically driven conspiracy to hide the truth. But these are not very satisfactory responses. Both sides have their data; indeed, their sources are mostly the same. Conspiracies to delude are unlikely to work for long. The chapter tries to probe more deeply into the foundations of current evidence and debates. The focus is on income inequality. Of course, there are also inequalities in wealth, and in 'non-income' dimensions of welfare, such as health, education, rights, and freedoms. But income inequality is the obvious place to start, given the attention it receives. The chapter's intended audience is not specialists on measurement, but economists and others in the public at large using and interpreting data on inequality.

The chapter demonstrates that the view one takes of global income inequality—the stylized facts one identifies—can be highly sensitive to relaxing some of the (often implicit) assumptions made in measurement. Those assumptions relate to both how one deals with certain systematic data deficiencies, and to the concept of 'inequality' one uses, including its ethical premises. The concepts favoured by economists and statisticians can differ substantially from those of the population at large. While the chapter does not come to a definitive conclusion as to which of the two narratives described above is closer to the truth, it is hoped that by making the assumptions explicit and comprehensible, a more constructive debate will be possible.

The next section provides an overview of what we already know about global income inequality, based on the prevailing approach in economics, though with some new empirics for developing countries. Section 3 turns to issues pertaining to the underlying survey-based data, recognizing that perceptions of inequality may be sensitive to aspects of reality not adequately captured in standard data sources. The rest of the chapter takes the data as given and turns instead to two conceptual issues. Section 4 examines the issue of what trade-offs one accepts among different levels of living, and points out that with sufficient ethical aversion to extreme inequality—in either tail of the distribution—one will conclude that global inequality is in fact rising. Section 5 turns to the distinction between absolute and relative inequality. The widespread use of relative measures rests on a 'scale invariance axiom' that is routinely assumed by economists measuring global inequality but it is unlikely to be widely endorsed by the public at large. Focusing instead on absolute inequality, there can be little doubt that global inequality is rising. But this also points to a potential trade-off between absolute inequality and absolute poverty—an important trade-off that has received rather little attention.

2 An Overview of the Evidence on Global Income Inequality

Looking back over 200 years, the best available evidence suggests that global income inequality was on a rising trend until about 1990 (Bourguignon and Morrisson 2002). This was mainly driven by much of today's rich world taking off economically from the early nineteenth century. Indeed, average inequality within countries was stagnant or even falling over much of this period, most notably over the middle fifty years of the twentieth century.

This is believed to have changed dramatically around the end of the twentieth century. The same measures suggest that an overall pattern of falling inequality between countries emerged, alongside rising average inequality within countries. Figure 2.1 shows the series of global inequality measures from Bourguignon (2016). We see the fall in global inequality, markedly so in the new millennium.[5] This has been driven by a decline in inequality between countries, which accounts for the bulk of total inequality.[6] Average inequality within countries has edged upwards.

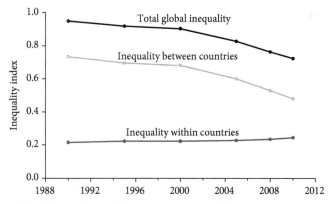

Figure 2.1 Global inequality and its between- and within-country components
Source: Estimates from Bourguignon (2016: Table 1).

---

[5] Anand and Segal (2008) provide a compilation of estimates of global inequality over the period 1960–2000 that suggest an ambiguous picture, although most estimates show a decline in the 1990s. However, since their series only goes up to 2000 it misses the more marked decline in the new millennium (Figure 2.1).
[6] Unlike the popular Gini index, for the Theil class of indices (one of which is used in Figure 2.1), the within and between components add up exactly to total inequality. (Exact aggregation for the Gini index only holds for non-overlapping distributions.)

With falling global inequality and a rising global mean income, global measures of poverty are expected to fall when judged against poverty lines that are fixed in real terms over time and across countries. This is intuitive, although it is theoretically possible for any standard poverty measure to respond perversely to lower inequality alongside a rising mean (Datt and Ravallion 1992). Nonetheless, Chen and Ravallion (2010) show that the intuitive expectation is confirmed by the data; indeed, falling poverty measures are found over a very wide range of poverty lines (and measures), up to (and beyond) the US official line.[7]

'Globalization' has been seen as a major driver of these changes. A number of observers have argued that globalization simultaneously decreased inequality between countries while increasing it within them; see, for example, Bourguignon (2016) and Milanovic (2016). While the role of globalization in determining global inequality is not the topic of this chapter, it can be noted that its causal role is not beyond dispute. Elsewhere, I have raised questions about the thesis that globalization has produced the pattern in Figure 2.1, drawing on the evidence from research on both growth and distributional changes (Ravallion 2018a).

There is much heterogeneity across countries and over time in the changes in the aggregate statistics for within-country inequality in Figure 2.1. Inequality has been rising in a majority of countries in the rich world, but not everywhere.[8] In a compilation of national Gini indices, estimated on a reasonably consistent basis, Atkinson and Morelli (2014) find that inequality has been increasing in recent years for about two-thirds of the 25 countries studied. (Only seven of the twenty-five are developing countries, and inequality has been increasing in four of those.) There appears to have been even more heterogeneity within the developing world. The developing countries with a trend increase in inequality over the past twenty years or so include the two most populous, China and India, which are clearly putting upward pressure on the (population-weighted) within-country component of global inequality, such as in Figure 2.1. However, inequality is falling in many developing countries; for example, there are clear signs that inequality has stabilized in China in recent years (Kanbur et al. 2017; Cai et al. 2018). There is also evidence of a process of inequality convergence across countries, with inequality tending to fall in high-inequality countries and rise in low-inequality countries, though the process appears to be slow (Ravallion 2003a).

To provide an overall description for the developing world, Figure 2.2a plots one of the Theil indices of inequality, namely the Mean Log Deviation (MLD) (also called Theil(0)), for the developing world only, and its within- and

---

[7] For recent evidence on both absolute and relative poverty see Ravallion and Chen (2019). For the latest estimates of absolute poverty measures across multiple poverty lines see the World Bank's *PovcalNet* site.

[8] Depending on the time period, one finds falling inequality in (for example) Belgium, France, Greece, Hungary, and Spain (OECD 2011; Morelli et al. 2014; Atkinson and Morelli 2014).

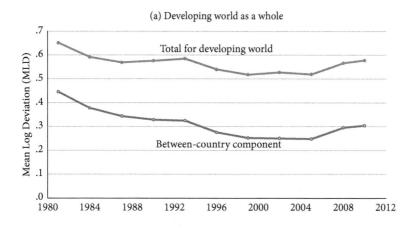

(a) Developing world as a whole

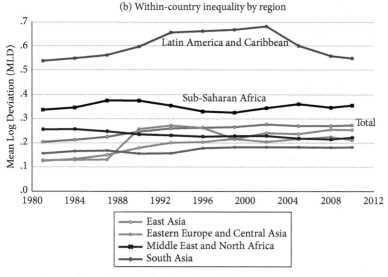

(b) Within-country inequality by region

Figure 2.2   Inequality within the developing world
Source: Author's calculations using *PovcalNet*.

between-country components.[9] The change in direction over the past few years appears to be mainly due to growth in China, which has surpassed the mean for the developing world. Panel (b) of Figure 2.2 gives a breakdown of MLD by region. Latin America and the Caribbean is the region with the highest average inequality among its countries, though it has been falling since the early 2000s. There has been a trend increase in average inequality among the countries of East Asia. Other regions have shown little trend either way.

---

[9] See Theil (1967). For an overview of these and other inequality measures see Cowell (2000).

These observations indicate that the idea of a common global force of economic integration driving up inequality everywhere can be readily dismissed. Inequality appears to fall in some developing countries when they are opened up to trade and grow in the aggregate, while inequality increases in other countries (Ravallion 2006). There are clearly many other forces in play. Indeed, during periods of economic growth we have seen falling inequality within developing countries about as often as we have seen rising inequality. This was first demonstrated by Ravallion and Chen (1997), and more recently by Ravallion (2004), using the longest available periods ('spells') between two national surveys for the same country with the same welfare indicator (either consumption or income). Using survey data up to the late 1990s, Ravallion (2004) found for 120 spells that the simple correlation coefficient between proportionate changes (annualized difference in logs) in the Gini index and those for mean household consumption or income was −0.06. Figure 2.3 provides an update to Ravallion (2004) using an extra ten or more years of survey data, thus capturing the higher growth rates we have seen since 2000; the median date of the second survey in the 144 spells is 2012. Inequality increased in about half the spells (70/144 for the Gini index and 68/144 for MLD). The update in Figure 2.3 indicates a small positive correlation (r = 0.18),[10] which is statistically significant at the 5 per cent level.

So there is more of a sign that the higher growth rates of mean household income seen in the new millennium have often come with increases in income inequality in developing countries. However, it is hardly a strong feature of even the new data in Figure 2.3. There are many instances of falling inequality in

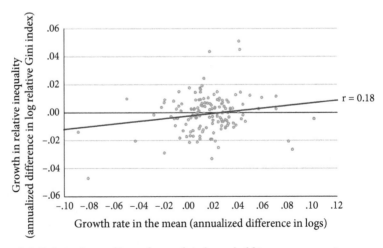

Figure 2.3 Relative inequality and growth in household income per capita
Source: Author's calculations.

---

[10] This also holds if one uses changes in MLD (r = 0.20).

growing economies. Indeed, inequality is falling in half (59/119) of the countries with positive growth in the mean in Figure 2.3. There is clearly a lot more to the story of what is driving the country-level distributional changes observed in the developing world.

This chapter will not go any further into explaining these changes in inequality at the country level. Rather, the focus will be on the numbers on global inequality, including both their statistical veracity and their conceptual basis.

3 Data Concerns

There are many data issues, related to the ways in which consumption and income are measured in practice, the design of the household surveys used, the price indices, and the census data.[11] This discussion focuses on those issues that are likely to be important to global inequality measures.

Let us begin by summarizing the standard practices underlying the estimates in the previous section. Almost all household surveys use personal interviews.[12] The household data refer to either consumption expenditure or disposable income, as reported by respondents for stipulated (often rather short) recall periods. Standard practice by statistics offices uses a survey instrument that can cover all income sources and/or market goods and services consumed, including imputed values for consumption from own production, as is important for farm households. However, while cash transfers received from government are included in the income aggregates, it appears to be rare to include imputed values for in-kind public services consumed. Consumption is used more often in developing countries, while income is more common in rich countries and Latin America. (Consumption is often preferred to current incomes as the latter tend to be more variable over time, especially in rural-based economies. Given that such variability is to some degree predictable, consumption will be a better indicator of current welfare.) When this chapter refers to 'income' this can be taken as an abbreviation for either consumption expenditure or disposable income.

It is well recognized that household income is not a sufficient statistic for average economic welfare within the household. The aim is typically to obtain a monetary metric of the typical welfare level within a household. The most common

---

[11] Further discussion of the data issues can be found in (*inter alia*) Gottschalk and Smeeding (1997), Anand and Segal (2008), and Ravallion (2016a, Part 2).

[12] The main option is phone interviews, though these are mainly found in rich countries. All the data issues discussed here apply to phone interviews. There is evidence (for Austria) that phone interviews impart an additional (downward) bias to inequality measures (Fessler et al. 2018).

method in practice is to divide household income (or consumption) by a deflator that reflects both prices and demographics (household size and composition).[13]

3.1 Surveying Errors

There are sampling errors, of course, though the national surveys used in measuring global inequality have large samples, and aggregating globally will probably further reduce the mean error. However, there are reasons to suspect that the within-country component in Figure 2.1 is systematically underestimated due to non-sampling errors.

An important source of bias is selective compliance with the randomized assignments done in sampling, such that there is a lower probability of rich people being included in the final sample used to estimate inequality measures. Such non-random compliance in surveys is a concern almost everywhere, and may be becoming more worrying over time. Traditional survey instruments are time consuming, often requiring many hours, often including multiple household members. With rising living standards, the opportunity cost of time doing surveys is likely to rise; yet surveys do not appear to be getting any shorter. Higher income households are likely to have a higher marginal cost of survey participation given the opportunity cost of time. It can also be hard to reach rich households due to gated communities and/or residences.

In theory, such selective compliance has ambiguous effects on the Lorenz curve and so does not necessarily imply that inequality measures are underestimated (Korinek et al. 2006). However, the evidence we have suggests that there is a bias. On re-weighting the data for the US, Korinek et al. (2006) estimate that correcting for selective compliance adds five percentage points to the Gini index, bringing it from 0.45 to around 0.50. This method requires a common support assumption; this fails if (for example) none of the super-rich participate in the survey.

There are also concerns about under-reporting of incomes even when there is a response, especially income from capital and illicit income sources. This too has theoretically ambiguous effects on standard inequality measures; if someone living well above the mean underreports their income in the survey then

---

[13] The deflator is interpretable as a 'poverty line' (the personal cost of a fixed reference utility level) and the ratio is variously called 'real income' (up to a scalar) or the 'welfare ratio' (Blackorby and Donaldson 1987). This is only an exact money metric of utility under homothetic preferences. More generally, one requires an equivalent income function giving the monetary income needed to attain the current utility level at fixed reference prices and household characteristics (King 1983). This idea can also be applied with heterogeneous (non-homothetic) preferences (see, e.g., Fleurbaey and Blanchet 2013). Applications are still scarce. An example in the context of measuring poverty can be found in Ravallion and van de Walle (1991).

this need not reduce the popular Gini index (and may even increase it), though such under-reporting will always reduce MLD.[14]

Reflecting both selective compliance and under-reporting, estimates using income tax records have indicated larger 'high-end' incomes than are found in surveys (Atkinson et al. 2011). Unlike household surveys, income reporting for tax purposes is required by law, often with penalties for non-compliance or false reports. However, the narrow coverage of income tax schemes in most developing countries makes this a less convincing approach in such settings, though the data from tax records that do exist can still provide a useful clue. Drawing on income tax records, Chancel and Piketty (2017) provide estimates (requiring many assumptions) of inequality measures for India that suggest considerably higher income inequality than those underlying the numbers for South Asia in Figure 2.2. Similarly, the finding in Figure 2.2 of relatively low inequality in the Middle East and North Africa, based on household surveys, changes when one draws on these other data sources to better reflect the high-end; see World Inequality Lab (2018) using their World Inequality Database (WID). Anand and Segal (2017) estimate global inequality measures by combining survey-based distributions with data on top incomes from the WID. Then the decline in global inequality is only evident from 2005, with little sign of a trend either way prior to that.

My expectation is that inequality within countries is both higher and rising more than the data in Figure 2.1 suggest, on the presumption that many newly affluent respondents are reticent to fully reveal their gains or even to participate in surveys. It is unclear what bias if any would be imparted to Figure 2.3.

3.2   Two Neglected Sources of Bias

Two data issues that are relevant to inequality measures stand out as especially neglected in the literature. The first relates to intra-household inequality. The standard (indeed, near universal) assumption is that there is equality within the household. This is almost certainly wrong, and the direction of bias is clear: we will underestimate overall inequality. Evidence on the magnitude of this bias is scarce. In one of the few cases in which we can estimate the distribution of consumption within households, Lambert et al. (2014) find a Gini index in Senegal of 0.60 when one attributes to each person the average per capita consumption of his or her household. If instead each individual is attributed the per capita consumption of his or her subgroup within the household, then the Gini index rises

---

[14] This follows from a result in Cowell and Flachaire (2018), namely that, when comparing two distributions that differ in one person's income, the greater the distance from equality, the higher the inequality.

to 0.63.[15] It is unclear how this source of bias would affect the time profile of inequality, though there is some evidence that gender inequalities are declining in some relevant domains, notably schooling (World Bank 2011). Then we might conjecture that the impact of this omission is becoming less important over time. If so, then this source of bias may attenuate the rise in average inequality within countries.

The second issue relates to prices. Differences in prices between countries are dealt with using purchasing power parity (PPP) rates of exchange. Since price levels tend to be higher in richer countries (especially due to higher wage rates, implying higher prices of non-traded goods), using PPPs rather than official exchange rates tends to reduce the level of inequality *between* countries. For example, Milanovic (2005) shows that the global Gini index using PPPs is 0.65, as compared to 0.81 using official exchange rates. PPPs are systematically revised at times in the light of the new price surveys across countries (as used to estimate the PPPs) and methodological changes. The PPPs from the 2011 round of price surveys saw upward revisions in the estimated real incomes for some developing countries (notably in Asia) implying lower global inequality measures (Inklaar and Rao 2017). It is well known that the price surveys that feed into the PPPs are biased toward urban areas, but the extent of this bias has varied across regions of the world. Ravallion (2018c) argues that the 2011 price surveys were less urban-biased in Asia than for prior years or other regions, and that this change accounts for some share of the impact of the PPP revisions on global inequality.

It is not common to include deflators for geographic cost-of-living differences *within* counties. Within-country inequality is likely to be overestimated due to this omission. Using the data that are available on regional price differentials for Canada and the US, Lessmann (2014) confirms that standard methods (ignoring spatial price differences) overestimate inequality measures, though the trends over time are little affected. For developing countries, however, the expectation is that spatial price differentials will be attenuated with economic development (notably through lower transport costs due to better infrastructure). Then correcting for this bias can be expected to reveal a steeper increase over time in inequality within countries.

Thus these two omissions in standard data sources—intra-household inequality and sub-national prices—point in opposite directions, both in terms of the levels and the trends over time.

---

[15] One subgroup is the head; others comprise one or more of the wives and her children. Other evidence can be found in Haddad and Kanbur (1990), Sahn and Younger (2009), and De Vreyer and Lambert (2018).

3.3 The Role of Nationality

In the prevailing practice among economists, 'countries' only have salience as arbitrary groupings of people. There is no concept of 'nationality' underlying Figures 2.1 and 2.2. Yet, many people seem to care more about inequality within their country of residence than globally.

There are competing views on the relevance of national borders to inequality and policy responses. Philosophers such as Singer (2010) argue that national borders, or distance, are not morally relevant to the case for helping disadvantaged people whom we can help. By this view, one *should* care about everyone, no matter where they live. This has been dubbed the 'cosmopolitan view'.[16] In the literature on inequality measurement, this view is seen as an implication of the 'anonymity' (or 'symmetry') axiom, which says that it does not matter who has which income. This is an ethical premise of standard global inequality and poverty measures. Against this view, there is a nationalistic approach whereby 'global' inequality is simply the average level of inequality in the world. For example, this is how Eurostat (2015) measure overall inequality in Europe. Brandolini and Carta (2016) postulate a social welfare function that treats people equally within the country of residence but puts lower weight on foreigners.

This chapter takes the cosmopolitan view. This does not deny that nations exist and that their governments typically take actions to address inequality within their borders. The institutional fact of nation states and the limitations of global institutions constrain what global redistribution can be achieved in practice. These real-world constraints do not, however, diminish the moral case for a cosmopolitan perspective on 'global inequality'—a perspective that values all people of the world equally, no matter where they may happen to live.

The cosmopolitan view still allows a role for nationality, independently of 'own-income'. The issue can be thought about in terms of omissions/errors in measuring individual welfare. Inequality and poverty measures are summary statistics of a distribution of money-metrics of welfare. The type of global inequality measure found in this literature implicitly characterizes individual welfare in a rather narrow way, as solely a function of individual consumption or income as measured in surveys. One way in which national income may matter independently of 'own-income' stems from the longstanding idea of relative deprivation. This postulates a welfare loss from economic gains to (say) co-residents that are not shared with the person in question. Then we can rationalize a nationalistic view that 'global inequality' is just the average national inequality across

---

[16] See the discussions in Caney (2005), Nagel (2005), and Brandolini and Carta (2016).

countries. This emerges as the limiting case in which only one's relative income within the country of residence matters.[17]

Against this view, it can be argued that there are also (positive) external welfare gains from living in a richer country that would not be reflected in survey-based 'own-incomes'. A case in point is Wagner's Law (Musgrave 1969), namely that the share of national income devoted to public services rises with income.[18] While Wagner's Law need not apply to all types of public spending or all countries, it is a plausible assumption that richer countries have better public goods and that these deliver gains in economic welfare that are not adequately captured in the survey-based measures of current disposable income or consumption expenditure used in measuring global inequality. Administrative and judicial capabilities tend to improve, creating more secure economic opportunities that need not be well reflected in current incomes. Mean income can also pick up income opportunities not reflected in the recall periods used in surveys. Studies of global subjective welfare suggest that people feel better off in richer countries at a given level of own household income; one such study concludes that 'a richer person in a rich nation would be better off than a rich person in a poor country' (Diener et al. 2013: 273).

In short, one can point to plausible arguments and some evidence to support the view that there are *positive* external effects of living in a richer country at given own income. This can stem from the likely positive correlation between national income and factors conducive to a higher long-run personal income, better public services, and greater security. None of these gains are likely to be properly reflected in current incomes as measured in surveys.

The implication is clear: the (large) differences in average incomes found between rich and poor countries create an extra (horizontal) inequality between their residents, not reflected in their observed current incomes. This is a source of downward bias in prevailing measures of the between-country component of global inequality. Yet the likelihood that living in a richer country delivers gains to economic welfare that are not reflected in survey-based incomes has been entirely ignored by past measures of global inequality. What does this imply quantitatively for measures of global inequality?

3.4 Testing Sensitivity to Allowing National Income to Matter

To test the sensitivity of global inequality measures to allowing national income to matter to individual welfare, one needs to adjust survey-based incomes. It is

---

[17] Note that the national mean of the ratio of own income to the national mean is unity for all countries, leaving no inequality between countries.

[18] For evidence of this see Akitoby et al. (2006) and Afonso and Alves (2017).

assumed that this adjustment does not change (relative) inequality within countries. All incomes within a given country are then multiplied by the constant that depends on the national mean, preserving the distribution within countries. Specifically, the adjusted income is $m_{jt}^{\alpha} y_{ijt}$ where $y_{ijt} (> 0)$. denotes the surveyed income of household i in country j at time t, m_{jt} is the corresponding mean in j, and α is a parameter reflecting the extra value attached to (log) national income.[19] Global inequality is then measured using the distribution of these adjusted incomes. The standard approach among economists (such as used in the estimates reported in Section 2) has $\alpha = 0$. When $\alpha = -1$ we have the strongly relative view of Easterlin (1974) and others, whereby only relative income matters $(y_{ijt}^{*} = y_{ijt}/m_{jt})$. (A value of $\alpha < -1$ can be ruled out under the assumption that y_{ijt}^{*} is non-decreasing in own income at given relative income.) For $-1 < \alpha < 0$, the welfare metric depends positively on both own income and relative income.[20] Then the adjusted (log) income is a weighted mean of log survey-based income and log relative income (i.e., the log of adjusted income is $(1+\alpha)\ln y_{ijt} - \alpha \ln(y_{ijt}/m_{jt})$). However, we can also allow that (on balance) a higher national mean implies higher real income at given own-income, based on the surveys, that is, $\alpha > 0$. Clearly this will yield a higher between-country component of global inequality. The higher the value of α, the greater the between-country inequality (Ravallion 2018b).

A clue to the value of a can be found in the literature on subjective welfare. In most of that literature, either the samples are micro-data drawn for one country, or the analysis is based on comparisons of means across countries. What we need is a study of 'global' micro-data. One such study is Helliwell et al. (2010), which reports regression coefficients of subjective wellbeing on own-income and national income (GDP per capita), both in logs; the ratio of the coefficient on log national income to that on log own-income gives an estimate of α.[21] The regressions suggest a positive value with an upper bound estimate around $\alpha = 0.5$. However, there are also indirect effects of national income through the other control variables used in Helliwell et al., so the true value of α is likely to be higher. For example, the indirect effect via life expectancy alone would add about 0.05 to the effect of log national income on satisfaction with life, which would raise the upper bound estimate for α to around 0.6 (Ravallion 2018b).

How much does the choice of α matter empirically? Clearly the strong form of relative deprivation theory $(\alpha = -1)$ implies that global interpersonal inequality is far lower than prevailing measures suggest since it is then entirely

---

[19] Alternatively, the effect of national income could be additive $(y_{ijt}^{*} \equiv y_{ijt}/\alpha m_{jt})$. There are two reasons to question this. First, it does not seem plausible that the gain from living in a rich country is constant for everyone in that country; it would seem more plausible that it is greater for higher-income households. Second, the additive form does not allow for relative deprivation whereby adjusted income has a positive weight on y_{ijt}/m_{jt}.

[20] This is the special case considered by Ravallion and Chen (2013) and Milanovic and Roemer (2016).

[21] Also see Helliwell (2008) and Diener et al. (2010).

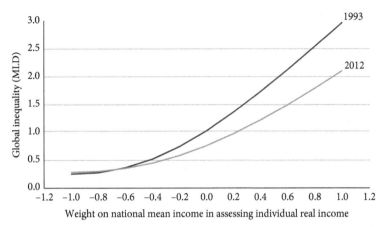

Figure 2.4 Global inequality for various weights on (log) national mean income
Source: Based on Ravallion (2018b).

within countries. This changes dramatically when one attaches a positive value to national income (at given own-income), such as when living in a richer country brings benefits in terms of access to non-market goods and services, and better opportunities for private support. Figure 2.4 shows how the global MLD varies with α for 1993 and 2012. Global inequality falls as long as $\alpha > -0.6$.[22] Also notice that the upward adjustment to the measure of global inequality rises sharply with higher α.

For even moderate α, (positive) global inequality is far higher than prevailing measures suggest, and far higher than found in the most unequal country. Indeed, the differences in levels of inequality due to even rather modest differences in how one values national mean income tend to swamp the differences seen over time in standard measures, or the differences we see between countries. They are also large relative to the impact of even a substantial underestimation of the incomes of the rich. Suppose, for example, that incomes of all the richest 1 per cent in the world are actually double the numbers in Lakner and Milanovic (2016a) for 2008.[23] This would add about 0.1 to MLD,[24] which is about the same as adding 10 per cent of log national mean income to log own income to allow for the gains from living in an economically-better off country.

---

[22] The intersection point is at $\alpha = -0.66$.

[23] Lakner and Milanovic estimate that in 2008 the world's richest 1 per cent had an average income of US$64,213 (converted at PPP for 2005) while the overall mean was US$4,097.

[24] Let all incomes of the richest p^r *proportion of the population, with income share* s^r, *be underestimated by a factor* k. *Then the change in MLD is* $(s^r - p^r) \ln k$.

In summary, the stylized fact that overall inequality has been falling since around 1990 is not robust, though one only finds rising inequality with a seemingly high negative weight on national income, such as due to a strong welfare effect of relative deprivation. The finding of falling between-country inequality since 1990 is robust whatever value (positive or negative) one attaches to national income in assessing individual economic welfare.

This discussion has focused on data-related issues. The rest of the chapter will largely take the data as given and focus on the conceptual foundations of prevailing measures.

4 Ethical Aversion to Extremes in Either Tail

It has long been recognized that an inequality index can be thought of as a summary statistic of the normative judgements made about how different levels of income are weighted in assessing social welfare. This was made explicit in Dalton (1920) and developed further in Atkinson (1970) who proposed a class of inequality measures in which the aversion to inequality is represented by an ethical parameter, reflecting the trade-offs allowed between incomes at different levels. (The discussion will return to this measure.)

We must first unpack Figure 2.1 to see how income gains were distributed. Milanovic (2013) and Lakner and Milanovic (2016a) provide an informative picture of the evolution of income distribution in the world. They plot the proportionate gain in income over 1988–2008 against fractiles of the income distribution, as reproduced in Figure 2.5; this is a version of a 'growth incidence curve' (GIC) (Ravallion and Chen 2003).[25] Figure 2.5 has been dubbed the 'elephant chart' since it traces the shape of an elephant's head with its trunk held high. On the right side we see rising inequality in the rich world; between the 80th percentile (from the bottom) and the top 1 per cent globally we see a steeply positive curve (the elephant's raised trunk), rising from near zero growth to over a 60 per cent gain for the top percentile. But we also see something striking—the

---

[25] The methodology used to construct the GIC in Figure 2.4 is explained in Lakner and Milanovic (2016a). Note that the version of the GIC in Lakner and Milanovic gives growth rates for ventiles (with the top 1 per cent separated out) rather than percentiles. This smooths their curve. The percentile version can be found in Corlett (2016). This shows negative growth rates among the poorest and in a neighbourhood of the eightieth percentile. These have been averaged out in the Lakner and Milanovic version, as also used in Milanovic (2016). The negative values at the bottom probably reflect compositional effects, given that the set of countries is not held fixed. This is consistent with the fact that the 'quasi-non-anonymous' GIC in Lakner and Milanovic (2016a: Figure 5) does not show any negative growth rates.

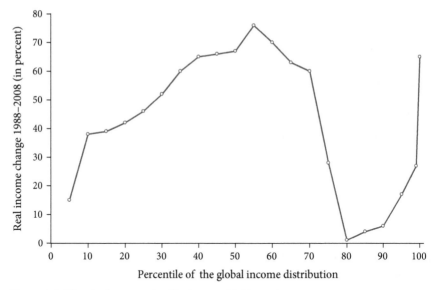

Figure 2.5 The elephant graph of Lakner and Milanovic

Source: Based on estimates in Lakner and Milanovic (2016a).

marked proportionate rise in incomes for those near the middle of the global distribution (the elephant's massive and expanding head). This came with considerably slower growth for the poorest decile.

Based on the elephant graph, Milanovic (2016) argues that the rich world's lower-middle class—by interpretation, those living around the 80th percentile of Figure 2.5—have seen little or no gain from globalization. This is in marked contrast to the middle class of the developing world, who have seen substantial gains in the wake of the falling incidence of absolute poverty.[26] The largest percentage gain in the elephant graph is close to the global median. In Milanovic's interpretation, the emerging middle class in the developing world have been the big gainers from globalization, while the losers were the (relatively) poor and middle class within the rich world.

Whether or not one agrees with Milanovic on the importance of globalization to the elephant graph, it is clear that this is a much more ambiguous picture of distributional change than suggested by the claim that 'global inequality is

---

[26] Ravallion (2010) argues that the developing world's middle class can be defined as those who are not poor by typical standards in poor countries, but are poor by standards of rich countries. By this definition the middle class has expanded greatly, and is now a huge segment of the population— around 50 per cent in 2005, and higher still today.

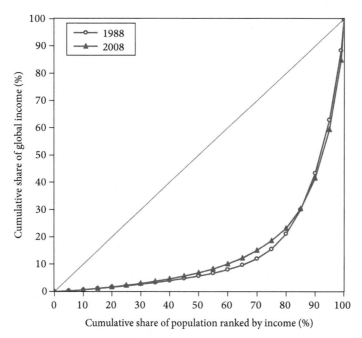

Figure 2.6 Lorenz curves for global income 1988 and 2008
Source: Based on estimates in Lakner and Milanovic (2016a).

falling'. The global Lorenz curves intersect internally, both at low percentiles and in the second decile from the top, as can be seen in Figure 2.6. While the overall Gini index fell (from 72 per cent to 71 per cent) this came with a marked inward shift of the Lorenz curve around the middle—between the 30th and 80th percentiles—and an outward shift among the top decile, and a declining share for the poorest 5 per cent. The Lakner–Milanovic estimates imply that the share of the world's top 1 per cent rose from 12 per cent to 15 per cent between 1988 and 2008. Some valid inequality measures (such as the Gini index and the Theil index, as in Figure 2.1) can show a decrease while other equally valid measures do not. This is an implication of the fact that there is not Lorenz dominance in Figure 2.6.[27]

Consider now the Atkinson (1970) index. This has a parameter ε reflecting the aversion to inequality; a higher value of ε implies that one is willing to incur a greater loss when transferring money from the rich to the poor (i.e., a lower share

---

[27] Lorenz dominance requires that one Lorenz curve is entirely within the other up to its end points. Such dominance implies an unambiguous ordering for all measures satisfying the Pigou–Dalton transfer axiom (Atkinson 1970).

actually reaching the poor) and yet still judge that social welfare has increased. More precisely, the Atkinson index can be written as $1-\left(\frac{1}{n}\sum_{i=1}^{n}\left(\frac{y_i}{\bar{y}}\right)^{1-\varepsilon}\right)^{1/(1-\varepsilon)}$ where y_i is the income of person $i=1,...,n$ while the overall mean is $\bar{y}$, and where $\varepsilon>1$ is the ethical parameter reflecting inequality-aversion;[28] the higher the value of the greater the loss one is willing to incur when transferring money from the rich to the poor and yet still judge that social welfare has increased. In Ravallion (2018a) I calculate that the Atkinson index of global inequality has fallen over 1988–2008 for $\varepsilon\leq4$ but that inequality has risen for $\varepsilon=5$. This is a high value for the Atkinson parameter compared to those found in the literature, which are rarely above 2. (Atkinson's (1970) illustrative calculations of his index tested sensitivity up to 2.5.) The upshot of these observations is that with sufficiently strong aversion to inequality, one will judge that global inequality has risen over this period.

Similarly to the Gini and Theil indices, the Atkinson index satisfies the Pigou–Dalton transfer axiom, namely that any (mean-preserving) income transfer for which the donor has a higher initial (and final) income than the recipient must reduce inequality. This axiom need not be universally accepted. In a survey I did in 2018 of my undergraduate students (using a confidential computer-based survey tool) I asked which of these two distributions had higher inequality: A: (2, 4, 6, 10) or B: (2, 5, 5, 10). About half (36/71) said A, consistent with the transfer axiom. But 31 per cent said B. I also asked the same question using the anonymous polling tool in Twitter. Out of 214 respondents in a 24-hour period, I again found that about half (53 per cent) ranked the two distributions consistently with the transfer axiom. By contrast, 21 per cent said B was more unequal while the remainder said that the extent of inequality was no different between A and B.

In exploring this further with my students, I found that almost all (92 per cent) said that (2, 4, 6) was more unequal than (3, 4, 5), consistent with the transfer axiom. So it is not that those who thought that (2, 5, 5, 10) was more unequal than (2, 4, 6, 10) generally rejected the transfer axiom. Rather (as came out in class discussion), they put extra weight on the greater inequality in the tails, notably among the 'rich'. The fact that the richest person, with an income of 10, had even more in B than the next richest was troubling to my students, and outweighed the more equal middle. This is an example of what can be called an ethical aversion to 'high-end inequality', and it may override the Pigou–Dalton principle, and not be reflected in any standard inequality index.

Of course, the fact that growth is positive for such a large segment of the population in Figure 2.5 is good news. This assures that we see a reduction in any standard measure of absolute poverty (for which the poverty line is fixed in real

---

[28] For $\varepsilon=1$ the Atkinson index is one minus the ratio of the geometric mean to the arithmetic mean.

terms over a wide range of possible poverty lines). Indeed, one finds first-order dominance over this period, for a very wide range of poverty lines, up to and beyond the US official line (Chen and Ravallion 2010, 2013).[29]

However, there has been much less progress for the world's poorest, who can reasonably be said to have been 'left behind'. We already saw a hint of this in the elephant graph (Figure 2.5). But this graph is highly aggregated at the bottom. We need a lens with higher magnification, and we need to fix the set of countries to avoid selection bias. To see how the poorest are doing we need to measure the floor to living standards—below which their density is zero and above which it is positive. The floor cannot be reliably measured by the lowest observed consumption or income in a survey, which is likely to be a noisy indicator. Elsewhere I have proposed that the floor should be estimated instead as the weighted mean consumption of those living below some level, with higher weight on people with lower observed consumption (Ravallion 2016b). When the weights decline linearly, the expected value of the floor is $z\left(1 - \frac{SPG}{PG}\right)$, where Z is the income level above which there is no chance of being the poorest person while SPG and PG are the squared-poverty gap and poverty gap indices using z as the poverty line. This measure indicates only very modest growth in the floor of the distribution of permanent consumption in the world, which is still barely above a survival level (Ravallion 2016b).

For the purpose of this chapter, Figure 2.7a provides an update of the estimates in Ravallion (2016b). I have set z at the World Bank's international poverty line of US$1.90 per person per day at 2011 purchasing power parity. From around 2000, the developing world has seen a substantial increase in the mean consumption, but this has clearly not been shared by the poorest. We see both absolute and relative divergence between the floor and the mean. One caveat on Figure 2.7a is that the data include income surveys (about one-third of the 2,400 household surveys on which the Figure 2.7 is based). Incomes can be zero or negative, but this need not be indicative of living standards. However, the results are essentially the same if one takes out the income surveys and only uses consumption, as can be seen in Figure 2.7b.

This finding that the poorest have seen rather little progress raises a serious moral concern about how the distribution of income is evolving in the world. The concern echoes social policy discussions, which have often put emphasis (at least in their rhetoric) on the need to raise the floor—for example, the desire

---

[29] First-order dominance implies an unambiguous poverty ranking for all additive measures (Atkinson 1987). Note that first-order dominance is not implied by the Lakner–Milanovic GIC. However, this reflects the fact that the set of countries is not fixed; when one holds countries constant, one obtains positive growth rates at all percentiles in their dataset (Lakner and Milanovic 2016a: Figure 5).

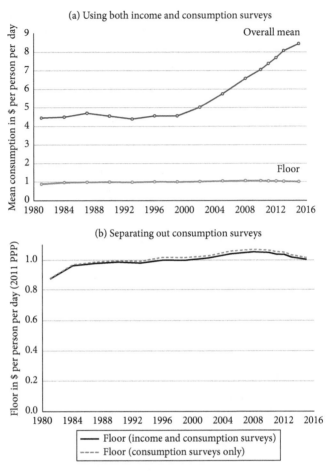

Figure 2.7 Consumption floor for the developing world
Source: Author's calculations.

to 'leave no one behind' is prominent in the United Nations Sustainable Development Goals (SDGs). In the period from the middle of the nineteenth to the middle of the twentieth century, during which time today's rich world virtually eliminated extreme absolute poverty, more progress appears to have been made in raising the consumption floor than we are seeing in the developing world today (Ravallion 2016b).

We have seen that introducing a stronger ethical aversion to inequality changes the assessment of whether global inequality is increasing. If one puts a very high weight on the poorest then one will also conclude that global inequality is rising. The same is true if one introduces greater aversion to rising high-end inequality. These two factors—the lack of progress for the poorest, and steep gains to the richest—thus point in the same direction.

The findings of this section also point to the limitations of some widely used inequality measures. As noted, the fact that there is not Lorenz dominance implies that some measures will show a decrease in global inequality and some will show an increase. This relates to the underlying differences in the ethical weights attached to changes at different income levels. Measures such as the ratio of the mean to the median and the inter-quartile range may be quite insensitive to what is happening at the tails, among the poorest and the richest, though (by the same token) they will be more robust to errors in the tails than other measures.

5 Absolute Inequality

The empirical literature has focused almost solely on measures of relative inequality, whereby the measure depends on the ratios of incomes. This class of measures follows from the scale invariance axiom (SIA) in the theory of inequality measurement, which says that the measure of inequality does not change when all incomes are multiplied by a constant. However, this *is* an axiom. It need not be accepted. The alternative axiom is translation invariance, which says that the inequality index is unaffected by adding a constant. This yields absolute inequality measures that depend instead on the absolute differences (not normalized by the current mean). The choice depends entirely on what axiom one prefers—scale invariance or translation invariance. There is no right or wrong answer, as theoretical papers on inequality measurement have long recognized.[30] Yet the bulk of the applied work on global inequality has used relative measures.[31] Indeed, this is typically done without even noting the fact that the option exists of using absolute measures.

Two examples illustrate the difference. Consider first the Gini index. The absolute Gini index is simply the average absolute difference between all pairs of incomes, $\Sigma_i \Sigma_j | y_i - y_j | / 2n^2$ (one can normalize by a fixed reference mean). By contrast, in calculating the relative Gini index all household incomes are normalized by the current mean. The second example is the standard deviation, $s = \left(\Sigma_i (y_i - \bar{y})^2 \right)^{1/2}$. This is clearly an absolute inequality measure, since adding a constant to all incomes leaves it unchanged. (The same is true of the variance) Consider instead the coefficient of variation, s^2) This is the corresponding relative inequality measure, in that multiplying by a constant leaves the measure unchanged.

[30] See, for example, Dalton (1920), Kolm (1976), Blackorby and Donaldson (1980), Chakravarty and Tyagarupananda (1998), and Bosmans and Cowell (2010).

[31] Exceptions are Ravallion (2003b, 2004, 2014), Atkinson and Brandolini (2010), Anand and Segal (2015), and Niño-Zarazúa et al. (2017).

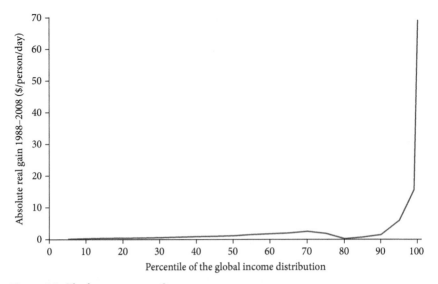

Figure 2.8 Elephant or serpent?

Note: Incidence of the absolute income gains corresponding to Figure 2.5.

Source: Author's calculation using the estimates made by Lakner and Milanovic (2016a).

There is no sign of a popular consensus on this issue. A number of experiments (all with university students to my knowledge) have found that 40–60 per cent of participants (in the UK, Israel, Germany, and the US) think about inequality in absolute rather than relative terms.[32] In the aforementioned surveys of my students at Georgetown I have found that the majority do not accept the SIA. For example, when asked which of the two income distributions, (1, 2, 3) and (2, 4, 6), has higher inequality (if either), 258 (56 per cent) out of 460 students said it was the latter distribution. When comparing (2, 4, 6) with (4, 8, 12), 57 per cent said that the latter had higher inequality. Similarly, in my aforementioned Twitter survey, out of 247 responses in a 24-hour period (21/22 November 2018), 48 per cent said that (2, 4, 6) had higher inequality than (1, 2, 3), while 45 per cent said inequality was the same. While these are hardly random samples drawn from any well-defined population, they are at least consistent with the view that many people view inequality as absolute, not relative.

Even if relative inequality does not change during a period of growth in mean income, the absolute income gains to the rich will obviously be greater than those for the poor, given existing inequality. We saw in the previous section that a focus on the poorest suggests rising inequality, both relative and absolute. Figure 2.8

---

[32] The literature on survey-based perceptions of inequality has followed Amiel and Cowell (1992), who found that 40 per cent of the university students they surveyed (in the UK and Israel) thought about inequality in absolute rather than relative terms. Harrison and Seidl (1994) report similar findings for a large sample of German university students.

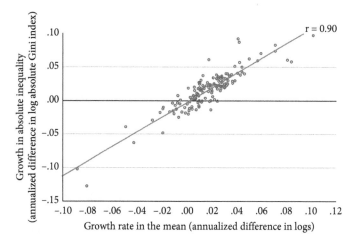

Figure 2.9 Absolute inequality and growth in household income per capita
Source: Author's calculations.

gives the absolute GIC—the US$ gains across percentiles of the whole distribution. Compared to Figure 2.5, the elephant's head has shrunk greatly relative to the trunk. Over this 20-year period, the absolute gain in mean daily income of the poorest 5 per cent was 7 cents per person, while for the richest 1 per cent it was almost US$70 (and the latter number could well be an underestimate, as noted in Section 2). In absolute terms, the developing world's middle class and (especially) its poor have gained rather little; it is only because they started off so poor that the elephant's head is so large in the (relative) GIC in Figure 2.5. While the relative Gini index fell slightly (from 0.72 to 0.71) the absolute version rose appreciably (from 0.72 to 0.90).[33]

We saw in Figure 2.3 that there is weak correlation between changes in the relative Gini index and growth rates. This becomes much stronger when one switches to the absolute Gini index, as can be seen in Figure 2.9. Higher rates of growth in the overall mean come with steeper increases in absolute inequality. This is hardly surprising, given that the absolute Gini index is (up to a scaler) the relative index times the mean. However, the comparison of Figures 2.3 and 2.9 underlines the sensitivity of statements about inequality and growth to the axiomatic foundations. Switch out one axiom and the picture changes a lot. The (many) people who view inequality as absolute rather than relative will probably see sharply rising inequality in growing economies. They are not wrong; they simply have a different concept of what 'inequality' means.

When combined with the tendency for measures of absolute poverty to fall with growth in mean income, the (strong) tendency for absolute inequality to rise

---

[33] For the purpose of this calculation I have normalized the indices such that the two are equal in 1988.

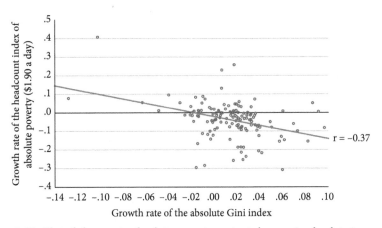

Figure 2.10 Plot of changes in absolute poverty against changes in absolute inequality across developing countries
Source: Author's calculations.

with that growth points to a trade-off between reducing absolute inequality and reducing poverty, as discussed in Ravallion (2005). Figure 2.10 illustrates this point, by plotting the annualized growth rate of the headcount index of absolute poverty (using US$1.90 a day) against the corresponding growth rate in the absolute Gini index (as used in Figure 2.9).[34] This pattern suggests that those who see inequality as absolute and give high priority to reducing it may well find themselves living in an absolutely poorer world. Greater clarity is needed on what trade-offs one is willing to accept between reducing absolute inequality and reducing absolute poverty.

Will we see absolute inequality start to decline at some point in the future? That depends on what absolute gaps we focus on and whether relative inequality is declining. If we are talking about the world's richest 1 per cent (say) and the poorest 1 per cent then it is plain that we will not see a declining absolute gap in the foreseeable future if recent trends continue, since we are not even seeing falling relative inequality between the two groups of people.

There is a range of 'middle' incomes for which recent trends do suggest declining absolute inequality over the next few decades. Compare the world's middle incomes—the 50th–60th percentiles, say (just above the global median)—with the income of the 80th–90th percentiles, that is, the group that Milanovic (2016) identifies as the rich world's 'middle class'. The elephant graph (Figure 2.5) shows that the former group saw incomes growing strongly at 3.6 per cent per annum over 1988–2008, while the latter group saw little growth (0.23 per cent per

---

[34] The correlation coefficient of −0.37 (n = 136) is significant at the 1 per cent level. If one drops the outlier with the highest rate of increase in the poverty rate (Figure 2.10) then the correlation coefficient drops to −0.28 (n = 135), but it is still significant at the 1 per cent level.

annum). The ratio of mean incomes in 2008 was 5.7 (Lakner and Milanovic 2016a: Table 3). Then it can be readily verified that absolute inequality between the two will decline, though it will take fifty-three years for the two income levels to converge if recent trends continue.[35] One might question whether a near zero growth rate of the rich world's middle class is sustainable. Suppose instead that this income group sees a 1 per cent per annum growth rate, with all else unchanged. Then absolute divergence between the rich world's middle class and the world's middle will rise for the next twenty years, and only then start to fall, vanishing after about seventy years.

Such calculations should be taken with a grain of salt. They only serve to illustrate that absolute inequality is likely to persist for some time even with falling relative inequality. Indeed, with current trends, the gap will rise between the world's richest and poorest, and may well also do so between the rich world's middle class and the new middle class of the developing world.

6 Conclusions

It is important to know how robust prevailing measures of global income inequality are to relaxing the (often implicit) assumptions made in measurement. This is not just an academic question. The measures used to inform public debates should accord with popular perceptions of what 'inequality' means. That is almost certainly not the case at present. And that provides a clue to understanding the differing narratives one hears on what is happening to inequality.

Within-country measures based on standard data sources may well underestimate inequality, though some data deficiencies point in the opposite direction. There are many issues, but one stands out in my view: selective compliance with the randomized assignments in surveys. This is a serious and (possibly) increasing concern for measuring inequality almost everywhere. This does not necessarily imply that inequality measures are underestimated, but the evidence so far suggests that they are. Appropriate re-weighting methods can address this problem in a way that is internally consistent with the survey, but may still miss the extremes. Triangulation with other data sources (such as income tax records when coverage and compliance are adequate) can also help correct the problem. Going forward, the technology of surveying may need to adapt if it is to produce

---

[35] Let t^* be the number of years required for the two incomes to equalize. Then $t^* = \dfrac{\ln(y_1/y_0)}{\ln(g_0/g_s)}$. where y_i is the base year income of group $i = 0,1$ (where $y_1 > y_0$) and g_i is the corresponding growth factor (1+growth rate).

distributional data that represent well the relevant populations. Better linkage across survey and administrative data bases will also help.

When one considers the conceptual foundations of prevailing approaches, one finds further reasons to question the robustness of the claim that global income inequality has been falling over the past thirty years. With sufficient ethical aversion to lack of progress by the poorest, or to steeply rising top incomes, one concludes that global inequality has been rising. A focus on the middle of the global distribution suggests that relative inequality is falling, though it will clearly be a long time (fifty or more years) before the developing world's emerging middle class catches up on average with the rich world's middle class.

Rising global inequality is also indicated if one holds a very strong concern about relative deprivation (or, equivalently, a highly nationalistic perspective on global inequality). However, a more serious omission in prevailing measures may well be that they do not allow for the benefits of living in a richer country at any given level of own-income as measured in surveys. With even a seemingly modest positive effect of national income on individual welfare, global inequality is far higher than we think, though still falling over time.

A credible argument suggesting that global inequality may in fact be rising is found in concerns about the commonly assumed (but contentious) 'scale invariance axiom'. It appears that many people do not accept the relativism implied by this axiom; instead, they look to the absolute gaps between 'rich' and 'poor' in assessing inequality. Then we see clear signs of rising absolute inequality in growing economies. We also see that the world's poorest are being left behind in the wave of higher rates of economic growth in the new millennium. While there are fewer people living near the world's floor of living standards, that floor has risen little despite overall economic growth. A measure based on the income gaps across the whole distribution indicates that absolute inequality has been rising globally with economic growth, and that can be expected to continue for some time given the level of current inequality.

The measurement issues reviewed here are salient to the debates on globalization. Different sides in that debate appear often to hold different ideas about what 'inequality' means (though at times one also hears claims that have no imaginable basis in reason or fact). Those who talk about the widening gap between rich and poor appear to have in mind absolute inequality, not relative inequality. Yet one cannot say that one of these concepts is right and the other wrong—the difference is solely based on the choice between two rival axioms in the theory of inequality measurement. The standard definition in terms of relativities can be questioned; if one does not accept the scale invariance axiom then one can justifiably reject relative measures in favour of absolute ones (satisfying the translation invariance axiom). In this respect, the measurement tools used in this literature appear to be woefully incomplete for informing the public discourse about 'inequality'.

In conclusion, the claim that global income inequality has been falling over the past few decades holds over a subset of the defensible measures, but only a subset. This ambiguity belies the (confident) claims one often hears, with one side predicting a far more equal world ahead, and the other claiming that development has failed. Given the scope for sensible people to disagree on the desirable properties of an inequality measure—and there is no scientific case for the near monopoly of relative measures in applied work by economists—more productive debates on globalization and development might be possible if both sides better understood what concepts of inequality they are using. To talk about 'inequality' without making explicit whether one means absolute or relative inequality is especially problematic. The non-robustness found in this chapter also points to the limitations of both a single concept of inequality and any single overall measure, such as the popular Gini index. A single measure is unlikely to be acceptable to everyone. Thankfully, the more flexible tools that are now available for representing distributional change, such as (absolute and relative) growth incidence curves, can be used to better inform public debates on this topic.

References

Afonso, A., and J. Alves (2017). 'Reconsidering Wagner's Law: Evidence from the Functions of the Government'. *Applied Economics Letters*, 24(5), 346–50.

Akitoby, B., B. Clements, S. Gupta, and G. Inchauste (2006). 'Public Spending, Voracity, and Wagner's Law in Developing Countries'. *European Journal of Political Economy*, 22(4), 908–24.

Amiel, Y., and F. Cowell (1992). 'Measurement of Income Inequality: Experimental Test by Questionnaire'. *Journal of Public Economics*, 47, 3–26.

Anand, S., and P. Segal (2008). 'What Do We Know about Global Income Inequality?' *Journal of Economic Literature*, 46(1), 57–94.

Anand, S., and P. Segal (2015). 'The Global Distribution of Income'. In A. Atkinson and F. Bourguignon (eds), *Handbook of Income Distribution*, Volume 2. Amsterdam: North-Holland.

Anand, S., and P. Segal (2017). 'Who Are the Global Top 1%?' *World Development*, 95, 111–26.

Atkinson, A. (1970). 'On the Measurement of Inequality'. *Journal of Economic Theory*, 2, 244–63.

Atkinson, A. (1987). 'On the Measurement of Poverty'. *Econometrica*, 55, 749–64.

Atkinson, A., and A. Brandolini (2010). 'On Analyzing the World Distribution of Income'. *World Bank Economic Review*, 24(1), 1–37.

Atkinson, A., and S. Morelli (2014). 'Chartbook of economic inequality'. ECINEQ Working Paper 324.

Atkinson, A., T. Piketty, and E. Saez (2011). 'Top Incomes in the Long Run of History'. *Journal of Economic Literature*, 49(1), 3–71.

Basu, K. (2018). 'Today's Huge Global Inequality...' Twitter, 13 October.

Beddoes, Z.M. (2012). 'The Great Levelling', CNBC.

Blackorby, C., and D. Donaldson (1980). 'A Theoretical Treatment of Indices of Absolute Inequality'. *International Economic Review,* 21(1), 107–36.

Blackorby, C., and D. Donaldson (1987). 'Welfare Ratios and Distributionally Sensitive Cost-Benefit Analysis'. *Journal of Public Economics,* 34, 265–90.

Bosmans, Kristof, and Frank Cowell (2010). 'The Class of Absolute Decomposable Inequality Measures'. *Economics Letters,* 109, 154–6.

Bourguignon, Francois (2016). *The Globalization of Inequality.* Princeton: Princeton University Press.

Bourguignon, Francois, and Christian Morrisson (2002). 'Inequality among World Citizens: 1820–1992'. *American Economic Review,* 92(4), 727–44.

Brandolini, Andrea, and Francesca Carta (2016). 'Some Reflections on the Social Welfare Bases of the Measurement of Global Income Inequality'. *Journal of Globalization and Development,* 7(1), 1–15.

Cai, Meng, Bjorn Gustafsson, Li Qinghai, Li Shi, Chuliang Luo, and Terry Sicular (2018). 'Inequality in the developing giants: China'. Paper presented at the UNU-WIDER conference, *Think Development, Think WIDER,* Helsinki, Finland.

Caney, Simon (2005). *Justice Beyond Borders: A Global Political Theory.* Oxford: Oxford University Press.

Chakravarty, S.R., and S. Tyagarupananda (1998). 'The Subgroup Decomposable Absolute Indices of Inequality'. In S.R. Chakravarty, D. Coondoo, and R. Mukherjee (eds), *Quantitative Economics: Theory and Practice, Essays in Honor of Professor N. Bhattacharya.* New Delhi: Allied Publishers Limited.

Chancel, Lucas, and Thomas Piketty (2017). 'Indian income inequality, 1922–2014: From British Raj to billionaire Raj?' Working Paper 2017/11. World Wealth and Income Database, Paris School of Economics.

Chen, Shaohua, and Martin Ravallion (2010). 'The Developing World Is Poorer than We Thought, but No Less Successful in the Fight against Poverty'. *Quarterly Journal of Economics,* 125(4), 1577–625.

Chen, Shaohua, and Martin Ravallion (2013). 'More Relatively Poor People in a Less Absolutely Poor World'. *Review of Income and Wealth,* 59(1), 1–28.

Corlett, Adam (2016). 'Examining an elephant: Globalization and the lower middle class of the rich world'. Resolution Foundation Report, London.

Cowell, Frank (2000). 'Measurement of Inequality'. In A.B. Atkinson and F. Bourguignon (eds), *Handbook of Income Distribution.* Amsterdam: North-Holland.

Cowell, Frank, and Emmanuel Flachaire (2018). 'Inequality measures and the rich: Why inequality increased more than we thought'. Mimeo, London School of Economics.

Cowen, Tyler (2014). 'Income Inequality Is Not Rising Globally. It's Falling'. *New York Times*, 19 July.

Dalton, Hugh (1920). 'The Measurement of the Inequality of Incomes', *Economic Journal* 30(9): 348–61.

Datt, Gaurav, and Martin Ravallion (1992). 'Growth and Redistribution Components of Changes in Poverty Measures: A Decomposition with Applications to Brazil and India in the 1980s'. *Journal of Development Economics*, 38, 275–95.

De Vreyer, Philippe, and Sylvie Lambert (2018). 'Intra-household inequalities and poverty in Senegal'. Mimeo, Paris School of Economics.

Diener, Ed, W. Ng, J. Harter, and R. Arora (2010). 'Wealth and Happiness across the World: Material Prosperity Predicts Life Evaluation, whereas Psychosocial Prosperity Predicts Positive Feeling', *Journal of Personality and Social Psychology*, 99(1), 52–61.

Diener, Ed, Louis Tay, and Shigehiro Oishi (2013). 'Rising Income and the Subjective Well-Being of Nations', *Journal of Personality and Social Psychology*, 104(2), 267–76.

Easterlin, Richard A. (1974). 'Does Economic Growth Improve the Human Lot? Some Empirical Evidence'. In P.A. David and W.R. Melvin (eds), *Nations and Households in Economic Growth*. Palo Alto: Stanford University Press.

Eurostat (2015). 'Income and Living Conditions'. Luxembourg: Eurostat.

Fessler, Pirmin, Maximilian Kasy, and Peter Lindner (2018). 'Survey Mode Effects on Measured Income Inequality'. *Journal of Economic Inequality*, 16(4), 487–505.

Fleurbaey, Marc, and Didier Blanchet (2013). *Beyond GDP Measuring Welfare and Assessing Sustainability*. Oxford: Oxford University Press.

Gottschalk, Peter, and Timothy Smeeding (1997). 'Cross-National Income Inequality Cross-National Comparisons of Earnings and Income Inequality', *Journal of Economic Literature*, 35, 633–87.

Haddad, Lawrence, and Ravi Kanbur (1990). 'How Serious Is the Neglect of Intra-Household Inequality?' *Economic Journal*, 100, 866–81.

Harrison, Elizabeth, and Christian Seidl (1994). 'Perceptional Inequality and Preferential Judgment: An Empirical Examination of Distributional Axioms'. *Public Choice*, 79, 61–81.

Helliwell, John (2008). 'Life satisfaction and quality of development'. NBER Working Paper 14507.

Helliwell, John, Chris Barrington-Leigh, Anthony Harris, and Haifang Huang (2010). 'International Evidence on the Social Context of Well-Being'. In Ed Diener, John Helliwell, and Daniel Kahneman (eds), *International Differences in Well-Being*. Oxford: Oxford University Press.

Hickel, Jason (2017). *The Divide: A Brief Guide to Global Inequality and Its Solutions*. London: William Heinemann.

Inklaar, R., and P. Rao (2017). 'Cross-Country Income Levels over Time: Did the Developing World Suddenly Become Much Richer?' *American Economic Journal: Macroeconomics*, 9(1), 265–90.

Kanbur, Ravi, Yue Wang, and Xiaobo Zhang (2017). 'The Great Chinese Inequality Turnaround', CEPR DP11892.

King, Mervyn A. (1983). 'Welfare Analysis of Tax Reforms Using Household Level Data'. *Journal of Public Economics*, 21, 183–214.

Kolm, Serge-Christophe (1976). 'Unequal Inequalities I'. *Journal of Economic Theory*, 12(3), 416–42.

Korinek, Anton, Johan Mistiaen, and Martin Ravallion (2006). 'Survey Nonresponse and the Distribution of Income'. *Journal of Economic Inequality*, 4(2), 33–55.

Lakner, Christoph, and Branko Milanovic (2016a). 'Global Income Distribution: From the Fall of the Berlin Wall to the Great Recession'. *World Bank Economic Review*, 30(2), 203–32.

Lakner, Christoph, and Branko Milanovic (2016b). 'Response to Adam Corlett's "Examining an elephant: globalisation and the lower middle class of the rich world"'. Mimeo, Graduate Center, City University of New York.

Lambert, Sylvie, Martin Ravallion, and Dominique van de Walle (2014). 'Intergenerational Mobility and Interpersonal Inequality in an African Economy'. *Journal of Development Economics*, 110, 327–44.

Lessmann, Christian (2014). 'Spatial Inequality and Development—Is There an Inverted-U Relationship?' *Journal of Economic Development*, 106, 35–51.

Milanovic, Branko (2005). *Worlds Apart: Measuring International and Global Inequality.* Princeton: Princeton University Press.

Milanovic, Branko (2013). 'Global Income Inequality in Numbers: in History and Now', *Global Policy*, 4(2), 198–208.

Milanovic, Branko (2016). *Global Inequality: A New Approach for the Age of Globalization.* Cambridge, MA: Harvard University Press.

Milanovic, Branko, and John E. Roemer (2016). 'Interaction of Global and National Income Inequalities'. *Journal of Globalization and Development*, 7(1), 109–15.

Morelli, Salvatore, Timothy Smeeding, and Jeffrey Thompson (2014). 'Post-1970 Trends in Within-Country Inequality and Poverty'. In *Handbook of Income Distribution*, Volume 2, edited by Anthony B. Atkinson and Francois Bourguignon. Amsterdam: Elsevier Science.

Musgrave, Richard (1969). *Fiscal Systems.* New Haven: Yale University Press.

Nagel, Thomas (2005). 'The Problem of Global Justice', *Philosophy and Public Affairs* 33(2), 15–27.

Niño-Zarazúa, Miguel, Laurence Roopez, and Finn Tarp (2017). 'Global Inequality: Global Inequality: Relatively Lower, Absolutely Higher'. *Review of Income and Wealth*, 63(4), 661–84.

OECD (2011). *Divided We Stand: Why Inequality Keeps Rising.* Paris: OECD.

Ravallion, Martin (2003a). 'Inequality Convergence'. *Economics Letters*, 80, 351–6.

Ravallion, Martin (2003b). 'The Debate on Globalization, Poverty and Inequality: Why Measurement Matters'. *International Affairs*, 79(4), 739–54.

Ravallion, Martin (2004). 'Competing Concepts of Inequality in the Globalization Debate'. In Susan Collins and Carol Graham (eds), *Brookings Trade Forum 2004*. Washington, DC: Brookings Institution.

Ravallion, Martin (2005). 'A Poverty-Inequality Trade-Off?' *Journal of Economic Inequality*, 3(2), 169–82.

Ravallion, Martin (2006). 'Looking Beyond Averages in the Trade and Poverty Debate', *World Development* (special issue on *The Impact of Globalization on the World's Poor*, edited by Machiko Nissanke and Erik Thorbecke), 34(8), 1374–92.

Ravallion, Martin (2010). 'The Developing World's Bulging (but Vulnerable) Middle Class'. *World Development*, 38(4), 445–54.

Ravallion, Martin (2014). 'Income Inequality in the Developing World'. *Science*, 344, 851–5.

Ravallion, Martin (2016a). *The Economics of Poverty: History, Measurement and Policy*. New York: Oxford University Press.

Ravallion, Martin (2016b). 'Are the World's Poorest Being Left Behind?' *Journal of Economic Growth*, 21(2), 139–64.

Ravallion, Martin (2018a). 'Inequality and Globalization: A Review Essay'. *Journal of Economic Literature*, 56(2), 1–23.

Ravallion, Martin (2018b). 'Global Inequality When Unequal Countries Create Unequal People'. *European Economic Review*, 111, 85–97.

Ravallion, Martin (2018c). 'An Exploration of the Changes in the International Comparison Program's New Global Economic Landscape'. *World Development*, 105, 201–16.

Ravallion, Martin, and Shaohua Chen (1997). 'What Can New Survey Data Tell Us about Recent Changes in Distribution and Poverty?' *World Bank Economic Review*, 11(2), 357–82.

Ravallion, Martin, and Shaohua Chen (2003). 'Measuring Pro-Poor Growth'. *Economics Letters*, 78(1), 93–9.

Ravallion, Martin, and Shaohua Chen (2011). 'Weakly Relative Poverty'. *Review of Economics and Statistics*, 93(4), 1251–61.

Ravallion, Martin, and Shaohua Chen (2013). 'A Proposal for Truly Global Poverty Measures'. *Global Policy*, 4(3), 258–65.

Ravallion, Martin, and Shaohua Chen (2019). 'Global Poverty Measurement When Relative Income Matters'. *Journal of Public Economics*, 177, 1–13.

Ravallion, Martin, and Dominique van de Walle (1991). 'The Impact on Poverty of Food Pricing Reforms: A Welfare Analysis for Indonesia'. *Journal of Policy Modeling*, 13, 281–99.

Sahn, David, and Stephen Younger (2009). 'Measuring Intra-Household Health Inequality: Explorations Using the Body Mass Index'. *Health Economics*, 18, S13–36.

Singer, Peter (2010). *The Life You Can Save: How to Do Your Part to End World Poverty.* New York: Random House.

Theil, Henri (1967). *Economics and Information Theory.* Amsterdam: North-Holland.

World Bank (2011). *World Development Report: Gender Equality and Development.* Washington, DC: World Bank.

World Inequality Lab (2018). *World Inequality Report.* Paris: Paris School of Economics.

3

Comparing Global Inequality of Income and Wealth

James Davies and Anthony Shorrocks

1 Introduction

The past half century has seen a huge expansion in the quantity and quality of available information on income distribution throughout the world.[1] Sample surveys are conducted more frequently, and in more countries, using methods for data collection and analysis that have improved beyond recognition. This has led growing numbers of researchers to study inequality trends over time within countries and to undertake comparisons between countries. More adventurous researchers have gone further and attempted to provide estimates of the distribution of income for the world as a whole.

This line of work prompted us a decade ago to initiate similar research on the distribution of global wealth, reported first in Davies et al. (2008, 2011) and continued more recently in the Credit Suisse Global Wealth Report and Databook (see Davies et al. 2018a, 2018b). The global wealth estimates are obtained from a synthetic wealth sample representative of all adults in the world and totalling more than a million observations in each year. For the present study, we have constructed a similar global income sample using the World Income Inequality Dataset. Together, these two synthetic datasets provide a unique opportunity to apply the same research methodology to both the income and wealth samples, enabling us to compare and analyse—for the first time—the level and trend of global income and wealth inequality this century.

To set the scene, Section 2 reviews past work on global income and wealth inequality. In Section 3 we discuss the choices faced in constructing our income and wealth samples, and the degree to which the income and wealth concepts are comparable. The trends in global income and wealth inequality this century are examined in Section 4. Section 5 explores the different ways in which between-country and within-country factors contribute to global inequality. Finally, in

[1] We thank Rodrigo Lluberas and Cinar Baymul for help in producing the global wealth and income microdata.

James Davies and Anthony Shorrocks, *Comparing Global Inequality of Income and Wealth* In: *Inequality in the Developing World*. Edited by: Carlos Gradín, Murray Leibbrandt, and Finn Tarp, Oxford University Press (2021).
© United Nations University World Institute for Development Economics Research (UNU-WIDER).
DOI: 10.1093/oso/9780198863960.003.0003

Section 6, we decompose the inequality trend since the year 2000 to show the separate influence of changes in inequality within countries and changes in mean income or wealth combined with population size. All of our decomposition exercises apply the Shorrocks–Shapley approach, which allows any inequality measure to be decomposed in an attractive manner.

2 Previous Studies of Global Inequality

Bourguignon and Morrisson (2002) provided the first estimates of global income inequality by combining data on the average level of income across countries with information on the distribution of income within countries, as captured by the quintile income shares. They concluded that global income inequality rose from the early nineteenth century up to the Second World War, and was then fairly steady until about 1980. These findings have been broadly confirmed in subsequent studies: see Anand and Segal (2008), Niño-Zarazúa et al. (2014), and Van Zanden et al. (2014).

Improved coverage and quality of data after 1980 expanded the opportunities for research, but also led to more variation regarding both the methodological approaches and the results. Bhalla (2002), Dowrick and Akmal (2005), and Sala-i-Martin (2006) are in broad agreement, reporting Gini values for global income inequality averaging 67.5 per cent around 1980. They also agree that global inequality rose slightly, or showed no change, from 1980 to the early 1990s, after which it declined (see Niño-Zarazúa et al. 2014 for details). Milanovic (2002, 2005) comes to a different conclusion for the period 1980–90, when he finds a noticeable rise in the Gini coefficient.[2] Dowrick and Akmal (2005) compared results derived using purchasing power parity (PPP) exchange rates, finding a downward trend using PPP values but an upward trend using market, or 'official', exchange rates. While, in principle, PPP rates may be preferred, Dowrick and Akmal (2005) concluded that both methods were subject to biases, and that if these are corrected there appears to be no trend.

Anand and Segal (2008) surveyed the literature, identifying limitations of the data and the methodology which led them to conclude that there was no firm evidence of either an upward or a downward trend in recent decades. Subsequent studies have tried to correct the problems identified by Anand and Segal. Examples are provided by Niño-Zarazúa et al. (2014) and Lakner and Milanovic (2016): both studies find a downward trend since 1990, but starting from a higher level than reported in previous studies—a Gini value above 70 per cent for 1985–8, for example.

---

[2] See table 1 of appendix 1 in Lakner and Milanovic (2013) for a summary of Milanovic's evolving estimates over his 2002, 2005, and 2012 articles.

In recent years much attention has been paid to data deficiencies in the top tail, which some authors have tried to correct by adjusting the tail to conform to a Pareto distribution. Atkinson (2007) revised the Bourguignon and Morrisson (2002) estimates in this way. Lakner and Milanovic (2016) found that such an adjustment increased the Gini by around 5 percentage points, but found also that the downward trend from 1988 to 2008 disappears. Similar conclusions were reached by Anand and Segal (2015), who adjusted the top tail by replacing the survey income share of the top 1 per cent by the share of the top 1 per cent in the World Top Income Database (Alvaredo et al. 2013). This adjustment raises the world Gini to 70.5 per cent in 1988 and to an even higher level (71.0 per cent) in 2005, resulting in a flat overall trend. Alvaredo et al. (2018) use the World Wealth and Income Database (successor to the World Top Income Database) to estimate the world distribution of income up to 2016, using top-tail-adjusted national income distributions. The results show that the shares of the top 1 per cent and 10 per cent trended upward from 1982 to 2006, and declined after 2007. The decline after 2007 was gradual for the share of the top 10 per cent but abrupt for the share of the top 1 per cent, being concentrated in the years 2008 and 2009.

Another recent development has been the evolution of world income databases, including attempts to produce consistent standardized series, and to fill in gaps in the temporal record (Lahoti et al. 2016; Solt 2009). The most advanced example is the Global Consumption and Income Project (GCIP), which generates distributions of both income and consumption for each year from 1960 to 2015. Lahoti et al. (2016) report that the Gini value for global consumption inequality fell from a high of 71 per cent in the 1970s and 1980s to a low of 64 per cent in 2013.

A common theme in studies of world income inequality is the divergence between inequality within countries, which has often moved upwards, and inequality between countries, which has generally trended down. Dowrick and Akmal (2005), Milanovic (2005), Anand and Segal (2008), and Lakner and Milanovic (2016) discuss the global inequality trend in terms of the net outcome of these two underlying factors, with the decline in between-country inequality due largely to the rise of mean income in China and, to an extent, in India.

Estimating the global distribution of household wealth was first attempted by Davies et al. (2008, 2011) for the year 2000. The overall strategy involved three main steps. First, estimates of the level of wealth per adult were produced for each country using household balance sheets where available, survey evidence for a few countries, and regression-based results elsewhere for countries with suitable data. Evidence on wealth distribution within countries was then assembled and combined with the wealth level estimate for each country to produce a large synthetic sample of wealth observations. Processing this sample yielded estimates of wealth distribution within each country and region, and for the world as a whole. Improvements and updates of these estimates have been reported each year since 2010 in the annual *Global Wealth Report* and *Global Wealth Databook* published by the Credit Suisse Research Institute (Davies et al. 2018a, 2018b). Davies et al. (2017) provides further details of the methodological revisions.

The level of world wealth inequality is exceptionally high. Davies et al. (2011) reported a Gini coefficient of 89.2 per cent for global wealth in the year 2000 using official exchange rates. Our more recent estimates make an adjustment to the top tail to try to correct for non-sampling error in wealth surveys. This adjustment tends to raise the estimated figure for global inequality, although more accurate data on average wealth levels across countries have mitigated its impact. Our latest estimates for 2000 suggest a Gini value of 90.4 per cent, and a figure of 84.8 per cent for the share of the global top 10 per cent, close to the 85.1 per cent reported in Davies et al. (2011).

To date, no other research team has offered an estimate of the global distribution of wealth—in sharp contrast to the world income distribution literature.[3] There are a number of reasons for this neglect of the wealth dimension of global inequality. One is that income may be considered more important than wealth, covering the flow of purchasing power from both human and non-human wealth, and hence appearing to be more comprehensive. Another reason for the neglect of global wealth inequality concerns data quality and availability. Although the number of countries with good wealth data continues to increase, there are currently only about thirty-five countries with a national household wealth survey. From our viewpoint this is not a stumbling block, because this list includes all the wealthiest countries as well as the most populous countries. We estimate that these countries cover about two-thirds of the global population and 95 per cent of world household wealth. To round out the picture, imputations can be made for the missing countries, as explained in Davies et al. (2017).

3 Data Issues

The results obtained for income or wealth distributions are often sensitive to the choices made in the construction of the income or wealth samples and in the way the samples are processed to obtain the results. Comparing income and wealth series raises additional issues, because there are potentially more dimensions which can affect comparability. It is therefore important to understand the way that the data are assembled and analysed.

---

[3] There has, however, been significant research on related aspects. Global wealth aggregates were studied by Goldsmith (1985) and the World Bank (2006, 2011), while many international comparisons of wealth distribution have been reported: see e.g. Bönke et al. (2017), Kessler and Wolff (1991), Klevmarken et al. (2003), and Wolff (1987). The Luxembourg Wealth Study (LIS Data Center 2016; Sierminska et al. 2006) and the ECB-coordinated Household Finance and Consumption Surveys in eighteen eurozone countries plus Poland and Hungary have made consistent wealth distribution data available across many countries. And increased interest in wealth distribution from an international perspective is reflected in Piketty (2014) and Alvaredo et al. (2018).

Our income sample is based on a revised version of the WIID database, adjusted to control for a variety of household characteristics. We use the adjusted Lorenz curve data corresponding to net household income per household member for the period 2000–15, which provides an observation for each country and year for which a record exists in the WIID database. Gaps in the database are filled by estimating Lorenz curves for countries and years which lack a WIID record. For each country and year, we then construct a synthetic income sample which conforms exactly to the Lorenz data, and scale the sample values and sample weights to match per-capita income and population size, respectively. Pooling these samples enables estimates of global inequality values to be produced.

The wealth sample refers to net household wealth per adult and is drawn from the micro wealth database underlying the material published in Davies et al. (2018a, 2018b). This yields a slightly longer series covering end-of-year values for 2000–17. The wealth sample differs from the income sample with regard to the reference population—adults rather than all individuals—and because the top tail values have been adjusted to match evidence from the Forbes billionaire records. In other respects, however, the global inequality estimates for wealth are produced in a similar way to those for income.

The definitions and methods used in our estimation of global income and wealth distributions reflect choices made with regard to a range of data issues. The options and choices made are outlined below in order to indicate how analysts could in principle produce different sets of results.

3.1 Income and Wealth Definitions

Several alternative income definitions have been used in the literature. The latest WIID dataset focuses on three of these: gross income, net income, and consumption. Gross income includes all sources of money income with no deduction for taxes. Net income is the same as gross income but is net of direct taxes—principally income tax. Consumption is measured by consumer expenditure. We work with net income in this chapter since it reflects the actual flow of purchasing power for a household.

In principle, our wealth definition corresponds with that in the official System of National Accounts (SNA): that is, the value of all assets owned by households minus household debts (European Commission et al. 2009). Both financial assets and real (or 'non-financial') assets are included. Real assets include producer durables and real estate, while financial assets include both liquid and non-liquid assets, the latter including the value of employer-based pension funds and private retirement savings. Human capital and state pensions are excluded, as is all capital owned by sectors other than households—for example, assets in public ownership. While the household balance sheet data we use are part of the SNA and therefore conform to this definition, household wealth surveys generally omit some assets or debts, perhaps because the benefits of including them are judged to be outweighed by the costs (e.g., in lengthening questionnaires and therefore reducing response rates).

3.2 Target Population

The target population for income could be restricted to its legal recipients, and that for wealth could be confined to its legal owners. In practice, distributional studies often aggregate both income and wealth within families or households, and the latter are taken as the target population. There is a good argument for that approach in the case of income, since a family's income is usually assumed to be used for the benefit of all its members. However, wealth represents deferred spending, and benefits of that future spending are more likely to accrue to the owners of the family's wealth, who are mainly its adult members, than equally to all current family members. For this reason, we take adults as the target population for wealth.

3.3 Income Sharing Rule

The default assumption in much work on income distribution is equal sharing of income within the family. This motivates looking at income on either a per capita or a household equivalent basis. In the case of wealth, however, this approach is not the natural one. First, as argued above, adults are the appropriate target population. Second, even within marriage the presumption of fully equal sharing only applies in a community property regime, which is observed in relatively few jurisdictions around the world (World Bank 2012). Much more common is a limited community property regime in which the property brought to a marriage or inherited while married is under individual ownership. And there are many countries, particularly in South Asia and Africa, in which property ownership within marriage is separate. Hence the most natural variable to consider, in principle, is individual adult wealth. In practice, it is often difficult to obtain estimates on that basis, but we prefer to use such estimates whenever they are available.

3.4 Exchange Rates

In order to pool income or wealth distributions across countries one must use some system of exchange rates. In the case of income, there is a strong argument for using purchasing power parity (PPP) rates. For wealth, however, it is not clear that PPP rates are superior to market or 'official' exchange rates. Wealth is highly concentrated, and the value of assets to wealthy owners is not determined solely by consumer prices in their home country. It also depends on consumer prices abroad if they spend a significant amount of time and money in other countries, and on asset prices both at home and abroad unless they do all their saving and investment domestically. While recognizing the case for using PPP rates, for reasons of both convenience and comparability, we applied official exchange rates to both the income and wealth data in this study.

3.5 Inequality Index

In studying economic inequality, it is important to use a range of summary indices which reflect inequality in different portions of the distribution. Here we use the shares of the top 10 per cent and the top 1 per cent as well as the Gini coefficient. We also report the ratio of the median to the mean. This index is not commonly reported, but it is intuitively attractive and experience suggests that it captures important aspects of inequality trends. For the decomposition exercises which we discuss below, there is a natural case for using indices from the Entropy family. However, the more sophisticated decomposition procedures that we employ circumvent most of the disadvantages of the other indices, making inclusion of the Entropy indices unnecessary.

3.6 Top Tail Adjustments

As noted earlier, some researchers have used top tail adjustments in their estimation of global income inequality. We make such adjustments to the wealth data, based on the annual Forbes world list of billionaires.[4] However, no top tail adjustment is made to incomes, as we have not yet found a satisfactory way to do that with our large sample of countries. This no doubt leads to a downward bias in our estimated level of global income inequality relative to the global wealth inequality figures. As mentioned previously, Anand and Segal (2015) and Lakner and Milanovic (2016) found that making a top tail adjustment removes the downward trend in global income inequality otherwise found in the period from about 1988 to 2008, so that observation should be borne in mind when interpreting our results.

---

[4] Available at: https:/www.forbes.com/billionaires/#64531bab251c (accessed 10 December 2018).

3.7 Time Period

Our wealth data are only available for this century, and any attempt to provide satisfactory estimates for earlier years poses great difficulties due to data limitations. The WIID data allow reasonable estimates to be constructed back to at least 1980, and possibly 1960. However, for reasons of comparability, we confine attention to income and wealth inequality trends over the course of this century.

4 Trends in Income and Wealth Inequality

We begin by considering the income inequality trajectory during the period 2000–15 for each of the selected indices. As displayed in Figure 3.1, the Gini coefficient value eased down from 78.9 per cent in 2000 to 77.4 per cent in 2005, after which the decline speeds up until 2010 and then levels off, the Gini reaching 73.3 per cent in 2015. The share of the top 10 per cent shows a similar pattern, falling from 67.9 per cent in 2000 to 61.4 per cent in 2015: in fact, the total decline (6.5 percentage points) over the fifteen-year period is almost identical to the total drop (6.6 percentage points) in the Gini value. The mean/median ratio also echoes this pattern, although the percentage decline is much greater, falling more than 40 per cent from an initial ratio of 6.4 in 2000 to a multiple of 3.7 in 2015. The outlier, so to speak, among the inequality indices is the share of the top 1 per cent, which is relatively flat over the period under consideration, declining just 0.8 percentage points from 21.2 per cent in 2000 to 20.4 per cent in 2015.

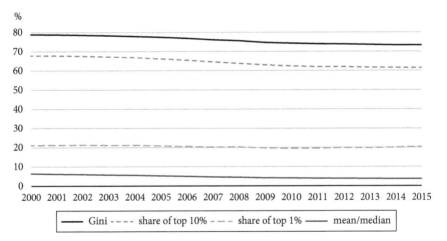

Figure 3.1 Income inequality trends 2000–15, selected indices
Source: Original estimates by the authors.

This assessment of inequality trends is broadly in line with the findings of previous studies. Niño-Zarazúa et al. (2014) and Lakner and Milanovic (2016), who looked at the trend up to about 2008, agree with us that inequality declined from 2000 to 2008 in the absence of a top tail adjustment. Alvaredo et al. (2018) found the opposite when the top tail is adjusted using income tax records, but, like us, they found a decrease in the period after 2007.

The wealth inequality series differ from the income inequality series in a number of important respects. As is evident from Figure 3.2, in every year and for each of the indicators, wealth inequality is significantly higher than income inequality. In part, this reflects the fact that top tail adjustments have been applied to the wealth sample, but not to the income sample. It may also reflect the fact that the wealth data refer to the distribution across adults while the income data refer to the distribution across individuals. However, even allowing for these considerations, it is likely that the wealth inequality values far exceed the income

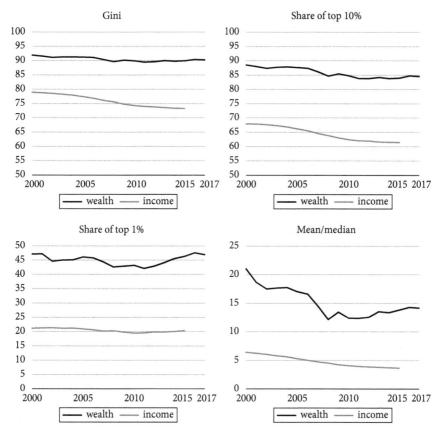

Figure 3.2 Trends in wealth inequality vs income inequality, selected indices
Source: Original estimates by the authors.

inequality values, as numerous past studies have shown. And it is unlikely that the way in which the sample data are constructed makes much difference to the pattern of inequality trends over time.

The trends in income and wealth inequality differ in various ways according to the inequality index selected. For the Gini coefficient, both series show a steady decline until 2008. But in the period since the global financial crisis, the wealth Gini shows no downward movement, and in fact is slightly higher (90.3 per cent) in 2017 than in 2008 (89.6 per cent). This levelling-off since 2008 contrasts with the continuing decline registered in the income inequality series. The initial similarity and the contrasting experience since 2008 are also apparent in the income and wealth shares of the top 10 per cent, and are evident as well in the comparison between the mean/median ratios for income and wealth, where the wealth series shows a very marked decline until 2008, followed by a mild upward trend in recent years.

Differences between the inequality trends for income and wealth are most apparent in the series for the share of the top 1 per cent. The wealth share declines markedly from 47.1 per cent in 2000 to 42.6 per cent in 2008 and on to 42.1 per cent in 2011, considerably more than the fall recorded for the income share of the top 1 per cent over this period. But since 2011 the wealth share of the top 1 per cent has climbed back to reach 47.5 per cent in 2016, more than reversing the earlier decline. This recent rise in the wealth share of the top 1 per cent likely reflects the prolonged and pronounced gains in equity prices seen in most countries over the past decade, and the disproportionate gains made by the very wealthiest individuals. If top tail adjustments are applied to the income series, a similar reversal in recent years might also appear, although it is unlikely to be as pronounced as in the wealth series, as suggested by the Alvaredo et al. (2018) results.

In summary, comparison of the inequality series for income and wealth suggest significant differences. First, the global inequality values for wealth are consistently higher than the corresponding values for income. Second, while both income and wealth inequality appear to have declined in the first decade of the century, the pattern has diverged in more recent years, with income inequality continuing to fall at a modest rate while wealth inequality has levelled off and probably even risen at the very top of the distribution. Both of these conclusions may be tempered if the income and wealth series are aligned by applying top tail adjustments to the income series. It is, however, likely that the differences would still persist.

5 Decomposing the Level of Income and Wealth Inequality

For a given population structure across countries, the level of global inequality is completely determined by the mean income or wealth of each country and the corresponding Lorenz, so we can write:

$$I = F(m_1, m_2, \ldots, m_n; L_1, L_2, \ldots, L_n) \tag{1}$$

where I is an inequality indicator, and m_k and L_k are respectively the mean and Lorenz curve of country $k = 1, 2, \ldots, n$. Expressed more simply, this becomes

$$I = F(B, W) \tag{2}$$

where $B = (m_1, m_2, \ldots, m_n)$ is the 'between-country' factor capturing differences in the average level of income and wealth between countries, and $W = (L_1, L_2, \ldots, L_n)$ is the 'within-country' factor representing relative differences in income and wealth within countries. To understand the determinants of the level and time path of global income and wealth inequality, it is useful to begin by identifying the contributions of these two core factors.

Let (B_1, W_1) denote the observed means and Lorenz curves, let B_0 refer to a situation in which all countries have the same mean income or mean wealth, and let W_0 indicate the situation in which income or wealth differences have been eliminated within all countries (so each country registers zero inequality). Then $F(B_0, W_0)$ represents complete equality in global terms. Note that $F(B_0, W_0) = 0$ for the Gini coefficient, but $F(B_0, W_0) = 10$ per cent when the share of the top 10 per cent is used as the indicator, and the corresponding baseline values for the share of the top 1 per cent and the mean/median ratio are 1 per cent and 1, respectively. The decomposition exercise therefore becomes one of splitting total inequality $F(B_1, W_1) - F(B_0, W_0)$ into the between-country and within-country components.

In the context of income inequality, the between-group contribution C_B is typically captured by calculating the level of inequality which would arise if the only source of inequality were differences in country means: in the above notation,

$$C_B = F(B_1, W_0) - F(B_0, W_0) \tag{3}$$

It is then natural to regard the remainder

$$F(B_1, W_1) - F(B_0, W_0) - [F(B_1, W_0) - F(B_0, W_0)] = F(B_1, W_1) - (B_1, W_0) \tag{4}$$

as the within-group contribution. However, to be consistent with (3), the within-group contribution should be expressed as

$$C_W = F(B_0, W_1) - F(B_0, W_0), \tag{5}$$

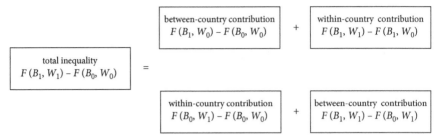

Figure 3.3 Alternative decomposition routes
Source: Authors.

in other words, the inequality which would occur if each country had its own observed Lorenz curve but the same mean income as all other countries (which implies that C_W is obtained by averaging the Lorenz curves across countries using the population sizes as weights). The remainder

$$F(B_1,W_1)-F(B_0,W_0)-[F(B_0,W_1)-F(B_0,W_0)]=F(B_1,W_1)-(B_0,W_1) \qquad (6)$$

then yields an alternative estimate of the between-group contribution. The problem for most researchers is that while C_B in equation (3) is relatively easy to compute (since it requires only information on country means), C_W in equation (5) is a more complex calculation requiring distributional information for all countries. Our global income micro database gives us a unique capacity to make the appropriate calculation, as we report later.

There remains the problem that C_B in (3) and C_W in (5) do not sum to total inequality, so the relative importance of the two factors is not immediately apparent. However, inspection of the alternative decompositions captured in Figure 3.3 suggests a simple solution: average the contributions across the two routes, as suggested by the Shorrocks–Shapley decomposition (Shorrocks 2013).

This yields the revised formula

$$C_B = [F(B_1,W_0)-F(B_0,W_0)+F(B_1,W_1)-(B_0,W_1)]/2 \qquad (7)$$
$$C_W = [F(B_0,W_1)-F(B_0,W_0)+F(B_1,W_1)-(B_1,W_0)]/2.$$

These between-country and within-country contributions sum to total inequality and are the ones reported presently.

The values we obtain for the between-country and within-country contributions to total global income inequality are illustrated in Figure 3.4 and recorded in more detail in Table 3.1. A clear picture emerges. For the Gini coefficient, the between-country component is roughly twice the level of the within-country term. Thus differences in mean incomes across countries account for about two-thirds of total inequality. However, the between-country component has trended

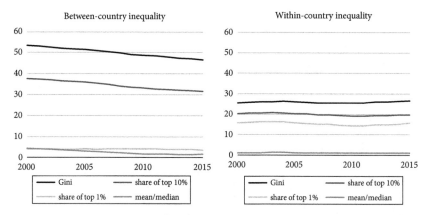

Figure 3.4 Between-country and within-country components of income inequality
Source: Original estimates by the authors.

Table 3.1 Shorrocks–Shapley decomposition of global income inequality

	Year	Total	Between	Within	Baseline	Between	%	Within	%
		Raw inequality values				Shorrocks–Shapley contribution			
Gini	2000	78.9	71.3	43.5	0	53.4	67.6	25.5	32.4
	2001	78.8	71.0	43.7	0	53.0	67.3	25.7	32.7
	2002	78.6	70.7	44.1	0	52.6	66.9	26.0	33.1
	2003	78.3	70.2	44.3	0	52.1	66.5	26.2	33.5
	2004	77.9	69.8	44.3	0	51.7	66.3	26.2	33.7
	2005	77.4	69.3	43.8	0	51.4	66.5	26.0	33.5
	2006	76.8	68.6	43.7	0	50.9	66.2	25.9	33.8
	2007	76.1	67.9	43.1	0	50.5	66.3	25.7	33.7
	2008	75.6	67.2	42.9	0	50.0	66.1	25.7	33.9
	2009	74.8	66.1	42.6	0	49.1	65.7	25.6	34.3
	2010	74.3	65.6	42.4	0	48.8	65.6	25.6	34.4
	2011	74.0	65.2	42.4	0	48.4	65.4	25.6	34.6
	2012	73.8	64.7	42.9	0	47.9	64.8	26.0	35.2
	2013	73.6	64.4	43.0	0	47.5	64.5	26.1	35.5
	2014	73.4	63.9	43.2	0	47.0	64.1	26.3	35.9
	2015	73.3	63.6	43.5	0	46.7	63.7	26.6	36.3
Share top 10%	2000	67.9	54.8	37.5	10	37.6	64.9	20.3	35.1
	2001	67.8	54.6	37.7	10	37.4	64.6	20.5	35.4
	2002	67.6	54.4	38.0	10	37.0	64.2	20.6	35.8
	2003	67.3	54.3	38.3	10	36.6	64.0	20.6	36.0
	2004	66.8	53.9	38.3	10	36.2	63.7	20.6	36.3
	2005	66.2	53.6	37.8	10	36.0	64.1	20.1	35.9
	2006	65.5	52.9	37.6	10	35.4	63.8	20.1	36.2
	2007	64.5	52.1	37.0	10	34.8	63.9	19.7	36.1

Continued

Table 3.1 *Continued*

		Raw inequality values			Shorrocks–Shapley contribution			
	Year	Total	Between	Within	Baseline	Between	%	Within	%
	2008	63.8	51.4	36.8	10	34.2	63.5	19.6	36.5
	2009	63.0	50.8	36.6	10	33.6	63.4	19.4	36.6
	2010	62.4	50.4	36.4	10	33.2	63.4	19.2	36.6
	2011	62.0	50.1	36.4	10	32.9	63.2	19.1	36.8
	2012	61.9	49.9	36.9	10	32.5	62.6	19.4	37.4
	2013	61.6	49.9	36.9	10	32.3	62.5	19.4	37.5
	2014	61.5	49.5	37.2	10	31.9	62.0	19.5	38.0
	2015	61.4	49.6	37.5	10	31.7	61.7	19.7	38.3
Share top 1%	2000	21.2	6.5	17.8	1	4.4	21.9	15.7	78.1
	2001	21.3	6.3	18.0	1	4.3	21.3	15.9	78.7
	2002	21.3	6.3	18.4	1	4.1	20.2	16.2	79.8
	2003	21.2	6.5	18.7	1	3.9	19.5	16.2	80.5
	2004	21.2	6.4	18.7	1	4.0	19.6	16.2	80.4
	2005	20.9	6.4	18.0	1	4.2	20.9	15.8	79.1
	2006	20.6	6.3	17.8	1	4.0	20.6	15.5	79.4
	2007	20.2	6.0	17.1	1	4.1	21.2	15.1	78.8
	2008	20.2	6.0	16.9	1	4.2	21.7	15.1	78.3
	2009	19.8	6.1	16.6	1	4.1	22.0	14.6	78.0
	2010	19.5	6.1	16.4	1	4.1	22.1	14.4	77.9
	2011	19.5	6.0	16.4	1	4.1	22.0	14.4	78.0
	2012	19.9	6.0	16.9	1	4.0	21.0	14.9	79.0
	2013	19.8	5.9	17.0	1	3.9	20.6	15.0	79.4
	2014	20.0	5.8	17.3	1	3.8	19.9	15.2	80.1
	2015	20.4	5.8	17.7	1	3.7	19.2	15.7	80.8
Mean/ median	2000	6.4	4.6	1.5	1	4.3	79.4	1.1	20.6
	2001	6.2	4.4	1.5	1	4.1	77.6	1.2	22.4
	2002	6.0	4.0	1.5	1	3.8	75.3	1.2	24.7
	2003	5.8	3.7	1.5	1	3.5	73.5	1.3	26.5
	2004	5.6	3.5	1.5	1	3.3	72.0	1.3	28.0
	2005	5.3	3.3	1.5	1	3.1	70.9	1.3	29.1
	2006	5.0	3.0	1.5	1	2.8	69.0	1.3	31.0
	2007	4.7	2.7	1.4	1	2.5	66.8	1.2	33.2
	2008	4.5	2.5	1.4	1	2.3	64.6	1.3	35.4
	2009	4.2	2.2	1.4	1	2.0	62.3	1.2	37.7
	2010	4.1	2.1	1.4	1	1.9	60.8	1.2	39.2
	2011	4.0	2.0	1.4	1	1.8	59.4	1.2	40.6
	2012	3.9	1.9	1.4	1	1.7	57.7	1.2	42.3
	2013	3.8	1.9	1.4	1	1.6	57.8	1.2	42.2
	2014	3.7	1.9	1.4	1	1.6	59.1	1.1	40.9
	2015	3.7	2.1	1.5	1	1.7	61.8	1.0	38.2

Source: Original estimates by the authors.

downward for the whole of this century while the within-country element has been quite stable, and has actually risen slightly since 2010. So while differences in country means still dominate global inequality, they have become progressively less important over the years. This suggests that rapid growth in the developing world, especially in China, has reduced income differences across countries and hence contributed substantially to the decline in overall global income inequality discussed in Section 4.

Decomposition of the share of the top 10 per cent reveals a similar pattern, although the contribution of differences in country mean income is somewhat less, and declines from 64.9 per cent in 2000 to 61.7 per cent in 2015. As regards the mean/median ratio, the between-country contribution was more than four times the within-country contribution in 2000 and accounted for 80 per cent of total inequality. But the relative contribution fell rapidly until 2010, after which it stabilized. Mean income differences across countries now account for a little over 60 per cent of the mean/median income ratio, almost exactly the same as for the Gini coefficient and the share of the top 10 per cent.

As might be expected, decomposition of the share of the top 1 per cent gives a very different outcome. Income differences within countries alone would produce a share of about 15 per cent for the top 1 per cent, considerably higher than the share of around 4 per cent associated with differences in mean incomes across countries. Furthermore, the proportion of global inequality attributable to within-country differences has remained close to 80 per cent for the entire period under consideration. The small contribution of the between-country component helps us understand why the downward trend in mean income differences across countries has not translated into a reduction in the income share of the top 1 per cent.

The corresponding decomposition of global wealth inequality is displayed in Figure 3.5. There are many similarities with Figure 3.4, but also many important differences. As regards the between-country component, the levels for each of the indicators are broadly similar, although for the share of the top 10 per cent and for the mean/median ratio the wealth values are roughly double those obtained for income. In addition, the flattening-out since 2010 is more evident in the wealth figures than in the income graphs. For the within-country component, the time profile remains flat for the mean/median ratio, but for the other indicators the trend is clearly upwards for most of the period under consideration.

The most significant difference between the wealth and income graphs is the much higher within-country contribution to global inequality. In fact, when the Gini coefficient, the share of the top 10 per cent, or the mean/median ratio is used, the within-country component is broadly similar to the between-country component, indicating that both factors account for roughly half of global wealth inequality. Furthermore, the contribution of within-country country differences has been increasing over time. For each of the selected inequality indicators, the contribution of within-country differences in wealth now exceeds the contribution of between-country differences (see Table 3.2 for details).

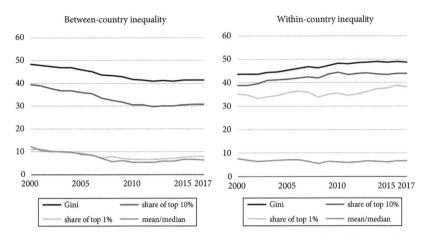

Figure 3.5 Between-country and within-country components of wealth inequality
Source: Original estimates by the authors.

Table 3.2 Shorrocks–Shapley decomposition of global wealth inequality

	Year	Total	Between	Within	Baseline	Between	%	Within	%
		Raw inequality values				Shorrocks–Shapley contribution			
Gini	2000	91.9	77.5	73.0	0	48.2	52.4	43.7	47.6
	2001	91.6	76.9	72.7	0	47.9	52.3	43.7	47.7
	2002	91.1	75.8	72.1	0	47.4	52.0	43.7	48.0
	2003	91.2	75.3	72.8	0	46.9	51.4	44.4	48.6
	2004	91.3	75.4	73.2	0	46.7	51.2	44.6	48.8
	2005	91.2	75.0	74.4	0	45.9	50.3	45.3	49.7
	2006	91.1	74.2	75.2	0	45.0	49.4	46.1	50.6
	2007	90.4	72.2	75.5	0	43.5	48.2	46.9	51.8
	2008	89.6	71.1	74.0	0	43.4	48.4	46.2	51.6
	2009	90.1	71.0	75.6	0	42.8	47.5	47.4	52.5
	2010	89.9	69.5	76.2	0	41.6	46.3	48.3	53.7
	2011	89.4	69.3	75.8	0	41.5	46.4	48.0	53.6
	2012	89.6	68.9	76.5	0	41.0	45.8	48.6	54.2
	2013	90.0	69.4	77.2	0	41.1	45.7	48.9	54.3
	2014	89.8	69.4	77.4	0	40.9	45.5	48.9	54.5
	2015	89.9	69.9	77.3	0	41.3	45.9	48.7	54.1
	2016	90.4	70.5	77.9	0	41.5	45.9	48.9	54.1
	2017	90.3	70.4	77.7	0	41.5	46.0	48.8	54.0
Share top 10%	2000	88.5	62.0	61.5	10	39.5	50.3	39.0	49.7
	2001	87.9	61.1	61.0	10	39.0	50.0	38.9	50.0
	2002	87.4	58.4	60.2	10	37.8	48.8	39.6	51.2
	2003	87.7	56.5	61.0	10	36.6	47.1	41.1	52.9
	2004	87.8	56.8	61.4	10	36.6	47.1	41.2	52.9
	2005	87.6	57.4	62.9	10	36.1	46.5	41.5	53.5
	2006	87.3	57.5	64.1	10	35.4	45.8	41.9	54.2
	2007	86.1	55.3	64.3	10	33.5	44.0	42.6	56.0

	2008	84.7	52.7	62.1	10	32.6	43.7	42.1	56.3
	2009	85.4	52.2	64.2	10	31.7	42.0	43.7	58.0
	2010	84.8	51.2	65.0	10	30.5	40.8	44.3	59.2
	2011	83.8	51.5	64.4	10	30.4	41.2	43.4	58.8
	2012	83.8	51.1	65.2	10	29.8	40.4	44.0	59.6
	2013	84.2	52.1	66.2	10	30.0	40.5	44.2	59.5
	2014	83.8	52.8	66.5	10	30.1	40.7	43.7	59.3
	2015	84.0	53.4	66.3	10	30.5	41.3	43.4	58.7
	2016	84.8	54.2	67.2	10	30.9	41.3	43.9	58.7
	2017	84.6	53.6	66.7	10	30.7	41.2	43.9	58.8
Share top 1%	2000	47.1	6.8	31.2	1	10.9	23.6	35.2	76.4
	2001	47.1	7.0	30.6	1	11.3	24.4	34.9	75.6
	2002	44.6	6.5	29.7	1	10.2	23.4	33.4	76.6
	2003	45.0	6.2	30.5	1	9.9	22.4	34.2	77.6
	2004	45.1	6.3	31.3	1	9.5	21.6	34.5	78.4
	2005	46.1	6.5	33.2	1	9.2	20.5	35.9	79.5
	2006	45.8	6.3	34.5	1	8.3	18.4	36.5	81.6
	2007	44.3	6.2	35.0	1	7.3	16.9	36.0	83.1
	2008	42.6	6.1	32.1	1	7.8	18.8	33.8	81.2
	2009	42.9	6.5	34.5	1	6.9	16.6	35.0	83.4
	2010	43.1	6.4	35.4	1	6.6	15.6	35.6	84.4
	2011	42.1	6.4	34.5	1	6.5	15.8	34.6	84.2
	2012	42.9	6.6	35.3	1	6.6	15.8	35.3	84.2
	2013	44.1	6.4	35.7	1	6.9	16.0	36.2	84.0
	2014	45.5	6.5	37.0	1	7.0	15.8	37.5	84.2
	2015	46.3	6.6	36.7	1	7.6	16.9	37.7	83.1
	2016	47.5	6.8	37.9	1	7.7	16.6	38.8	83.4
	2017	46.9	6.8	37.3	1	7.7	16.8	38.2	83.2
Mean/median	2000	21.0	7.3	2.8	1	12.3	61.3	7.7	38.7
	2001	18.6	6.4	2.8	1	10.6	60.3	7.0	39.7
	2002	17.5	6.1	2.7	1	9.9	60.2	6.6	39.8
	2003	17.7	6.1	2.8	1	10.0	59.9	6.7	40.1
	2004	17.7	5.7	2.8	1	9.8	58.6	6.9	41.4
	2005	17.0	4.8	3.0	1	8.9	55.5	7.1	44.5
	2006	16.6	4.4	3.1	1	8.5	54.3	7.1	45.7
	2007	14.5	3.7	3.2	1	7.0	52.0	6.5	48.0
	2008	12.1	2.8	2.9	1	5.5	49.5	5.6	50.5
	2009	13.5	2.6	3.2	1	5.9	47.7	6.5	52.3
	2010	12.4	2.4	3.3	1	5.2	46.1	6.1	53.9
	2011	12.4	2.5	3.2	1	5.3	46.7	6.1	53.3
	2012	12.6	2.4	3.4	1	5.3	46.0	6.2	54.0
	2013	13.6	2.7	3.5	1	5.9	46.7	6.7	53.3
	2014	13.4	2.7	3.5	1	5.8	46.8	6.6	53.2
	2015	13.8	3.8	3.5	1	6.5	50.9	6.3	49.1
	2016	14.3	3.5	3.6	1	6.6	49.7	6.7	50.3
	2017	14.2	3.2	3.6	1	6.4	48.6	6.8	51.4

Source: Original estimates by the authors.

The evidence discussed in Section 4 suggests that global income inequality is on a downward trend. Wealth inequality also shows no significant upward trend since 2000, although there is evidence of a rise since the financial crisis in 2007–8. These facts are at variance with the widespread feeling that both income and wealth inequality have risen in recent years. Our decompositions of global income and wealth inequality into the between-country and within-country components cast light on this conundrum. In global terms, between-country differences have been an equalizing influence; but within-country differences show no significant decline over time and some tendency to increase. This is particularly true in the context of wealth inequality, where there is strong evidence that wealth differences within countries have increased significantly during this century.

6 Decomposing the Inequality Trend of Income and Wealth

The evidence discussed in the previous section hints at the relative contributions of within-country and between-country factors to the trend in inequality over time. It suggests that changes in country means are likely to dominate changes in income inequality over time for inequality indices other than the share of the top 1 per cent, but that changes in inequality within countries have a more significant impact when it comes to wealth inequality over time. However, when changes over time are examined, we also have to make allowance for changes in the population size of countries. This could be considered as an additional factor, but given that its contribution is likely to be limited, we treat it as part of the between-country component.

It is useful to start by considering two counterfactual questions. First, what would the global inequality trend look like if inequality within countries was frozen at the year 2000 values, but the mean incomes and population sizes of countries changed in the way observed since the turn of the century? Second, how would the global inequality trend appear if mean incomes and population sizes were kept at the 2000 values, but inequality within countries changed as observed in the intervening years? Figure 3.6 displays the corresponding income inequality graphs for each of our chosen inequality indices. The results are striking. First, changes in the mean incomes and population sizes of countries have had a continuous equalizing impact for all of this century. Second, for three of the indicators—the Gini coefficient, the share of the top decile, and the mean/median ratio—if income distribution within each country had remained unchanged this century, global inequality would still have evolved in almost exactly the way that transpired. For these three indicators, therefore, changes in mean incomes and population sizes account for virtually all of the downward movement in income inequality, and this is largely true of any subperiod too.

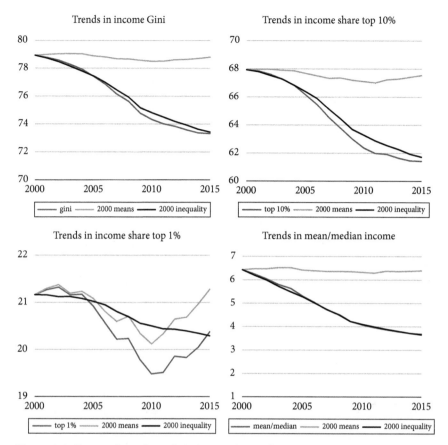

Figure 3.6 Counterfactual trends in income inequality
Source: Original estimates by the authors.

For the share of the top 1 per cent, the picture is slightly different. Over the whole period 2000–15, changes in mean incomes and population sizes again account for almost 100 per cent of the fall in global inequality; but in the period 2000–10, the share of the top 1 per cent fell by roughly twice as much as would have been predicted from the changes in mean incomes and population sizes, leaving a significant residual due to inequality reductions within countries. Then this process went into reverse, with the top 1 per cent rising sharply within countries after 2010, overcoming the continuing equalizing effect of changes in means and population to produce a significant increase in the global share of the top 1 per cent.

For wealth inequality, the results of the counterfactual exercises are even more striking in some respects, although slightly different. When inequality within countries is held at the 2000 values, Figure 3.7 shows that trends in country mean

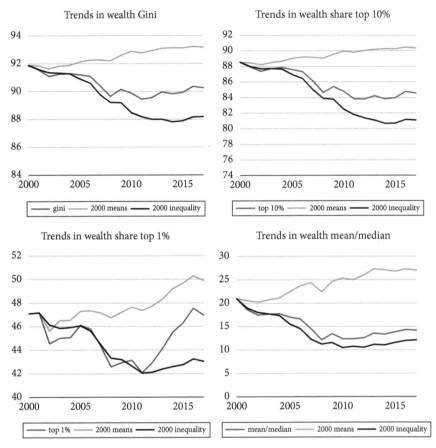

Figure 3.7 Counterfactual trends in wealth inequality

Source: Original estimates by the authors.

wealth and population sizes cause global wealth inequality to fall sharply during the first decade of this century. This is similar to the findings for income, although unlike income the trend reverses in recent years for each of the indices considered.

The most noticeable difference between the wealth and income graphs concerns the time path traced out when mean wealth and population sizes are held at the year 2000 values. Once country growth rates are discounted in this way, for each of the indicators global wealth inequality rises markedly over the course of this century, and more or less continuously. For the share of the top 1 per cent there is even evidence that the rise in wealth inequality accelerated in the aftermath of the global financial crisis. While wealth inequality may have fallen in certain individual countries, the results show that, on balance, wealth inequality within countries has clearly risen whichever inequality indicator is used.

As regards the time path of wealth inequality discussed in Section 4, it now becomes evident that the observed trend is a compromise between two strong opposing forces: the evolution of the between-country factors tending to reduce global wealth inequality for at least the first decade, and the evolution of within-country inequality driving movement in the opposite direction. The observed series suggest that the between-country factors dominated in the early years of the century, while the rise in within-country inequality has been the decisive force more recently.

To provide a more formal assessment of the between-country and within-country contributions to the income and wealth inequality change since the year 2000, we revert to the terminology used in the previous section and express the change in inequality from time 0 to time T as

$$\Delta I = F(B_T, W_T) - F(B_0, W_0) = S_B + S_W \tag{8}$$

where

$$S_B = \frac{1}{2}\left(F(B_T, W_0) - F(B_0, W_0) + F(B_T, W_T) - F(B_0, W_T)\right) \tag{9}$$

and

$$S_W = \frac{1}{2}\left(F(B_0, W_T) - F(B_0, W_0) + F(B_T, W_T) - F(B_T, W_0)\right) \tag{10}$$

denote the Shorrocks–Shapley between-country and within-country components, respectively. Note that S_B is the change in inequality obtained using the fixed within-country distributions observed in the initial year averaged with the change in inequality using the fixed within-country distributions observed in the final year. The within-country contribution S_W has a parallel interpretation.

The results recorded in Table 3.3 confirm the impressions gained from Figures 3.6 and 3.7. When the change in income inequality over the period 2000–15 is split into the two components, the between-country component is seen to account for virtually all of the reduction in inequality, leaving little or no contribution from the within-country changes. This is true for each of the inequality indicators considered. Thus we can conclude that the fall in income inequality this century is almost entirely attributable to changes in country mean incomes and population sizes.

For the change in wealth inequality over the period 2000–17, the between-country factor again dominates. However, the overall decline in wealth inequality is seen to be the net outcome of a substantial fall in inequality due to changes in

Table 3.3 Shorrocks–Shapley decomposition of changes in global income and wealth inequality

	Counterfactual values				Shorrocks–Shapley contributions		
	$F(B_D,W_D)$	$F(F_D,W_T)$	$F(F_T,W_D)$	$F(B_T,W_T)$	S_B	S_W	Total
Income							
Gini	78.9	78.8	73.4	73.3	−5.5	−0.1	−5.6
Share top 10%	67.9	67.5	61.7	61.4	−6.2	−0.4	−6.5
Share top 1%	21.2	21.3	20.3	20.4	−0.9	0.1	−0.8
Mean/median	6.4	6.4	3.7	3.7	−2.7	0.0	−2.7
Wealth							
Gini	91.9	93.2	88.2	90.3	−3.3	1.7	−1.6
Share top 10%	88.5	90.3	81.1	84.6	−6.6	2.6	−4.0
Share top 1%	47.1	49.9	43.0	46.9	−3.5	3.4	−0.2
Mean/median	21.0	27.0	12.1	14.2	−10.9	4.0	−6.8

Source: Original estimates by the authors.

country means offset by an increase in inequality caused by a rise in wealth inequality within countries. Broadly speaking, the magnitude of the (negative) between-country component is roughly double the contribution of the (positive) within-country component, although the contributions are similar (and hence almost net out to zero) for the share of the top 1 per cent.

7 Conclusion

There is a widespread belief—among researchers as well as the general public—that economic inequality has been rising in recent years. However, it is difficult to square this belief with the numerous studies which show that income inequality has declined this century, and our previous work on wealth inequality, which suggests little change.

Our findings help to reconcile the two viewpoints. For both income and wealth, and for all the inequality indices considered, the degree of inequality attributable to differences in mean income and wealth across countries accounts for much, if not most, of the level of global inequality. As regards changing inequality over time, changes in mean income and wealth and population sizes have induced a strong downward element to the trend in global inequality regardless of the inequality index selected. There has been little underlying movement in income inequality within countries to offset the between-country trend. However, the evidence suggests that the underlying wealth inequality has risen significantly this century, although not by enough to offset the between-country contribution.

One may ask what policy implications this study could have. The answer depends partly on what future trends are expected. An important driver of rising within-country wealth inequality since 2008 has been the rise in equity prices, which has raised the share of the top 1 per cent in particular. In part that rise has been due to low interest rates. If interest rates rise towards more normal levels, stock market performance will likely be affected. It is also possible that widespread concern about rising inequality will lead to higher taxes on top incomes and perhaps also wealth. These trends could stabilize within-country inequality. On the other hand, the decline of between-country inequality may slow or come to a halt since further increases in China's mean income and wealth, both now above the global means, will begin to raise between-country inequality, rather than reduce it, as in the past.

Our conclusion is that global income and wealth inequality are not likely to fall significantly in the near future, and may show little trend for some time. One may therefore ask what steps could be taken to lower global inequality. More progressive income taxation and/or the introduction of wealth taxes have been recommended by some observers. Others worry about the possible consequences for growth. Fortunately, there are policies that should be able both to reduce inequality and stimulate growth. Keeping inflation low, providing tax-sheltered retirement saving opportunities, ensuring the availability of sound mortgage finance, and making education universally accessible at all levels through grants and loans, for example, are sound policies that can make ordinary people better off and increase both their income and wealth. In addition, cracking down on crony capitalism and breaking up monopolies and oligopolies would reduce wealth concentration at the top and increase growth by fostering stronger competition. These policies are likely to reduce not only within-country inequality but also between-country inequality, since they would have their most dramatic impact in poor countries. Between-country inequality could also be attacked through improvements in the ways in which foreign aid is provided and by opening first-world markets fully to imports from the third world.

References

Alvaredo, F., A.B. Atkinson, T. Piketty, and E. Saez (2013). "'The World Top Incomes Database" – New Website'. Paris School of Economics. Available at: www.parisschoolofeconomics.eu/en/news/the-top-incomes-database-new-website/ (accessed 10 December 2018).

Alvaredo, F., L. Chanel, T. Piketty, E. Sae, and G. Zucman (2018). *World Inequality Report 2018*. Cambridge, MA: Harvard University Press.

Anand, S., and P. Segal (2008). 'What Do We Know about Global Income Inequality?' *Journal of Economic Literature*, 46(1): 57–94.

Anand, S., and P. Segal (2015). 'The Global Distribution of Income'. In A.B. Atkinson and F. Bourguignon (eds), *Handbook of Income Distribution*, Vol. 2A. Amsterdam: Elsevier.

Atkinson, A.B. (2007). 'Measuring Top Incomes: Methodological Issues'. In A.B. Atkinson and T. Piketty (eds), *Top Incomes over the Twentieth Century: A Contrast Between Continental European and English-Speaking Countries*. Oxford: Oxford University Press.

Bhalla, S.S. (2002). 'Imagine There's No Country: Poverty, Inequality, and Growth in the Era of Globalization'. Washington, DC: Institute for International Economics.

Bönke, T., M. Grabka, C. Schröder, and E.N. Wolff (2017). 'A Head-to-Head Comparison of Augmented Wealth in Germany and the United States'. NBER Working Paper 23244.

Bourguignon, F., and C. Morrisson (2002). 'Falling Inequality in Latin America: Policy Changes and Lessons'. WIDER Policy Brief 2014/001. Helsinki: UNU-WIDER.

Davies, J.B., R. Lluberas, and A. Shorrocks (2017). 'Estimating the Level and Distribution of Global Wealth, 2000–2014'. *Review of Income and Wealth*, 63: 731–59.

Davies, J.B., R. Lluberas, and A. Shorrocks (2018a). *Global Wealth Report*. Zurich: Credit Suisse Research Institute.

Davies, J.B., R. Lluberas, and A. Shorrocks (2018b). *Global Wealth Databook*. Zurich: Credit Suisse Research Institute.

Davies, J.B., S. Sandstrom, A. Shorrocks, and E.N. Wolff (2008). 'The World Distribution of Household Wealth'. In J.B. Davies (ed.), *Personal Wealth from a Global Perspective*. Oxford: Oxford University Press.

Davies, J.B., S. Sandström, A. Shorrocks, and E.N. Wolff (2011). 'The Level and Distribution of Global Household Wealth'. *Economic Journal*, 121: 223–54.

Dowrick, S., and M. Akmal (2005). 'Contradictory Trends in Global Income Inequality: A Tale of Two Biases'. *Review of Income and Wealth*, 51(2): 201–29.

European Commission, IMF, OECD, United Nations, and World Bank (2009). *The System of National Accounts 2008*. Available at: https://unstats.un.org/unsd/nationalaccount/docs/-SNA2008.pdf (accessed 4 December 2018).

Goldsmith, R.W. (1985). *Comparative National Balance Sheets, A Study of Twenty Countries, 1688–1978*. Chicago: University of Chicago Press.

Kessler, D., and E.N. Wolff (1991). 'A Comparative Analysis of Household Wealth Patterns in France and the United States'. *Review of Income and Wealth*, 37(3): 249–66.

Klevmarken, N.A., J.P. Lupton, and F.P. Stafford (2003). 'Wealth Dynamics in the 1980s and 1990s: Sweden and the United States'. *Journal of Human Resources*, 38(2): 322–53.

Lahoti, R., A. Jayadev, and S. Reddy (2016). 'The Global Consumption and Income Project (GCIP): An Overview'. *Journal of Globalization and Development*, 7(1): 61–108.

Lakner, C., and B. Milanovic (2013). 'Global Income Distribution: From the Fall of the Berlin Wall to the Great Recession'. Policy Research Working Paper 6719, World Bank Development Research Group.

Lakner, C., and B. Milanovic (2016). 'Global Income Distribution: From the Fall of the Berlin Wall to the Great Recession'. *World Bank Economic Review*, 30(2): 203–32.

LIS Data Center (2016). 'New Luxembourg Wealth Study (LWS) Database is Launched'. Available at: www.lisdatacenter.org/news-and-events/new-luxembourg-wealth-study-lws-is-launched/ (accessed 4 December 2018).

Milanovic, B. (2002). 'True World Income Distribution, 1988 and 1993: First Calculation Based on Household Surveys Alone'. *The Economic Journal*, 112(476): 51–92.

Milanovic, B. (2005). *Worlds Apart: Measuring International and Global Inequality*. Princeton: Princeton University Press.

Niño-Zarazúa, M., L. Roope, and F. Tarp (2014). 'Global Interpersonal Inequality Trends and Measurement'. WIDER Working Paper 2014/004. Helsinki: UNU-WIDER.

Piketty, T. (2014). *Capital in the Twenty-First Century*. Cambridge, MA: Harvard University Press.

Sala-i-Martin, X. (2006). 'The World Distribution of Income: Falling Poverty and…Convergence, Period'. *Quarterly Journal of Economics*, 121(2): 351–97.

Shorrocks, A. (2013). 'Decomposition Procedures for Distributional Analysis: A Unified Framework Based on the Shapley Value'. *Journal of Economic Inequality*, 11: 99–126.

Sierminska, E., A. Brandolini, and T.M. Smeeding (2006). 'Comparing Wealth Distribution across Rich Countries: First Results from the Luxembourg Wealth Study'. LWS Working Paper 1. Luxembourg: LIS Cross-National Data Center.

Solt, F. (2009). 'Standardizing the World Income Inequality Database'. *Social Science Quarterly*, 90(2): 231–42.

Van Zanden, J.L., J. Baten, P. Foldvari, and B. van Leeuwen (2014). 'The Changing Shape of Global Inequality 1820–2000; Exploring a New Dataset'. *Review of Income and Wealth*, 60(2): 279–97.

Wolff, E.N. (ed.) (1987). *International Comparisons of the Distribution of Household Wealth*. Oxford, Toronto: Clarendon Press.

World Bank (2006). *Where Is the Wealth of Nations? Measuring Capital for the 21st Century*. Washington, DC: World Bank.

World Bank (2011). *The Changing Wealth of Nations: Measuring Sustainable Development in the New Millennium*. Washington, DC: World Bank.

World Bank (2012). *Women, Business and the Law—Removing Barriers to Economic Inclusion*. Washington, DC: World Bank.

4

Empirical Challenges Comparing Inequality across Countries

The Case of Middle-Income Countries from the LIS Database

Daniele Checchi, Andrej Cupak, and Teresa Munzi

1 Introduction

In the past few decades, the focus in research on income inequality has been predominantly on the high-income OECD countries (see, e.g., Atkinson and Brandolini 2001). More recently, research has turned to an analysis of top-income share and its historical development (e.g. Atkinson et al. 2011), again covering mostly high-income Anglo-Saxon and Nordic countries. The research analysing income inequality in middle-income and developing countries from the Middle East and North Africa (MENA) region, Asia, sub-Saharan Africa, and Latin America is still evolving.

Some of the recent examples, and perhaps the closest studies to ours in terms of the focus on middle-income countries, are studies by Alvaredo and Gasparini (2015) and Lakner and Milanovic (2016). Lakner and Milanovic (2016) analyse global income inequality with international data (combining different household surveys) covering the period 1988–2008. The authors show that the global Gini index reached 70.5 per cent in 2008 and report that the income inequality levels were quite stable over the analysed time period, though inequality levels varied between sub-regions. The lowest income inequality was observed for India, with the Gini spanning from 31.1 per cent in 1988 to 33.1 per cent in 2008. Mature economies experienced growth in the Gini from 38.2 per cent to 41.9 per cent during the same time period. The highest inequality levels were observed in sub-Saharan Africa, increasing from 53.5 per cent in 1993 to 58.3 per cent in 2008. According to the authors, the fastest increase in inequality was observed in China, where the Gini index rose from 32.0 per cent in 1988 to 42.7 per cent in 2008, overall representing an increase of 33.5 per cent.

Daniele Checchi, Andrej Cupak, and Teresa Munzi, *Empirical Challenges Comparing Inequality across Countries: The Case of Middle-Income Countries from the LIS Database* In: *Inequality in the Developing World.* Edited by: Carlos Gradín, Murray Leibbrandt, and Finn Tarp, Oxford University Press (2021). © United Nations University World Institute for Development Economics Research (UNU-WIDER). DOI: 10.1093/oso/9780198863960.003.0004

Alvaredo and Gasparini (2015) show that national income inequality for developing countries first increased during the 1980s and 1990s, and then dropped during the 2000s. They also explore possible determinants of changing inequality over time and across countries, finding an inverse U-shaped relationship between the Gini coefficient and log gross national income (GNI) per capita, consistent with the Kuznets hypothesis. Despite caveats related to consistency and comparability of microdata from low-income countries, the authors highlight that significant progress has been made in measuring and monitoring income inequality and poverty.

Other examples studying income inequality and poverty in developing and middle-income countries are those by Assaad et al. (2016, 2017) for the MENA countries, Piketty and Qian (2009) for China and India, Gasparini et al. (2011) for Latin America, and Novokmet et al. (2017) for Russia. Regarding the empirical evidence based on the LIS data, Gornick et al. (2009) were among the first to report inequality trends for the Latin American countries. More recently, the LIS data source has been utilized to demonstrate income inequality and (child) poverty in middle-income countries; see, for example, Rasch (2017) and Evans et al. (2018).

The main goal of our study is to update the existing evidence on income and expenditure/consumption inequality, focusing on a set of middle- and high-income countries from Asia (East and South), the MENA region, and Latin America. To present the results in a comparative perspective, we also add high-income countries from neighbouring areas. Before going into data analysis, we take advantage of LIS Datacentre experience in harmonizing income and consumption microdata from middle-income countries to illustrate some caveats to be considered when executing cross-country comparative research involving both affluent and less developed countries.

From the empirical point of view, the main contribution of this study is twofold. First, we extract household- and individual-level income and consumption aggregates for which we compute various inequality measures. Then we merge the computed indicators (country-level averages) with macroeconomic characteristics obtained from the World Bank Indicators database. Our final database covers almost forty years (from 1976 to 2016), with an unbalanced panel of twenty countries, summing to 150 observations.

By using descriptive and regression analyses, we aim to uncover possible correlations between recent trends in income and expenditure/consumption inequality measures and compositional population statistics related to educational attainment and gender participation in the labour market. We also explore the different magnitudes of correlation between our inequality measures and some institutional indicators capturing countries' economic stage development.

As such, our empirical analysis updates the findings of Alvaredo and Gasparini (2015) and Lakner and Milanovic (2016) on inequality trends in middle-income countries by including more recent years. In the second part, we contribute to the macro-level analysis of Roine et al. (2009), who analyse macroeconomic determinants of economic inequality in a panel of sixteen high-income countries.

The chapter unfolds as follows. Section 2 discusses the main challenges when harmonizing microdata from developing and middle-income countries. In Section 3 data and variables are presented, while Section 4 describes the applied methodology. Empirical results are presented and discussed in Section 5. Finally, Section 6 concludes and offers policy implications.

2 The Challenges of Harmonizing Data from Middle-Income Countries

From its inception in the 1980s, LIS has been historically focused on high-income countries. A pilot project was carried out in 2007 with the collaboration of a team at the World Bank in order to study the feasibility of including middle-income countries in the LIS database. Following the decision to go ahead with this expansion, LIS has made some conceptual adjustments and changes to its list of harmonized variables in order to accommodate more diverse labour market characteristics, social benefit structures, consumption patterns, transnational income flows, and within-country variability.

Among the main changes achieved with the major template revision, which took effect in 2011, the following were mostly aimed at, at the same time, maximizing its applicability to datasets from both high- and middle-income countries:

- Adjustment of the disposable household income (DHI) concept, such that it also includes non-monetary income from labour and from public and private third parties. The main reason for this enlargement of the DHI concept stemmed from the fact that in many middle-income countries the proportion of non-monetary incomes from own-consumption and social and/or private assistance-based transfers was too important to be left out, and in fact these amounts are much more often available in middle-income countries than in high-income countries, where many data providers do not even collect them, given their irrelevance.
- Adjustment of the concept of household member to ensure that persons who are physically present in the household but whose incomes do not contribute to the household income (namely live-in domestic servants, boarders,

and lodgers) are not accounted for in the creation of total household income or the calculation of the equivalence scale.

- Inclusion of a number of living arrangement variables allowing for a better analysis of multi-unit/multi-generation households, so that, if available, information on partnership and parenthood of adults outside the nuclear family is retained.
- Inclusion of variables containing information on an array of new topics, including rural/urban indicator, farming activity indicator, type of dwelling, involvement in marginal/informal work, and characteristics of a second job.

Additional challenges are typically found when dealing with income microdata from these sources, as discussed presently. Because of the diversity of *rural versus urban areas*, in many middle-income countries income surveys either only cover urban areas, where it is easier to capture incomes, or use very different instruments (including different sampling and questionnaires) for the urban and rural areas.[1]

The definition of *household membership* (and ensuing treatment of individual incomes when creating household-level incomes) is of particular relevance in middle-income countries. Family members temporarily absent are sometimes treated as household members, sometimes not, and it is often difficult to distinguish the two situations—this is particularly challenging when adults are temporarily absent to work elsewhere (e.g. the case of absent household heads or spouses) as it considerably changes the way their incomes should be accounted for (include their total income as labour incomes or only the part that they send back to the family as remittances).

Multi-generational households, and more generally large or *complex households*, are much more common; depending on who is defined as the household head (the older or middle generation in the case of three-generational households), the characteristics of the household—often based on the head and its nuclear family—will differ. In the case of polygamy, many of the usual indicators that are typically based on the head and a single spouse become much more difficult to create.

When turning to the labour market information, and especially to the *employment definition*, it should be noted that in many surveys of middle-income countries, the labour market module follows the method of the 'catch-all' question on

---

[1] This issue proved particularly challenging with the Chinese survey, where the integration of the three different samples (urban, rural, and rural-to-urban migrants) into a unique national sample required some adjustments to the weights and to the variables themselves that risked the quality of the resulting file (to the point that for the year 2007, where the issue was particularly severe, LIS decided not to make the Chinese data public).

employment: after responding that he or she does not have a job or does not work, an interviewee is asked a series of questions to determine whether he or she has done any activity in order to help the family (such as cultivating fruits and vegetables, selling products in the street, carrying out services for other persons, helping out in a household business, etc). Given the large extent to which these activities are performed by women and children in many middle-income countries, considering these activities as ILO employment (under the argument that they fall under either the category of paid work for at least one hour, or of unpaid family work) increases the employment rates considerably, creating large gaps between population with positive earnings and population employed, as well as potentially creating a bias versus those countries that do not include such questions.[2]

A related point concerns child labour. In most middle-income countries, information about the labour market is collected for children as well, in order to analyse its diffusion. Some surveys have a special section for children only; in other cases (some of) the same questions asked for adults are also asked for children. In both cases, the creation of a fully comparable labour market participation rate (or employment rate) between those different countries becomes very tricky. In addition, there are typically many questions on unofficial work, non-regular activities, household production, and illegal labour (not registered, not covered by social insurance, not taxed) in order to capture some measure of *informal labour*. These questions are typically very different from survey to survey (often referring to the institutional set up of the country), and are almost impossible to harmonize.

Finally, the wide extent of persons having *multiple jobs* makes the harmonization (and hence ensuing comparison) of job characteristics challenging, especially when the questionnaires ask about different types of work in different sections of the questionnaire (e.g. work in a family business separately from work on the farm separately from other jobs). This is troublesome because (a) it is often not clear if the persons report the same jobs in several sections of the questionnaire, hence incurring the risk of double-counting the jobs; (b) it becomes difficult to determine which is the main job.

When looking at the income variables, several issues are at stake when considering middle-income countries. First and foremost, indicators of inequality, poverty, and well-being are still prevalently based on *consumption rather than income*

---

[2] A very clear example of this arises in Peru (with data from the National Household Survey— ENAHO), which, together with Switzerland, is the country that exhibits the highest employment rate of all LIS countries. Like in the surveys of most other Latin American countries, individuals are first asked if they have a job; if they respond that they do not, then they are asked if they have carried out any activity to help out the family, and the question includes a long list of possible marginal activities. The very high number of persons who answer negatively to the first question and positively to the second implies that the employment mostly consists of marginal employment. It is, however, very likely that the way the question is formulated invites many people who would not have answered positively with a different question, to answer positively.

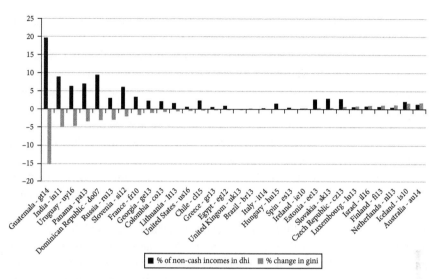

Figure 4.1 Impact of non-monetary incomes
Source: Authors, based on data from the LIS database.

data, which often implies that income microdata are either non-existent or insufficient for the purpose of calculating robust income indicators (not collected, collected but not provided, collected but not exhaustive to capture the totality of household income). As already mentioned, the enlargement to the middle-income countries group has been followed by a necessary adjustment of the concept of total disposable income to include also *non-monetary incomes* from labour (notably own-consumption of products stemming from farming activities) and public and private transfers (notably public and private assistance as benefits in-kind): see Figure 4.1.

Whereas the adjustment was necessary to get a more unbiased picture of the households' standards of living in those countries, the inclusion of those incomes in the data has often proven to be particularly tricky. The first problem is due to the fact that the coverage of the non-monetary incomes collected by the different surveys differs widely across countries, hence implying a situation in which comparability is at stake. For example, in surveys that are mostly focused on consumption, the value of most goods and services consumed but not paid for (either because they are own-produced or because they are received from the employer, the government, charitable institutions, or other private households) is collected with great detail and precision, whereas in other types of surveys the data on the availability of those goods becomes much more scarce.

Another problem arises with the non-monetization of quantities of goods and services; at this stage, LIS has taken the approach of only including those incomes that have been monetized by the data provider, thus increasing the potential bias due to the fact that in some countries, for purely practical rather than conceptual reasons, the final income concept includes more non-monetary incomes than is the case in others.

Somewhat arbitrary assumptions are to be made in the case that non-monetary incomes are collected in different sections of the questionnaire (among the consumption variables, among the household-level incomes from household activities, and among individual-level labour incomes); it becomes clear that those amounts will certainly overlap to some extent, and the creation of a final amount that does not include any under- or over-counting of some income sources proves extremely hard to obtain.

Independently from (but related to) the issue of the non-monetary incomes, another problematic area is that of the *self-employment incomes* in general— especially those from farming activities and informal activities. As those incomes are more irregular and difficult to measure by nature, the reliability of a total household income variable which is composed in large part of those types of incomes naturally becomes much more difficult. In addition, when it is collected at the household level only (as is often the case in middle-income countries where surveys have specific sections about the household activities), the creation of a comprehensive measure of total individual labour income becomes impossible, hence restricting the possibility of using such an important variable in many analyses: see Figure 4.2.

Other than the measurement of the income itself, its classification into the different income subcomponents can also become more problematic in middle-income countries. One particular issue refers to the classification of *employer-provided pensions and benefits into labour income versus social security*: while benefits provided by the employer (such as allowances and subsidies paid together with the

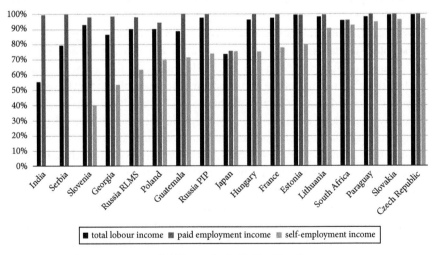

Figure 4.2 Labour income availability at the individual level
Source: Authors, based on data from the LIS database.

basic wage income) have typically been considered as labour income in high-income countries, when moving to middle-income countries it becomes clear that some of those benefits were actually replacing an almost non-existent social security and were thus much closer to social security benefits than labour income. Similarly, the usual distinction between *social insurance, assistance, and universal benefits* has often proved irrelevant in middle-income countries, where the employment-related benefits stem purely from the willingness of the employer and not from the benevolence of the government, and most of the—strictly speaking, public—benefits are targeted to the very poor.

The *treatment of taxes and social security contributions* also differentiates middle- from high-income countries (Figure 4.3). The issue in high-income countries is centred on the difference between the countries/surveys that provide income data gross of taxes and contributions and those that provide the data after such deductions. More specifically, in the first case all the incomes provided are gross, and the totality of taxes and contributions are deducted from total gross income to obtain the concept of disposable income; on the other hand, for countries that provide each income source already net of taxes and contributions, the sum of all income subcomponents is already net of taxes and contributions, and hence corresponds to the concept of disposable income. As a result, while at the level of total disposable income the variables are perfectly comparable, the comparability is reduced by the fact that at the subcomponent level some datasets provide gross incomes and others net incomes. For middle-income countries the challenge concerning the treatment of taxes is rather different. The very low reliance on direct taxes in most middle-income countries makes the above-mentioned issue almost irrelevant, as the difference between 'gross' and 'net' datasets is very tiny. It actually becomes problematic to even simply distinguish the surveys

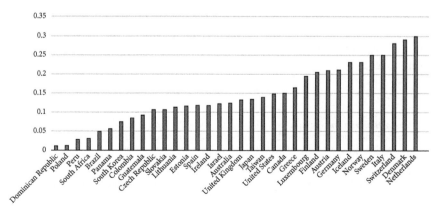

Figure 4.3 Taxes and social security contributions as a percentage of total gross income

Source: Authors, based on data from the LIS database.

between gross and net, as the situation is either a mixture of the two (in some cases with only wage income being gross of taxes and contributions and all others net), or simply is not defined at all by the data provider itself.[3] Several middle-income countries even provide the income data only in gross terms, without indication of the amount of taxes and contributions paid on them, which results in having to simulate taxes and contributions in order to obtain a measure of disposable income comparable to other countries.[4] In any case, even in the presence of full information on taxes and contributions, the low reliance on direct taxes relative to indirect ones in middle-income countries adds a bias to the comparability of well-being indicators based on DHI. If indirect taxes were also taken into account, the true difference in high- and middle-income countries' inequality might even be greater than is shown by the figures.

From a more technical point of view, an issue that can often become serious, especially in data from middle-income countries (but not necessarily confined to those), is the presence of a large number of observations with *missing (or inconsistent) data*. When the percentage of households with missing (or zero) total disposable income goes beyond a certain threshold,[5] and especially when the data provider does not account for this in the calculation of the weights, the potential bias due to the non-random distribution of those households is large enough to put at risk any country-level analysis of the income distribution. See Figure 4.4 for an overview of the percentage of households with missing DHI in a selection of LIS countries.

All in all, in spite of the efforts made at the various levels of the data production chain (survey conception, implementation, data editing, and data harmonization), there remain some important gaps in order to ensure perfect consistency of the income micro-datasets coming from high- and middle-income countries, and the question of whether those two sets of data can be analysed within the same framework or whether they should be kept separate remains an important one. LIS has adopted the view that a common framework is possible, but cannot stress enough the importance of highlighting all the caveats that go with such an approach.

---

[3] This is the case, for example, in India, where, given the almost irrelevance of taxes, the data provider does not specify whether the incomes should be reported before or after such deductions. The end result is therefore a mix of the two depending on the observations, without any indication as to what the situation is for each observation.

[4] This is the case in the National Household Sample Survey (PNAD) of Brazil, the Colombian Great Integrated Household Survey (GEIH), and the Continuous Household Survey (ECH) of Panama.

[5] LIS typically uses 10 per cent as the threshold requiring some careful treatment, and 20 per cent as the maximum acceptable threshold for reliable income estimates. For Tunisia, for example, LIS obtained data from the only existing income microdata (the Tunisian Labor Market Panel Survey—TLMPS), but after data inspection decided not to include it in the LIS database due to an excessively large portion of the sample having missing household income (about half of the households).

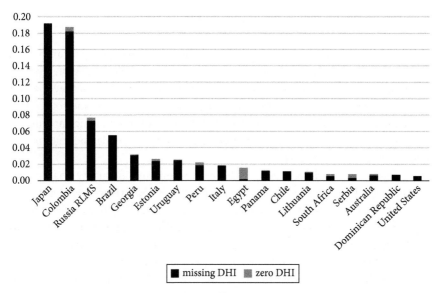

Figure 4.4 Extent of missing or zero income
Source: Authors, based on data from the LIS database.

3 Data and Variables

3.1 Dataset

The present sample of countries is drawn from the LIS database, the largest available income database of harmonized microdata collected from about fifty countries, spanning five decades. In addition to broad coverage of countries across the world, its advantage is a large set of standardized variables, making the results directly comparable. LIS datasets contain household- and individual-level data, such as labour income, capital income, social security and private transfers, taxes and contributions, expenditures, employment conditions, and usual demographics.

In our empirical analysis we primarily focus on middle-income countries, including Brazil, China, India, Mexico, Russia, and South Africa. To present the results in a comparative perspective, we consider other middle-income countries (Colombia, Paraguay, Uruguay) and some high-income countries (Chile, Hungary, Israel, Mexico, Poland, Slovenia, South Korea, Taiwan, and the USA) as potential benchmarks. In the regression analysis, we expand the country sample to include other high-income countries (Australia, Austria, Italy, and Peru).[6]

---

[6] The choice of the benchmark countries is mostly influenced by the country's sample length, reliability of the survey data, regional diversity, and finally the country's economic environment with

3.2 Variables

Our main outcome (household-level) variables are household pre-tax market income (consisting of labour and capital income), household disposable income, and household monetary consumption, as well as the total individual-level labour income. Note that values in all outcome variables were bottom- and top-coded[7] and equivalized, applying the square root scale. The covariates, which are further used in the empirical part, include basic information on gender, education, and employment status of individuals.

In addition to variables used in the microeconomic inequality analysis, we consider a set of macroeconomic country-level characteristics that have been shown to be significant determinants of economic inequality (e.g., Alvaredo and Gasparini 2015; Davies et al. 2017; Roine et al. 2009). Similarly to previous studies, the macroeconomic characteristics considered include GDP per capita, share of agriculture in GDP, share of urban households, life expectancy, age dependency ratio and share of government spending in GDP.[8] A natural question here is what the associations between inequality and such macroeconomic indicators should look like. Following Roine et al. (2009), we summarize the impact of the main contextual variables. First, standard Kuznets theory predicts different inequality levels across a country's development path, suggesting an inverse U-shape relationship between GDP per capita and inequality. Standard theory also suggests that the growth of financial markets goes hand in hand with lower inequality. In terms of trade liberalization, the standard Heckscher–Ohlin theory predicts that trade openness should favour the rich, hence increasing inequality levels. Finally, central government spending (as a proxy for the welfare state) is believed to equalize incomes of households.

4 Methodology

In our empirical analysis, we first compute a set of inequality indicators for income and consumption aggregates, as well as for major population subgroups. Then we correlate the estimated inequality measures with some country-level macroeconomic indicators. We obviously anticipate that in all cases causality may

respect to the core countries (i.e. matching gross domestic product (GDP) per capita, trade openness, financial development, etc). A comprehensive overview of the sample countries and years available is presented in Table A1 of Checchi et al. (2018). In Table A2 of the same paper we report descriptive statistics for the covariates.

[7] The values in main outcome variables were bottom-coded at 0 and top-coded at ten times the median of the corresponding non-equivalized variable.

[8] A full list of country characteristics along with their definitions is presented in Table A3 of Checchi et al. (2018).

go in both directions, and therefore these are to be considered as mere descriptive statistics. In the next two subsections we briefly summarize our methodological framework.

4.1 Inequality Measures

In this section we describe the inequality measures that we apply to the main outcome variables: household-level disposable income and total consumption, and individual-level labour income. For the reader's convenience, we briefly recall the definition of the main inequality indicators we are going to use in the analysis. Following Cowell (2011), let us consider a population of households (individuals), indexed by $i = 1,...,n$ with income (consumption) y_i, the arithmetic mean of the income (consumption) for the population is given by $\bar{y} = \frac{1}{n}\sum_{i=1}^{n} y_i$. The main inequality indicator that we present through the paper is the *Gini index*, which can be written as follows:

$$Gini = \frac{1}{2n^z \bar{y}} \sum_{i=1}^{n} \sum_{j=1}^{n} \left| y_i - y_j \right|.$$

A second inequality measure that we apply is the *Atkinson index*, which is given by:

$$A_\epsilon = 1 - \left[\frac{1}{n} \sum_{i=1}^{n} \left[\frac{y_i}{\bar{y}} \right]^{1-\epsilon} \right]^{\frac{1}{1-\epsilon}},$$

where ϵ represents the weighting parameter measuring aversion to inequality. In our case, we compute the Atkinson index for ϵ taking values of 0.5, 1, and 2. The higher the parameter, the stronger the expression of inequality aversion captured by the index.

The third and final inequality measure we consider is the *mean log deviation index*, which can be written as:

$$MLD = \frac{1}{n} \sum_{i=1}^{n} log\left(\frac{\bar{y}}{y_i} \right)$$

and has the advantage of being exactly decomposable in a between-group and within-group component. In our case, we consider groups created out of gender and three educational categories.

In addition to the three inequality metrics discussed previously, we compute some percentile ratios and income shares. The *percentile ratio* exhibits the proportion of one income group over the other. Instead of analysing the distribution as a whole, it compares two points of the distribution. In our case we compare the average income of the richest 90 per cent of the households (individuals) to the poorest 10 per cent. The *income shares* measure gives an overview of what share of the total income is held by a certain subpopulation group. In our analysis, we focus on the bottom 50 per cent, top 90 per cent, and 95 per cent of households (earners).

4.2 Regression Analysis

In the second stage of our empirical framework, we run a set of country-level regressions in which we correlate the computed (average) inequality measures to macroeconomic indicators capturing the country's economic development. We estimate the relationships by the following linear regression:

$$\textit{Inequality}_{it} = \beta_0 + \beta X'_{it} + \delta_i + u_{it},$$

where the left-hand side variable is a specific inequality indicator estimated for country i in period t, X'_{it} and presents a vector of country-level characteristics including indicators such as GDP per capita, employment rate, educational attainment in the population, life expectancy, etc, along with the corresponding coefficients β to be estimated. We also control for country fixed effects δ_i in the regressions. Note that controlling for time fixed effects is more problematic, since the survey years are not coincident among countries.

5 Results

5.1 Descriptive Analysis

We start our analysis of inequality trends by showing the inequality levels for the BRICS middle-income countries (Brazil, China, India, Russia, and South Africa). We also add figures for the USA as a benchmark country. To cross-check the picture emerging from the LIS database, we also include inequality measures and income shares from external sources: for inequality measures we collected additional data from the UNU-WIDER WIID database,[9] whereas for income shares, we considered data from the World Inequality Database.[10]

---

[9] www.wider.unu.edu/project/wiid-world-income-inequality-database.
[10] https://wid.world.

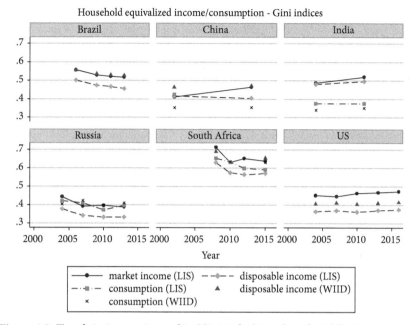

Figure 4.5 Trends in income inequality (Gini index) in selected middle-income countries (USA as benchmark)

Note: Gini indices obtained from the WIID database are per capita, therefore they exhibit higher levels compared to the equivalized LIS numbers (except India for consumption).

Source: Authors, based on data from the LIS database and WIID database.

In Figure 4.5, the first aspect to be considered is that inequality in market incomes is always higher than inequality in disposable incomes, the average difference being around 5 percentage points, with consumption inequality (when available) taking an intermediate value (this is true in Russia and South Africa).[11] One might notice that household consumption is covered only for a subset of countries in the LIS database. Pearson correlation between the Gini index of household disposable income and the Gini index of household (monetary) consumption is 0.87. This might imply that where information on consumption is not available, we could infer a trend for consumption inequality based on the income inequality data, and vice versa.

Moving on now to consider inequality trends, from Figure 4.5 we observe that inequality is on a declining trend in the case of Brazil: for example, the Gini index of household disposable income declined from 50 per cent in 2006 to 46 per cent in 2013. The decline in inequality in Latin America is a known phenomenon

[11] The average Gini indices for BRICS countries in LIS are 0.51, 0.46, and 0.47 for gross market incomes, disposable incomes, and consumption respectively. The corresponding averages obtained from WIID are 0.49 and 0.44 for disposable incomes and consumption.

(see Cornia 2014) that extends to most Latin American countries available in our dataset. Among the suggested explanations, one may consider a drop in the skill premium following an expansion of secondary education and the adoption of a new development model by a growing number of progressive governments which adopted prudent but more equitable macroeconomic, tax, social assistance, and labour policies. For example, Lustig et al. (2013) argue that overall decrease in income inequality in Latin American countries was dominated by a decline in labour income inequality that occurred due to expansion of employment and hours worked. These changes raised the incomes of, especially, the poor (roughly defined as the bottom half of the distribution), at the expense of the élites (again roughly identified as the top 5 per cent or 10 per cent in the distribution; see Figure 4.6).

Going back to Figure 4.5, for China and India we can hardly talk of any trend, as there are only two data points available for each country in the LIS database. With this caveat in mind, we observe that in the case of China inequality in market income is on the rise, while the (admittedly limited) redistributive activities of the public sector contained this trend, leading to a constant inequality in terms of disposable incomes: in fact, the Gini index of pre-tax market incomes rose from 41 per cent to 46 per cent between 2002 and 2013, while the Gini index of

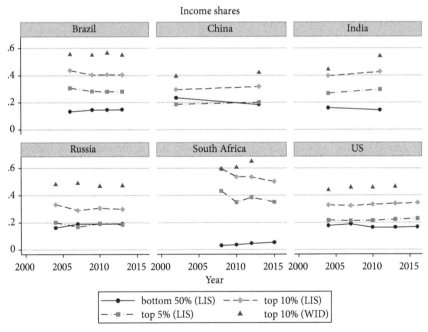

Figure 4.6 Evolution of income shares held by households with incomes below the 50th, and above the 90th and 95th percentiles

Source: Authors, based on data from the LIS database and the WIID database.

household disposable income spans around 40 per cent.[12] The rising trend in pre-tax income inequality is confirmed in other studies, though it may hide an even higher peak reached around the year 2008 (Jain-Chandra et al. 2018; Ghosh 2012). Income shares observed in Figure 4.6 suggest that most of the gains from growth accrued to the richest 10 per cent (though LIS data underestimate this share due to inability to capture the top incomes, as detectable when comparing with WID top incomes data). Contrary to the Latin American experience, differences in educational attainment at tertiary level and the skill premium are identified as drivers of the increase in income inequality (Jain-Chandra et al. 2018).

According to LIS data, India experienced a similar increase in market income inequality between 2004 and 2011, with the Gini index of pre-tax household income rising from 0.49 to 0.52, while the corresponding figures for disposable incomes rose from 0.48 to 0.49 (confirming that in middle- and low-income countries the distinction between the two income concepts is conceptually weak—see Section 2). In the case of India, we can only compare the consistency of our results against the WIID database for household consumption, showing that the trends for consumption inequality are very similar between LIS and WIID (see again Figure 4.5). Income shares indicate a robust expansion of the élites, though it is weaker than what is recorded by corresponding WID data for the top 10 per cent: see Figure 4.6. The rising trend would reverse a declining trend detected in the beginning of the previous decade, as a consequence of trade liberalization undertaken by local governments at the end of the previous century (Krishna and Sethupathy 2012). Chancel and Piketty (2017), in a recent paper, conclude that economic transformation from a socialist planning to a capitalist economy was the main driver of unequal distribution of income and wealth in India. Over a comparable time interval, we do not find an equivalent trend in income inequality for countries available in the LIS database, since both Taiwan and South Korea exhibit rather stable inequality trends: see Checchi et al. (2018: Figure A2).

Inequality trends for Russia presented in Figure 4.5 indicate a declining trend in income inequality, with the Gini index of household disposable income dropping from 41 per cent in 2000 to 33 per cent in 2013.[13] A possible reduction in inequality found in LIS data stands in sharp contrast to results from top incomes analysis: Novokmet et al. (2017) claim that official inequality estimates vastly underestimate the concentration of income in Russia. While income shares of the top 10 per cent exhibit a declining trend in LIS survey data, tax records indicate

---

[12] In the case of China, the LIS figures for household disposable income inequality are somewhat lower compared to numbers from the external WIID database (due to different equivalency scale applied). Note that trends in both cases are very similar, with the two lines being almost parallel.
[13] As in the case of India, we can only compare the validity of our computed inequality measures for household consumption: Figure 4.5 shows that consumption inequality computed on LIS data is somewhat lower than corresponding figures from the WIID database.

an opposite trend.[14] The Russian declining trend in inequality is partly in contrast with other Central and Eastern European countries (Hungary, Poland, and Slovenia), as detectable in Checchi et al. (2018: Figure A3).

Finally, we consider income inequality trends for South Africa (see again Figure 4.5). Among all the countries considered here, income inequality in South Africa, measured by all three indices, is by far the highest. Based on the Gini index of DHI, this inequality was as high as 63 per cent in 2008. It had gradually dropped to 57 per cent by 2015. As regards consistency with external data sources, we can only compare consumption inequality against the WIID figures. As there are only two points available, we cannot confirm whether the trends are well captured. Nevertheless, one might notice that consumption inequality has opposite trends between 2008 and 2010 based on LIS and WIID figures. When cross-checking with national sources, the problem of data quality (coverage, weights, imputations) emerges immediately, since various data imputations of missing income values may produce alternative trends, though all of them are on the rise.[15] This is also confirmed by the trend in income shares of the top 10 per cent from WID, while in the LIS data the corresponding top-income share would have lost approximately 10 percentage points. In the case of South Africa, there is no other sub-Saharan country available in the LIS database. The closest country to compare the trends against is Israel, where the ethnic divide is also rather pronounced. Apart from the lower level of aggregate inequality, in the latter country inequality seems also to be declining (see Checchi et al. 2018: Figure A4).

Overall, we may conclude that the inequality trend in BRICS countries exhibits different patterns, with Latin America and Eastern Europe on a declining trend while Eastern Asia and South Africa are on the rise. Despite the enormous differences in economic structure among these countries, we make an attempt to investigate whether common causes may underlie these changes. We resort to the common within/between decomposition analysis based on the mean log deviation index, and we focus on personal labour earnings, where the identification of common sources of inequality (like gender and education) is easier. In Figure 4.7 we report the result of such a decomposition, where two covariates are considered—gender and education—and consequently the employed population is divided into

---

[14] 'The Gini coefficient jumped from about 0.3–0.4 in self-reported survey data to over 0.6 using the leaked tax data, and the top 10% income share moved from about 30% to over 50% of total income' (Novokmet et al. 2017: 13).

[15] 'Using Sequential Regression Multiple Imputation (SRMI) to impute values for reported zero or missing incomes, Yu (2009) found a strong increase (seven or eight points) in the Gini coefficient between 1996 and 2001 (Table 4.3). Supporting evidence comes from other studies employing alternative measures: Leibbrandt et al. (2006) found an increase in the Gini from 0.68 to 0.73 using one method, and from 0.74 to 0.79 using another; Simkins (2004) found that the Gini coefficient for households grew from 0.66 to 0.69; and Ardington et al. (2005) concluded that the Gini coefficient rose from 0.74 to 0.82. There is thus agreement about the trends, though the levels vary widely' (Van Der Berg 2010: 12).

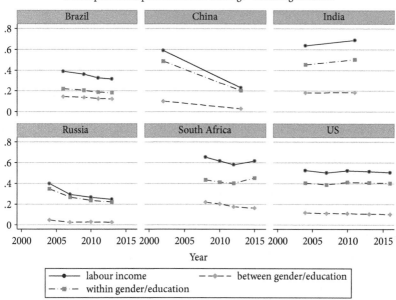

Figure 4.7 Inequality decomposition in labour incomes
Source: Authors, based on data from the LIS database.

six groups (two genders by three educational attainments). The between-group component (the inequality that would have been observed had each group member an income equivalent to the group mean) is intended to capture the return to education and/or the gender gap contributions to inequality: in all countries this dimension declines, though from different starting points. In previously centrally planned economies, this dimension of inequality was almost non-existent, while for the other countries it reached between one-third and one-half of observed earnings inequality. Within-group inequality (namely the inequality that can be attributed to unobserved components) is on the rise in India and South Africa, while a strong reduction can be observed in China. The limitation of this approach is the exclusion of people without labour earnings from the analysis, which makes these countries not strictly comparable. Nevertheless, the decomposition indicates that traditional inequality drivers—gender and education—see a reduction of their explanatory power with reference to income inequality.

5.2 Regression Results

We now turn to a multivariate analysis in an expanded sample that includes other countries in the same area and/or at a similar level of development. Detailed summary statistics of the variables considered are reported in Table 4.1. We can

Table 4.1 Descriptive statistics of variables used in the empirical analysis

Variable	Obs.	Countries	Mean	Std. dev.	Min.	Max.
Gini index equivalized household factor income	148	21	0.43	0.08	0.27	0.71
Gini index equivalized disposable household income	150	21	0.37	0.10	0.21	0.63
Atkinson index equivalized household factor income e = 0.5	148	21	0.17	0.06	0.06	0.43
Atkinson index equivalized household factor income e = 1	148	21	0.35	0.09	0.12	0.74
Atkinson index equivalized household factor income e = 2	148	21	0.82	0.13	0.31	1.00
Income share bottom 50 per cent (based on household factor income)	144	21	0.19	0.05	0.03	0.30
Income share top 10 per cent (based on household factor income)	147	21	0.33	0.07	0.22	0.60
Income share top 5 per cent (based on household factor income)	147	21	0.21	0.06	0.12	0.43
Income share top 1 per cent (based on household factor income)	147	21	0.07	0.03	0.03	0.17
Gini index personal labour earnings	143	20	0.40	0.08	0.21	0.57
Atkinson index personal labour earnings e = 0.5	143	20	0.14	0.05	0.04	0.27
Atkinson index personal labour earnings e = 1	143	20	0.28	0.10	0.08	0.50
Atkinson index personal labour earnings e = 2	143	20	0.60	0.19	0.18	0.97
MLD personal labour earnings	143	20	0.34	0.15	0.08	0.69
MLD personal labour earnings—between six groups (sex and education)	143	20	0.08	0.04	0.02	0.22
MLD personal labour earnings—within six groups (sex and education)	143	20	0.26	0.11	0.07	0.53
Decile ratio p90/p10 of personal labour earnings	143	20	9.92	7.18	2.50	32.00
Employment rate among men (16–65)	150	21	0.72	0.09	0.40	1.00
Employment rate among women (16–65)	150	21	0.51	0.12	0.20	1.00
Share female low education 15–65	150	21	0.25	0.11	0.07	0.47
Share female high education 15–65	150	21	0.08	0.06	0.01	0.28

Share male low education 15–65	150	21	0.23	0.10	0.08	0.46
Share male high education 15–65	150	21	0.07	0.05	0.01	0.19
Age dependency ratio (% of working-age population)	138	20	0.52	0.09	0.36	0.90
Life expectancy at birth (years)	138	20	75.13	4.85	53.72	83.09
Log GDP per capita	135	20	9.30	0.95	6.43	10.96
Urban population (% of total)	139	20	0.73	0.13	0.29	0.95
Government expenditure (% of GDP)	129	20	0.29	0.11	0.11	0.51
Government spending on education (% of GDP)	103	19	4.63	0.99	2.25	6.70
Agriculture, forestry, and fishing, value added (% of GDP)	122	20	0.05	0.04	0.01	0.20
Market capitalization of listed domestic companies (% of GDP)	107	19	61.96	49.29	2.08	246.47

Source: Authors, based on data from the LIS database and the World Bank Indicators database.

see that our countries differ in terms of the computed inequality indicators (e.g. Gini index of the household disposable income ranges from 0.20 to 0.63), but also in terms of underlying social conditions (e.g. life expectancy ranges from 53 to 83 years).

We also explore existing correlations between income inequality measures and a set of institutional variables.[16] We present four scatterplots in Figure 4.8. The results of these unconditional correlations suggest that income inequality (captured by the Gini index of household disposable income) is negatively correlated with the log of GDP per capita (measured in current US dollars), share of public expenditure (percentage of GDP), and life expectancy (years). On the other hand, the age dependency ratio is positively linked with income inequality. This might suggest that in countries with an ageing population and limited replacement pension systems, income inequality becomes an issue. We are fully aware that such graphs do not imply any causal relationships and do not consider potential covariance among these variables. To cope with these problems in a more consistent approach, we move to multivariate regressions.

[16] Note that from now onward we extend the sample of country/year in order to get a more precise estimation of the variable correlations. We are thus working with 21 countries and 150 observations, with an average of 7.4 surveys per country. The countries are (number of surveys in brackets): Australia (8), Austria (9), Brazil (4), Chile (12), China (2), Colombia (4), Hungary (8), India (2), Israel (11), Italy (12), South Korea (4), Mexico (12), Paraguay (6), Peru (4), Poland (9), Russia (5), Slovenia (6), South Africa (4), Taiwan (11), the USA (12), and Uruguay (5). Note that for South Korea personal labour earnings are not collected.

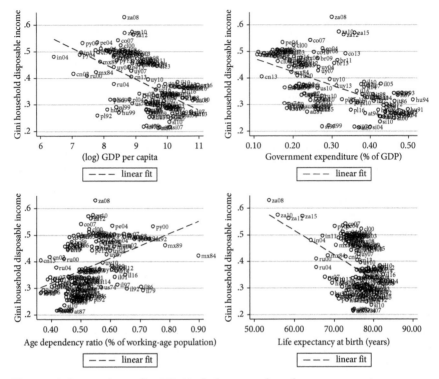

Figure 4.8 Income inequality (Gini index) versus selected macroeconomic country characteristics

Note: Gini index of DHI (top-coded and equalized according to the OECD equivalence scale) presented on the vertical axis.

Source: Authors, based on data from the LIS database and the World Bank Indicators database.

The results of our multivariate analysis are presented in Tables 4.2–4.4. In Table 4.2 we consider three outcome variables (factor household income, DHI, and personal labour earnings), three inequality indicators (Gini index, Atkinson index with alternative risk aversion coefficients— $\epsilon = 0.5$ and $\epsilon = 2$ —and alternative income shares). Since we do not control for country fixed effects (though residuals are clustered at country level), these are to be intended as simple conditional correlations, meant to explore the data. Among the most persistent results we notice that compositional variables (employment rates and educational attainment by gender) exhibit significant correlations, though with inconsistent patterns. On the contrary, GDP per capita turns out always to be insignificantly correlated with any inequality measure, similarly to proxies for production composition (agriculture share, trade openness) and public expenditure. Two variables exhibit positive correlation with inequality: one is a proxy for financial development (the market capitalization of listed domestic companies) and the other is a measure of urbanization (though it is positively associated with total income inequality, but negatively associated with labour earnings). However, the

Table 4.2 Regression analysis: OLS including all contextual variables

Variables	1	2	3	4	5	6	7	8	9	10	11	12
	Household factor income (labour + capital)						Household disposable income			Personal labour earnings		
	Gini index	Atkinson e = 0.5	Atkinson e = 2	share bottom50	share top90	share top95	Gini index	Atkinson e = 0.5	Atkinson e = 2	Gini index	Atkinson e = 2	p90p10
Employment rate among men (16–65)	0.13	0.07	−0.40*	0.19*	0.09	0.09	0.26	0.19	−0.24	0.63***	1.28***	47.16***
	[0.120]	[0.106]	[0.214]	[0.070]	[0.086]	[0.073]	[0.180]	[0.117]	[0.504]	[0.138]	[0.298]	[10.954]
Employment rate among women (16–65)	0.06	0.06	0.34**	−0.15**	−0.01	−0.02	−0.07	−0.04	0.3	−0.09	0.06	2.49
	[0.114]	[0.101]	[0.133]	[0.061]	[0.078]	[0.062]	[0.120]	[0.080]	[0.386]	[0.093]	[0.227]	[13.946]
Share female low education 15–65	−1.22***	−0.68***	0.76	0.41	−0.88***	−0.79***	−0.96	−0.55	−2.51**	−0.67**	0.35	−19.8
	[0.302]	[0.230]	[0.677]	[0.264]	[0.277]	[0.199]	[0.572]	[0.351]	[0.835]	[0.254]	[0.588]	[45.905]
Share female high education 15–65	−0.60**	−0.43**	−0.52	0.2	−0.39*	−0.34*	−0.29	−0.18	−1.52*	−1.05***	−1.82	−85.09**
	[0.236]	[0.199]	[0.707]	[0.225]	[0.213]	[0.174]	[0.311]	[0.199]	[0.855]	[0.282]	[1.198]	[37.238]
Share male low education 15–65	1.25***	0.80***	−0.32	−0.34	0.82***	0.75***	0.97*	0.60*	2.40***	0.67***	0.29	28.92
	[0.290]	[0.234]	[0.742]	[0.309]	[0.275]	[0.210]	[0.545]	[0.336]	[0.658]	[0.191]	[0.773]	[43.557]
Share male high education 15–65	0.01	0.06	0.64	0.29	−0.13	−0.12	−0.01	0	0.99	1.71**	4.42*	145.17*
	[0.330]	[0.243]	[0.662]	[0.291]	[0.332]	[0.286]	[0.390]	[0.252]	[0.700]	[0.623]	[2.226]	[70.498]

Continued

Table 4.2 *Continued*

Variables	1	2	3	4	5	6	7	8	9	10	11	12
	Household factor income (labour + capital)						Household disposable income			Personal labour earnings		
	Gini index	Atkinson e = 0.5	Atkinson e = 2	share bottom50	share top90	share top95	Gini index	Atkinson e = 0.5	Atkinson e = 2	Gini index	Atkinson e = 2	p90p10
Age dependency ratio (% of working-age population)	0.27* [0.098]	0.14* [0.079]	−0.31* [0.151]	−0.19*** [0.063]	0.16* [0.076]	0.1 [0.059]	0.26* [0.137]	0.13 [0.093]	0.43 [0.363]	0.30* [0.155]	0.3 [0.465]	29.95 [20.890]
Life expectancy at birth (years)	−0.01*** [0.003]	−0.01** [0.003]	0 [0.004]	0.00** [0.002]	−0.01*** [0.003]	−0.01*** [0.002]	−0.01* [0.005]	−0.01* [0.003]	0 [0.010]	−0.01*** [0.003]	−0.01 [0.006]	−0.53* [0.278]
Log GDP per capita	0.01 [0.018]	0.01 [0.016]	0.09** [0.033]	0 [0.012]	0 [0.014]	0 [0.013]	−0.02 [0.023]	−0.02 [0.016]	0.02 [0.065]	0.01 [0.026]	0.04 [0.067]	3.24 [3.560]
Urban population (% of total)	0.15** [0.064]	0.07 [0.054]	−0.17 [0.116]	−0.12*** [0.037]	0.17** [0.062]	0.15** [0.060]	0.17 [0.082]	0.09 [0.062]	−0.32* [0.184]	−0.09 [0.096]	−0.71*** [0.192]	−32.75*** [8.638]
Government expenditure (% of GDP)	−0.08 [0.067]	0.03 [0.049]	0.06 [0.207]	0.08 [0.050]	−0.07 [0.053]	−0.06 [0.044]	−0.11 [0.133]	−0.03 [0.086]	−0.14 [0.255]	−0.21* [0.093]	−0.40* [0.218]	−8.21 [13.887]
Government spending on education (% of GDP)	0 [0.010]	0 [0.008]	−0.04** [0.013]	−0.01 [0.008]	0.01 [0.008]	0 [0.006]	0 [0.015]	0 [0.009]	−0.09* [0.047]	0.03*** [0.006]	0.06** [0.023]	2.73*** [0.752]

Agriculture, forestry, and fishing, value added (% of GDP)	0.2 [0.314]	-0.07 [0.268]	-0.02 [0.644]	-0.37* [0.181]	0.22 [0.293]	0.23 [0.284]	-0.06 [0.522]	-0.2 [0.362]	-0.6 [1.155]	0.07 [0.617]	-1.23 [1.573]	19.6 [75.907]
Trade openness (% of GDP)	0.02 [0.028]	0.01 [0.026]	-0.05 [0.047]	0 [0.019]	0.01 [0.024]	0.01 [0.024]	0 [0.039]	0 [0.027]	-0.27*** [0.084]	0.05 [0.047]	0.16 [0.094]	6.82 [5.833]
Market capitalization of listed domestic companies (% of GDP)	0.06*** [0.014]	0.05*** [0.013]	0.01 [0.030]	-0.02*** [0.007]	0.05*** [0.012]	0.04*** [0.012]	0.08*** [0.019]	0.05*** [0.014]	0.16** [0.057]	0.09*** [0.025]	0.14** [0.056]	7.28** [2.604]
Observations	75	75	75	74	75	74	77	77	77	71	71	71
R-squared	0.85	0.793	0.515	0.795	0.88	0.872	0.857	0.848	0.556	0.831	0.669	0.632

Note: Robust standard errors in brackets. Standard errors clustered at country level. *** $p < 0.01$, ** $p < 0.05$, * $p < 0.1$.

Source: Authors, based on the LIS database and World Bank Indicators database.

Table 4.3 Regression analysis: country fixed effects selecting some contextual variables

Variables	1	2	3	4	5	6	7	8	9	10
	Household factor income (labour + capital)					Household disposable income		Personal labour earnings		
	Gini index	Atkinson e = 2	share bottom50	share top90	share top95	Gini index	Atkinson e = 2	Gini index	Atkinson e = 2	p90p10
Employment rate among men (16–65)	−0.26** [0.113]	0.12 [0.138]	0.18** [0.076]	−0.19* [0.101]	−0.11 [0.080]	−0.13 [0.095]	−0.71* [0.325]	−0.34** [0.122]	−0.66 [0.410]	3.72 [15.151]
Employment rate among women (16–65)	0.12 [0.102]	−0.40*** [0.161]	−0.04 [0.069]	0.06 [0.108]	0.02 [0.087]	0 [0.133]	0.26 [0.265]	0.28** [0.094]	0.44 [0.332]	−1.84 [16.612]
Share female low education 15–65	0.14 [0.087]	−0.48 [0.129]	−0.12 [0.101]	0.14 [0.082]	0.19** [0.072]	0.02 [0.079]	−0.86 [0.220]	0.13 [0.120]	−0.13 [0.400]	−15 [17.744]
Share female high education 15–65	−0.08 [0.144]	−0.44 [0.426]	0.32 [0.238]	−0.11 [0.091]	−0.1 [0.085]	0.03 [0.114]	−0.04 [0.552]	−0.23 [0.094]	−0.42 [0.267]	−92.87*** [31.871]
Share male low education 15–65	0.23** [0.212]	−0.13 [0.639]	−0.03 [0.108]	0.18 [0.213]	0.16* [0.150]	0.04 [0.209]	0.59** [0.777]	0.08 [0.160]	−0.42 [0.778]	−22.99 [19.263]
Share male high education 15–65	0.97*** [0.177]	0.99 [1.045]	−0.63*** [0.185]	0.84*** [0.108]	0.70*** [0.160]	0.4 [0.234]	3.25** [1.278]	1.09*** [0.094]	3.33** [0.980]	136.31*** [40.248]
Age dependency ratio (% of working-age population)	0.05 [0.112]	−0.31* [0.150]	−0.09 [0.122]	0.02 [0.112]	0.06 [0.084]	0.03 [0.116]	0.34 [0.417]	−0.18** [0.077]	−0.63*** [0.158]	−33.59* [12.440]
Life expectancy at birth (years)	0.01 [0.005]	0.02** [0.006]	0 [0.004]	0 [0.005]	0 [0.004]	0 [0.004]	0.01 [0.009]	0.01** [0.004]	0.02** [0.008]	1.62** [0.720]

	(1)	(2)	(3)	(4)	(5)	(6)	(7)	(8)	(9)	(10)
Log GDP per capita	-0.02	-0.01	0.01	-0.02	-0.01	-0.02	-0.09**	-0.05**	-0.13***	-4.57**
	[0.016]	[0.025]	[0.012]	[0.015]	[0.014]	[0.014]	[0.033]	[0.017]	[0.039]	[1.987]
Urban population (% of total)	0.08	-0.4	-0.4	0.37	0.44**	0.06	-0.12	-0.98**	-3.15***	-188.85***
	[0.328]	[0.659]	[0.311]	[0.305]	[0.209]	[0.305]	[1.072]	[0.374]	[0.809]	[61.310]
Government expenditure (% of GDP)	-0.19*	-0.2	-0.03	-0.15	-0.11	-0.12	-0.51	-0.12	-0.07	3.18
	[0.098]	[0.220]	[0.076]	[0.093]	[0.075]	[0.104]	[0.313]	[0.125]	[0.335]	[15.923]
Observations	127	127	123	126	126	129	129	122	122	122
R-squared	0.289	0.271	0.326	0.234	0.216	0.179	0.331	0.373	0.332	0.311
Number of countries	21	21	21	21	21	21	21	20	20	20

Note: Robust standard errors in brackets. Standard errors clustered at country level. Country fixed effects included. *** $p < 0.01$, ** $p < 0.05$, * $p < 0.1$.

Source: Authors, based on the LIS database and World Bank Indicators database.

Table 4.4 Regression analysis: country fixed effects selecting some contextual variables—most recent observations (year > 2000)

Variables	1	2	3	4	5	6	7	8	9	10
	Household factor income (labour + capital)					Household disposable income		Personal labour earnings		
	Gini index	Atkinson e = 2	share bottom50	share top90	share top95	Gini index	Atkinson e = 2	Gini index	Atkinson e = 2	p90p10
Employment rate among men (16–65)	0.11 [0.170]	0.54 [0.348]	0.07 [0.114]	0.1 [0.143]	0.13 [0.145]	0.16 [0.108]	0.37 [0.389]	−0.06 [0.146]	−0.42 [0.508]	2.05 [26.774]
Employment rate among women (16–65)	−0.25 [0.146]	−0.79* [0.388]	0.12 [0.115]	−0.21 [0.133]	−0.22 [0.127]	−0.24** [0.092]	−0.78** [0.365]	0.05 [0.166]	0.07 [0.629]	9.72 [32.745]
Share female low education 15–65	−0.29 [0.565]	−2.05 [1.984]	−0.04 [0.421]	−0.11 [0.502]	−0.2 [0.474]	−0.62 [0.413]	−5.16*** [1.798]	−0.08 [0.488]	−0.68 [2.336]	−29.26 [83.711]
Share female high education 15–65	0.07 [0.400]	0.47 [1.279]	−0.07 [0.286]	0.19 [0.292]	0.14 [0.227]	0.11 [0.261]	−0.8 [1.124]	−0.22 [0.731]	−1.59 [1.956]	−101 [130.952]
Share male low education 15–65	0.11 [0.527]	0.11 [1.345]	0.14 [0.357]	0.18 [0.513]	0.31 [0.500]	0.43 [0.434]	1.66 [1.175]	−0.33 [0.450]	−1.65 [1.987]	−96.12 [66.203]
Share male high education 15–65	−0.31 [0.433]	−1.45 [1.039]	0.33 [0.201]	0.08 [0.332]	0.22 [0.289]	0.02 [0.347]	1.9 [1.269]	−0.47 [0.695]	0.33 [2.645]	−99.34 [100.619]
Age dependency ratio (% of working-age population)	0.13 [0.189]	−0.86* [0.428]	−0.07 [0.140]	−0.04 [0.147]	−0.12 [0.116]	0.02 [0.151]	0 [1.007]	0.4 [0.267]	1.31* [0.689]	66.45 [50.825]
Life expectancy at birth (years)	0 [0.005]	0.01 [0.008]	0 [0.004]	−0.01 [0.005]	0 [0.004]	0 [0.003]	0 [0.008]	0 [0.005]	0.01 [0.014]	1.04 [0.936]
Log GDP per capita	−0.01 [0.014]	−0.07*** [0.024]	0.01 [0.008]	−0.01 [0.013]	−0.01 [0.011]	−0.02* [0.010]	−0.17*** [0.049]	−0.01 [0.020]	−0.02 [0.050]	1.35 [2.713]

	(1)	(2)	(3)	(4)	(5)	(6)	(7)	(8)	(9)	(10)
Urban population (% of total)	-0.08	-0.62	-0.03	0.11	-0.07	-0.39	-0.72	-0.08	-0.32	-137.18
	[0.641]	[1.211]	[0.393]	[0.499]	[0.429]	[0.481]	[1.005]	[0.662]	[1.734]	[105.797]
Government expenditure (% of GDP)	-0.09	-0.52	-0.04	-0.05	-0.06	-0.17*	-0.89**	-0.1	-0.72*	-2.74
	[0.095]	[0.405]	[0.092]	[0.080]	[0.065]	[0.074]	[0.335]	[0.157]	[0.391]	[21.288]
Observations	83	83	81	83	82	83	83	79	79	79
R-squared	0.306	0.243	0.354	0.359	0.287	0.428	0.346	0.196	0.15	0.198
Number of countries	21	21	21	21	21	21	21	20	20	20

Note: Robust standard errors in brackets. Standard errors clustered at country level. Country fixed effects included. *** $p < 0.01$, ** $p < 0.05$, * $p < 0.1$.

Source: Authors, based on data from the LIS database and the World Bank Indicators database.

main limit of this approach is the missing values on some variables (as can easily be detected in Table 4.1, where market capitalization and public expenditure are absent in one-third of the sample).

For this reason, in Table 4.3 we adopt a more parsimonious model, in order to raise the number of observations. We also abandon the Atkinson index (with $\in = 0.5$), given its high correlation with the Gini index ($\rho = 0.98$ for household factor income), and we introduce country fixed effects.[17] We currently find that educational attainment in the male population tends to polarize the income distribution, thus raising inequality, while employment rates reduce it. The GDP per capita and the population urban share are now negatively associated with labour market inequality, though still uncorrelated with total income inequality. However, the timespan covered by these regressions is rather wide, spanning from 1974 to 2016. Therefore, we have chosen to restrict the sample period to most recent observations, in order to obtain a model more compatible with the BRICS sample (which is only observed after the year 2000).

In Table 4.4 we present our preferred model, which contains a limited number of statistically significant coefficients, especially when looking at inequality in factor incomes or in personal labour earnings. However, more consistent results emerge when considering household disposable incomes (columns 6 and 7 of Table 4.4), irrespective of whether we use the Gini index or the Atkinson index with $\in = 2$, which focuses more on lower values: inequality declines when more women enter the formal labour market (female employment rate), when public expenditure increases, and when GDP per capita rises.[18]

6 Concluding Remarks

In this chapter we have presented recent developments in income and consumption inequality, focusing on a set of middle-income countries (Brazil, China, India, Russia, and South Africa) that have been recently added to the LIS database and for which there is limited coverage and comparability in the empirical literature.

We started by discussing the main challenges when harmonizing income and consumption survey microdata from the middle-income countries, and what implications this has for the analysis of economic inequality.

In our empirical exercise, we first estimated a variety of income (consumption) inequality indicators separately for each country and year for the whole

---

[17] Year fixed effects cannot be included since LIS surveys are available in neighbouring years, but not necessarily coincident ones.
[18] We have also considered a random-effect model, as well as relaxing the error clustering assumption, without finding more statistical significance in the results. Only life expectancy obtains a significant negative sign, but we acknowledge that causality may go in both directions.

population, as well as for subpopulation groups. We described the trends of these five countries against of the trends of neighbouring countries, finding declining trends in inequality in Brazil, Russia, and South Africa, against rising trends in East Asia (India and China). By then merging inequality indicators with World Bank Indicators data, we created an unbalanced panel database covering around twenty-one countries over the time period from 1976 to 2016. Our panel data analysis updates the findings of Roine et al. (2009), who estimated macroeconomic determinants of economic inequality for fifteen high-income countries.

Results from the country-level panel regressions revealed the following patterns. For our analysed sample of countries, the relationship between income inequality and GDP per capita exhibits a negative correlation, jointly with the (female) employment rate. It is also negatively correlated with public expenditure in GDP, while other controls (such as trade openness, share of agriculture, financial openness) come out as not significant when country fixed effects are taken into account. None of the country-level correlation results implies a causal relationship. However, the robustness of the results would be reinforced were more countries to be available in the sample—especially the low-income ones, which differ in many economic circumstances from the high-income countries. Therefore, the LIS Datacenter aims in future to acquire more microdata from other low- and middle-income countries, in addition to those already covered in the database.

References

Alvaredo, F., and L. Gasparini (2015). 'Recent Trends in Inequality and Poverty in Developing Countries'. In A.B. Atkinson and F. Bourguignon (eds), *Handbook of Income Distribution*. Amsterdam: Elsevier.

Ardington, C., D. Lam, M. Leibbrandt, and M. Welch (2005). 'The sensitivity of estimates of post-apartheid changes in South African poverty and inequality to key data imputations'. Working Paper 106. Cape Town: Southern Africa Labour and Development Research Unit, University of Cape Town.

Assaad, R., C. Krafft, H. Nazier, R. Ramadan, A. Vahidmanesh, and S. Zouari (2017). 'Estimating poverty and inequality in the absence of consumption data: an application to the Middle East and North Africa'. Working Paper 1100. Giza: Economic Research Forum.

Assaad, R., C. Krafft, J. Roemer, and D. Salehi-Isfahani (2016). 'Inequality of opportunity in income and consumption: the Middle East and North Africa region in comparative perspective'. Working Paper 1003. Giza: Economic Research Forum.

Atkinson, A.B., and A. Brandolini (2001). 'Promise and Pitfalls in the Use of "Secondary" Data-sets: Income Inequality in OECD Countries as a Case Study'. *Journal of Economic Literature*, 39(3): 771–99.

Atkinson, A.B., T. Piketty, and E. Saez (2011). 'Top Incomes in the Long Run of History'. *Journal of Economic Literature*, 49(1): 3–71.

Chancel, L., and T. Piketty (2017). 'Indian income inequality, 1922–2014: from British Raj to Billionaire Raj?' Discussion Paper 12409. Washington, DC: CEPR.

Checchi, D., Cupak, A., Munzi, T., and Gornick, J. (2018). 'Empirical challenges comparing inequality across countries: the case of middle-income countries from the LIS database'. WIDER WP No. 2018/149. Helsinki: UNU-WIDER.

Cornia, G.A. (ed.) (2014). *Falling Inequality in Latin America: Policy Changes and Lessons*. Oxford: Oxford University Press.

Cowell, F. (2011). *Measuring Inequality*. Oxford: Oxford University Press.

Davies, J.B., R. Lluberas, and A.F. Shorrocks (2017). 'Estimating the Level and Distribution of Global Wealth, 2000–2014'. *Review of Income and Wealth*, 63(4): 731–59.

Evans, M., A. Hidalgo, and M. Wang (2018). 'Universal child allowances in 14 middle income countries: options for policy and poverty reduction'. Working Paper 738. Esch-Belval: LIS Cross-National Data Center in Luxembourg.

Gasparini, L., G. Cruces, L. Tornarolli, and D. Mejía (2011). 'Recent Trends in Income Inequality in Latin America [with Comments]'. *Economia*, 11(2): 147–201.

Ghosh, M. (2012). 'Regional Economic Growth and Inequality in India during the Pre- and Post-Reform Periods'. *Oxford Development Studies*, 40(2): 190–212.

Gornick, J.C., M. Jäntti, and A. Leguizamon (2009). 'Adding five Latin American datasets to the Luxembourg Income Study (LIS) Database: data assessment and first comparative results'. Technical Paper 3. Esch-Belval: LIS Cross-National Data Center in Luxembourg.

Jain-Chandra, S., N. Khor, R. Mano, J. Schauer, P. Wingender, and J. Zhuang (2018). 'Inequality in China: trends, drivers and policy remedies'. Working Paper 18/127. Washington, DC: IMF.

Krishna, P., and G. Sethupathy (2012). 'Trade and Income Inequality in India'. In J. Bhagwati and A. Panagariya (eds), *India's Reforms: How They Produced Inclusive Growth*. Oxford: Oxford University Press.

Lakner, C., and B. Milanovic (2016). 'Global Income Distribution: From the Fall of the Berlin Wall to the Global Recession'. *World Bank Economic Review*, 30: 203–32.

Leibbrandt, M., L. Poswell, P. Naidoo, M. Welch, and I. Woolard (2006). 'Measuring Recent Changes in South African Inequality and Poverty Using 1996 and 2001 Census Data'. In H. Bhorat and R. Kanbur (eds), *Poverty and Policy in Post-Apartheid South Africa*. Cape Town: HSRC Publishing.

Lustig, N., L.F. Lopez-Calva, and E. Ortiz-Juarez (2013). 'Declining Inequality in Latin America in the 2000s: The Cases of Argentina, Brazil, and Mexico'. *World Development*, 44(C): 129–41.

Luxembourg Income Study (LIS) (n.d.). Luxembourg Income Study. Database. Esch-Belval: LIS Cross-National Data Center in Luxembourg.

Novokmet, F., T. Piketty, and G. Zucman (2017). 'From Soviets to oligarchs: inequality and property in Russia, 1905–2016'. Working Paper 23712. Cambridge, MA: NBER.

Piketty, T., and N. Qian (2009). 'Income Inequality and Progressive Income Taxation in China and India, 1986–2015'. *American Economic Journal: Applied Economics*, 1(2): 53–63.

Rasch, R. (2017). 'Measuring the Middle Class in Middle-Income Countries'. *Forum for Social Economics*, 46(4): 321–36.

Roine, J., J. Vlachos, and D. Waldenström (2009). 'The Long-Run Determinants of Inequality: What Can We Learn from Top Income Data?' *Journal of Public Economics*, 93(7–8): 974–88.

Simkins, C. (2004). 'What Happened to the Distribution of Income in South Africa between 1995 and 2001'. Johannesburg: University of the Witwatersrand.

Van Der Berg, S. (2010). 'Current poverty and income distribution in the context of South Africa history'. Working Paper 22/10. Stellenbosch: Stellenbosch University, Department of Economics.

World Bank (n.d.). World Development Indicators. Database. Washington, DC: The World Bank. Available at: https://data.worldbank.org.

Yu, D. (2009). 'The comparability of Census 1996, Census 2001 and Community Survey 2007'. Working Paper 21/2009. Stellenbosch: Stellenbosch University, Department of Economics.

PART III
INEQUALITY IN FIVE DEVELOPING GIANTS

5

Brazil

What Are the Main Drivers of Income Distribution Changes in the New Millennium?

Marcelo Neri

1 Introduction

1.1 Overview

Since the beginning of the 1970s, Brazil has been known as one of the most unequal countries in the world (Bacha and Taylor 1978; Fishlow 1972; Langoni 1973; Ramos 1993).[1] Its per capita income inequality presented high instability but no clear trend until 2001. After the start of the new millennium, inequality fell every single year until 2014 (Barros et al. 2006; Kakwani et al. 2014; Neri 2004). Earnings inequality also presented a falling trend in this period (Ferreira et al. 2016; IPEA 2013; Neri and Camargo 2002).

In 2003, the income-equalizing movement was coupled with an acceleration of GDP growth and, on top of that, mean household income grew even faster. The above-mentioned inequality trend has a clear parallel with the rest of Latin America, while its household income growth is at odds with other countries of the region and with Brazil's own National Accounts statistics. As a result, until 2014, Gini index-based social welfare grew three times faster than GDP. In this period, Brazil followed a 'middle path', in which the well-being distribution improved simultaneously on these three fronts. Roughly speaking, social welfare growth was evenly divided between: (i) falling inequality of household income; (ii) the differential of mean income between surveys and National Accounts; (iii) and real GDP growth (Neri 2014).

This chapter describes the evolution of Brazilian income distribution and its close determinants between 1994 and 2015. Encompassing both inequality and

---

[1] The Brazilian component of the UNU-WIDER Inequality in the Giants project comprises seven studies co-authored by Marcelo Neri (FGV, lead), Tiago Bonomo (FGV), Marcos Hecksher (IPEA), Cecilia Machado (FGV), Valdemar Neto (FGV), José Nogueira (UFPE), Manuel Camillo Osorio (FGV), Pedro Silva (IBGE), and Rozane Siqueira (UFPE). Neri (2018) presents a more complete version of this chapter. The papers that were the basis of this study were presented at the UNU-WIDER conferences held in Helsinki and Quito and at the National Meetings of Brazilian Economists (ANPEC) held in Natal, Rio de Janeiro, and Sao Paulo. We are grateful for the comments provided at these conferences.

Marcelo Neri, *Brazil: What Are the Main Drivers of Income Distribution Changes in the New Millennium?* In: *Inequality in the Developing World.* Edited by: Carlos Gradín, Murray Leibbrandt, and Finn Tarp, Oxford University Press (2021).
© United Nations University World Institute for Development Economics Research (UNU-WIDER).
DOI: 10.1093/oso/9780198863960.003.0005

mean income rates of growth is key to providing a comprehensive picture of impacts in terms of social welfare within Brazil and world inequality. Moreover, measurement and causal issues that affect inequality have implications on the mean income, and *vice versa*. This means analysing the second moment of income distribution without losing sight of the first moment, or of the existing synergies between them. The other general point in all the contributions to this project is that changes of inequality and mean income should be emphasized, not only their respective levels. This helps us to address the various period-of-analysis restrictions across different datasets. Differences across time are also a way to deal with measurement issues and to identify causality.

The key objective here is to assess the relative role of different public policy ingredients in income distribution changes. The channels behind these changes are diverse, such as increasing education levels; falling education and experience premiums; the diffusion of social programmes such as conditional cash transfers (CCTs); the expansion of contributory and non-contributory social security benefits and other programmes linked to the minimum wage, which also rose sharply in this period, to name just a few examples.

1.2 Organization

In these studies, we offer a description and an interpretation of the main causes of income distribution changes in Brazil in the past twenty-five years. Section 2 presents an overview of the main socioeconomic developments and the main economic challenges ahead. We attempt to time the evolution of income distribution and surveys methodology, setting 2003–15 as the central period of analysis. We also assemble the main aspects of mean income growth and inequality trends in this period using household surveys.

The rest of the chapter attempts to fill the gaps about income distribution changes in the previous literature. I connect the main questions of the overall project and specific contributions by exploring new empirical possibilities, applying various techniques to a vast array of datasets. Table 5.1 presents a schematic view of the main empirical strategies pursued, described in sequence.

Identified administrative records such as RAIS (*Registro Anual de Informações Sociais* from the Labour Ministry) allows us to look at the upper part of the earnings distribution and test the main determinants of overall earnings distribution changes. In particular, RAIS makes it possible to construct merged employer–employee records and to measure the role of firms mediating labour earnings inequality (Section 3).

Next, the 1996 and 2014 special supplements to the national household survey PNAD (*Pesquisa Nacional de Amostras a Domicílio* from the Brazilian Institute of Geography and Statistics (IBGE)), with additional information on the individuals'

Table 5.1 Inequality in Brazil by topic, technique, dataset, period of time, and income concept

Paper/Inequality topic	Technique	Dataset/Period used	Income concept
1. Firm effects	J-Divergence decompositions	RAIS 1994–2015 (matched employer–employee records)	Individual formal earnings
2. Intergenerational transmission of education & returns estimation	Omitted variables, measurement error and Markov regressions	PNAD supplements 1996 & 2014 (household survey)	Individual earnings
3. Missing incomes imputation	Combine regressions and stochastic imputation	PNAD 2001–15 (household survey)	Per capita (all sources)
4. Fiscal policy instruments	Dynamic microsimulation	PNAD + POF + AR 2003–15 (income & expenditures surveys and administrative records)	Per capita (all sources)
5. Top incomes	Pareto interpolation	PNAD + PIT - 2007–15 (household survey and income tax records)	Individual (all sources)

Source: Elaborated by the author.

education background, is also used. This information allows us to assess intergenerational education changes before and after the bulk of Brazilian income inequality reversal, in addition to better analyse the changes in the returns to education—in particular, how measurement errors and omitted variables biases affect education's impact on the earnings distribution (Section 4).

Besides exploring new data sources, the project analyses available surveys through a new lens. Although PNAD is the main Brazilian household survey used in inequality studies, it is the only official survey with no explicit imputation for missing incomes values. A new imputation methodology is another by-product proposed here. Brazil has a well-established tradition of welfare measurement but has not paid much attention to issues such as imputed rents and income measurement period, an issue also addressed here (Section 5). In particular, PNAD does not ask questions on direct or indirect taxes and some of the questions on the official cash transfers are not very detailed. Consequently, we developed a microsimulation framework that details the role played by individual fiscal instruments in income distribution changes using actual data across different points in time (Section 6).

Finally, Brazil recently released detailed personal income tax (PIT) tabulations from the Brazilian Internal Revenue Service. Combining these with household surveys gives us a clearer view of the top end of the income distribution. Once again, we address mean income growth and social welfare changes and their causes, adding new insights to the previous literature (Section 7). Section 8 presents the main conclusions of the chapter.

2 Brazilian Social and Economic Developments

This section presents the big picture of Brazilian evolution in the past three decades, using international social indicators such as the Human Development Index (HDI), Millennium Development Goals (MDGs), and Sustainable Development Goals (SDGs), with an emphasis on poverty and shared prosperity goals. We connect these developments with the economic policy agenda, especially regarding structural reforms. We also attempt to relate Brazilian income distribution changes to related measurement issues. Finally, we assess the role played by different policy-related components in income distribution trends for the 2003–15 period. The overall objective here is to set the stage for the specific contributions of the project.

2.1 Poverty

The first and main goal of the MDGs was to reduce poverty by 50 per cent between 1990 and 2015. In this period, the proportion of extremely poor fell by 73.3 per cent in Brazil and 70.2 per cent worldwide. This global poverty reduction occurred due to the combined economic miracles in China and India, nations that once housed half of the world's poor (Deaton 2013). Throughout the 1990–2015 period, Brazil had direct elections for president, and since 1994 it has achieved price stability, which is no small achievement for a nation that held the world inflation record between 1970 and 1995. Poverty reduction in Brazil between 1990 and 2015 had a roughly equal contribution from two components: income growth and inequality reduction. This trend reversed in 2015, when extreme poverty rose by 23.5 per cent.

2.2 Human Development

In 1991, about 85 per cent of all Brazilian municipalities had very low HDI. In 2010, this statistic was 0.6 per cent. There was a profound social transformation. The problem is that Brazilian governments disconnected its social policy from its economic agenda and, as a result, presented stagnated labour productivity and increasing fiscal imbalances.

The inconsistencies between social and economic progress can be captured in the three HDI components. Federal public spending as a proportion of GDP in Brazil rose from 10.8 per cent in 1991 to 19.7 per cent in 2016. The main driving force of public spending was social security payments. In 1980, life expectancy was 62.5 years; by 2016, it reached 75.8 years. That is, in every three-year period, life expectancy advanced by more than a year. Fertility also fell sharply. The population pyramid aged considerably, yet Brazil did not implement broad pension reform. Brazil spends 13 per cent of its GDP on pensions and retirement benefits, while Japan, the longest-living nation in the world, spends 10 per cent. Japan's share of people over 65 years old is currently 350 per cent higher than Brazil's. However, Brazil's elderly population share is set to multiply by five in the next fifty years.

Education has also advanced in Brazil. In 1990, 16 per cent of children aged between 7–14 were out of school. By 2018, this share was less than 2 per cent, with low quality of inputs. Brazil increased school enrollment but required only four hours a day of school time. In 1980, the adult population had only three years of schooling, on average, while in 2015 it had eight years. Although education has increased, labour productivity has not. In 1980, Brazil's productivity was equal to South Korea's. Today it is just one third of the Korean productivity level, due to several factors, including lack of education quality and connection with economic demands, an inhospitable business environment, closure to immigration, and a lack of engineers. Brazil has followed an educational agenda focused on expanding citizenship that has its merits, as the above-mentioned life-expectancy increase suggests, but that has had little impact on labour productivity.

In addition, there has been an increase in mean labour remuneration above mean labour productivity (Neri 2014). Disaggregated data reveal that the wage gains distribution has not been accompanied by improvements in the remuneration fundamental, namely productivity distribution (Alvarez et al. 2017). The social advancements manifested in the transformation of the trilogy of HDI components were largely disconnected from productivity and fiscal adjustment considerations, the two main Brazilian macroeconomic challenges.

2.3 Inclusive Growth

From 1930 to 1980 Brazil had the second highest GDP growth worldwide, behind only Japan. From 1980 onwards, growth reduced but there was progress with regard to democracy and in terms of social dimensions. After 2000, inequality fell every single year until 2014. In 2003, the income-equalizing movement was coupled with an acceleration of GDP growth, and mean household income grew even faster.

The inequality fall was around the mean for Latin America countries, while the excess of household income growth with respect to GDP is Brazil-specific. Between 2002 and 2012 Brazil was third among the seventeen Latin American countries in terms of household income growth but tenth in terms of GDP growth. In most of the world's emerging or developed countries, the growth in

GDP was larger than the rise in household incomes and inequality. These contrasts make Brazil an interesting case to study.

In late 2015, the main Brazilian household surveys, PNAD and PME (*Pesquisa Mensal de Emprego*), were replaced by a new national survey, PNADC (*Pesquisa Nacional de Amostras a Domicilio Contínua*), which shows a major reversal of all previous distributive-growth trends. In particular, from the first quarter of 2015 onwards, every annual variation showed an inequality increase, until the third quarter of 2019. This means that per capita labour inequality rose for eighteen quarters in a row, which is a duration unprecedented in Brazilian series. Therefore, it should be noted in PNADC data a rise and fall of Brazilian mean earnings and their equality between 2012 and 2019. Social welfare trends based on labour income sources also depict a mountain shape graph throughout the period, where 2012 and 2017 both represent the basis of the mountain and 2014 its peak.

2.4 Shared Prosperity

Given the major revision in the main Brazilian household surveys at the end of 2015 and the changing inequality trends noted above, we focus on the 2003–15 period, looking first at individual incomes of different groups to capture horizontal inequality trends. Mean income grew in real terms by 3.79 per cent per year, while the income of traditionally marginalized groups grew at faster yearly rates: blacks (4.8 per cent), females (5 per cent), north-east region (5 per cent), rural areas (5.3 per cent), illiterate individuals (5.6 per cent), mulattos (6 per cent), and spouses (6 per cent).[2]

SDG 10 captures inequality by focusing on the income growth of the poorest 40 per cent of the population (Basu 2001; Kakwani et al. 2014). It is interesting to compute how much the yearly growth rate between 2003 and 2015 in the mean income of the whole population (3.79 per cent) differs from that of the bottom 40 per cent (6.39 per cent). The −2.60 per cent difference in favour of the bottom 40% of the population is a useful measure of inequality trends. We can disentangle, in an additive fashion, the main drivers of this inequality fall, namely: other income sources (-0.65 per cent); years of schooling (−2.02 per cent); hourly wages per year of schooling (−0.51 per cent); hours worked (0.29 per cent); occupation rate (0.09 per cent); and labour supply (0.41 per cent). This labour ingredients decomposition suggests that the faster growth of the bottom 40 per cent is mostly due to an expansion in population's years of study and a decrease of income returns from schooling. The other point worth noting is that the impact of

---

[2] Other productive attributes of workers that are in general positively related to earnings, such as technical education, formalization, job tenure, and firm size, increased their share in the workforce, but individuals without those attributes presented the highest wage growth rates in the period of falling inequality (Neri 2014).

other income sources on mean growth and inequality is relatively small, suggesting the dominance of labour earnings effects in inequality trends.

Another policy perspective is to disentangle different per capita income sources inequality trends. Fiscal microsimulation exercises reveal that in the 2003–15 period market incomes inequality fell by 2.2 per cent per year; when we add to that official cash transfers, gross income inequality fell 2.7 per cent. If we consider the effect of direct taxes, inequality fell by 2.69 per cent, a similar amount. Finally, when we consider the effects of indirect taxes, final income inequality fell by 2.56 per cent. Section 6 provides details using the Gini index, the role played by specific private income sources, and official cash transfers.

Disposable income-based mean and inequality trends are similar to those based on gross income. If we move to the upper disposable income shares, the respective 2003–15 period yearly growth rates fall: whereas the bottom half grows by 5.91 per cent, the upper half grows by 3 per cent, the top 10 per cent by 2.19 per cent, and the top 1 per cent by 2.02 per cent.

Finally, we need to complete the missing pieces of the pure growth puzzle. Household income grew on average 1.88 per cent a year above GDP in the 2003–15 period. This difference is almost the same as the difference between labour remuneration and labour productivity. We are able to decompose for the 2003–13 period the 1.9 per cent a year difference. Only 18 per cent is due to nominal and timing differences, which is good news—first, because for social welfare purposes consumer price index is more relevant than implicit deflators; and second, because it puts the burden of the difference explanation outside National Accounts versus household surveys information sets.

Instead, we must look at differences between the GDP implicit deflator and the official consumer price index (IPCA) inflation rates. We see that 20.7 per cent of the residual gap is due to terms of trade (meaning domestic demand over total demand in an open economy); 29.3 per cent is due to differences between private consumption and domestic demand; and the residual half is due to differences between consumer price index and the private consumption implicit deflator. Social welfare growth cannot be sustained if the costs of goods and services purchased in the markets rises less than the cost of producing them captured by the implicit deflator.

We have based our understanding of income distribution trends in Brazil during this century and their main policy determinants on the main national household survey (PNAD). This takes into account the impact of different income sources (labour, rents, social security, official cash transfers) and of classical labour ingredients (participation, unemployment, working hours, hourly wages, school premiums). We have also decomposed the reasons behind the gap between mean household income and GDP growth (nominal differences), and related to deflators (terms of trade, domestic demand, and consumption). In the rest of the chapter we will incorporate, step by step, new data and methodological possibilities explored in the project to provide a more detailed picture.

3 Are Firm Effects Driving Formal Earnings Inequality?

The vast majority of the empirical literature on income distribution in developing countries uses household surveys.[3] Brazil established this tradition in the early 1970s. Recently, a series of studies have documented inequality changes based on PIT records. Establishment-level administrative records are also available in Brazil, but these have rarely been used in studies on income inequality. RAIS (*Registro Anual de Informações Sociais*) is a matched employer–employee database containing around 30 million observations per year on workers over the past two decades. RAIS depicts formal employment and wage differentials dynamics. It is a powerful complement to other data sources (Alvarez et al. 2017; Engbom and Moser 2017). This section documents the evolution and the main determinants of earnings inequality in the Brazilian formal sector from 1994 to 2015 using RAIS.

A broad inequality diagnosis using Lorenz curves and the main inequality indexes used in the literature, such as earnings ratios across different percentiles, the Gini index, and the Theil indexes, shows a consistent formal earnings inequality fall. Using RAIS, we also compare these results with broader household surveys, which also present falling trends. For example, the Gini of labour earnings in RAIS fell by 12.5 per cent between 1995 and 2015, while the concentration index obtained with PNAD data fell by 19.3 per cent in the same period.

3.1 Top Earnings

RAIS allows us to measure wages at the very upper end of the formal earnings distribution. In spite of the overall fall in inequality, the monotonic decrease of earnings growth throughout the income distribution continues only until the ninetieth percentile; above this point the trend is reversed. This evidence is in line with PIT data, which is explored in Section 7 (Medeiros et al. 2015a, 2015b).

J-Divergence measures allow us to disentangle the role played by specific categories of different variables, including income itself. The share of inequality explained by the top 10 per cent, 1 per cent, and 0.1 per cent rose between 1995 and 2015: by 20.2 per cent, 43.1 per cent, and 90.1 per cent, respectively. Similarly, despite falling mean schooling returns, the share of inequality explained by those with a high school diploma rose by 29.5 per cent in the same period (Hecksher et al. 2017; Rohde 2016).

---

[3] This section is based on Neri et al. (2018a). Machado et al. (2018), which also belongs to this project on gender inequality using RAIS, was omitted to align with the topics studied in other countries' studies.

3.2 Breaking Down Inequality

Standard inequality decompositions based on information theory help us to understand the main determinants of formal earnings dispersion. These include workers' characteristics (such as gender, race, age, education, and spatial location) and firms' characteristics (sector of activity, firm size, legal nature, etc). In general, the results indicate the predominant role played by the 'within' component in explaining total inequality, for the entire historical series of 1994–2015. However, looking at the 'between' effect for the educational categories, we observe a relatively higher contribution. For instance, in 1994, schooling explained 24.1 per cent of the total inequality measured by the J-Divergence index, while in 2015 this statistic reached 32.8 per cent.

As we found for several individual workers' characteristics above, the 'between-within' decomposition for firms' characteristics shows the predominance of the 'within' component in determining total inequality. Nonetheless, when we look at a highly disaggregated level by considering firm fixed effects (i.e. each firm being a category itself), the results show a remarkable contribution of individual firms. For the 1994–2015 period, the contribution of firm-specific factors explains around 65 per cent of total inequality in each year considered. In 2015 the portion of the total inequality, as measured by the J-Divergence index, explained by the between component reached 64.7 per cent.

Taken together, our findings suggest that, among several workers' characteristics, differences in schooling were a primary factor in explaining total inequality in the Brazilian formal labour market. Firm fixed effects have an even more pronounced explanatory power.

3.3 Inequality Changes

When one looks at the changes observed from 1994 to 2015, the power of individual firm effects to explain the fall in inequality observed is 64.5 per cent. Applying the same type of analysis across time to different characteristics, we also found the following contributions to inequality fall: education (−4.3 per cent), gender (2.55 per cent), age (8.8 per cent), macroregion (1.96 per cent), sector of activity (9.92 per cent), nature of the firm (−2.61 per cent from 1995 to 2015), and firm size (3.06 per cent). The firm effects explain the total inequality fall between 1994 and 2015 around three times more than the combined contribution of all the other characteristics considered.

The other striking result is the increasing impact of education on inequality in this period, which is not intuitive. This effect disappears with a more recent period of analysis. From 2001 onwards, there is a clearer inequality downward trend; hence, it may also be advisable to consider this period. Education explained

33.3 per cent of the marked inequality fall observed and thus assumes the role of the second highest explanatory variable on the inequality fall observed from 2001 to 2015. Once again, firm effects explain most (75.9 per cent) of the inequality fall observed between 2001 and 2015. This means that the gross explanatory power of individual firms to explain inequality in the Brazilian formal labour market is almost twice that for education. In sum, in the context of inequality change, firms also appear as the main driving variable.

We mention here only the results for people who finished high school but have no college education, to discuss the broader determinants of inequality within education groups (Alvarez et al. 2017; Machado et al. 2018). The baseline model with basic sociodemographic categories explains 25.8 per cent of the overall variance of logs of earnings. When we add occupation and sectoral dummies, the cumulative explanatory power reaches 39.7 per cent. If we add firm fixed effects, it reaches 77.8 per cent.

3.4 Main Findings

This section has documented the evolution and the main close determinants of earnings inequality in the Brazilian formal sector from 1994 to 2015 using establishment-level administrative records. Changes in the earnings distribution in the formal sector share are among the trends observed in household surveys, which evidence, in particular, a marked fall in inequality between 2001 and 2014. However, the distributive decompression is observed only until the ninetieth percentile, which is in line with PIT-based evidence. The analysis of specific groups shows that the share of inequality explained by the top 1 per cent and 0.1 per cent income-earners rose by 43 per cent and 91 per cent, respectively. We will come back to top income issues, looking at broader income concepts, in Section 6.

In 2015, schooling explained 33 per cent of overall inequality. Firm effects explain 65 per cent of total inequality. Firms are also central to explaining the marked inequality fall observed. Moreover, firms seem to drive overall inequality in developed countries such as the US and Germany (Card et al. 2013; Song et al. 2015).

4 What Is the Role of Educational Background?

Education changes are often viewed as the main driver of changes in earnings distribution.[4] In the case of Brazil, there is low intergenerational mobility and strong dependence on family background. In contrast with most other countries,

---

[4] This section is based on Neri and Bonomo (2018).

Brazil has experienced a strong reduction in educational premiums in the past two decades. However, omitted variable and measurement error biases possibly affect the econometric estimates of these effects.

There was also a sharp fall in individual labour earnings inequality between 1996 and 2014. Coincidentally, supplements to the national household sample survey (PNAD) on family background in these two specific years allow us to clarify the role played by falling education returns. This section takes advantage of this information to provide new estimates of the returns to education in Brazil using traditional Mincerian regressions, quantile regressions, and *pseudo-* panels. We also study the intergenerational transmission of education in Brazil using Markovian regressions.

The main questions posed here are: How has intergenerational mobility in education evolved? (Behrman et al. 2001; Ferreira and Velloso 2003; Lam and Schoeni 1993). What has been the evolution of wage premiums with respect to schooling? And, in particular, how has parents' education affected the returns and the educational level of their children? (Card 2001; Lam et al. 2015).

4.1 Intergenerational Inertia

Brazil is a country marked by low intergenerational mobility in education. For example, in 2014, in households where the father had completed higher education, 70.7 per cent of their children achieved the same level and 7.09 per cent got a Master's or a PhD degree. But how has educational mobility evolved in recent years? A simple Markovian model shows a strong reduction in the mean intergenerational persistence of education between the years 1996 and 2014, which went from 0.7 to 0.47. It is important to stress that this result still places Brazil among the countries with the highest levels of education inertia across generations (between Germany with 0.2 in 1997 and Colombia with 0.7 in 2001). Indeed, Brazil is now closer to where Mexico and Peru were placed at the end of the last century.

Cohort effects regarding intergenerational mobility show that the fall in the persistence of education is stronger for younger cohorts, coinciding with the fall in education premiums when we take into account family background data in the regressions.

Finally, quantile regressions enable us to assess how the intergenerational persistence in education changed along the income distribution between 1996 and 2014. Comparing directly the coefficients for the two years, we find that, except for the first tenth, the persistence is smaller for 2014 than for 1996, especially in the middle and upper part of the income distribution. In fact, we find stronger reductions in the intergenerational persistence of education for the richest individuals.

4.2 Education Premiums

The two PNAD supplements allow us to address econometric issues of omitted variable and attenuation bias. First, omitting parents' education information while accounting for selectivity issues reduces education premium estimates by 24 per cent. Perhaps more importantly, the fall in education premium is heavily underestimated when we do not take into account family background. Quantile regressions show that the highest fall in returns occurred for intermediary levels of education and income. Cohort effects also show that the reduction in the education premium has been going on over several generations.

Information on which member of the family responded to the survey questionnaire was used to assess measurement error, controlling for availability bias. We find evidence of attenuation bias, reducing schooling returns by between 14 per cent and 32 per cent.

4.3 Main Findings

The empirical exercises performed show that the fall in education premium in Brazil is underestimated when we do not take into account family background impacts. In particular, when we measure omitted variables bias for the years 1996 and 2014, we find that they did not cancel each other out over time. This result reinforces the importance of using two points in time to address the close determinants of earnings inequality fall.

Although the fall in the intergenerational persistence of education in Brazil (from 0.7 in 1996 to 0.47 in 2014) is contemporaneous with the introduction and dissemination of CCT programmes such as *Bolsa Escola* and *Bolsa Família* with the same objectives, a causal connection between these factors cannot be established at this point.

5 Does Missing Income Affect Distribution?

Incomes are information-sensitive and vulnerable to non-response in any household survey.[5] PNAD, collected by the *Instituto Brasileiro de Geografia e Estatística* (IBGE), is the main household survey used in inequality studies in Brazil (the others are the Demographic Census, PME, PNADC, and POF). However, it is the only one with no explicit imputation for missing income values. The incidences of missing values and null incomes are in proportions that vary over time.

---

[5] This section is based on Hecksher et al. (2018).

The trend of inequality reduction observed in PNAD in the twenty-first century might be affected by the treatment that is given to both the null and unavailable incomes. In addition, some inequality indexes with useful special properties cannot be estimated in the presence of null incomes. This section opens with a description of the new imputation methodology developed. Then follows a thorough analysis of the impact of null and unavailable incomes on income distribution-related statistics.

5.1 New Imputation Method

PNAD investigates multiple sources of income that were received in a given month, relative not only to the people interviewed, but to all eligible residents of each sampled household. Generally, income non-response on surveys tends to be more frequent at top incomes. This is identified as differential non-response and therefore requires a statistical treatment to correct the resulting estimates for potential bias. This issue results from the way the survey is conducted (on the PNAD, the reference period corresponds to one month only) and does not occur with comparable surveys in many other countries (De Waal et al. 2011).

The income imputation process began by fitting the regression models with observations classified as potential donors. The expected theoretical relations between the income variables to be imputed and all the other variables available in PNAD guided the initial choice of the potential predictor variables to be considered in each model. Then, using 2015 data, model selection was performed considering the complex sampling design of PNAD when testing the statistical significance of the predictor variables. In 2015, 2.9 per cent of the (weighted) sample had per capita household income altered by the imputation procedure.

The process of imputing individual incomes generally resulted in higher mean incomes and slightly higher levels of inequality than the ones estimated in 2001 and 2015 without the imputation. The increase in mean incomes caused by imputation is higher in 2001 than in 2015. Therefore, after imputation in these two years, real growth in labour income decreases from an annual average of 1.52 per cent to 1.48 per cent, and the annual growth in per capita household income decreases from 2.53 per cent to 2.46 per cent. On the other hand, the estimates of the Gini index for labour income and per capita household income increase by 0.003 in 2001 and 0.002 in 2015. Thus, the Gini index fall in both indicators between 2001 and 2015 becomes only 0.001 more intense.

We also study the behaviour of inequality in terms of poverty alleviation objectives. The idea is to increase the weights given to the bottom part of the per capita income distribution since traditional measures such as the Gini index place more weight on the upper part of the income spectrum. Any income increase up to the seventy-fifth percentile approximately yields Gini index reductions in Brazil.

Here we focus on the P^1 measure using the US\$3.20/day PPP poverty line, in which the imputation process reduces 2015 poverty by 16.8 per cent or 0.9 percentage points. Poverty differences across time are much smaller, not exceeding 0.4 percentage points. In our benchmark scenario, these differences amount to 0.1 percentage point. Although poverty levels present some differences, poverty change estimates—at least in the 2001–15 period—are not affected by imputation procedures. Imputation procedures in PNAD provide a bridge to the new PNADC, bringing poverty rates closer.

5.2 Policy-Related Marks and Imputed Rents

Our analysis takes advantage of strong points of the methodology to add a rent imputation into income-based social measures and to study 'pressure points' associated with minimum wage law in Brazil. With respect to the latter, in our simulated income exercises, social security benefits and earnings among informal employees are affected by wage floors together with low-skilled formal employees, preserving key policy-related features of Brazilian income distribution.

Poverty with imputed rent estimates is, as expected, lower. For example, in 2015 using the US\$3.20/day PPP line, the poverty gap (P^1) is 48.9 per cent lower. The P^1 between 2001 and 2015 falls from 8.4 to 5.8 percentage points using imputed rents. Using Datt–Ravallion-type decomposition the share of poverty fall explained by inequality reduces from 45.87 per cent to 30.38 per cent. Although imputed rent does reduce the relative importance of the inequality component of poverty reduction, it does not affect the Gini coefficient trends.

5.3 Main Findings

Missing income data in Brazilian surveys is more frequent among people expected to be extremely poor or extremely rich than in the middle of predicted income distribution, potentially affecting inequality measurement. We propose a new imputation method and apply it to PNAD. Our method preserves both random variability and empirical relations between variables. It also preserves discontinuities related to Brazilian institutional factors such as labour earnings and various official cash transfers with values exactly equal to the minimum wage. The imputed values preserve yearly specificities of different income sources distributions among different groups (e.g. employers, self-employed, formal employees, and informal employees). From 2001 to 2015, imputation increases the level of mean income, decreases the main poverty indicators, and slightly increases inequality indexes. It reduces the mean income growth rate but does not affect inequality or poverty trends in the period.

6 How Did Taxes and Transfers Steer Distributive Changes?

After being stuck around 0.60 for decades, the Gini coefficient declined every year from 2001 to 2014, reaching a Gini of 0.52.[6] However, the main Brazilian household surveys neither provide information on taxes paid by households nor on some relevant transfers. International comparisons of income inequality show that Brazil presents high market income inequality and the state does a poor redistributive job when transforming it into disposable income inequality. Previous studies assessed the distributional incidence of the Brazilian tax and benefit system at specific points in time (Higgins and Pereira 2013; Immervoll et al. 2009; SEAE/MF 2017). There is no previous microsimulation study in Brazil using different surveys over time.

The objective here is to shed light on the role of fiscal policy in determining inequality and poverty trends in Brazil. For this purpose, we estimate the redistributive effects of the fiscal system in the period 2003–15 using PNAD surveys plus nationwide expenditure surveys (POF). We also applied microsimulation techniques, and public tax and spending accounts.

6.1 Welfare Decomposition

The decomposition methodology derived step by step in the original paper allows us to evaluate causes and consequences in an integrated manner through growth and inequality components pointing to Gini social welfare function and standard poverty measures. It enables the assessment of the societal well-being level in a given year through its two main components (mean income and equality). The method also allows us to disentangle the contribution of specific official spending and taxation to both mean income and social welfare growth over time. The decomposition methodology further yields direct policy targeting indicators, comparing the welfare gains generated through each policy in comparison with its associated fiscal costs. Table 5.2 synthesizes the outcome of this methodology with additive static and dynamic properties.

We have focused on simulated per capita disposable income changes between 2003 and 2015. Gini index-based social welfare grew by 4.86 per cent per year in this period. This annual welfare increase can be disentangled into a component of mean income growth (3.48 per cent per year) on the one hand, and a component of equality growth (1.37 per cent) on the other. The respective welfare growth rate for disposable income is higher than those for initial income (4.36 per cent) and final income (4.47 per cent), but not for gross income (4.91 per cent). The only

---

[6] This section is based on Neri et al. (2018b).

Table 5.2 Income, equality, and social welfare: contribution to growth ordered by disposable income

Income type	2003–15 (annual)		
	Mean income	Equality	Welfare
Initial income	0.0276	0.0072	0.0349
Cash transfers	0.0110	0.0055	0.0165
Public pensions	0.0083	0.0016	0.0099
Poor elderly/disability benefits	0.0010	0.0013	0.0023
Wage bonus + Family wage	0.0004	0.0003	0.0008
Unemployment benefit	0.0004	0.0004	0.0008
Family grant	0.0013	0.0022	0.0034
Gross income	0.0387	0.0127	0.0514
Direct taxes	0.0038	−0.0010	0.0028
Personal income tax	0.0018	−0.0013	0.0005
Social security contribution	0.0021	0.0003	0.0023
Disposable income	0.0348	0.0137	0.0486
Indirect taxes	0.0080	0.0029	0.0109
Final income	0.0269	0.0108	0.0377

Source: Author's calculation based on PNAD/IBGE microdata.

two cash transfers that had a higher contribution to equality than to mean income growth were the Family Grant and the Poor Elderly/Disability Benefits (69 per cent and 30 per cent, respectively). Direct and indirect taxes contributed negatively to welfare growth, reducing the annual growth rate. However, direct taxes contributed to inequality reduction, since the PIT contribution to equality growth (0.13 per cent) offset the negative impact of the workers' contribution to social security on income distribution (−0.03 per cent). Indirect taxes also had a negative impact on equity (−0.29 per cent), thus increasing inequality.

6.2 Poverty

Our analysis of inequality links with concentration curves and emphasizes the impact of fiscal policies on poverty indicators, increasing the weight attributed to the lower end of the income distribution. We apply standard Ravallion–Datt poverty decomposition to growth and inequality components to assess their relative roles. Around 57 per cent of our benchmark poverty measure fall was explained by the mean income growth component, and 43 per cent by the inequality fall component. Using the same US\$3.20/day line, the poverty fall in the 2003–15 period amounted to approximately 69 per cent. This means that the poverty fall in Brazil was nearly twice the one expected by the UN's first MDG, in less than half the period.

The model outcomes allow us to assess the anti-poverty role played by specific fiscal instruments among various taxes and cash transfer programmes. The Family

Grant, the best targeted policy, was in action between 2003 and 2015. If one compares the Family Grant poverty impact with the second-best targeted cash transfer programme, each monetary unit spent generated a 119.7 per cent higher impact. The Family Grant concentration curve dominates the perfect equity line and all official cash transfers considered. Thus, the Family Grant gives relatively more to the poorest. Its contribution to the rise of social welfare is 2.7 times its contribution to the rise of mean income. However, since its creation in 2003, the programme has become less and less targeted towards the poor, maybe as a consequence of its steep expansion over time (Campello and Neri 2013).

Targeting differences also affects aggregate demand multipliers on GDP. Campello and Neri (2013) presents these multipliers within a social accounting matrix framework: Family Grant (1.78); Poor Elderly/Disability Benefits (1.19), Wage Bonus and Family Wage (1.06), unemployment insurance (1.06), and social security benefits (0.53, including public pensions). This means that the contractionary effects of fiscal adjustments, in particular social security reforms, can be mitigated by increasing pro-poor public spending, such as through the Family Grant. Incidentally, the minimum wage[7] acts as the numeraire of the benefits and/or eligibility criteria of almost all official cash transfers, including social security benefits. The only relevant transfer insulated from minimum wage effects is the Family Grant. This means that minimum wages do not have a very progressive impact profile in terms of Brazilian government transfers. The highest minimum wage impact is a little above the median per capita income.

6.3 Main Findings

This section interacts household survey data with fiscal rules and explores an analytical framework applied to cover income distribution and poverty changes observed over two decades of Brazilian fiscal policy. Per capita disposable income for the poorest fifth of the population in 2015 was 153 per cent higher than in 1995, compared with a growth of 20 per cent for the richest fifth, once inflation was accounted for. The welfare growth of 4.86 per cent per year between 2003 and 2015 is due more to mean income growth (72 per cent) than inequality reduction (28 per cent).

The Gini coefficient reduction caused by cash benefits increased from 3.5 percentage points in 1995 to 8.9 percentage points in 2015. The results suggest that official cash transfers accelerated the growth of social welfare (+1.65 per cent), while direct and indirect tax changes operated in the opposite direction (reductions of 0.28 per cent and 1.09 per cent, respectively). In a time of tight fiscal constraints,

---

[7] The Brazilian minimum wage increased by 79 per cent in real terms in the 2003–15 period.

the Family Grant should be a model for all official cash transfers, vindicating any budget adjustment decisions in terms of cost-efficiency. Gini reductions due to the introduction of more progressive taxes are still limited in Brazil and are another area of reform towards higher equality.

The poverty gap fall according to the US$3.20/day poverty line was explained almost equally by income growth and inequality reduction between 2003 and 2015. This indicates that Brazil followed a sort of middle path driven by distributive and growth dimensions.

7 Combining PIT Records and Surveys: Words of Caution

7.1 A Wider Scope

The assumption that Brazilian PIT tabulations for 2007–15 are representative of top incomes trends suggests that mean income experienced an unnoticed 'economic miracle', while household surveys, national accounts, and other sources incurred underestimation errors.[8] We evaluate the impacts of combining surveys with PIT in terms of growth, inequality, and social welfare. While the previous literature focused on the impacts of these data combination exercises on inequality, there are new sources of understanding about the economic causes and social consequences behind them (Medeiros et al. 2015a, 2015b).

First, if the level of inequality measured rises when higher top incomes replace previous lower estimates based on surveys, this same exercise also increases unequivocally, by construction, the mean and the social welfare level associated with it. Not only is this true for social welfare functions found in the economic literature, but it also satisfies the Pareto efficiency criteria; that is, everyone is better off, or at least remains the same as before. We refer to a country more unequal but more prosperous, or the same for all segments in the population.

Second, a similar story seems to hold for income distribution comparisons across time. While the empirical evidence analysed here shows that the movement of these combined estimates presents a slower inequality trend fall, income mean growth trends also rise at a much faster pace, which poses possibly higher social welfare growth rates than suggested by household surveys and new measurement-related issues. In fact, the social welfare index proposed by Sen (1973)—which results from multiplying mean income by the Gini inequality index complement—grows faster when PNAD's top incomes are replaced by PIT data.

After combining PNAD and PIT, the poorest 60 per cent of the adult population still increased their share of the total income. The richest 10 per cent also had

---

[8] This section is based on Neri and Hecksher (2018).

a growth rate (3.2 per cent) higher than average (2.9 per cent), but not as high as rates observed in the third and fourth tenths (7.5 per cent and 3.8 per cent, respectively).

7.2   Is All This Money New?

Annual growth of PIT taxpayers' average declared income (10.1 per cent) was much higher than that of GDP (3 per cent) from 2007 to 2011. Would the rich filers of PIT have experienced an 'economic miracle' unnoticed by the National Accounts? Not necessarily. Deflators and formalization can explain the difference. From 2007 to 2015, this income growth gap is smaller: 4.88 percentage points per year (ppy), reduced to 2.75 ppy when we use nominal values neutralizing differences in deflators used. Almost all the remaining difference can be explained by the formalization of incomes, which reduces the gap by 2.56 ppy to 0.19 ppy—less than 4 per cent of the original discrepancy.

As part of the formalization movement, new laws encouraged 5.7 million people to register, from 2009 to 2015, as individual microentrepreneurs, whose incomes, up to a legal ceiling imposed, could be declared as exempt by PIT filers or dependants, allowing an extra tax deduction in the last case. These new incentives may have increased the declared share of small business exempt incomes— the ones that grew the most among all declared income sources.

7.3   Taxpayers vs Demography

The use of income tax data to adjust for estimates about the income distribution assumes that individuals earn at least what they declare to the government, on the basis that no one would want to pay higher taxes than necessary. But the argument does not apply to non-taxable income sources, which grew three times faster than taxable incomes from 2007 to 2015.

The observed rise of exempt retirement income of people 65 years old or above is consistent with a reduction in the number of elderly declarants and their reallocation as dependants of their sons and daughters. From 2007 to 2015, the declarant population aged 41 or above fell by 15.9 per cent, while in PNAD it grew by 30.3 per cent. At the same time, the number of dependants per person up to 40 years of age doubled. All of this was in contrast with well-established demographic trends. What seems to explain this discrepancy is new incentives introduced in the tax system.

After 2008, the obligation to submit a PIT form in order to obtain a valid fiscal number (CPF) was abandoned, which may have affected the choice to move to dependant status in the PIT records. Tax legislation allows the individual to declare as dependants their parents and grandparents and to incorporate their social security benefits and pensions up to a threshold as exempt income. This institutional change created an additional incentive for younger people to incorporate their parents' incomes in their PIT declarations as dependants. Besides explaining the gap in age structure between PNAD and PIT, this may also have contributed to the marked rise in exempt income after 2008 and its impact on PIT income growth.

7.4 Main Findings

In the economic evaluation of income distributions, one should not look at their second moment without considering the first. A wider scope also leads to additional evidence with respect to measurement issues. Trying to correct top incomes of PNAD based on PIT tabulations slows the inequality fall from 2007 to 2015 but accelerates both mean income and social welfare growth. This difference was more dramatic in the 2007–11 period. The annual growth of PIT taxpayers' mean declared income (10.1 per cent) was much higher than that of GDP (3 per cent). Deflators and formalization of workers can explain most of this gap.

We document a rise in exempt non-taxable incomes and changes in the profile of tax filers and their dependants that are very different from the well-known demographic changes in Brazil. Exempt incomes drove PIT income growth. As the population ages, PIT taxpayers become younger and declare more dependants and non-taxable incomes. At least part of this difference is linked to changes in the incentives provided by Brazilian tax laws. It is risky to make conclusions on the trend of Brazilian inequality taking available PIT tabulations at face value.

8 Conclusions

This paper synthesizes the main results of the Brazilian component of the UNU-WIDER 'Inequality in the Giants' project. We assess the main drivers of income distribution changes and related measurement issues during the past quarter of a century. We provide the beginnings of an integrated picture of Brazilian income distribution using household surveys, disentangling the effects of various policy-related components on inequality, mean income, and social welfare growth rates. The chapter fills the blanks of this analysis using other data sources and various techniques.

In 1990, after fifty years of strong growth performance and dismal social indicators, Brazil's social performance began to trend upwards. Up to 2015, there was a poverty reduction of 73 per cent, above the global fall of 70 per cent. There was also an improvement of the Brazilian HDI above global trends. Life expectancy at birth increased by one year in every three-years period. However, social security parameters remained unchanged, implying increasing fiscal deterioration. At the same time, the recovery of part of the secular delay in Brazilians years of study occurred without any noticeable progress in labour productivity. Similarly, the gain in individual labour remuneration was independent of productivity gains. It was as if the social improvement observed missed the economic fundamentals that could provide greater long-term sustainability. The recent Brazilian crisis illustrates that. The crisis emerged initially in macroeconomic indicators in 2012 but social indicators kept improving and suffered only a major deterioration from 2015 onwards.

Nevertheless there was a major income distribution change in this millennium that is worth analysing. In the 2003–15 period, Gini-based social welfare grew three times faster than GDP, while for the bottom 5 per cent it was a fivefold difference. Social welfare growth was roughly evenly divided into falling inequality, real GDP growth, and the differential of mean incomes between surveys and National Accounts. We decompose these different pieces of income distribution trends considering the impact of different income sources, labour market ingredients, and price deflators. Social programmes' expansion, education expansion's impacts on earnings distribution, and consumer price inflation below producers' costs inflation were the highlights.

We brought in new data and methods to create a more detailed picture. When PIT data are used to substitute the top end of income distribution in household surveys, inequality falls less but mean incomes and social welfare growth rates are also much higher. We are also able to reconcile these discrepancies with the expansion of non-taxable income sources. Income inequality was very high and had no clear trend until 2001, but after that, according to most data sources, it experienced a falling trend that lasted until 2014. Most of the inequality fall was driven by earnings inequality, which was dominated by firm effects, at least in the formal sector. Minimum wage rises seemed to affect this channel, creating a wedge between labour productivity and remuneration but also affecting informal employees. Falling schooling returns also played a key role in earnings inequality, especially if one takes into account the effects of parents' educational background. Education expansion reduced intergenerational education inertia.

Missing values did not affect income inequality measured trends. Nor did the choice of whether to use gross or disposable incomes concepts. Direct and indirect taxes played against the inequality reduction trend, while official monetary benefits worked in the other direction, in particular conditional cash transfer programmes. The Family Grant programme had a much lower fiscal cost/social benefit ratio than all other programmes, most of which were indexed to the rising minimum wage in Brazil. Minimum wage hikes exerted a direct effect on fiscal accounts without much impact on the bottom part of the income distribution.

References

Alvarez, J., F. Benguria, N. Engbom, and C. Moser (2017). 'Firms and the decline of earnings inequality in Brazil'. IMF Working Paper 17/278. Geneva: International Monetary Fund.

Bacha, E., and L. Taylor (1978). 'Brazilian Income Distribution in the 1960s: "Facts", Model Results and the Controversy'. *Journal of Development Studies*, 14(3): 271–97.

Barros, R., M. Foguel, and G. Ulyssea (eds) (2006). *Desigualdade de renda no Brasil: uma análise da queda recente. [Income Inequality in Brazil: An Analysis of the Recent Fall]* [in Portuguese]. Brasília: IPEA.

Basu, Kaushik (2001). On the Goals of Development. In G. M. Meier and J. E. Stiglitz (eds), *Frontiers of Development Economics: The Future in Perspective*. World Bank Publications.

Behrman, J., A. Gaviria, and M. Székely (2001). 'Intergenerational Mobility in Latin America'. Working Paper 452. Washington, DC: Inter-American Development Bank.

Campello, T., and M.C. Neri (eds) (2013). *Programa Bolsa Família: uma década de inclusão e cidadania [Family Grant Programme: A Decade of Inclusion and Citizenship]* [in Portuguese], 1st edition, vol. 1. Brazil: IPEA.

Card, D. (2001). 'Estimating the Return to Schooling: Progress on Some Persistent Econometric Problems'. *Econometrica*, 69(5): 1127–60.

Card, D., J. Heining, and P. Kline (2013). 'Workplace Heterogeneity and the Rise of West German Wage Inequality'. *The Quarterly Journal of Economics*, 128(3): 967–1015.

De Waal, T., J. Pannekoek, and S. Scholtus (2011). *Handbook of Statistical Data Editing and Imputation*. Hoboken: John Wiley.

Deaton, A. (2013). *The Great Scape: Health, Wealth and the Origins of Inequality*. Princeton and Oxford: Princeton University Press.

Engbom, N., and C. Moser (2017). 'Earnings inequality and the minimum wage: evidence from Brazil'. CESifo Working Paper 6393. Munich: CESifo Group.

Ferreira, F.H., S.P. Firpo, and J. Messina (2016). 'Understanding recent dynamics of earnings inequality in Brazil'. In B.R. Schneider (ed.), *New Order and Progress: Development and Democracy in Brazil*. New York: Oxford University Press.

Ferreira, S., and F. Velloso (2003). 'Mobilidade Intergeracional de Educação no Brasil' [Intergenerational Mobility of Education in Brazil] [in Portuguese]. *Pesquisa e Planejamento Econômico*, 33(3): 481–513.

Fishlow, A. (1972). 'Brazilian Size Distribution of Income'. *American Economic Review*, 52(2): 391–402.

Hecksher, M., M. Neri, and P.L.N. Silva (2018). 'The measurement and evolution of inequality, growth and poverty with new imputation procedures'. WIDER Working Paper 2018/128. Helsinki: UNU-WIDER. Available at: https://www.wider.unu.edu/publication/new-imputation-procedures-measurement-inequality-growth-and-poverty-brazil.

Hecksher, M., P.L.N. Silva, and C. Courseil (2017). *Preponderância dos ricos na desigualdade de renda no Brasil (1981–2016): Aplicação da J-divergência a dados domiciliares e tributaries.* [*The Role of the Rich in Brazilian Inequality (1981–2016): Application to Surveys and Tax Records*] [in Portuguese]. Tese de Mestrado ENCE/IBGE.

Higgins, S., and C. Pereira (2013). 'The Effects of Brazil's High Taxation and Social Spending on the Distribution of Household Spending'. CEQ Working Paper 7. New Orleans: Tulane University.

Immervoll, H., H. Levy, J.R.B. Nogueira, C. O'Donoghue, and R.B. Siqueira (2009). 'The Impact of Brazil's Tax–Benefit System on Inequality and Poverty'. In S. Klasen and F. Nowak-Lehmann (eds), *Poverty, Inequality, and Policy in Latin America.* Cambridge, MA: MIT Press.

IPEA (2013). 'Duas décadas de desigualdade e pobreza no Brasil medidas pela PNAD/ IBGE'. [Two Decades of Inequality and Poverty in Brazil Using PNAD/IBGE] [in Portuguese]. *Comunicados do IPEA*, 159. Brasília: IPEA.

Kakwani, N., M. Neri, and F. Vaz (2014). 'Growth and Shared Prosperity in Brazil'. Annals of the 42th meeting of Brazilian Economic Association (Anpec), held in Natal. Available at: https://www.anpec.org.br/encontro/2014/submissao/files_I/ i12-e54e711753a63e8ce47ab4deab7c6c13.pdf.

Lam, D., A. Finn, and M. Leibbrandt (2015). 'Schooling inequality, returns to schooling, and earnings inequality'. WIDER Working Paper 2015/050. Helsinki: UNU-WIDER.

Lam, D., and R. Schoeni (1993). 'Effect of Family Background on Earnings and Returns to Schooling: Evidence from Brazil'. *Journal of Political Economy*, 101(4): 710–40.

Langoni, C.G. (1973). *Distribuição da Renda e Desenvolvimento Econômico do Brasil.* [*Income Distribution and Development in Brazil*] [in Portuguese], 3rd edition (2005). Rio de Janeiro: Editora FGV.

Machado, C., M. Neri, and V.P. Neto (2018). 'The gender gap and the life-cycle profile in the Brazilian formal labour market'. Wider Working Paper 2018/156. Helsinki: UNU-WIDER. Available at: https://www.wider.unu.edu/publication/gender-gap-education-and-life-cycle-profile-brazilian-formal-labour-market.

Medeiros, M., P.H.G.F. Souza, and F.Á. Castro (2015a). 'O Topo da Distribuição de Renda no Brasil: Primeiras Estimativas com Dados Tributários e Comparação com Pesquisas Domiciliares, 2006–2012'. [The Top End of Income Distribution in Brazil: First Estimates and Comparisons with Tax Records and Surveys 2006–2012] [in Portuguese]. *Dados—Revista de Ciências Sociais*, 1(58): 7–36.

Medeiros, M., P.H.G.F. Souza, and F.Á. Castro (2015b). 'A Estabilidade da Desigualdade de Renda no Brasil, 2006 a 2012: Estimativa com Dados do Imposto de Renda e Pesquisas Domiciliares'. [Stability of Income Inequality in Brazil, 2006 to 2012: Estimates with Tax Records and Surveys] [in Portuguese]. *Ciência & Saúde Coletiva*, 20(4): 971–86.

Neri, M. (2004). *Evolução recente da miséria* [*The Recent Evolution of Poverty*] [in Portuguese]. Rio de Janeiro: Centro de Políticas Sociais.

Neri, M. (2014). 'As Novas Transformações Brasileiras'. [New Brazilian Social Transformations] [in Portuguese]. In J.P.R. Velloso (ed.), *Desacorrentando Prometeu: Um Novo Brasil: Brasil das Reformas e das Oportunidades*. Rio de Janeiro: INAE.

Neri, M. (2018). 'What are the main drivers of Brazilian income distribution changes in the new millennium?' WIDER Working Paper 2018/186. Helsinki: UNU-WIDER. Available at: https://www.wider.unu.edu/publication/what-are-main-drivers-brazilian-income-distribution-changes-new-millennium.

Neri, M., and T. Bonomo (2018). 'Returns to Education, Intergenerational Mobility, and Inequality Changes in Brazil'. WIDER Working Paper 156/2018. Helsinki: UNU-WIDER. Available at: https://www.wider.unu.edu/publication/returns-education-intergenerational-mobility-and-inequality-trends-brazil-0.

Neri, M., and J.M. Camargo (2002). 'Distributive Effects of Brazilian Structural Reforms'. In R. Baumann (ed.), *Brazil in the 1990s: A Decade in Transition*. New York: Palgrave.

Neri, M., and M. Hecksher (2018). 'Top incomes impacts on growth, inequality and social welfare: combining surveys and income tax data in Brazil'. WIDER Working Paper 2018/137. Helsinki: UNU-WIDER. Available at: https://www.wider.unu.edu/publication/top-incomes%E2%80%99-impacts-inequality-growth-and-social-welfare.

Neri, M., C. Machado, and V.P. Neto (2018a). 'Earnings inequality in the Brazilian formal sector: the role of firms and top incomes between 1994 and 2015'. WIDER Working Paper 2018/157. Helsinki: UNU-WIDER. Available at: https://www.wider.unu.edu/publication/earnings-inequality-brazilian-formal-sector.

Neri, M., R. Siqueira, J.R. Nogueira, and M. Osorio (2018b). 'Fiscal redistribution in Brazil: 2003–2015', WIDER Working Paper 2018/136. Helsinki: UNU-WIDER. Available at: https://www.wider.unu.edu/publication/fiscal-redistribution-brazil.

Ramos, L. (1993). *A Distribuição de Rendimentos no Brasil 1976/85* [*Income Distribution in Brazil 1976/85*] [in Portuguese]. Brasília: IPEA.

Rohde, N. (2016). 'J-Divergence Measurements of Economic Inequality'. *Journal of the Royal Statistical Society: Series A (Statistics in Society)*, 179(3): 847–70.

SEAE/MF (Secretaria de Acompanhamento Econômico/Ministério da Fazenda) (2017). *Efeito Redistributivo da Política Fiscal no Brasil* [*Redistributive Effect of the Tax Policy in Brazil*] [in Portuguese]. Brazil: Secretaria de Acompanhamento Econômico, Ministério da Fazenda.

Sen, A. (1973). *On Economic Inequality*. Oxford: Clarendon Press.

Song, J., D.J. Price, F. Guvenen, N. Bloom, and T.Von Wachter (2015). 'Firming up inequality'. NBER Working Paper 21199. Cambridge, MA: National Bureau of Economic Research.

6

China

Structural Change, Transition, Rent-Seeking and Corruption, and Government Policy

Shi Li, Terry Sicular, and Finn Tarp

1 Introduction

In the late 1970s, China embarked on a major programme of economic transition and reform. Since that time, China's economy has been transformed from a socialist planned economy to a predominately market economy characterized by a combination of state, private, and mixed ownership forms. This transformation has been accompanied by remarkable economic growth and structural change, with positive consequences for household incomes and standards of living. Over the past forty years household incomes have risen six-fold, poverty has declined dramatically, and in recent years a new class of the ultra-rich has emerged.

These developments have naturally led to questions about trends in inequality in China, the topic of a growing literature that has employed a variety of empirical approaches and available data. Here we give a summary of the major trends in household income inequality in China, but our main aim is to go one step further and explain these trends in the context of China's broader economic development and transition.

In our view, the evolution of income inequality in China over the past forty years is the net result of four interleaved stories. The first is a standard development story characterized by structural change, growing market integration, and labour absorption, which together are associated with a Kuznets inverted-U path of inequality. The second is an economic transition story, in which the shift from a planned to a market economy generates increased differentiation of incomes. The third is a story of incomplete transition, which generates opportunities for rent-seeking, corruption, and hidden income, with obvious implications for inequality. The fourth is a story of government efforts to moderate inequality, which efforts have expanded over time and led to the establishment of a range of new social and welfare programmes.

Below, we discuss in turn each of these stories and their relationship to the evolution of China's income inequality. We begin with a review of major trends in income inequality in China since the late 1980s.

Shi Li, Terry Sicular, and Finn Tarp, *China: Structural Change, Transition, Rent-Seeking and Corruption, and Government Policy* In: *Inequality in the Developing World*. Edited by: Carlos Gradín, Murray Leibbrandt, and Finn Tarp, Oxford University Press (2021). © United Nations University World Institute for Development Economics Research (UNU-WIDER). DOI: 10.1093/oso/9780198863960.003.0006

2   Income Inequality in China: Major Trends

Although different studies provide somewhat different estimates of China's Gini coefficient and related variables, general agreement exists regarding the key trends. Here we highlight several of the main trends and report inequality estimates mainly from a recent set of studies based on the China Household Income Project (CHIP) surveys—specifically, Cai and Yue (2018), Gustafsson and Wan (2018), Li et al. (2018), and Luo et al. (2018)—as well as chapters from Sicular et al. (2020). The CHIP surveys are large, nationwide, repeated (1988, 1995, 2002, 2007, and 2013), cross-section household sample surveys spanning all major regions of China. Using the CHIP data, researchers have traced a consistent, detailed picture of incomes and inequality in China from the late 1980s through to 2013. The findings of the CHIP studies are generally consistent with those reported elsewhere.

What are the main findings of these studies? First and most importantly, from the late 1980s through to 2007 China experienced a long-term increase in income inequality. As shown in Figure 6.1, which shows estimates based on the CHIP data as well as official estimates from the National Bureau of Statistics (NBS), during these two decades China's income Gini rose from 0.38 to 0.49, so that by 2007 inequality in China was at a level similar to that in Mexico and not much lower than in Brazil, both countries with moderately high inequality by international

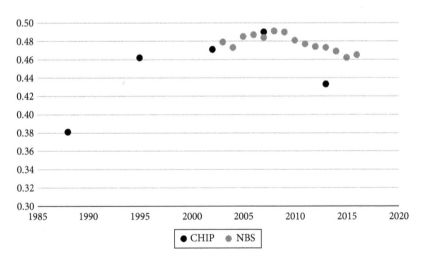

Figure 6.1 China's Gini coefficient

Note: The NBS Gini coefficients are those published by the NBS using its estimates of household income per capita. The CHIP Gini coefficients are calculated using the CHIP survey data and an estimate of household income per capita that adjusts the NBS income variable in several ways, such as to include estimates of imputed rent on owner-occupied housing and of the implicit subsidies on subsidized rental housing.

Source: Authors' illustration based on Luo et al. (2018), Department of Household Surveys (NBS 2016b: 407), and China Net (2017).

standards. More recent estimates, however, reveal that thereafter inequality began to decline.

The recent decline in China's inequality is the subject of some discussion and debate. It is generally believed that household survey samples do not fully capture the ultra-rich population and that consequently income inequality estimates based on household survey data understate actual inequality. In China this problem has recently become a concern due to the expansion of private wealth and the emergence of a growing class of the super-rich.

Some recent studies attempt to address this problem. Li et al. (2018) use available information about the income and wealth of China's super-rich to construct a top-income dataset, which is then combined with the CHIP household survey data as the basis for revised estimates of inequality. The results are striking. China's 2013 Gini coefficient jumps to over 0.6, noticeably higher than the Gini calculated from the original CHIP survey data. Luo et al. (2020) carries out a similar exercise. This study uses data from the Hurun and Forbes rich lists to construct the top tail of the income distribution. The resulting estimates of China's Gini coefficient are higher in both 2007 and 2013, but especially in 2013. This study's estimates imply that between 2007 and 2013 China's Gini coefficient increased by at least 10 per cent and perhaps by as much as 40 per cent. Such exercises necessarily rely on incomplete information, and so the resulting estimates are imprecise. Nevertheless, they raise questions about the apparent decline in China's inequality since 2007.

A second main finding is that China's twenty-year-long rise in inequality was not due to declining incomes of poorer segments of the population. In fact, incomes rose substantially throughout the income distribution, including for the poor. The income increases, however, were more rapid for richer segments of the population. This pattern is apparent in the growth incidence curves of household income per capita between various rounds of the CHIP survey (Figure 6.2).

Third, the trends in China's inequality both before and since 2007 are associated with changes in regional and sectoral income gaps, specifically the widening and then narrowing of income gaps between urban and rural areas and among regions. As shown in Table 6.1, the ratio of urban to rural incomes rose from 2.5 in 1988 to a high of 4.0 in 2007, after which it declined back to 2.6. The ratio

Table 6.1 China's regional and urban/rural income gaps

	1988	1995	2002	2007	2013
Urban/Rural	2.45	2.58	3.2	4.02	2.56
East/Centre	1.42	1.75	1.86	1.84	1.53
East/West	1.62	2.16	2.05	2.23	1.59

Source: Authors' calculations based on data from CHIP (China Institute for Income Distribution n.d.) and Luo et al. (2018).

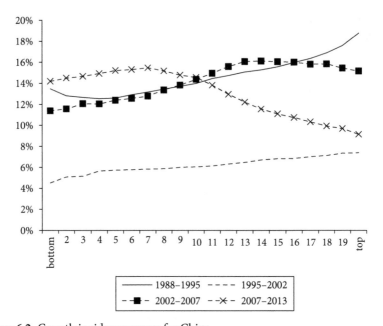

Figure 6.2 Growth incidence curves for China

Note: Growth of household income per capita, constant prices, by ventile.

Source: Authors' calculations based on data from CHIP (China Institute for Income Distribution n.d.) and Luo et al. (2018).

between incomes in the relatively rich East and in the poorer Centre and West regions shows a similar rise and fall.

Fourth, trends in China's inequality have been associated with underlying changes in the sources of household income and their distribution. The rise in inequality from the 1980s through to 2007 was associated with a declining share of income from more equally distributed sources, especially agriculture, and an increasing share of income from more unequally distributed sources of income such as assets (Figure 6.3). It also reflects changes in the distribution of some major sources of income. Notably, inequality in the distribution of wage earnings, which since the early 2000s has been the largest single source of household income, rose from 1988 through to 2007, after which it declined.

Wages are the most important component of income but only part of the inequality story. In urban China the share of wage earners has in fact been declining and non-wage sources of income have played an increasingly important role in income distribution. An important component of non-wage income in China is government transfers. A study by Cai and Yue (2018) finds that during the period 2002–13 government social security transfers increased substantially and became more equalizing. Nevertheless, China's largest single transfer programme—pensions—is very unequally distributed. Pensions, which on average account for more than 10 per cent of household income in China, go overwhelmingly to a

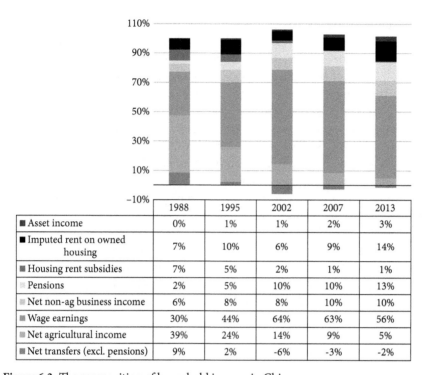

	1988	1995	2002	2007	2013
■ Asset income	0%	1%	1%	2%	3%
■ Imputed rent on owned housing	7%	10%	6%	9%	14%
■ Housing rent subsidies	7%	5%	2%	1%	1%
■ Pensions	2%	5%	10%	10%	13%
■ Net non-ag business income	6%	8%	8%	10%	10%
■ Wage earnings	30%	44%	64%	63%	56%
■ Net agricultural income	39%	24%	14%	9%	5%
■ Net transfers (excl. pensions)	9%	2%	-6%	-3%	-2%

Figure 6.3 The composition of household income in China
Source: Authors' calculations using data from CHIP (China Institute for Income Distribution n.d.) and adaptation from Luo et al. (2018).

minority of the population—urban retirees. Without pensions, urban retirees would be poor, but the size of urban pensions is so large that their pension incomes make them relatively rich. Consequently, on the margin, government pensions are dis-equalizing.

3 Economic Development, Structural Change, and the Kuznets Inverted U

The Kuznets inverted-U hypothesis postulates that, with growth and development, inequality will initially increase but eventually, at higher levels of per capita income, will level off and decline. Evidence on whether countries follow the Kuznets inverted U is mixed; nevertheless, the hypothesis provides a useful framework for understanding key mechanisms that can drive inequality during development.

One mechanism underlying the inverted U is the spread of growth across the economy through linkages. Economic growth typically starts in a few sectors and regions. The benefits of initial growth go to a relatively small share of the population in those sectors and regions, thus creating inequality. Over time, if linkages exist to the rest of the economy and if growth continues, the benefits can spread more widely. For example, if factor markets are sufficiently developed to permit mobility, then labour and capital with low returns can move to opportunities that yield higher returns. Over time, such movement will equalize the returns to capital and incomes. The resulting regional catch-up, migration, and structural change help move the economy along to the downward section of the inverted U.

In countries with surplus labour the inverted U is associated with a Lewis-type path of economic development. In such economies, during the initial stages of growth most of the population is in the traditional sector, which is characterized by low productivity, surplus labour, and underemployment or disguised unemployment. Surplus labour in the traditional sector supplies cheap labour to the modern sector and allows a 'grace period' during which the modern sector can expand rapidly with low wage costs. Growth during this phase benefits investors and entrepreneurs as well as relatively better paid workers in the modern sector, causing inequality to rise. With continued growth, however, the labour surplus is absorbed and eventually exhausted. In the later stages of development, labour scarcity leads to rising wages nationwide, thus moderating inequality. According to this scenario, the inverted U is associated with structural change, labour mobility, and changes in the composition of income between incomes from capital versus labour.

Studies of income inequality in China show evidence of regional catch-up associated with structural change, migration, and changes in employment and income composition. As shown in Table 6.1 and consistent with the Kuznets hypothesis, inter-regional income gaps in China widened from 1988 through 2007, during which period income growth in relatively rich eastern China outpaced that in central and western regions. From 2007 to 2013, however, the between-region gaps shrank, reflecting regional catch-up. Of relevance to the Lewis model, the urban–rural income gap also widened and reached a maximum of 4.0 in 2007, a very high level by international standards. After 2007, this trend reversed and the urban–rural income gap narrowed (Table 6.1).

China's experience of ongoing, large-scale migration—and, in recent years, rising wages and shortages of unskilled labour—is consistent with the Lewis story. At the start of the economic reform era, China was generally believed to have been a labour surplus economy characterized by a large labour force overwhelmingly employed in low-productivity agriculture. The shift from collective farming to household farming increased farm productivity and freed rural workers, who then began to transfer into higher productivity non-farm employment. The aggregate statistics in Figure 6.4 reveal the structural change in employment that has been ongoing since the 1980s, such that by the early 2000s fewer than half of employed workers in China were primarily employed in agriculture.

This shift out of agriculture and into other sectors is visible in household survey data. Using data from a nationally representative rural household survey,

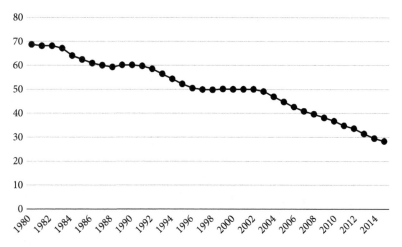

Figure 6.4 Primary sector employment in China as a share of total employment (per cent) 1980–2015

Note: Share of employed persons at year end based on primary sector of employment.

Source: Authors' calculations based on NBS (2016c) data.

Huang and Rozelle (2012) trace changes over time in the proportion of rural workers engaged in on-farm versus off-farm work. They find that the proportion employed solely in agriculture declined from about 70 per cent in 1995 to 45 per cent in 2007. Conversely, the proportion engaged in off-farm employment rose from 30 per cent in 1995 to 55 per cent in 2007. Roughly one-third of those with off-farm employment, however, also continued to engage in farming.

Changes in incomes and inequality are broadly consistent with the Lewis story. The Lewis story predicts that the structural shift in employment from agriculture to other sectors will not immediately lead to rising wages for urban workers or incomes for the remaining rural population. Such has been the case for China. Hoken and Sato (2017) analyse long-term growth in rural incomes using the CHIP survey data and find that rural income per capita grew slowly over the period 1988–2002. Thereafter, growth in rural income accelerated to about 8 per cent between 2002 and 2007 and to more than 10 per cent between 2007 and 2013. Wages for migrants and for unskilled labour in urban China followed a similar path.

With respect to the wage patterns of rural–urban migrant workers, as discussed in Lu (2012), in the late 1990s the wage growth for migrant workers was quite low, but after 2002 it began to increase. Figure 6.5 shows the average annual growth rate of wages of rural–urban migrant workers since the early 2000s, revealing slow wage growth in 2002 followed by wage growth of 6 per cent or faster thereafter.

These trends in rural incomes and migrant wages influenced the urban–rural income gap, an important contributor to the rise and recent fall in China's

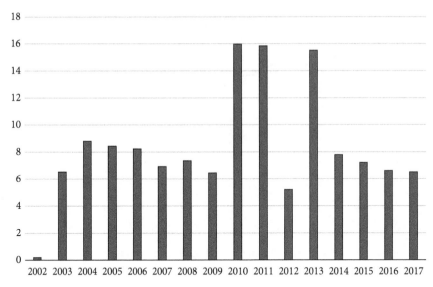

Figure 6.5 Wage growth of rural–urban migrant workers in China (%)

Note: Wage growth is in real terms (constant prices).

Source: Authors' calculations for 2009–17 are based on the NBS Rural Migrant Workers Survey (NBS 2010, 2012, 2013, 2014, 2015, 2016a, 2017a); for 2002–8 the estimates are based on Lu (2012).

national inequality. Decomposition of national inequality by groups between and within the urban and rural sectors reveals that the urban–rural income gap's contribution to overall inequality rose from roughly 30 per cent in the late 1980s and mid-1990s to 40 per cent in 2002, and further to 50 per cent in 2007, finally dropping back to 30 per cent in 2013 (Luo et al. 2018).

Although China's path of development is broadly consistent with the Lewis story, several factors modified or distorted its evolution. First, a baby boom in the 1960s caused a demographic bulge that resulted in rapid growth of the working-age population from the 1980s through the early 2000s, creating downward pressure on wages. Thereafter, the effects of the one-child policy began to kick in, causing a marked slowdown in growth in the labour supply after 2000.

Second, as will be discussed more fully below, incomplete transition has led to ongoing labour market segmentation and hindered labour mobility. Restrictions on migration through the household registration (*hukou*) system have loosened over time but have not yet been removed. Also, the incomplete reform of farm-land property rights has affected the willingness of rural households to leave farming. Knight et al. (2011) argue that ongoing segmentation of the labour market has caused labour scarcity in urban areas and labour surplus in rural areas to coexist. Recent increases in the wages of unskilled workers and migrant workers should be understood in this context.

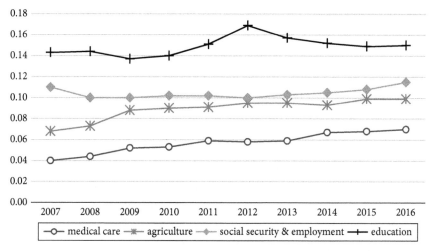

Figure 6.6 The shares of fiscal spending on education, medical insurance, social security, and agriculture in total budgetary expenditures in China

Note: Calculated using budgetary fiscal expenditure data published by the National Bureau of Statistics.

Source: Authors' calculations based on NBS (2017b) data.

Aside from structural change and the absorption of surplus labour, economic development can influence income distribution through several other mechanisms. With development comes strengthened fiscal capacity, which allows the public sector to play a larger role in redistribution through taxes and transfers and as a provider of social programmes. China's public sector was large during the Maoist era, but with the implementation of economic reforms fiscal revenues shrank considerably, reaching a low point in the mid-1990s (Lin 2009). Following fiscal reforms in 1994 and with continued economic growth, China's public sector recovered (Lin 2009). With that recovery, and especially since 2003, more resources began to be devoted to building a stronger social welfare system.

Figure 6.6 shows expenditures on education, social security, and welfare programmes such as *dibao* (the minimum income guarantee) as a share of total budgetary expenditures, which have grown during this period.[1] Government spending on social security and employment programmes has remained at around 11 per cent of total budgetary expenditures. The shares of budgetary spending on health and agriculture have increased. The rising share of expenditures on agriculture reflects a series of pro-rural policies starting under the Hu–Wen administration. These pro-rural policies have included grain subsidies and farm

---

[1] Apart from budgetary revenue and expenditures, the government also has extra-budgetary revenue and expenditures, which are currently around 10 per cent of their budgetary counterparts. During the period 2007–10, extra-budgetary spending on education accounted for 36–43 per cent of total extra-budgetary expenditures.

supports, in addition to the new rural pension scheme, new rural medical insurance scheme, and new rural poverty-alleviation programmes such as the rural *dibao* programme. Many poor and low-income rural households have benefited from these policies. The distributional impact of China's expanding social welfare programmes will be discussed more fully in Section 5.

Development can go hand in hand with increased trade and globalization, with implications for income distribution through its differential impact on regional development as well as on the distribution of wage earnings. China has in fact experienced a marked increase in its levels of trade, especially since its entry into the WTO at the end of 2001 (Figure 6.7). China's trade expansion did not occur equally among regions and provinces. It started in the eastern coastal region, which is closest to international markets, and gradually spread inland to the central and western regions. Consequently, China's opening to international markets contributed to the widening of regional income gaps. Furthermore, rapid growth of exports increased the demand for unskilled workers and helped to accelerate the absorption of China's rural surplus labour. The trade story thus helps explain why the wages of unskilled workers and rural migrant workers have increased more rapidly than the wages of other workers in recent years. The role of trade in China's distributional story has received little attention in the literature. Research on this topic would be valuable.

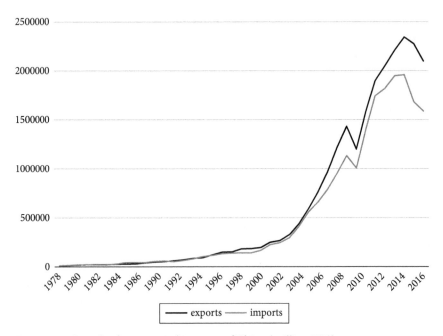

Figure 6.7 Growth of exports and imports of China (million US$)
Note: Calculated using data published by the National Bureau of Statistics.
Source: Authors' calculations based on NBS (2017b) data.

4 Economic Transition

Socialist economies differ from market economies in three major regards. First, the allocation of goods, labour, and capital is done through planning rather than markets. Second, wages are set administratively, and the distribution of income is based on labour or work performed and governed by the principle of egalitarianism. Third, private ownership is minimized; capital and assets are owned by the state and collectives. Private individuals do not receive income from capital.

During much of the Maoist era, these three pillars of socialism characterized China's economy. In rural areas, home to most of the population, production was carried out by collective farms that organized labour and paid workers in an egalitarian fashion based on work points. Urban labour was governed by planned allocation of workers to jobs, typically for lifetime employment in the same work unit, with wage scales fixed by planners. The wage structure minimized wage differentials, which were largely based on seniority. In both rural and urban areas, individuals and households did not own private property, although rural households were allowed to construct their own housing. This system did not eliminate income gaps—gaps persisted between the urban and rural sectors, and in rural areas between richer and poorer localities—but overall income inequality was exceedingly low. Available estimates of the Gini coefficient for the 1970s are generally at or below 0.3, very low by international standards, especially for a large, diverse economy (Xue et al. 2014).

Economic transition refers to reforms in these three pillars of socialism. Starting in 1978, China embarked on such a transition. The transition in rural areas began in the early 1980s with the replacement of collective farming by household farming under the household responsibility system. Although the household responsibility system did not constitute full privatization—land continued to be collectively owned—some property rights were transferred to households. Households were now given the rights to make production decisions and to keep the earnings from their productive activities. Incomes were now determined by the returns to farming by individual households rather than through egalitarian distribution by collective farms.

Concurrently, the government transformed the system of allocation in rural areas. Step by step it eliminated the planning of farm production, procurement and sales, and prices. By the 1990s agricultural products were largely allocated through markets. The government also lifted restrictions on the expansion of local rural industry. The ensuing rapid development of the so-called township and village industries, which operated outside of the plan, generated employment and income for the rural population, although with variation among regions and localities so that access to such employment and income was uneven.

Not surprisingly, these transition measures led to a marked upswing in rural inequality. Most estimates of the Gini coefficient in rural China for the late 1970s and early 1980s are around 0.2 (Xue et al. 2014). Estimates based on the CHIP data for 1988 (Hoken and Sato 2017) show a substantially higher 0.353, rising further to 0.419 in 1995.

After the mid-1990s, rural inequality declined and then remained fairly stable through 2007 (Hoken and Sato 2017; Luo et al. 2018). The decline and then stabilization of rural inequality suggests that by the mid-1990s the increase in inequality associated with the rural economic transition in ownership, allocation, and income distribution had played out. Meanwhile, the ongoing expansion of off-farm employment, which by the mid-1990s had become pervasive both due to local township and village enterprises and increasingly through migration, also began to moderate inequality.

Transition in the urban sector progressed more slowly. The planned allocation of labour and wages continued through the 1980s; however, firms were encouraged to pursue profits and were given more flexibility to decide on worker pay, for example through bonuses tied to performance. Flexibility in terms of labour allocation also increased as new workers were increasingly hired on contracts outside of the plan instead of being allocated to lifetime jobs in work units.

In this initial period of transition, urban workers retained substantial job security, but wage inequality began to increase. Table 6.2 shows an increase in the Gini of urban wage earnings from 0.23 in 1988 to 0.30 in 1995; inequality of urban household income per capita also rose.

These gradual transition steps continued until the late 1990s, when China undertook a radical restructuring of the urban economy. At this time the government opened the door to the bankruptcy, mergers, and ownership reform of inefficient state-owned enterprises (SOEs) and collective enterprises. Enterprises were now permitted to fire and lay off workers. The result was the breaking of the 'iron rice bowl'. Millions of urban workers were laid off or became unemployed, with adverse effects on their incomes. In the short term, urban income inequality rose, primarily due to layoffs and unemployment (Meng 2004). The restructuring, however, was accompanied by a reduction of restrictions on the private sector and the reinvigoration of the medium and small-scale enterprises, which were sold off or converted to shareholding. Expansion of these sectors generated jobs.

Table 6.2 Gini coefficients of urban wages and income per capita in China, 1988–2013

	1988	1995	2002	2007	2013
Wage earnings	0.230	0.301	0.345	0.379	0.384
Household income per capita	0.231	0.332	0.311	0.335	0.352

Notes: Calculated using the CHIP data for urban workers and individuals with urban household registration.

Source: Authors' illustration based on Gustafsson and Ding (2017), and Gustafsson and Wan (2018).

Consequently, by the early 2000s urban employment had largely recovered (Gustafsson and Wan 2018).

A more lasting effect of the urban restructuring was the transformation of the urban wage structure. Seniority-based wage differentials shrank, and wage differentials based on productivity, for example as reflected in rapidly increasing returns to education, widened (Deng and Li 2009; Gustafsson and Wan 2018; Zhang et al. 2005). As wages increasingly reflected heterogeneous productive characteristics such as ability and education, the Gini of urban wages rose further to 0.345 in 2002 (Table 6.2).

Notably, despite rising inequality of wage earnings, during these same few years the inequality of urban household income per capita declined (Table 6.2). This apparent inconsistency between inequality trends for urban wages and urban household income per capita reflects the growing importance of other sources of urban income, including government social programme transfers.

From the early 2000s on, the government has generally refrained from direct interventions in the labour market, relying on indirect regulatory measures such as the labour contract and minimum wage laws and stimulus spending. Urban wage inequality has continued to rise, with the Gini of urban wage earnings reaching 0.384 in 2013 (Table 6.2). Unlike in previous decades, however, these recent trends are largely due to shifts in the demand and supply for labour, resulting, for example, from changes in labour demand due to growth, structural change, and technological change, and in labour supply due to education expansion and demographic changes. From the early 2000s the inequality of urban income per capita has also increased, with the Gini rising to 0.35 in 2013 (Table 6.2).

The urban restructuring involved reforms in ownership. For the first time in decades, urban individuals and households became property owners. As noted already, at this time the government officially condoned the development of private ownership of businesses and enterprises, which generated not only employment but also business income and profits for owners and investors. At the same time the government undertook the privatization and marketization of urban housing.

Experiments with urban housing reform had started earlier, but in 1998 the central government adopted the policy nationwide. Within four years (by 2002), 80 per cent of urban public housing had been sold to occupants (Wang 2001; Yang and Chen 2014: Chapter 2). The housing reforms meant that although many urban workers lost their jobs, they gained ownership of their housing, and at concessionary prices.

The distribution of benefits from the housing reform was not equal, however. Households that happened to be located in work units that had more resources or that were located in more favourable districts or cities, and individuals who had more status, seniority, or power within their work units, obtained a larger transfer of housing wealth. Furthermore, the housing reform only benefited workers with formal urban employment, not informal workers or migrant households. In the ensuing years, urban housing prices have appreciated rapidly but unevenly. The consequences for income distribution are evident in the rising share of asset and property income in total income and their growing contribution to income inequality (Figure 6.3; Luo et al. 2018).

Transition has affected not only each of the rural and urban sectors, but also the linkages between the two sectors. Under the planned economy, China's household registration (*hukou*) system highly restricted geographic mobility. Aside from the return of sent-down urban youth to their cities of origin in the early 1980s, mobility continued to be very limited until the mid-1990s, when rural workers began to engage in short-term migration. Migration increased over time, and especially from 2000. Since 2000, the pace of urbanization has also accelerated. In the early 1990s more than 80 per cent of China's population was rural and rural–urban migration was minimal; in 2002 the rural population share was 64 per cent and rural–urban migrants accounted for 3 per cent of the population; in 2013 the rural population share had fallen to 46 per cent and the rural–urban migrant share had risen to 13 per cent (Luo et al. 2018).

The resulting massive human relocation from rural to urban China has had implications for inequality. Luo et al. (2020) obtain a rough estimate of the impact of migration on inequality by calculating the Gini coefficient including and excluding rural–urban migrants. For 2013, including migrants reduces the national Gini modestly from 0.45 to 0.43. This calculation likely understates the impact of migration on inequality because it does not capture the indirect and general equilibrium effects of migration.

Migration and also urbanization have expanded income-earning opportunities for and transformed the composition of income of the rural population. They have affected urban labour markets, greatly expanding the supply of unskilled and low-skilled labour (Gustafsson and Wan 2018). They have influenced trends in the urban–rural income gap, a major contributor to national inequality (Luo et al. 2018).

Since 2000, the composition of household income has also changed due to the growing private sector as well as self-employment, rising housing prices, the ageing population, and increasing public transfers. At the national level, the share of wage income decreased from 2002 to 2013 by 5.5 percentage points (Figure 6.3). Moreover, wage income has become more equally distributed among households, as its concentration rate decreased from 0.64 in 2002 to 0.48 in 2013 (Luo et al. 2018). This has contributed to the reduction in income inequality.

Nevertheless, trends in wage income have differed between the urban and rural sectors. From 2002 to 2013, urban households experienced a declining share of wage income from 83 per cent to 60 per cent, while for rural households the share of wage income rose from 32 per cent to 34 per cent (calculated from Luo et al. 2018). The declining share of wage income of urban households was accompanied by increasing shares of pension income, which rose from 16 per cent to 19 per cent;

family business income, which rose from 3 per cent to more than 6 per cent; and imputed rent on owner-occupied private housing, which rose from 7 per cent to 15 per cent. It is important to realize that although these growing income components have become more equally distributed, their distribution remains relatively unequal. Pension income, for example, is more unequally distributed than wage income (Luo et al. 2018).

5 Incomplete Transition

Although China has made much progress in its economic transition over the past forty years, aspects of the transition remain incomplete. Here we discuss several aspects that have significant consequences for inequality.

Well-functioning markets require strong underpinnings in the form of market regulations, corporate governance, and enforceable legal systems. In China these underpinnings are weak. The resulting problems are most visible in asset markets. In both urban and rural areas, property rights to land and housing are not enforceable. Local governments can expropriate land and housing from individual households to make way for new development. The affected households are often compensated poorly, while the new development enriches local officials and developers. Stock markets, which were established in the 1990s and expanded rapidly in the 2000s, remain extremely volatile. Elliott (2015) explains the volatility as arising due to incomplete reforms and ongoing direct government intervention:

> Firms are almost totally shielded by government policy from the possibility of a hostile takeover or a forced change of management unless there is a dominant shareholder. Similarly, many company heads can determine dividend levels without great concern over shareholder preferences. Further, corporate governance is weak enough that management is often in a position to divert company assets for their own purposes. Widespread corruption makes this even more of a problem, especially for the many firms where a government entity owns a substantial stake.

Incomplete transition in these areas of property rights contributes to a growing concentration of asset wealth and income. Individuals with existing wealth, connections, or power can take advantage of the incomplete market reforms to enrich themselves. Recent studies on the distribution of wealth in China find that wealth inequality has increased substantially (Knight et al. 2017; Li and Wan 2015). The combination of high income inequality, the rapid rise of housing prices, privatization of SOEs and other assets, and corruption of government officials contributes to growing wealth inequality.

The unequal distribution of wealth contributes to income inequality. Nearly a quarter of household income growth during the period 2007–13 was due to increases in income from property, including asset income plus imputed rents on owner-occupied housing (Luo et al. 2018). During this same period the share of income from property increased from less than 10 per cent of household income in 2002 to 17 per cent in 2013 (Figure 6.3). Because property income is unequally distributed, these trends have had negative implications for income inequality.

Incomplete transition in capital and land property markets has contributed to the emergence of an ultra-rich class and the rapid growth of their assets. China's capital market is subject to government intervention and manipulation, enabling those close to government officials to have more opportunities to obtain bank loans and become successful businessmen. Li et al.'s (2018) top-income dataset reveals the importance of land and real estate markets. Most of the super-rich in this dataset come from the real estate and IT industries. The Forbes Rich List has also shown growth in the number of billionaires from these two sectors in recent years.

Incomplete reform of the state enterprise sector has contributed to weak corporate governance. State ownership in China has declined substantially but continues to dominate key sectors and firms. SOEs have been transformed into shareholding corporations in which the state owns the majority of, or controlling, shares. Despite these reforms, SOEs continue to have privileged status and receive special treatment in terms of industrial policies and access to loans and finance. Their relationship with the state and the Communist Party remains murky, such that corporate governance is compromised. With respect to income distribution, these characteristics of SOEs create opportunities for corruption and unequal wealth accumulation.

In addition, the insulation of SOE employment and compensation from labour market forces contributes to inequality in wage earnings and benefits. Gustafsson and Wan's (2018) estimates of Mincer urban wage equations for each year of the CHIP survey reveal that after controlling for individual characteristics such as education and experience, SOE wages remain higher than those in all other ownership sectors except the foreign-owned enterprise sector; moreover, since 1995 the magnitude of the SOE wage premium has increased.

The *hukou* system is another area of incomplete transition. Despite substantial loosening of restrictions on migration, a variety of policies and related factors continue to impede labour mobility. The result is ongoing segmentation of the labour market, which tends to elevate wage differentials among regions and between urban and rural workers. Rural migrant workers with rural *hukou* are discriminated against in terms of employment opportunities, compensation, and access to public services in urban areas. They are referred to as 'second class' (Démurger et al. 2009).

Another important area of incomplete transition is rural land ownership. Rural households have only partial property rights to their farmland. They have the right to cultivate and earn income from their land, and increasingly they have the right to transfer land through rental markets, but they do not have the right to sell their land or use it as collateral. Moreover, they are not protected against confiscation of their land by local governments. The incomplete reform of rural land property rights distorts the distribution of income in ways that increase inequality. It creates an imbalance between poorer rural and richer urban households in terms of their ability to benefit from their real property. It reduces farm productivity and thus depresses income from agriculture, which is the most equalizing component of income. The depressed income from agriculture creates heightened incentives to seek off-farm work. Yet, the fact that rights to the land can be lost if it is not cultivated hinders mobility. These factors distort patterns of income and inequality.

6 Distributional Policies

In the first decades of the economic reform, China followed a development strategy that emphasized growth of the 'productive forces', that is, a strategy that placed priority on growth of GDP, development of the underlying factors of production, and improved productivity. In reaction to the overly egalitarian policies of the Cultural Revolution, distributional concerns were placed on the back burner, especially after Deng Xiaoping's southern tour in 1992, when he proclaimed that China should 'let some people get rich first'. China did not totally ignore distributional issues at that time—for example, it invested in a major programme of rural poverty alleviation. Less attention, however, was paid to distributional trends elsewhere. Through the 1980s and 1990s, China's rapid GDP growth was accompanied by unprecedented increases in income inequality. By the late 1990s, income inequality in China was approaching levels found in countries considered to be relatively unequal by international standards.

Concerns about rising inequality led to a shift in development strategy in the early 2000s, when China launched the 'Hu–Wen New Policies' (*Hu–Wen xinzheng*), including the 'Scientific Outlook on Development' (*kexue fazhan guan*) and 'harmonious society' (*hexie shehui*) programmes, which emphasized sustainable and equitable growth. Over the following decade China embarked on an ambitious programme to improve its social welfare system, with the aim of achieving universal coverage of social security and social insurance programmes. As of 2013, the main components of these programmes were largely in place, and improvements have continued since.

The major components of China's social welfare system are pensions, health insurance, and cash transfers to the poor. Pensions had previously only existed for urban workers with formal employment. In 2009, the government extended pensions to rural China with the launch of the New Rural Pension Scheme. By 2012, this new programme reportedly covered 100 per cent of China's rural counties (Wang 2014). Although the amount of rural pension payments has remained low, it has increased over time. Still, rural pension benefit levels differ among provinces and counties, with higher payments in the more developed regions. In 2015, for example, rural pension income was 470 yuan per person per month for rural residents of Beijing, as compared to 85 yuan in the western province of Gansu.

In 2011, China extended pension benefits in urban areas with the introduction of the new basic urban pension scheme, which was aimed at urban residents without formal employment and those who were ineligible for the pre-existing urban employee pension programmes. In 2014, the new rural and urban basic pension schemes were merged. According to official NBS statistics, enrolment in the combined rural and urban basic pension programmes grew rapidly from essentially zero in 2007 to 497.5 million in 2013. As of 2015, enrolment exceeded 500 million, and pension recipients numbered 148 million.

Like pensions, health insurance had previously been limited to formal sector urban employees. In 2009, health insurance was extended to rural areas nationwide with the adoption of the New Rural Cooperative Medical Scheme. According to official statistics, the programme's coverage increased from 252 million people in 2007 to 487 million people in 2013, with a coverage rate exceeding 95 per cent; during the same period, contributions from individuals and governments rose from about 50 yuan per person to more than 300 yuan per person (Meng and Xu 2014). In 2007 the government took a further step and initiated Urban Resident Basic Medical Insurance, a voluntary programme providing health insurance to urban residents who do not have formal employment. By 2009, this programme was offered in almost all of China's cities (Liu and Zhao 2014). Enrolment in the programme rose from 43 million people in 2007, its first year, to 296 million people in 2013, and further to 377 million people in 2015.

By increasing the affordability of medical care, these health insurance programmes have the potential to improve health outcomes and labour productivity, and thus reduce the use of household savings for self-insurance. In these ways China's health insurance programmes can have an indirect but positive impact on household income. Nevertheless, participant contributions and levels of reimbursement vary regionally, and levels of reimbursement remain low.

China has pursued an active poverty reduction agenda in rural areas since the 1980s. In the early years, China's rural poverty programmes were designed to reduce poverty by developing the local economy. They funded economic development in designated poor rural regions and counties, with the idea that low economic development in the poor localities was the main cause of poverty. This strategy, together with macroeconomic growth more broadly, contributed to a marked reduction in poverty.

By the 2000s, the pattern of poverty in China had become more dispersed and required a different approach. In response, China adapted its poverty alleviation strategy and began targeting smaller areas (e.g. villages instead of counties) and households. The Minimum Livelihood Guarantee or *dibao* programme, a means-tested cash transfer programme targeted at households, was first established in cities in 1999 and was expanded significantly in urban areas in the early 2000s. Official statistics indicate that by 2007 the number of recipients in the urban *dibao* programme was 23 million, since which time the numbers have remained at about 20 million.

A similar, rural *dibao* programme was initiated on a pilot basis in 2004 and adopted in rural areas nationwide in 2007. The rural *dibao* programme grew rapidly to 54 million recipients in 2013. Concurrently, the generosity of the rural programme rose, with rural *dibao* expenditures per recipient increasing from 446 yuan per person per year in 2007 to 1,609 yuan per person per year in 2016 (Golan et al. 2017). The expansion of the urban and rural *dibao* programmes has had both direct and indirect impacts on measured income levels and inequality.

Cai and Yue (2018) evaluate the distributional impact of China's expanding social welfare programmes, specifically the impact of China's pension programmes (formal sector, urban resident, and rural resident pension programmes), the minimum guaranteed income or *dibao* programme, medical insurance reimbursements, farmer subsidies, and some other smaller programmes. The study compares the impact of these social security programme transfers in 2002, at the start of the new efforts to build a comprehensive social welfare system, to that in 2013, when much of the system was in place.

The study finds that the amount of social security transfers increased markedly between 2002 and 2013, rising from 9 per cent to 14 per cent of household income before taxes and transfers. The effects of the programmes on income inequality, however, were mixed. On the positive side, the transfers reduced inequality in the sense that measured inequality including the transfers is lower than that excluding the transfers. Moreover, the transfers became more equalizing over time, a reflection of the introduction and expansion of programmes to previously uncovered rural and informal urban residents.

On the negative side, the extent to which China's social welfare programmes served as a mechanism for redistribution was compromised by the fact that their benefits went disproportionately to the wealthier, urban population. This imbalance is largely due to the formal sector pension programme, which accounted for more than 80 per cent of total social welfare transfers in both 2002 and 2013. Importantly, formal sector pensions went almost entirely to the relatively well-off formal urban population (Cai and Yue 2018).

Aside from China's pension, *dibao*, health, and other social welfare programmes, a few other government programmes with distributional objectives deserve mention. First, since the late 1990s the Chinese government has adopted major initiatives to expand rural secondary education and to increase university enrolments. Official statistics indicate that the progression rate from junior to senior secondary school rose from 50 per cent in 2000 to 81 per cent in 2007, and further to 91 per cent in 2013. According to UNESCO data, gross enrolment rates in secondary education rose from 61 per cent in 2000 to 73 per cent in 2007, and further to 96 per cent in 2013; tertiary enrolment rates rose from 8 per cent in 2000 to 21 per cent in 2007 and 30 per cent in 2013.

The expansion of secondary and tertiary education has helped narrow gaps in education levels (e.g. between women and men). These changes in educational attainment have implications for recent trends in income and inequality. For example, Gustafsson and Wan (2018) reports that the returns to education rose from 1988 to 2007 but declined thereafter. Gustafsson and Wan (2018) attributes the decline in the returns to education in part to the increased supply of workers with university education.

Second, minimum wage policies, initially adopted in the 1990s, have targeted the low-wage segment of China's urban labour market. In the early years of these programmes, minimum wage levels were low and not strictly enforced. After implementation of the New Labour Contract Law in 2008, minimum wage levels and their enforcement have increased. To some extent these efforts are the result of political competition by local governments responding to the central government's call for a higher wage share in national income. For instance, in July 2010 Hainan province and Henan province increased their provincial minimum wages by 30 per cent and 33 per cent, respectively. In 2011, at least five provinces raised their minimum wages by more than 20 per cent, and in 2012–13 twenty-seven provinces increased their minimum wages (Li et al. 2014). Several studies have investigated the consequences of these minimum wage policies on the urban wage distribution (Li and Ma 2015; Lin and Yun 2016; Ma and Li 2017).

7 Conclusions

From the late 1970s through the early 2000s, income inequality in China rose from a low level to one that is relatively high by international standards. Standard estimates indicate that the level of inequality has plateaued and declined modestly since 2007, suggesting that China may have turned the corner in the Kuznets inverted U. Potential bias in recent estimates of China's inequality due to the increased difficulty of capturing China's emerging ultra-rich class, however, raises questions about the path of China's inequality in the past decade.

China is both a developing economy and an economy in transition. Consequently, conventional development theories only go partway to explaining China's story of inequality. The special dynamics of income inequality in China during the past forty years need explanations that reflect China's unique development path, the completed aspects of its economic transition, and the still incomplete facets of its economic transition. China's economic transition has been successful in many regards, but some facets of the transition remain incomplete. The transition aspect of China's economy may have elongated the rise of income inequality beyond what one would expect based on Lewis's two-sector model, and China's incomplete transition has likely dampened the mechanisms that would normally bring about the downturn in the Kuznets inverted U.

Incomplete reform of the *hukou* system has contributed to a persistent income gap between urban and rural households, despite the large number of rural migrants moving into cities. Delayed political reform has led to continued, excessive government intervention into economic activities, corruption, rent-seeking, and an excessive number of super-rich businessmen and disguised rich officials. Partial reform of the state-owned enterprise sector has preserved its monopolistic position in some sectors and has contributed to wage differentials among sectors.

How does China's experience with rising income inequality relate to that in other developing countries? First, China's experience highlights the importance of income growth for poor and low-income households. Despite the increase in income inequality, China has not yet experienced severe social instability. This is likely due in part to the fact that, unlike some other developing countries, poor and lower-income households have enjoyed substantial income growth. Thus, even though income inequality has risen to a relatively high level, the poor as well as the rich enjoyed the benefits of China's rapid economic growth. By some definitions, then, Chinese economic growth has been inclusive.

Second, China's experience highlights the importance of redistributive government policies and programmes. Evidence suggests that in recent years the expansion of redistributive policies has begun to play a role in moderating income inequality. Such policies are important not only for their actual impact on income distribution, but also for their symbolic function. They signal the regime's commitment to a certain vision of social welfare.

What will be the direction of China's income inequality in the future? China's past experience suggests that future trends will depend on whether China is able to address several challenges. First, the contribution of labour market segmentation and incomplete and distorted capital markets to widening income inequality highlights the need to pursue measures that promote well-functioning, equitable market mechanisms. Second, direct redistributive policies must be accompanied by steps to fight the corruption and rent-seeking that result from government interventions and weaknesses in the political system.

Third, recent, encouraging trends in income inequality may not be sustainable if wealth inequality continues to rise. Steps are needed to address the widening inequality of wealth and broaden opportunities for wealth accumulation by lower-income groups. Our findings thus suggest that China's future ability to transition from a high-inequality to a low-inequality economy is not guaranteed. It will require ongoing vigilance, further economic and political reforms, and the strengthening and expansion of redistributive policies.

References

Cai, M., and X. Yue (2018). 'The Redistributive Role of Government Social Security Transfers on Inequality in China'. Mimeo.

China Institute for Income Distribution (n.d.). 'CHIP Dataset Homepage'. [Online]. Available at: http://ciid.bnu.edu.cn/chip/index.asp (accessed August 2018).

China Net (2017). 'Ning Jiwei: China's Gini Coefficient Is Generally Declining, and the Urban–Rural Income Gap Is Narrowing'. [Online]. Available at: http://finance. china.com.cn/news/gnjj/20170120/4077373.shtml (accessed August 2018).

Démurger, S., M. Gurgand, S. Li, and X. Yue (2009). 'Migrants as Second-class Workers in Urban China? A Decomposition Analysis'. *Journal of Comparative Economics*, 37(4): 610–28.

Deng, Q., and S. Li (2009). 'What Lies Behind Rising Earnings Inequality in Urban China? Regression-based Decompositions'. *CESifo Economic Studies*, 55(3–4): 598–623.

Elliott, D.J. (2015). 'Op-ed: China Will Struggle with Its Stock Markets Until It Completes Reforms', The Brookings Institution. Available at: https://www.brookings. edu/opinions/china-will-struggle-with-its-stock-markets-until-it-completes-reforms/ (accessed August 2018).

Golan, J., T. Sicular, and N. Umapathi (2017). 'Unconditional Cash Transfers in China: Who Benefits from the Rural Minimum Living Standard Guarantee (Dibao) Program?' *World Development*, 93(5): 316–36.

Gustafsson, B., and S. Ding (2017). 'Unequal growth: how household incomes and poverty in urban China have developed since 1988, with an emphasis on the period from 2007 to 2013'. University of Western Ontario Centre for Human Capital and Productivity Working Paper 2017–18. Available at: https://ir.lib.uwo.ca/cgi/viewcontent.cgi?article=1130&context=economicscibc (accessed August 2018).

Gustafsson, B., and H. Wan (2018). 'Wage growth and wage inequality in urban China: 1988–2013'. WIDER Working Paper 2018/163. Helsinki: UNU-WIDER.

Hoken, H., and H. Sato (2017). 'Public policy and long-term trends in inequality in rural China 1988–2013'. Western University Centre for Human Capital Productivity Working Paper No. 2017–16. Available at: https://ir.lib.uwo.ca/economicscibc/125/ (accessed August 2018).

Huang, J., and S. Rozelle (2012). 'China's labor transition and the future of China's rural wages and employment'. Background Paper for World Development Report 2013. Available at: http://siteresources.worldbank.org/EXTNWDR2013/Resources/8258024-1320950747192/8260293-1320956712276/8261091-1348683883703/WDR2013_bp_China_Labor_Transition.pdf (accessed August 2018).

Knight, J., Q. Deng, and S. Li (2011). 'The Puzzle of Migrant Labor Shortage and Rural Labor Surplus in China'. *China Economic Review*, 22(4): 585–600.

Knight, J., S. Li, and H. Wan (2017). 'The increasing inequality of wealth in China, 2002-2013'. University of Western Ontario Centre for Human Capital and

Productivity Working Paper 2017–15. Available at: https://ir.lib.uwo.ca/cgi/view-content.cgi?article=1127&context=economicscibc (accessed August 2018).

Li, Q., S. Li, and H. Wan (2018). 'Top incomes in China: data collection and the impact on income inequality'. WIDER Working Paper 2018/183. Helsinki: UNU-WIDER.

Li, S., and X. Ma (2015). 'Impact of Minimum Wage on Gender Wage Gaps in Urban China'. *IZA Journal of Labor and Development*, 4(1): 1–22.

Li, S., and H. Wan (2015). 'Evolution of Wealth Inequality in China'. *China Economic Journal*, 8(3): 264–87.

Li, S., L. Ye, and L. Xiong (2014). 'Understanding impacts of minimum wage policy on labor market in China'. Presentation at the International Conference on Minimum Wage Policy, Hong Kong University of Science and Technology, September.

Lin, C., and M.-S. Yun (2016). 'The Effects of the Minimum Wage on Earnings Inequality: Evidence from China'. In L. Cappellari, S.W. Polachek, and K. Tatsiramos (eds), *Income Inequality Around the World* (Research in Labor Economics, Volume 44). Bingley, UK: Emerald Group Publishing Limited.

Lin, S. (2009). 'The rise and fall of Chinese government revenue'. EAI Working Paper 150. Singapore: National University of Singapore East Asian Institute. Available at: http://www.eai.nus.edu.sg/publications/files/EWP150.pdf (accessed August 2018).

Liu, H., and Z. Zhao (2014). 'Does Health Insurance Matter? Evidence from China's Urban Resident Basic Medical Insurance'. *Journal of Comparative Economics*, 42(4): 1007–20.

Lu, F. (2012). 'Wage Trend of Rural Migrant Workers: 1979–2010'. *China Social Sciences* (in Chinese), 7: 47–67.

Luo, C., S. Li, and T. Sicular (2018). 'The long-term evolution of income inequality and poverty'. WIDER Working Paper 2018/153. Helsinki: UNU-WIDER.

Luo, C., T. Sicular, and S. Li (2020). 'Overview: Incomes and Inequality in China, 2007–2013'. In T. Sicular, S. Li, H. Sato, and X. Yue (eds), *Changing Trends in China's Inequality: Evidence, Analysis and Prospects*. New York: Oxford University Press.

Ma, X., and S. Li (2017). 'The effects of minimum wage on wage distribution in urban China: evidence from the CHIP data'. Western University Centre for Human Capital and Productivity Working Paper 2017–24. Available at: https://ir.lib.uwo.ca/economicscibc/136/ (accessed August 2018).

Meng, Q., and K. Xu (2014). 'Progress and Challenges of the Rural Cooperative Medical Scheme in China'. *Bulletin of the World Health Organization*, 92(6): 447–51.

Meng, X. (2004). 'Economic Restructuring and Income Inequality in Urban China'. *Review of Income and Wealth*, 50(3): 357–79.

NBS (2010). '2009 Migrant Workers Monitoring Survey Report'. [Online]. Available at: http://www.stats.gov.cn/ztjc/ztfx/fxbg/201003/t20100319_16135.html http://www.stats.gov.cn/ztjc/ztfx/fxbg/201003/t20100319_16135.html (accessed 18 December 2018).

NBS (2012). '2011 China Migrant Workers Survey and Monitoring Report'. [Online]. Available at: http://www.stats.gov.cn/ztjc/ztfx/fxbg/201204/t20120427_16154.html (accessed 18 December 2018).

NBS (2013). '2012 National Migrant Workers Monitoring Survey Report'. [Online]. Available at: http://www.stats.gov.cn/tjsj/zxfb/201305/t20130527_12978.html (accessed 18 December 2018).

NBS (2014). '2013 National Migrant Workers Monitoring Survey Report'. [Online]. Available at: http://www.stats.gov.cn/tjsj/zxfb/201405/t20140512_551585.html (accessed 18 December 2018).

NBS (2015). '2014 National Migrant Workers Monitoring Survey Report'. [Online]. Available at: http://www.stats.gov.cn/tjsj/zxfb/201504/t20150429_797821.html (accessed 18 December 2018).

NBS (2016a). '2015 Migrant Workers Monitoring Survey Report'. [Online]. Available at: http://www.stats.gov.cn/tjsj/zxfb/201604/t20160428_1349713.html (accessed 18 December 2018).

NBS (2017a). '2016 Migrant Workers Monitoring Survey Report'. [Online]. Available at: http://www.stats.gov.cn/tjsj/zxfb/201704/t20170428_1489334.html (accessed 18 December 2018).

NBS (2016b). *China Yearbook of Household Survey 2016*. Beijing: China Statistics Press.

NBS (2016c). *China Statistical Yearbook 2016*. Beijing: China Statistics Press.

NBS (2017b). *China Statistical Yearbook 2017*. Beijing: China Statistics Press.

Sicular, T., S. Li, X. Yue, and H. Sato (eds) (2020). *Changing Trends in China's Inequality: Evidence, Analysis and Prospects*. New York: Oxford University Press.

Wang, D. (2014). 'China's pension system reform'. Presentation at the Regional Consultation on Strengthening Income Support for Vulnerable Groups in Asia and the Pacific, UNESCAP Subregional Office for East and North-East Asia, Incheon, Republic of Korea, 26–27 March. Available at: http://www.unescap.org/sites/default/files/ISS-Meeting_item3-dewen-wang.pdf (accessed June 2017).

Wang, Y. (2001). 'Urban Housing Reform and Finance in China: A Case Study of Beijing'. *Urban Affairs Review*, 36(5): 620–45.

Xue, J., C. Luo, and S. Li (2014). 'Globalization, Liberalization and Income Inequality: The Case of China'. *Singapore Economic Review*, 59(1): 1450002 (21 pages).

Yang, Z., and J. Chen (2014). *Housing Affordability and Housing Policy in Urban China*. New York, NY: Springer.

Zhang, J., Y. Zhao, A. Park, and X. Song (2005). 'Economic Returns to Schooling in Urban China 1988–2001'. *Journal of Comparative Economics*, 33(4): 730–52.

7

India

Inequality Trends and Dynamics: The Bird's-Eye and the Granular Perspectives

Hai-Anh H. Dang and Peter Lanjouw

1 Introduction

Income inequality is a topic of longstanding interest in India. Historically, attention has tended to focus on the lower tail of the welfare distribution—on poverty—rather than on overall income inequality.[1] This would seem appropriate given the very high levels of absolute poverty that have long prevailed in India. Recently, however, as economic growth in India has accelerated, and as absolute poverty rates have started to fall fairly rapidly, there has been a turn also to questions about the broader distributional impact of India's growth trajectory. There are deep concerns about the possible consequences of rising inequality for social stability.

An important dimension of inequality in India pertains to widespread horizontal inequalities. India's complex caste structure translates into significantly different opportunities and aspirations across population segments. Religious, gender, and even spatial differences also play a role in shaping wellbeing. It is important to accommodate these horizontal inequalities into any analysis of the evolution of India's overall income distribution.

This chapter reports on a recently completed research project that seeks to inform the debate on inequality in India by offering a bird's-eye view of inequality trends and dynamics at the all-India level over three decades up to 2011/12, and contrasting this with similar evidence at the level of the Indian village or the urban block. We explore dynamics by reporting 'snapshots' of inequality at different time periods, but also by tracing the movement of people within the income

[1] This chapter is part of a larger study on inequality in India, which itself is part of the UNU-WIDER project, Inequality in the Giants, looking at inequality in a set of populous countries. We are grateful to UNU-WIDER and in particular to Finn Tarp and Carlos Gradín for supporting this work. We have benefited from conversations with and guidance from Chris Elbers, Himanshu, Murray Leibrandt, Shi Li, Abhiroop Mukhopadhyay, Rinku Murgai, Marcelo Neri, Nicholas Stern, David Garcés Urzainqui, Roy van der Weide, and participants at the 2018 UNU-WIDER conference Think Development, Think WIDER in Helsinki. Any errors are our own.

Hai-Anh H. Dang and Peter Lanjouw, *India: Inequality Trends and Dynamics: The Bird's-Eye and the Granular Perspectives* In: *Inequality in the Developing World*. Edited by: Carlos Gradín, Murray Leibbrandt, and Finn Tarp, Oxford University Press (2021). © United Nations University World Institute for Development Economics Research (UNU-WIDER). DOI: 10.1093/oso/9780198863960.003.0007

distribution over time. We ask, for example, whether a rise in inequality is characterized by a simple stretching-out of the income distribution, or is also associated with switches in relative position within the income distribution. We consider, further, aspects of income mobility within, and across, generations.

We start, in Section 2, with a review that assesses the available evidence on inequality trends and dynamics in India from a variety of perspectives. At the all-India level, inequality is broadly found to have risen between 1983 and 2011/12, particularly in the early 2000s, but to differing degrees depending on the dimension considered and the measurement method employed. Section 3 goes on to interrogate the all-India-level evidence, with the detailed story of economic development in the north Indian village of Palanpur since the late 1950s. Inequality has also risen in Palanpur—the consequence of a process of structural transformation that can also be discerned at the all-India level. Section 4 shows that local-level inequality (within-village in rural areas; within-block in urban areas) accounts for the bulk of overall inequality in India; understanding what occurs at the local level is thus important for understanding overall inequality. The importance and direction of change of local-level inequality is, moreover, argued to vary considerably across India's states.

Section 5 reveals that nationally representative data point to rising intra-generational income mobility over time. This is consistent with the idea that inequality of lifetime income may be lower than what is observed in a given year. However, the evidence also suggests that while poverty has fallen, most of the poor who have escaped poverty continue to face a high risk of falling back into poverty. Moreover, those who remain poor are increasingly chronically poor, and may be particularly difficult to reach via the introduction or expansion of safety nets.

Section 6 moves on to examine inter-generational education mobility in India. There is little conclusive evidence of improved mobility over time. We enquire into the possible impact of promoting greater inter-generational mobility (thereby reducing the stark inequalities of opportunity that prevail). Not only would such efforts promote social justice, but evidence is presented to show that they could also stimulate inequality-dampening economic growth. A plausible route through which this could occur is via rising education levels, particularly among the poor. Section 7 offers some concluding remarks.

2 Inequality Levels and Trends in India: A Bird's-Eye View

Himanshu (2019) scrutinizes evidence from India to present a general picture of rising inequality in recent decades. While the picture is fairly consistent, the patterns are not always equally pronounced across all indicators of wellbeing. Tax data from the World Inequality Database (WID) database are examined to assess extent of income/wealth concentration at the top of the income distribution. The analysis proceeds further to briefly consider inequality in human development indicators.

2.1 Monetary Inequality

Since the 1950s the National Sample Survey (NSS) Organization has fielded a series of national household surveys suitable for tracking household consumption. Himanshu (2019) draws on the 'thick' rounds (with larger sample sizes) of the NSS surveys to examine trends between 1983 and 2011/12 (the most recent available round). His inequality measures are based on the mixed recall period (MRP) consumption aggregates that are the basis of India's official poverty estimates.[2]

Table 7.1 reports Gini indexes between 1993/4 and 2011/12 after correcting for spatial cost-of-living differences using the deflators implicit in India's official poverty lines. Such price indices are not available for the 1980s. Consumption inequality at the all-India level can be seen to have risen moderately since the early 1990s. The trend increase is more marked when based on the variance of log of consumption expenditure—which gives higher weight to inequality at the lower tail of the income distribution. The increase was sharpest between 1993/4 and 2004/5 and most pronounced in urban areas.

Table 7.1 Inequality trends in real consumption expenditure

	Gini coefficient of consumption expenditure					
	Nominal MPCE			Real MPCE		
	Rural	Urban	Total	Rural	Urban	Total
1983	0.27	0.31	0.30	n/a	n/a	n/a
1993/94	0.26	0.32	0.30	0.25	0.31	0.28
2004/05	0.28	0.36	0.35	0.27	0.36	0.31
2009/10	0.29	0.38	0.36	0.27	0.38	0.32
2011/12	0.29	0.38	0.37	0.27	0.37	0.33
	Variance of log of consumption expenditure					
	Nominal MPCE			Real MPCE		
	Rural	Urban	Total	Rural	Urban	Total
1993/94	0.20	0.31	0.26	0.19	0.29	0.23
2004/05	0.22	0.39	0.32	0.21	0.37	0.26
2009/10	0.24	0.42	0.35	0.21	0.40	0.29
2011/12	0.25	0.41	0.36	0.21	0.39	0.29

Notes: Real mean per capita expenditures (MPCE) are MRP consumption estimates corrected for cost-of-living differences across states, between rural and urban areas, and over time, using deflators implicit in the official poverty lines.

Source: Himanshu (2019). Reproduced here with permission of UNU-WIDER.

[2] Most NSS consumption rounds collect data using a uniform recall period (URP) of thirty days for all consumption items. A mixed recall period (MRP) aggregate with longer (365 days) recall for some (mainly non-food) items was introduced, alongside URP consumption, in the mid-2000s. For earlier years, Himanshu (2019) reconstruct a comparable MRP aggregate using the unit-record data.

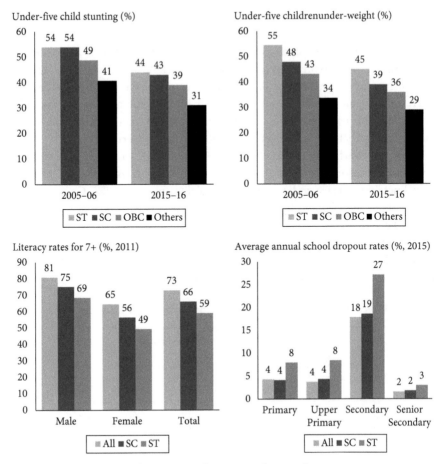

Figure 7.1 Disparities in human capital outcomes, by social group

Note: Reproduced here with permission of UNU-WIDER.

Sources: Himanshu (2019). Nutrition outcomes from the National Family Health Surveys (2005/06 and 2015/16), literacy outcomes from the 2011 Population Census, and dropout rates from the National University of Education Planning and Administration (2015).

Figure 7.1 reports the Gini index of income inequality from the 2004/5 and 2011/12 India Human Development Surveys (IHDS). The IHDS is a nationally representative household panel survey that collects data on both consumption and income. Estimates based on this survey indicate that nominal income inequality in India was about 0.54 in both 2004/5 and 2011/12, but showed a marginal increase in terms of real income.[3] IHDS-based estimates of consumption inequality are lower than estimates of income inequality but, as in the NSS, show

---

[3] Corrected for spatial price differentials, the Gini coefficient of real incomes is 45.3 in 2005 and 45.9 in 2012.

an increase over time. It is noteworthy that estimates of income inequality place India among the highest inequality countries internationally.

As suggested previously, an important note of caution in assessing survey-based levels and trends in inequality is that household surveys may not capture well the economic status of richer households. This seems particularly problematic with (NSS) consumption-based analysis in the light of the growing gap over time between aggregate consumption from the NSS surveys and private consumption in the national accounts (NAS). There are good reasons why the two aggregates should differ (for instance, due to differences in definition) but the gap in India is particularly large.[4] It is difficult to know how much of the gap is due to errors in NAS consumption versus NSS survey methods, with the possibility of errors on both sides. To the extent that under-reporting of consumption or non-compliance is likely to be greater among the rich, inequality would be underestimated.

An emerging set of studies attempt to overcome the limitations of survey data on the rich by drawing on income tax data, in combination with household survey-based income or consumption data, to examine the changing shares of income accruing to rich households across a range of countries. For India, Chancel and Piketty (2017) have extended an earlier analysis by Banerjee and Piketty (2005) to develop a time series from 1922 to the present.

While there has been some debate on the reliability of inequality estimates based on combining household survey and tax data, the evidence compiled by Chancel and Piketty (2017) combines to present a picture of extreme inequality in India.[5] By 2016, India was second only to the Middle Eastern countries in terms of the income share of the top 10 per cent. But it was also the country with the highest increase in the share of top incomes in the past thirty years, the share of the top 10 per cent increasing from 31 per cent in 1980 to 56 per cent in 2016 (World Inequality Lab 2018).

Rongen (2018) offers an alternative approach to gauging the impact of under-coverage of the rich from the NSS surveys. His approach combines survey data with a database of house prices that can be used as predictors of income or consumption.[6] Rongen (2018) re-estimates inequality in Mumbai by this method and finds little support for the contention that the NSS survey data underesti-mate inequality in that city. Further research into the suitability of this method to empirical application with NSS data is warranted, but the results do suggest that debates about the levels and trends of monetary inequality in India are unlikely to end soon.

---

[4] The ratio of NSS to NAS consumption declined from about 60 per cent in 1991 to 39 per cent in 2011/12 (Datt et al. 2016).

[5] While the method adopted by Piketty and others is similar to what has been used in other countries where tax data have been used to estimate income distribution for the entire population, there have been concerns over the appropriateness of the method—for details see Atkinson (2007: 18–42); Leigh (2007); Leigh and Posso (2009); and Sutch (2017).

[6] Van der Weide et al. (2018) developed this approach in a study of inequality in Egypt. Correcting for under-coverage of the rich in Egypt in this way raises the estimated Gini from 0.39 to 0.52.

2.2 Non-Monetary Indicators: Health and Education

India has made substantial gains in health and education outcomes in the past few decades. Himanshu (2019) documents that over the period 1991–2013 life expectancy at birth increased by more than seven years, the infant mortality rate fell by half, the share of births in health facilities more than tripled, the maternal mortality ratio fell by about 60 per cent, and the total fertility rate fell to almost replacement level. India's District Information System for Education (DISE) indicates that the education system has also expanded rapidly, leading to gross enrolment ratios of 100 and 91 in primary and upper primary grades, respectively.[7]

But the picture is not uniformly positive. While India has outpaced the world in reductions in consumption poverty, progress on nutrition outcomes has been less remarkable. Child stunting (associated with poorer socioeconomic outcomes later in life), which affected nearly half (48 per cent) of the under-five child population in 2005/6, has reduced, but still afflicted 38 per cent of children in 2015/16. Under-five child wasting (weight-for-height) has shown no improvement, stagnating at one-fifth of the population. India also ranks poorly in global indices such as the Global Hunger Index and the Human Capital Index, reflecting the challenges that remain and the need for sustained progress.[8]

National averages mask disparities across social groups, states, and rural–urban areas, reflecting inequalities in opportunity to access basic services. Figure 7.1 shows differences in selected health and education outcomes by social groups. Although there have been improvements across all social groups, Scheduled Tribes (STs) and Scheduled Castes (SCs) persistently have worse outcomes.[9] In 2015/16, 44 per cent of under-five children in STs were stunted, compared with 31 per cent of children from general caste households. Even larger disparities are evident in the rates of underweight children, and those gaps are not closing.

Gaps between social groups are also evident in education outcomes, although outcomes are better in education than in health, and gaps in enrolment rates among school-age children have been closing (Himanshu 2019). Literacy rates have improved for all groups, but in 2011 literacy rates in SCs and STs were 66 per cent and 59 per cent, respectively, compared with the national average of 73 per cent. The disparity between social groups can also be seen in the average annual dropout rates at all levels of school education. Except for primary education, the dropout rates were higher than average for SC children. The rates were much higher for ST children at all levels of school education.

---

[7] National University of Educational Planning and Administration (2015).

[8] The 2017 Global Hunger Index ranks India in 100th place out of the 119 countries that were included.

[9] Thorat and Sabharwal (2011) provide evidence on caste-based disparities in nutrition outcomes through the 1990s and early 2000s.

The intersection of gender, location, and social groups exacerbates these gaps. In 2011, more than 80 per cent of men were literate, while the rate was only 65 per cent for women. Female literacy among STs is even lower, at below 50 per cent. The literacy rate of rural women is 62 per cent, while the rate is much higher among urban women, at 81 per cent. The corresponding rates for men are 83 per cent and 91 per cent, respectively.

3 Inequality at the Village Level: A Granular View

India's rural population resides mainly in villages—the 2011 Census reports roughly 800 million people living in more than 600,000 villages. Most of rural India's workforce (60 per cent) remains primarily involved in agriculture, but in recent decades this sector's growth has lagged behind that of other sectors in the economy. The deceleration in agricultural growth has been offset by the emergence and growth of the non-farm sector: in 2011/12 non-farm workers accounted for 40 per cent of the workforce, nearly double the ratio observed only ten years earlier (Himanshu 2019).

Elbers and Lanjouw (2019) study the distributional impact of this structural transformation of the rural Indian economy at the level of an individual village, Palanpur, in western Uttar Pradesh. There are grounds for interest in local-level distributional outcomes. In rural areas people are likely to see the local village population as their reference group. Thinking about the magnitude and direction of change in inequality is thus likely to be influenced by village-level trends.

3.1 Inequality in Palanpur: 1957–2015

Palanpur was the subject of intensive study on seven occasions between 1957/8 and 2015. Surveys were conducted in 1957/8, 1962/3, 1974/5, 1983/4, 1993, 2008/9, and 2015. In each survey year detailed quantitative and qualitative data, covering a very wide range of topics, were collected for the entire village population, with fieldwork conducted over an extended period—often a year or longer.[10]

The population of Palanpur grew from just over 500 in 1957/8 to roughly 1,250 in 2008/9—an annual population growth rate that was similar to that recorded for India as a whole. Both distributional change and structural transformation in Palanpur are closely linked to the village caste structure. Although there are eight caste groups in the village, the three main castes in the village are Thakurs, Muraos, and Jatabs. Thakurs are the largest caste in the village numerically and

---

[10] Himanshu et al. (2018) provide an in-depth analysis of economic development in Palanpur over the seven decades covered by the surveys.

they continue to be powerful economically. They were the first to move into the non-farm sector in a major way but have now been joined by other castes. Muraos, on the other hand, are a traditionally cultivating caste and take pride in their agricultural skills. Alongside the relative decline of agriculture in village income, Muraos have seen their economic status decline somewhat in relative terms. Jatabs, at the bottom of the village hierarchy, remained economically and socially marginalized until around 2005, but have become increasingly involved in casual non-farm wage activities and are now seen as an increasingly important community within the village. They have therefore experienced significant upward mobility over the years.

Throughout the study period, Palanpur has essentially been a village of small farmers, with a relatively low proportion of landless households. Since the late 1950s, the village has seen agricultural practices transformed in connection with the spread of irrigation; the introduction of new seed varieties, fertilizers, and pesticides; the emergence of rental markets for agricultural equipment; and the introduction of new crops. Key to the agricultural development process has been the expansion of irrigation from around half of village land at the beginning of the survey period to 100 per cent by the 1974/5 survey, as well as intensification of farm mechanization that has been both land-augmenting and labour-saving. Additional forces of agricultural change include the shift of cropping patterns towards higher-value crops.

Over time, an increasing number of villagers have become involved in the non-farm sector. Non-farm activities represented roughly two-thirds of total primary employment by 2015 and accounted for nearly 60 per cent of average household income in 2008/09 (Table 7.2). Better access to towns and cities via improvements in railways and communications infrastructure, particularly mobile phones, has helped villagers find jobs and has led to a growing number travelling outside Palanpur, on a commuting basis, for employment.

Jobs in the non-farm sector can largely be categorized into two kinds: low-paying casual and menial activities, versus regular jobs (often government-provided) and some profitable self-employment units. But even the lower-paying jobs are more remunerative than agricultural labour, and often offer additional spells of employment that can be combined with some continued involvement in agriculture. The casual non-farm sector registered the highest growth in employment over the survey period, notably in activities related to the construction sector. Self-employment has seen the fastest income growth in Palanpur by a substantial margin. The embrace of entrepreneurship has been striking. Regular wage jobs have declined both relatively and absolutely and there has been very little growth in the number of these jobs since the early 1990s.

While full migration from Palanpur is not common and has not increased as a proportion of households, the related practice of villagers commuting from Palanpur on a daily basis, or for short periods, is now both common and increasing over time. Commuting allows villagers to continue to reside in Palanpur and

Table 7.2 Income shares in Palanpur over time (%)

Income source		Year				
		1957/58	1962/63	1974/75	1983/84	2008/09
Household income	Cultivation	58.5	56.7	58.4	50.2	30
	Livestock income	19.8	21.5	22	13.7	10.4
	Non-cultivation (see breakdown)	21.7	21.8	19.6	35.4	59.6
	Total income share	100	100	100	100	100
Non-cultivation income (% contribution to total income)						
Agricultural labour income	Casual labour—farm	7.3	3.5	1.8	1.5	0.9
Other non-cultivation income	Other farm income	1.2	0.6	0.1	2.7	10.7
	Rental	0	0.2	0.6	0	1.6
Non-farm income	Casual labour—non-farm	1.1	1	0	7	6.1
	Self-employment	1.3	3.5	1	3	19.8
	Regular employment	7.5	8.9	15.7	20	16.1
	Jajmani income	1.3	0.6	0.4	1	0.2
	Remittances	2	1.9	0	0.2	3.6
	Other non-farm	0	1.7	0	0.2	0.6

Source: Himanshu et al. (2018), reproduced with copyright-holder's permission.

maintain some involvement in cultivation while they access an ever wider range of non-farm job opportunities in the surrounding area and nearby towns and cities.

The richness of data covering all households in Palanpur permits an analysis of the dynamics of poverty, inequality, and mobility at a level of detail not normally available from secondary data sources. Poverty in Palanpur was extensive in the early survey years—more than 80 per cent of the population was classified as poor during the 1950s and 1960s. The growth in incomes associated with expanding irrigation in the late 1950s and the 1960s, and the green revolution technologies and methods that evolved in the late 1960s and early 1970s, led to a sharp decline in poverty, the headcount ratio falling to less than 60 per cent by 1974/5, remaining at roughly that level in 1983/4, and then falling again sharply after 1983, declining to below 40 per cent by 2008/9.

Table 7.3 indicates that between 1957/8 and 1962/3, inequality represented by the Gini coefficient rose from 0.336 to 0.353; it then fell back by 1974/5. The decline between 1962/3 and 1974/5 was likely linked to the expansion of irrigation and the intensification of agriculture: by 1974/5, all village land was irrigated. Between 1974/5 and 1983/4, inequality increased but remained lower than its 1957/8 and 1962/3 levels. A combination of factors helps to explain the rise. With the ongoing intensification of agriculture, the Muraos as a group experienced

Table 7.3 Inequality of individual incomes

Measures of inequality	Survey years				
	1957/58	1962/63	1974/75	1983/84	2008/09
Gini coefficient	0.336	0.353	0.272	0.310	0.379
Coefficient of variation	0.650	0.755	0.530	0.578	0.769
Atkinson Index					
e = 1	0.173	0.191	0.137	0.170	0.229
e = 2	0.319	0.344	0.206	0.366	0.444
Theil L measure					
GE(0)	0.19	0.213	0.147	0.186	0.26
No. of observations	529	585	750	977	1,255
No. of households	100	106	112	143	233
No. of individuals (households) with missing income	0	0	5(1)	8(3)	37(12)

Source: Himanshu et al. (2018), reproduced with copyright-holder's permission.

improved relative prosperity due to higher returns from cultivation. By 1983/4 the Muraos had even surpassed the Thakurs in terms of per capita income. In addition, in 1983/4, new non-farm employment opportunities were increasingly available, and were taken up mostly by villagers from economically better-off backgrounds. In 2008/9, the Gini index, at 0.379, was at a higher level than in any other survey year. A decomposition exercise assessing the contribution to total inequality of different income sources points to non-farm income as accounting for the bulk of inequality in the later survey years.

The Palanpur data can be further analysed to study patterns of mobility. Over the entire survey period since the 1950s there is evidence of the increasing mobility of households across income quintiles, with a falling share of households ranked in the same quintile between survey rounds. Among the factors that seem to have contributed are the decline in per capita landholding and the expansion of non-farm employment opportunities. While access to non-farm jobs has been uneven, with the relatively affluent and socially networked being more successful in finding regular, high-paying jobs, the spread of non-farm activities to lower-ranked households in more recent years has also allowed at least some of those at the bottom to improve their fortunes.

The long time horizon covered by the Palanpur study offers an opportunity to look beyond intra-generational mobility to inter-generational mobility, and indeed to compare changes in inter-generational mobility. Elbers and Lanjouw (2019) point to a father–son inter-generational income elasticity for the interval 1983/4–2008/9 that is higher than that for the interval 1957/8–1983/4. This implies that inter-generational mobility has fallen: the father's income is a better predictor of his son's income in the 1983/4–2008/9 interval than in the preceding interval.

Elbers and Lanjouw (2019) build a simple model of a village economy that permits the study of drivers of inequality in isolation, with a view to acquiring a better understanding of the kind of inequality trends observed in a village like Palanpur. They scrutinize how the distribution of welfare has been shaped by the key forces of change, and examine a few counterfactual scenarios with a view to gauging how welfare might have evolved in their absence. Their simulations suggest that moving out of agriculture has played an important role in contributing to poverty reduction, and that it has not necessarily added to village-level inequality. If anything, the counterfactual exercise implies that inequality would have been even higher if occupational diversification had not taken place. The analysis indicates that the common perception of rural non-farm diversification resulting in higher inequality may require nuancing.

4 Dynamics of Spatial and Local Inequality

Analysis of inequality at the village level offers useful insights into the drivers of inequality in a country like India. Systematic evidence on the evolution of inequality in spatial units smaller than districts and states remains scarce, however. This evidence gap has largely been due to a lack of representative data for individual towns and villages. Mukhopadhyay and Garcés Urzainqui (2018) implement imputation techniques that draw upon census and satellite data to chronicle the evolution of local-level inequality in India over the period 2004–11. Their analysis offers estimates of the importance of inequalities that exist within and between disaggregated spatial units.

Delving into the spatial distribution of inequality is of interest given the widely shared perception that gains from growth in India have been spatially uneven. There is a sense that a 'biased' growth process is making India 'look more and more like islands of California in a sea of sub-Saharan Africa' (Sen and Drèze 2013). Indian cities have been singled out by their contrasting landscape of flourishing well-off residential areas and deprived slums. It is natural to wonder whether the national trend of increasing urban inequality is also reproduced at small scale—within urban blocks, for example. Concerning rural areas, on the one hand, there is evidence that points towards widening differences between rural areas—Narayan and Murgai (2016) show that rural poverty is becoming increasingly concentrated in poor states—while on the other hand, Li and Rama (2015) find substantial spill-overs from proximity to 'top locations' in rural areas, suggesting the existence of localized patterns of rural development, with some villages catching up and others lagging behind. The Palanpur study suggests that inequality within villages has been rising. It is not obvious which of these phenomena will predominate when we aggregate up to the national level. It is thus well worth tracking the evolution of inequality at the finest spatial level possible.

The analysis by Mukhopadhyay and Garcés Urzainqui (2018) defines spatial units at the lowest Indian administrative level: blocks (sub-districts) in urban areas and villages in rural areas. They estimate a regression model of district-level real consumption expenditure per capita on a host of district-level characteristics for which information is available, as well as for lower levels of aggregation, such as physical geography, demography, structure of employment, and night-time luminosity. The analysis is based on consumption expenditure data from NSS surveys for 2004/5 and 2011/12 and thus enables temporal comparisons. Their prediction model is used to impute per capita consumption expenditure for all rural villages and urban blocks of India. After successfully validating the predictions of the model against NSS data at levels where such comparisons are feasible, Mukhopadhyay and Garcés Urzainqui (2018) compute inequality measures for the country, as well as for its states, based on imputed consumption at the village and urban block level. This is tantamount to asking how much inequality would exist in India as a whole, and in each state, if one were to assume that there was no inequality within villages or within urban blocks such that overall inequality arose only because of differences in average consumption *between* villages and blocks. This allows Mukhopadhyay and Garcés Urzainqui to then deduct this calculation of spatial inequality from their direct measure of total inequality, to arrive at an estimate of the percentage of state or national total inequality that can be attributed to within-village (or within-block) inequality.

Table 7.4 presents total inequality of India (rural and urban separately), and its decomposition into within- and between-spatial units. In rural India, 75 per cent of overall inequality is accounted for by within-village inequality. Although income inequality has increased slightly in rural areas, the within-village proportion has stayed roughly constant over time. The absence of a rise in inequality between villages contrasts with the observation of rapidly rising inequality *between districts*. It seems that while districts may be diverging from one another, the villages within the districts have not seen a similar divergence. In urban areas, the within-block component accounts for an even larger share—88 per cent—of total inequality. This share has also been stable but has been accompanied a significant increase in overall inequality. Again, in urban India there is clear evidence of divergence across districts, but little divergence across blocks within them. What clearly emerges from these calculations is that national-level inequality can be viewed as a kind of aggregation of local-level inequalities. Understanding inequality trends at the national level requires understanding of what is occurring at the local level.

Table 7.4 Decomposing inequality in India

	2004	2011
All India (NSS)	0.188 (100 per cent)	0.210 (100 per cent)
Imputation-based inequality (between spatial units)	0.050 (27 per cent)	0.055 (26 per cent)
Residual: within spatial unit	0.138 (73 per cent)	0.155 (74 per cent)
Rural India (NSS)	0.140 (100 per cent)	0.143 (100 per cent)
Rural inequality based on village-level imputation (between)	0.035 (25 per cent)	0.037 (25 per cent)
Residual: within village	0.105 (75 per cent)	0.106 (75 per cent)
Urban India (NSS)	*0.234 (100 per cent)*	*0.264 (100 per cent)*
Urban inequality based on urban blocks (between)	0.028 (12 per cent)	0.033 (13 per cent)
Residual: within urban block	0.206 (88 per cent)	0.231 (87 per cent)

Source: Mukhopadhyay and Garcés Urzainqui (2018). Reproduced here with permission of UNU-WIDER.

Section 2, and also Table 7.4, suggest that all-India consumption inequality did not increase markedly between 2004/5 and 2011/12. One might conclude that, the importance of local inequality as a share of total inequality notwithstanding, this period was not associated with significant movements in the inequality domain. This conclusion can be questioned once the analysis by Mukhopadhyay and Garcés Urzainqui (2018) is taken to the state level. The analysis unveils considerable heterogeneity in the evolution of inequality at the local level. Thus, the relative stillness in overall inequality hides a diverse landscape of changing inequalities. In particular, states show very different trends, with between-locality and within-locality inequalities often moving in different directions. By way of example, Kerala and Bihar show rising within-locality inequality but falling between-locality inequality. Overall inequality in Bihar remained stable (and low, with a Theil index of 0.08 in 2004/5 and 2011/12) but the share deriving from within-locality inequality increased from just over half to nearly three-quarters. In Kerala overall inequality increased (the Theil index rising from 0.258 to 0.310), with the share attributed to local inequality rising from an already very high 95 per cent to as much as 97 per cent. This heterogeneity becomes even more evident where separate within and between indices are calculated for rural and urban strata.

Having pointed to the heterogeneity of results at the state level, Mukhopadhyay and Garcés Urzainqui (2018) move to the district level and explore how changes in inequality relate to baseline average consumption and its growth. Their findings suggest that higher growth is strongly associated with increases in overall inequality, and low growth with reductions in such inequality, both within and between spatial units. Mukhopadhyay and Garcés Urzainqui (2018) then move on to regress changes in total, within, and between inequalities at the district level, on changes in covariates over time. Their results show that increased urbanization is correlated with a fall in spatial inequalities between villages. However, it has a positive correlation with the rise of overall inequality in rural areas, and with rising local as well as spatial inequalities in urban regions. Similarly, employment—particularly regular employment—is correlated with a fall in inequality between spatial units (especially in the rural sector) but is associated with increased within-inequality. Increases in literacy rates are unambiguously associated with slower inequality growth: improvements in literacy are correlated with slower growth in total inequality and, especially, within-inequality, both in rural areas and overall. The expansion of access to banking services is robustly associated with slower growth in inequality. In rural areas and for the district as whole, the associated decrease takes place through spatial inequality, while it is local inequalities that are most affected in urban areas. Similarly, access to sanitation (arguably a strong proxy for pro-poor intervention) is associated with more sluggish growth in spatial inequalities. In general, the correlation exercise reveals that structural factors are often associated with countervailing developments in spatial and local inequalities. They may lower the one while simultaneously increasing the other. These opposing forces often lead to a false impression that there is no dynamism in inequality in India.

5 Poverty, Vulnerability, and Mobility in India

Beyond studying levels and trends in inequality there is interest also to investigate the underlying processes that characterize changes in inequality. Notably, the patterns of relative income mobility that underpin changes in inequality are rarely documented in nationally representative studies, let alone well understood. Yet, mobility patterns interact closely with inequality levels. As noted by Krugman (1992), 'if income mobility were very high, the degree of inequality in any given year would be unimportant, because the distribution of lifetime income would be very even'.

Assessing the degree of income mobility requires analysis of panel data, as only such data permit the tracking of households over time. Collecting panel data, however, can be very costly and can also pose logistical and capacity-related challenges. Such datasets are accordingly rare. Dang and Lanjouw (2018a) overcome this data challenge in India by employing recently developed statistical techniques that allow them to construct synthetic panels from repeated cross-sections of the NSS surveys (Dang and Lanjouw 2013, 2018b, 2018c; Dang et al. 2014). The methods are predicated on strong assumptions which are often difficult to check.

In their study of India, Dang and Lanjouw (2018a) validate the synthetic panel approach with the IHDS data—the one nationally representative panel dataset that has been collected in India in recent years. Finding that the method appears to work well, they then appeal to the common timing of the IHDS data with the NSS data for 2004/5 and 2011/12, and the representative sampling design of both data sources, to suggest that the method is also likely to work well for mobility comparisons based on the NSS rounds.

5.1 Mobility Levels and Trends

Dang and Lanjouw (2018a) explore the idea of dividing the Indian population into three groups, comprising the poor, the 'vulnerable', and the secure. They specify a vulnerability line—analogous to a poverty line, but set at a consumption level above which one can be safely assumed to be secure from falling back into poverty. The vulnerable are thus those with a consumption level above the poverty line, but below this vulnerability line. Dang and Lanjouw (2018a) consider two approaches to setting the vulnerability line. The first arbitrarily sets a vulnerability line equal to twice the national poverty line. The second estimates a vulnerability line associated with an average risk of falling into poverty for the 'vulnerable' of at least 20 per cent. These two approaches yield similar vulnerability lines. Dang and Lanjouw (2018a) then move on to estimate transitions in and out of the three categories of poor, vulnerable, and secure, based on synthetic panels that are constructed using five 'thick' (large-sample) rounds of the NSS for 1987/8, 1993/4, 2004/5, 2009/10, and 2011/12.

Dang and Lanjouw (2018a) estimate that between the 1987/8 and 1993/4 survey years, about 30 per cent of the population experienced some consumption mobility. Of those that moved, only a very small percentage of the population was associated with jumps of more than one cell. For example, only 0.2 per cent of the population was secure in 1993/4 having been poor in 1987/8, and only 0.3 per cent of the population was poor in 1993/4 having been secure in 1987/8. In terms of conditional mobility (i.e. the estimate of mobility conditional on initial position), about 75 per cent of the poor in 1987/8 remained poor in 1993/4, and 64 per cent of the vulnerable remained vulnerable over this period. Interestingly, nearly half (45 per cent) of the secure transitioned downward into the vulnerable group between 1987/8 and 1993/4.

In the years following 1993/4, poverty decline started to accelerate and welfare transitions also increased. Of course, the interval in this case is somewhat longer than was considered in the previous period, and one might expect more mobility over longer periods. However, the rising average consumption levels occurring over this period would suggest, a priori, an increased likelihood of the population crossing the fixed standard of living captured by an absolute poverty line (and its associated vulnerability lines). So, the rise in mobility captured in this way is likely real. In terms of conditional mobility, just under two-thirds of the poor in 1993/4 remained poor in 2004/5 (compared with three-quarters in the preceding interval), and between 51 and 61 per cent of the vulnerable (depending on choice of vulnerability line) remained vulnerable (down from 64 per cent). Downward mobility among the secure also declined, from about 45 per cent in the 1987/8–1993/4 interval to less than a third in 1993/4–2004/5.

Mobility rose further in the 2004/5–2011/12 interval to around 45 per cent of the population. Interestingly, however, although conditional mobility by the poor into the category of the secure did increase in comparison with the earlier intervals, it remained a rather rare event: regardless of the choice of vulnerability line, less than 10 per cent of the poor were able to make this transition across

Table 7.5 Welfare transition dynamics based on synthetic panel data, India 1987/88–2011/12 (%)

Panel A: Vulnerability line equals twice poverty line		2011			
		Poor	Vulnerable	Secure	Total
1987	Poor	18.4	23.0	4.9	46.4
		(0.1)	(0.0)	(0.0)	(0.1)
	Vulnerable	6.0	22.4	13.7	42.1
		(0.0)	(0.0)	(0.0)	(0.0)
	Secure	0.3	3.5	7.7	11.5
		(0.0)	(0.0)	(0.1)	(0.1)
	Total	24.7	48.9	26.3	100
		(0.1)	(0.0)	(0.1)	
Panel B: Vulnerability line corresponding to V-index = 0.2		2011			
		Poor	Vulnerable	Secure	Total
1987	Poor	18.4	19.7	8.2	46.4
		(0.1)	(0.0)	(0.0)	(0.1)
	Vulnerable	5.6	15.3	15.2	36.1
		(0.0)	(0.0)	(0.0)	(0.0)
	Secure	0.7	4.2	12.6	17.6
		(0.0)	(0.0)	(0.1)	(0.1)
	Total	24.7	39.2	36.1	100
		(0.1)	(0.0)	(0.1)	

Notes: The vulnerability index is defined as twice the poverty line (i.e. 893.4 rupees) in Panel A and that corresponding to a vulnerability index of 0.2 in 2004/05–2011/12 (i.e. 770 rupees) in Panel B. All numbers are in 2004 prices for all rural India. The all-rural-India poverty line is 446.68 rupees for 2004/05. All numbers are estimated with synthetic panel data and weighted with population weights, where the first survey round in each period is used as the base year. Bootstrap standard errors in parentheses are estimated with 1,000 bootstraps adjusting for the complex survey design. Household head's age range is restricted to between 25 and 55 for the first survey and adjusted accordingly for the second survey in each period. Estimation sample sizes are 95,391 and 55,757 for the first and second period, respectively.

Source: Dang and Lanjouw (2018a). Reproduced here with permission of UNU-WIDER.

two welfare classes between 2004/5 and 2010/11. The picture of poverty decline emerging from this assessment is that, although the poor did see improvements in living standards during the 2000s, they generally continued to face a heightened risk of falling back into poverty.

Table 7.5 considers consumption mobility over the longer interval of 1987/8–2011/12, in an effort to enquire into longer-term welfare transitions. A striking observation is that, although poverty declined markedly over this entire period, a very significant percentage did not experience mobility out of poverty. About 40 per cent of the poor in 1993/4 were still poor in 2011/12 (Panels A and B).

Thus, while mobility has risen in India, with growing numbers of the poor transitioning upward into the category of the vulnerable (and even some graduating to secure status), those who were poor in 2011/12 largely comprised the long-term, or chronically, poor. This picture accords with a narrative of poverty decline accompanying accelerating economic growth in India, but with the poor increasingly comprising the structural, long-term poor, who have been non-participants in the growth process. It is important to note that, although intuitive, this picture is far from inevitable: one could also have imagined a growth process involving a great deal of 'churning' in which households escape and fall back into their respective consumption classes, and the poor in any one year largely consist of previously vulnerable and secure households. A potential concern emerging from the patterns we observe is that poverty reduction will become increasingly difficult to achieve through a general growth process that fails to address the structural factors that prevent the chronically poor from escaping poverty.

6 Inequality of Opportunity and Economic Growth

In a recent global study, Narayan et al. (2018) identify India as a country with some of the lowest rates of inter-generational mobility in the world. Prompted by this finding, van der Weide and Vigh (2018) provide an in-depth study of inter-generational mobility for India. They build a database at the state-region level for India that tracks socioeconomic mobility and human capital accumulation at the subnational (NSS region) level over the past thirty years. The database is built using various rounds of the NSS (1983, 1987, 1993, 1999, 2004, and 2011). It includes a large range of variables, including household expenditure growth for the low, middle, and upper-income classes; inequality in household expenditure per capita; demographics; employment variables; domestic infrastructure connectivity; financial inclusion; and selected political variables (i.e. voter turnout and political competition). In their analysis, van der Weide and Vigh (2018) focus on a measure of 'upward mobility' captured by the expected rank of a child (in the child education distribution) whose parents are in the bottom 50 per cent of the parental education rank distribution.

6.1 Inter-Generational Mobility in Education

Van der Weide and Vigh (2018) show that there is a positive correlation between the father's and son's education levels. Their results suggest that gains in human capital accumulation at all education levels of fathers were highest in the late 1980s and 2000s and that increases in average educational attainment are driven primarily by increases among the sons of less educated fathers. Importantly, they find that while persistence declined at the lower end of the father's educational distribution, it increased at the top end, as high school graduation is becoming more common in India.

Van der Weide and Vigh (2018) also capture a different aspect of inter-generational education persistence, using the share of education inequality that is explained by the father's education level. They find that the relative importance of parental education in education inequality has not changed much in recent decades. It has remained at around 10 per cent despite the declining overall inequality in education. Based on their indicators of mobility, the overall assessment of van der Weide and Vigh (2018) is that there is little evidence that inter-generational socioeconomic mobility in India has improved over time.

6.2 Impacts of Inter-Generational Mobility on Consumption Growth

Van der Weide and Vigh (2018) examine next the impacts of inter-generational mobility on per capita consumption growth. In particular, using state-regions as the unit of analysis, they attempt to identify the causal effect of inter-generational mobility on growth of household expenditure per capita at different percentiles of the consumption distribution. They run a regression of the change in log per capita household expenditure on a measure of relative inter-generational mobility, controlling for a number of other variables such as the first lag of log per capita household expenditure, other time-varying state-region characteristics, zone fixed effects, and year fixed effects. In an effort to mitigate the possibility of endogeneity bias, van der Weide and Vigh (2018) implement an IV estimation model where the instrument for inter-generational mobility consists of the local share of the Brahmin caste in 1931 and the local share of Scheduled Tribes in 1961, both interacted with national trends in inter-generational mobility. Specifically, they regress inter-generational mobility on the local shares of Brahman and Scheduled Tribes interacted with the six time-period dummy variables to allow for non-linear time trends, and use the predicted values from this regression as their instrument.

The regression coefficients corresponding to inter-generational mobility are plotted in Figure 7.2. Several observations from this stand out. First, inter-generational mobility is found to have a positive effect on growth for all percentiles, although the effects are not statistically significant. Second, the effect is visibly

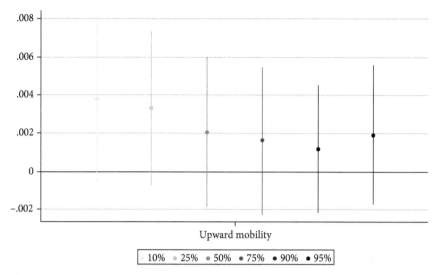

Figure 7.2 Impacts of upward mobility on consumption growth (at different percentiles: IV regression 1 (90% confidence bound)
Note: Reproduced here with permission of UNU-WIDER.
Source: Van der Weide and Vigh (2018).

larger (and almost significant) at lower percentiles. This is consistent with the hypothesis that higher inter-generational mobility is good for growth, particularly for inclusive growth, as those held back by an uneven playing field tend to be concentrated towards the bottom of the income distribution. This finding also predicts a negative relationship between inter-generational mobility and inequality: higher mobility is associated with inclusive growth, which in turn is associated with lower inequality.

Van der Weide and Vigh (2018) further hypothesize that human capital accumulation denotes an important channel via which inter-generational mobility impacts on growth and on the degree of 'inclusivity' of growth. To explore the plausibility of this conjecture, they consider changes in years of schooling for individuals with different parental education backgrounds as dependent variable. These estimates confirm that mobility has a positive and significant effect on human capital accumulation of individuals with less than highly educated parents, while the effect is insignificant for individuals with highly educated parents (for whom it matters less whether the playing field is level or not). This result is robust to the choice of controls.

7 Conclusion

Following the economic reforms of the early 1990s, India entered the twenty-first century with historically unprecedented per capita growth rates. Poverty reduction also accelerated and was justly celebrated. There is great concern, however, that this growth was being accompanied by rising inequality. This chapter has sought to inform the debate on inequality in India by offering a bird's-eye view of inequality trends and dynamics at the all-India level over three decades up to 2011/12 and contrasting this with a 'granular' picture at the level of the Indian village or urban block. The chapter further unpacks inequality dynamics by attempting not just to report 'snapshots' of inequality at different periods, but also to trace the movement of people within the income distribution over time. This analysis of income mobility is motivated by the sense that normative views about changes in inequality are likely to vary according to whether a rise in inequality is, for example, characterized by a simple stretching-out of the income distribution—leaving individuals in the same relative position but just further apart in absolute income—or is also associated with shifts in relative position within the income distribution. Again, the assessment of mobility is informed both by evidence at the very local level and by aggregate, national-level trends. Close attention is paid to the circumstances and fortunes of population groups defined in terms of characteristics that should not, ideally, be associated with differing outcomes. The study attempts to encapsulate these horizontal inequalities into a measure of inequality of opportunity as captured by inter-generational mobility in education outcomes.

Our evidence points to rising inequality between 1983/4 and 2011/12, but to differing degrees depending on the dimension being considered and the measurement method employed. This national trend is consistent with observations in the north Indian village of Palanpur over a period of six decades. It is also consistent with the pattern of structural transformation that has been under way in India in recent decades. We show further that local-level inequality (within-village in rural areas; within-block in urban) accounts for the bulk of overall inequality in India. Understanding what occurs at the local level is thus important for understanding inequality at the all-India level.

The Palanpur study further provides a window on patterns of income mobility, both within and across generations, and suggests that there is evidence that year-to-year changes in relative position are increasing. Our estimates at the national level based on synthetic panel data constructed at the household level confirm rising intra-generational income mobility over time. This is consistent with the idea that inequality of lifetime income may be lower than what is observed in a given year. However, the evidence also suggests that while poverty has fallen, most of the poor who have escaped poverty continue to face a high risk of falling back into poverty. Moreover, those who remain poor are increasingly chronically poor, and may be particularly difficult to reach via the introduction or expansion of safety nets.

While intra-generational mobility may be improving, the evidence on inter-generational mobility is less promising. In Palanpur, there is little evidence to suggest that mobility across generations has improved: father's income remains an important, possibly even strengthening, predictor of his son's income. These findings are consistent with our all-India findings of a negative relationship between inter-generational mobility and inequality: higher mobility is associated with inclusive growth, which in turn is associated with lower inequality. Furthermore, inter-generational mobility is found to have a positive effect on growth for all percentiles, and specifically stronger effects at lower percentiles. Mobility also has a positive and significant effect on human capital accumulation of individuals with less than highly educated parents. Although the analysis points to clear welfare improvements that could be expected to derive from greater inter-generational mobility, both our national-level and our granular-level analysis uncovered little conclusive evidence of improving inter-generational mobility in India over time. The suggestion is that growth has been less inclusive than might have been hoped, and this has been reflected in rising inequality. Looking forward, these findings point to tremendous challenges as the overall growth environment deteriorates in the aftermath of the Covid-19 pandemic.

References

Atkinson, A.B. (2007). 'Measuring Top Incomes: Methodological Issues'. In A.B. Atkinson and T. Piketty (eds), *Top Incomes over the Twentieth Century: A Contrast between Continental European and English-Speaking Countries*. Oxford and New York: Oxford University Press.

Banerjee, A., and T. Piketty (2005). 'Top Indian Incomes, 1922–2000'. *The World Bank Economic Review*, 19(1): 1–20.

Chancel, L., and T. Piketty (2017). 'Indian income inequality, 1922–2014: from British Raj to Billionaire Raj?' CEPR Discussion Paper 12409. London: Centre for Economic Policy Research.

Dang, H., and P. Lanjouw (2013). 'Measuring poverty dynamics with synthetic panels based on cross-sections'. Policy Research Working Paper 6504. Washington, DC: The World Bank.

Dang, H., and P. Lanjouw (2018a). 'Welfare dynamics in India over a quarter century: poverty, vulnerability, and mobility 1987–2012'. WIDER Working Paper 2018/175. Helsinki: UNU-WIDER.

Dang, H., and P. Lanjouw (2018b). 'Poverty Dynamics in India between 2004 and 2012: Insights from Longitudinal Analysis Using Synthetic Panel Data'. *Economic Development and Cultural Change*, 67(1): 131–70.

Dang, H., and P. Lanjouw (2018c). 'Measuring Poverty Dynamics with Synthetic Panels Based on Cross-Sections'. Mimeo. Washington, DC: The World Bank.

Dang, H., P. Lanjouw, J. Luoto, and D. McKenzie (2014). 'Using Repeated Cross-Sections to Explore Movements in and out of Poverty'. *Journal of Development Economics*, 107: 112–28.

Datt, G., R. Murgai, and M. Ravallion (2016). 'Growth, Urbanization and Poverty Reduction in India'. Policy Research Working Paper 7568. Washington, DC: The World Bank.

Elbers, C., and P. Lanjouw (2019). 'The distributional impact of structural transformation in rural India: model-based simulation and caste-study evidence'. WIDER Working Paper 2019/33. Helsinki: UNU-WIDER.

Himanshu (2019). 'Inequality in India: a review of levels and trends'. WIDER Working Paper 2019/42. Helsinki: UNU-WIDER.

Himanshu, P. Lanjouw, and N. Stern (2018). *How Lives Change: Palanpur, India and Development Economics*. Oxford: Oxford University Press.

Krugman, P. (1992). 'The Rich, The Right and the Facts'. *The American Prospect*, 11: 19–31.

Leigh, A. (2007). 'How Closely Do Top Income Shares Track Other Measures of Inequality?'. *Economic Journal*, 117(524): 619–33.

Leigh, A., and A. Posso (2009). 'Top Incomes and National Savings'. *Review of Income and Wealth*, 55(1): 57–74.

Li, Y., and M. Rama (2015). 'Households or Locations? Cities, Catchment Areas and Prosperity in India'. Policy Research Working Paper 7473. Washington, DC: The World Bank.

Mukhopadhyay, A., and D. Garcés Urzainqui (2018). 'The dynamics of spatial and local inequalities in India'. WIDER Working Paper 2018/182. Helsinki: UNU-WIDER.

Narayan, A., and R. Murgai (2016). 'Looking back on two decades of poverty and well-being in India'. Policy Research Working Paper 7626. Washington, DC: World Bank.

Narayan, A., R. van der Weide, A. Cojocaru, C. Lakner, S. Redaelli, D. Mahler, R. Gupta, N. Ramasubbaiah, and S. Thewissen (2018). *Fair Progress? Economic Mobility across Generations Around the World*. Washington, DC: World Bank.

National Sample Survey (NSS) (various). *National Sample Survey Report*. Delhi: Ministry of Statistics and Programme Implementation.

National University of Educational Planning and Administration (2015). School Education in India, U-DISE 2014–2015 (Provisional Estimates). Available at: http://udise.in/Downloads/Publications/Documents/Analytical_Table-14-15.pdf (accessed December 2018).

Rongen, G. (2018). 'A new inequality estimate for Urban India? Using house prices to estimate inequality in Mumbai'. WIDER Working Paper 2018/181. Helsinki: UNU-WIDER.

Sen, A., and J. Drèze (2013). *An Uncertain Glory: India and Its Contradictions*. Princeton: Princeton University Press.

Sutch, R. (2017). 'The One Percent across Two Centuries: A Replication of Thomas Piketty's Data on the Concentration of Wealth in the United States'. *Social Science History*, 41(4): 587–613.

Thorat, S., and N.S. Sabharwal (2011). 'Addressing the Unequal Burden of Malnutrition'. *India Health Beat*, 5(5). Available at: www.bpni.org/Article/Policy-Note-Number-5.pdf (accessed December 2018).

van der Weide, R., C. Lakner, and E. Ianchovichina (2018). 'Is Inequality Underestimated in Egypt? Evidence from House Prices'. *Review of Income and Wealth*, 64(s1): S55–79.

van der Weide, R., and M. Vigh (2018). 'Intergenerational mobility, human capital accumulation, and growth in India'. WIDER Working Paper 2018/187. Helsinki: UNU-WIDER.

World Inequality Lab (2018). *World Inequality Report*. Available at: https://wir2018.wid.world/ (accessed December 2018).

8

Mexico

Labour Markets and Fiscal Redistribution 1989–2014

Raymundo Campos-Vazquez, Nora Lustig, and John Scott

1 Introduction

Mexico is an upper middle-income country with a Gini coefficient hovering around 0.5, which places it in the group of high-inequality countries.[1] Since the mid-1980s, Mexico has opened up to international trade and, with the rise of computers and digitalization, has experienced changes in production technology. In addition, its labour force has become considerably more educated: the proportion of individuals with primary levels of education or lower declined from 67 per cent in 1990 to 33 per cent in 2015 and the share of individuals with a college education more than doubled between 1990 and 2015, when it reached around 15 per cent. The past thirty years have also been marked by a significant increase in social spending and a retooling of social programmes. All these changes have affected the demand and supply of labour and the extent to which the state has engaged in fiscal redistribution. What has been the evolution of income inequality during this momentous period? To what extent have market forces and fiscal policy contributed to the observed trends?

After discussing the evolution of income inequality and its components, in this chapter we focus on two main drivers of overall inequality: labour markets and fiscal redistribution. In particular, we apply state-of-the-art decomposition techniques to analyse the proximate determinants of labour income inequality, and we apply fiscal incidence analysis to estimate the first-order effects of changes in social spending and taxation on the distribution of income and poverty. This paper can be viewed as a sequel to Esquivel et al. (2010) and Campos-Vazquez et al. (2014). The former studied the dynamics of income inequality in Mexico up until 2006 and the latter until 2010.

Using results from Mexico's National Survey on Households' Income and Expenditures (ENIGH, by its Spanish acronym), Section 2 presents the evolution

[1] The authors wish to thank Alma S. Santillan for her excellent research assistance. Any errors and omissions are the authors' responsibility.

Raymundo Campos-Vazquez, Nora Lustig, and John Scott, *Mexico: Labour Markets and Fiscal Redistribution 1989–2014* In: *Inequality in the Developing World*. Edited by: Carlos Gradín, Murray Leibbrandt, and Finn Tarp, Oxford University Press (2021). © United Nations University World Institute for Development Economics Research (UNU-WIDER). DOI: 10.1093/oso/9780198863960.003.0008

in overall income inequality from the late 1980s until 2014.[2] The evolution of income inequality during this period can be summarized as follows: between 1989 and 1994, inequality increased; between 1994 and 2006, inequality declined; and between 2006 and 2014, inequality was again on the rise. Section 2 also identifies the influence of the main income components (labour income, capital income and pensions, transfers, and remittances) on the evolution of inequality. As will be seen in what follows, the key component that underlies the 'rise–decline–rise again' pattern was the evolution of labour income inequality. Thus, Section 3 focuses on the role of demand, supply, and institutional factors in accounting for the evolution of labour income inequality. Lastly, the decomposition exercise in Section 2 also shows that transfers were not only an equalizing force, but were increasingly so. Hence, Section 4 analyses the evolution of fiscal redistribution with a focus on transfers and other relevant characteristics of the fiscal system. Section 5 concludes.

2 The Level and Evolution of Income Inequality and Poverty: 1989–2014

2.1 Inequality: Trends and Proximate Determinants

As shown in Figure 8.1, income inequality increased between the late 1980s and mid-1990s and then declined until about 2006. Since then, there appears to have been an upward trend. More precisely, the Gini coefficient for per capita disposable monetary income[3] rose from 0.534 to 0.555 between 1989 and 1994 and declined to 0.506 in 2006. It then rose to 0.531 in 2014. It is worth noting that during the 1989–2014 period, average incomes sometimes rose and sometimes fell, depending on the overall growth performance of the economy. Average incomes fell sharply in 1995 as a result of Mexico's financial crisis. However, from 1996, average incomes recovered at the same time as inequality fell. This auspicious situation came to a halt after 2008, when Mexico suffered the consequences of the Great Recession. Between 2008 and 2014, average incomes fell, and inequality experienced an upward trend.

2.2 Top Incomes: Survey-Based and Administrative Data

Our microdata-based analysis in this chapter uses the National Survey on Households Income and Expenditures (ENIGH). However, household surveys

---

[2] Household surveys and their respective documentation are available in INEGI (1989, 1992, 1994, 1996, 1998, 2000, 2002, 2004, 2006, 2008, 2010, 2012, 2014). Household surveys for 2016 and 2018 exist, but unfortunately, due to drastic methodological changes undertaken by the National Statistical Institute (or INEGI, by its Spanish acronym), the results would not be comparable with previous surveys.

[3] See Campos-Vazquez et al. (2014) for income definitions. 'Income' here includes labour income and non-labour income.

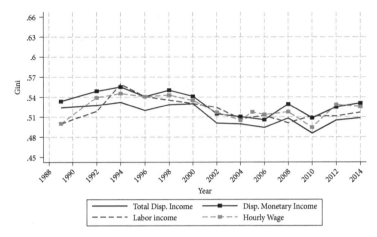

Figure 8.1 Gini coefficient, 1989–2014

Note: Total disposable income, disposable monetary income[4] and labour income are in per capita terms and include all members of the household regardless of age. Hourly wage is restricted to individuals aged 18–65 years. Labour income refers to the income obtained from main job and includes own business' income for the self-employed. Households where head reported zero income were excluded.

Source: Authors' calculations based on the National Survey of Household Incomes and Expenditures (INEGI 1989, 1992, 1994, 1996, 1998, 2000, 2004, 2006, 2008, 2010, 2012, 2014).

suffer from serious under-reporting and under-coverage, especially for incomes at the top that can yield biased inequality indicators. People at the top may be difficult to reach due to statistical and sampling issues; if rich people are a small group, then the likelihood of them being captured by the survey is also small. Moreover, even if captured in the sampling process, rich people may be more reluctant than the average individual to answer the full questionnaire, and this may be particularly the case for questions about income.

One common approach for addressing these limitations is to correct the information in household surveys using administrative data and generate a new distribution and concomitant indicators.[5] Alvaredo et al. (2017) combined data from ENIGH with the universe of personal income taxpayers, obtained from the Mexican Tax Administration Service (roughly 2–2.5 million taxpayers per year), and the universe of employer-reported information on wages for formal workers. The latter contains information on gross, taxable, and net labour income for about 20–25 million workers per year.

Using different correction methods, Alvaredo et al.'s (2017) results indicate that that survey-based top shares are substantially underestimated. For example, in

---

[4] The difference between disposable income and disposable monetary income is that the latter does not include imputed rent for owner-occupied housing or consumption of own production. The Gini coefficient for disposable income is lower by 2 to 3 Gini points. In the section on fiscal redistribution we use disposable income, and that is why the Ginis are lower than those presented here.

[5] See Lustig (2018a) for a survey of the issues and correction methods proposed in the literature.

2010, the survey-based income share of the top 10 per cent equalled 47.6 per cent. In contrast, with corrections the share is approximately 60 per cent. This is an active area for further research.

2.3 Poverty

Although the task of this chapter does not include the analysis of poverty, the persistence of extreme poverty throughout the period analysed is remarkable. The incidence of extreme poverty in 2014 (20.6 per cent) was similar to the level observed in 1994 (21.2 per cent), and only slightly lower than in 1984 (23.5 per cent). The persistence of extreme income poverty is all the more remarkable given the expansion of programmes targeted at the poor, a topic that will be discussed in the section on fiscal redistribution.

3 The Evolution and Determinants of Labour Income Inequality

As observed in Figure 8.1,[6] inequality of labour income per capita, labour income per worker, and the hourly wage increased from the late 1980s up to the mid-1990s and then declined up to the middle of the first decade of the twenty-first century. Since then and up to 2014, the data suggest a slight upward trend. Understanding the main drivers of labour income inequality is key to the understanding of the determinants of overall income inequality.

3.1 Labour Income Inequality: Characteristics and Returns

Labour income inequality is affected by two main factors: the distribution of (observable and unobservable) characteristics of workers (education, experience, gender, etc) and the returns to those characteristics. Workers' characteristics, in turn, are affected by circumstances (gender, race, talent, and so on), households' decisions (e.g. to enrol or not in post-secondary education, who marries whom, and so on), and policy (e.g. expanding access to education). Returns to households' characteristics depend on market forces (i.e. demand and supply of workers of different skills and experience) and institutional/policy factors (e.g. minimum wage policy and the unionization rate).

In order to separate the contribution of characteristics and returns, research on the proximate determinants of labour income inequality relies on decomposition techniques. Many decomposition procedures are employed in the literature. Most

---

[6] Based on Campos-Vazquez and Lustig (2017).

are variations on the Oaxaca–Blinder decomposition.[7] In this chapter, we follow the same approach. We employ the 're-centred influence function' (RIF) procedure proposed by Firpo et al. (2009) to decompose effects into characteristics and returns effects (as in the typical Oaxaca–Blinder decomposition).[8]

As discussed in Campos-Vazquez and Lustig (2017), we start our analysis by calculating the difference in average labour income for each quantile between the initial and end years for every quantile in segments of 1 per cent (that is, from the 1st to the 99th percentile). Then we estimate the RIF regression for each quantile and the initial and end years. Once the parameters are estimated, we proceed to apply the basic Oaxaca–Blinder decomposition for each quantile (1st–99th percentile). That is, we calculate β^{v} where t is the final year and s is the initial year. Note that the $\hat{v}(Y_t) - \hat{v}(Y_s) = \hat{\beta}_s^y(\overline{X}_t - \overline{X}_s) + \overline{X}_t(\hat{\beta}_t^y - \hat{\beta}_s^y)$, are for the entire sample, as in the traditional Oaxaca–Blinder. In our application, we set up the initial years as 1989, 1994, and 2006 and the final years as 1994, 2006, and 2014, respectively. The term $\hat{\beta}_s^y(\overline{X}_t - \overline{X}_s)$ refers to the characteristics effects, and the term $\overline{X}_t(\hat{\beta}_t^y - \hat{\beta}_s^y)$ refers to the return or price effects to observable characteristics included in X as well as unobservable ones (which is why this term is often referred to as the 'unexplained component'). We use as reference the wage distribution in the initial year (for each decomposition).

Research shows that in Mexico changes in labour income inequality can be largely linked to changes in the relative wage between skilled and unskilled workers, that is, in the returns to skill. In particular, the rise in inequality during this period is associated with an increase in returns to schooling.[9] Applying the RIF method proposed by Firpo et al. (2009) and the Oaxaca–Blinder decomposition method, Campos-Vazquez et al. (2014) show that the increase in earnings inequality between 1989 and 1994 is primarily driven by a rise in the returns to characteristics (schooling and experience), as shown by the upward sloping curve in Figure 8.2, Panel a. The distribution of characteristics remains almost flat. In other words, had relative returns remained at the 1989 level, inequality would not have increased.

From the mid-1990s up to the mid-2000s, labour income inequality steadily declined (Figure 8.1).[10] Applying the RIF method, Campos-Vazquez et al. (2014)

---

[7] We can divide the decomposition into four groups: (i) reweighting procedures (DiNardo et al. 1996); (ii) residual-imputation procedures (Almeida dos Reis and Paes de Barros 1991; Juhn et al. 1993) (iii) quantile decomposition procedures (Machado and Mata 2005); and (iv) RIF procedures (Firpo et al. 2009).

[8] See more details in Campos-Vazquez and Lustig (2017).

[9] This result was found in many other studies, including Bouillon et al. (1999), Meza González (1999), Bouillon (2000a, 2000b), Legovini et al. (2005), Lopez-Acevedo (2004, 2006), Popli (2011), and Campos-Vazquez et al. (2014).

[10] It is not only the Gini coefficient and other summary indicators for hourly wages and labour income that decline; firm data, for instance, show a decline in the relative wage of white- over blue-collar workers (Esquivel 2011).

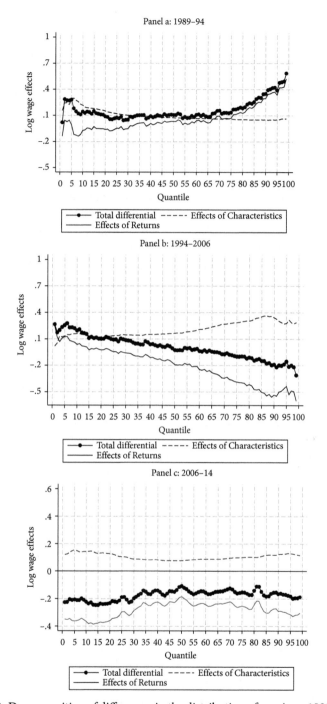

Figure 8.2 Decomposition of differences in the distribution of earnings: 1989–2014

Notes: Calculations using ENIGH. RIF decomposition method proposed by Firpo et al. (2009), which decomposes the change in the monthly wage in characteristics and returns. Smoothed lines with a simple moving average with weights 0.4 for the current observation and 0.3 for the lead and lag. Total differential is the total change in hourly wages (in logs); effects of characteristics (education and experience) and effects of returns are the portions that can be ascribed to changes in characteristics and returns, respectively.

Source: Panels a and b: based on Campos-Vazquez et al. (2014: Figure 7.4). Panel c: based on Campos-Vazquez and Lustig (2017).

show that the decline in earnings inequality between 1994 and 2006 is primarily driven by a fall in the returns to characteristics (schooling and experience), as shown by the downward curve in Figure 8.2 Panel b. The effect of changes in the distribution of characteristics (education, experience, female, and urban) was, in contrast, unequalizing, as shown by the upward curve for the effect of characteristics. If returns had remained unchanged in this period, the change in characteristics in the population would have resulted in higher levels of inequality. The effect of returns to those characteristics contributed to equalizing the labour income distribution by such an amount that they compensated for the inequality-increasing effects induced by characteristics. The puzzle is why changes in characteristics were unequalizing during a period in which, for example, there was substantial educational upgrading and the distribution of years of schooling became more equal. This seemingly contradictory result was first noted by Bourguignon et al. (2005), who called it the 'paradox of progress'. These authors show that this puzzling result is the mathematical consequence of the convexity in (i.e. increasing) returns to skill (this result has been found in other Latin American countries: Gasparini et al. 2011).

From 2006 to 2014, labour income inequality shows an upward trend. Figure 8.2 Panel c shows that the characteristics effect is no longer unequalizing but is flat. The returns effect is somewhat unequalizing because it is negative, especially for the lower centiles. Note that all wages fall but the decline is a bit more pronounced for the bottom of the distribution. Thus, the increase in labour income inequality during this period appears to be driven by a worsening situation for those at the bottom of the distribution rather than an improvement for those at the top, whose incomes also appear to fall slightly more than the group in the middle.

3.2 Relative Wages: Demand, Supply, and Institutions

In the previous section we showed that an important determinant of the evolution of labour income inequality is the evolution of relative returns to characteristics, that is, the relative wages for workers of different skills (with skills measured by years of education and experience). Relative wages, in turn, are affected by market forces—demand and supply of workers of different skills—and by institutional factors such as the minimum wage and unionization rate. In order to examine the effect of supply and demand on relative wages, we follow the Bound and Johnson (1992) method.

Assuming a simple CES (constant elasticity of substitution) production function with elasticity of substitution, σ, constant across skills, it is possible to determine the effect of supply and demand on relative wages:[11]

---

[11] See formula 3 on page 377 and formula A8 on page 390 of Bound and Johnson (1992).

$$\Delta\%\left(\frac{\overline{w}^C}{\overline{w}^S}\right)=\frac{1}{\sigma}\Delta\%(Demand)-\frac{1}{\sigma}\Delta\%(Supply)+\xi$$

The residual term ξ contains the effect of skill-biased technical change and institutional factors such as the minimum wage and unionization rate (sometimes called non-competitive factors).

Changes in demand could come from changes in trade patterns or develop-ments in technology, for example. However, they are unobserved. Data show only labour supply (by years of education and experience) but not real labour demand. Researchers then traditionally use the difference between the change in relative wages or returns and relative supply as an approximation to changes in demand and institutional factors, such as changes in the unionization rate and the value of the real minimum wage as well as technical change (where institutional factors and technical change are captured by the residual). If institutional factors remain unchanged during the period of analysis, the difference can be considered an approximation of changes in relative demand and technical change.

What was the evolution of labour supply during the period of analysis? As shown in Figure 8.3, relative supply of workers with college and high school

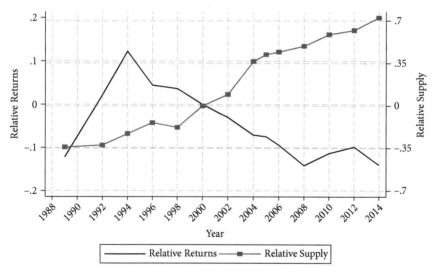

Figure 8.3 Relative returns and relative supply of workers by education, college, and high school vs rest

Notes: Sample restricted to individuals or workers aged 20–64 years. Base year is 2000. The figure calculates the relative return and relative supply of the group mentioned in the subtitle. The relative return line is calculated as the log of the ratio in the average labour income of college and high school workers over the rest of workers adjusting the weights using administrative data and the relative supply is calculated as the log of the ratio of individuals with a college and high school degree over the rest).

Source: Authors' calculations based on ENIGH (INEGI 1989, 1992, 1994, 1996, 1998, 2000, 2004, 2006, 2008, 2010, 2012, 2014).

education vis-à-vis the rest increased throughout, but the rate was higher between 1998 and 2006, when labour income inequality declined. As for institutional factors, both the unionization rate and the real minimum wage declined during the period of rising labour income inequality (1989–94) and remained roughly flat until 2014, the period in which labour income inequality first declined (1996–2006), and then again began to rise from 2006. In other words, if demand and technological change had been constant throughout the entire period, one would have expected labour income inequality to fall from 1996 onwards because of the increase in the supply of skilled workers and its effect on relative wages.

We now turn to the estimates from applying the Bound and Johnson (1992) decomposition. The results in Table 8.1 can be interpreted as follows. If we take, for example, the period of rising labour income inequality of 1989–94, we see that relative wages for skilled workers rose by 24.4 per cent. If the change in relative demand and institutional factors had been zero instead of positive, the relative wages of skilled workers would have fallen by 5.5 per cent. In contrast, if the supply of skilled workers had not increased, relative wages would have risen by 30 per cent. Given that the real minimum wage and the unionization rate fell during this period, one cannot ascribe the rise in the skill premium entirely to demand factors. Both demand and institutional factors likely played a role.

As discussed in Campos-Vazquez and Lustig (2017), the fact that demand for skilled workers increased during the 1989–94 period is considered a rather surprising effect. Given Mexico's abundance in low-skilled workers, a key question is why demand for higher-educated individuals increased at a time when theory would have predicted the opposite. Mexico experienced a large opening of its economy in 1986 when it joined the precursor to the World Trade Organization,

Table 8.1 Bound and Johnson decomposition: 1989–94; 1994–2006; 2006–14 (assuming an elasticity of substitution σ = 2 and comparing college and high school-educated workers with rest of workers)[12]

	Change Log Labour Income	Change in Supply Effect	Change in Demand Effect[a]
1989–94	0.244	−0.055	0.300
1994–2006	−0.216	−0.336	0.119
2006–14	−0.046	−0.141	0.096

Notes: Labour income for workers aged 20–65 years.

[a] This effect includes not only demand but also institutional factors and technological change.

Source: Authors' calculations based on ENIGH (INEGI 1989, 1994, 2006, 2014).

[12] Results for σ = 1 and for college educated versus the rest are qualitatively similar and are available upon request.

the General Agreement on Tariffs and Trade (or GATT). Due to the relative abundance of less skilled labour, the Stolper–Samuelson theorem would have predicted that liberalization would lead to a decrease in the relative wage of high-skilled workers and, therefore, a fall in inequality. However, as noted by Cragg and Epelbaum (1996) and Esquivel and Rodríguez-Lopez (2003), the opposite occurred. What drove this seemingly contradictory outcome? There are several persuasive explanations that offer an answer to the puzzle.

First, there is evidence that the most protected industries during the previous period were low skill-intensive sectors (e.g. textiles) and, thus, trade liberalization reduced the relative price of these industries and, as a consequence, the relative wage of the low-skilled (Hanson and Harrison 1999; Feliciano 2001; Robertson 2004, 2007). Second, there is evidence that during this period there was skill-biased technical change and a change in the composition of output that gave skill-intensive industries a higher share (Airola and Juhn 2005; Cragg and Epelbaum 1996; Esquivel and Rodriguez-Lopez 2003). Third, changes in the pattern of foreign direct investment (FDI) favoured skill-intensive firms. With trade liberalization, FDI also increased primarily through the expansion of *maquiladoras*. These establishments import most of their inputs and assemble the product to export (mainly to the USA). Using industry and state-level data from 1975 to 1988, Feenstra and Hanson (1997) track the impact of FDI on employment and wages. They find that the outsourcing of US multinationals caused an increase in the number of establishments in Mexico that favoured skill-intensive industries (Hanson 2003; Kurokawa 2011).

In other words, there is no real contradiction with the standard Stolper–Samuelson theorem: trade opening benefited skill-intensive industries relatively more because, contrary to expectations, low-skill industries had been relatively more protected before. This change, combined with skill-biased technical change and the change in the composition of output towards more skill-intensive sectors, favoured wages of skilled workers and increased labour income inequality.[13]

In addition to the positive impact on skilled workers' wages stemming from trade liberalization and skill-biased technical change, the evolution of the minimum wage and unionization rate might have played a role. From 1988 to 1996 the real minimum wage lost close to 50 per cent of its value and the unionization rate declined by roughly 40 per cent. If the sharp decline in minimum wages and the unionization rate are correlated with workers' bargaining power, they could affect the distribution of labour income because of their downward pressure on the wages of the low-skilled. In the case of unionization,

---

[13] In addition to the impact of trade liberalization and its implications on the demand for skills, there may be an adverse effect on their supply: e.g. more job opportunities available in the *maquiladoras* could cause a higher high-school dropout rate. For instance, Atkin (2016) finds that for every twenty-five jobs created, one student dropped out of school at grade 9 (final year of middle school).

there is evidence that its decline before NAFTA affected the wage structure. Using ENIGH, Fairris (2003) and Fairris and Levine (2004) conclude that the fall in the unionization rate from 1984 to 1996 explains 11 per cent of the increase in wage inequality. In terms of minimum wages, Bosch and Manacorda (2010) analyse the effect of the minimum wage on the wage structure and wage inequality during the 1989–94 period and in later years. They find that all of the increase in inequality in the bottom part of the distribution is caused by the fall in the real minimum wage. This is mainly due to the fact that the minimum wage affects other wages close to the minimum wage (lighthouse effect). In particular, Kaplan and Perez-Arce Novaro (2006) argue that although the minimum wage binding process has declined over time (at least until 1996), it affects other wages in the distribution (a similar result is provided by Fairris et al. 2008). Cortez (2001) analyses both aspects (unionization and minimum wages) and concludes that the increase in wage inequality can be fully explained by the decline in institutional forces.

During the 1994–2006 period, when labour income inequality (and overall inequality) declined, relative wages for the skilled fell by 21.6 per cent. Since the real minimum wage and the unionization rate were flat, this result must be the outcome of the relative strength of supply versus demand forces. As can be observed, and in contrast with the 1989–94 period, the dampening effect on the skill premium stemming from the increase in relative supply strongly dominates the increase in demand for skilled workers.

Although the RIF method does not disaggregate the returns into their various components, the result shown in Figure 8.2 (Panel b) is consistent with the fall in the relative returns to education shown in Figure 8.3, where it can be seen that the relative supply of college-educated (skilled) workers rose substantially during this period while the relative returns declined. This means that: (i) supply of skilled labour during this period outpaced demand; (ii) institutional factors moved in favour of the unskilled; or (iii) both.[14] The real minimum wage and the unionization rate remained largely constant during this period. Thus, changes in institutional determinants cannot drive the decrease in wage inequality.[15] As Campos-Vazquez et al. (2014) suggest, the change in the skill premium during this period is the result of a combination of a rising supply of workers with college education and a slow-down in demand for skilled workers. So, what drove the slow-down in demand growth for skilled workers?

Robertson (2004, 2007) argues that although trade benefited more skill-intensive industries in the 1980s and early 1990s, with NAFTA this process was reversed. After NAFTA, the relative price of tradable goods continued to decline over time. This potentially explains the decline in the skill premium given that NAFTA favoured skill-intensive industries. Thus, this process drives, in part, the

[14] The gross enrolment rate almost doubled in the 1994–2004 period (Campos-Vazquez 2013).
[15] There is evidence that the minimum wage is currently not binding and has not been binding since the mid-1990s. For a detailed and recent explanation of the role of minimum wages in Mexico see Escobar Toledo (2014).

decline in wage inequality. Other explanations that have been proposed for the decline in inequality include international migration, labour market distortions, and technical change that may have hurt older skilled workers. Migration increased during this period, probably due to the large negative effects of the 1995 crisis. Mishra (2007) shows that the increase of migration to the USA by low-skilled workers caused a decrease in their relative supply (holding everything else constant), which in a traditional supply-and-demand model would increase their wages.

Other research has shown that misallocation across firms induced by labour market distortions may have contributed to the decline in labour income inequality. Levy and Lopez-Calva (2016) argue that these distortions limit the growth of the high-productivity sectors, which are also more skill-intensive. As a result, there is a 'surplus' of workers with post-secondary education, who end up having to work in low-productivity firms, where their wages are lower. The misallocation of workers with high levels of education into low-productivity firms may be one of the drivers of the fall in absolute wages for college-educated workers and the stagnation of wages at the bottom.[16] Campos-Vazquez et al. (2016) explore the reasons behind the decline in absolute wages for college-educated workers. They observe that older cohorts are worse affected than younger cohorts and argue that the displacement of older educated workers may have been a result not only of technological change making skilled workers redundant but also of younger workers, who can be paid lower wages, being more adept in the use of the new technologies. Hence, it seems that the changes in the composition of output induced by NAFTA, the misallocation of skilled labour because of labour market distortions, and the characteristics of technological change were behind the slow-down in demand growth for skilled workers.

During the last period analysed here, when inequality was again on the rise (2006–14), the picture is less clear. As was shown above, during this period all labour income fell, but it fell more for the bottom of the distribution and for those at the very top. The latter is probably due to a continuation—albeit weaker—of the supply- and demand-side dampening forces on the skill premium observed in the previous period. The higher decline of incomes at the bottom is probably due to a decline in the demand for low-skilled workers as a consequence of how Mexico's growth was hit by the Great Recession in the United States. Further research is needed to understand the labour market dynamics that prevailed during this recessionary period.

4 Fiscal Redistribution: 1996–2015

Based on results in Scott et al. (2017), here we analyse the redistributive and poverty-reducing effects of the fiscal system—that is, taxes (personal and

---

[16] Halliday et al. (2016) obtain similar results using firm heterogeneity.

indirect), transfers (in cash and in kind), and (mainly) consumption subsidies—for the period 1996–2014 (and a simulation of policy changes for 2015),[17] though the tax side is only included for the 2008–14 period.

The period of analysis is of particular interest as it covers a number of significant changes in social and fiscal policy. First, after contracting during the 'lost decade' of the 1980s, social and other redistributive spending, such as energy consumer subsidies and agricultural subsidies, almost tripled from 1988 to 2012 (they have since declined from this historical maximum—by 17 per cent by 2018). Second, cash transfers became significantly more pro-poor, benefiting the rural poor in particular. The crown jewel of social policy reforms was the launch of the flagship conditional cash transfer programme PROGRESA in 1997 (which has changed its name and scope several times since).[18] PROGRESA involved a reallocation of costly generalized food subsidies from urban (particularly metropolitan) areas with low impact on extreme poverty and malnutrition, to cash transfers targeted at the extreme poor in rural areas.[19] In addition, some agricultural transfers were delinked from prices and output levels and, thus, they were able to reach poor, non-commercial farmers; also, a self-targeted temporary workfare programme was introduced to address seasonal and disaster-related unemployment. In addition, the coverage of basic education increased significantly both through supply-side measures and the demand-side increase in attendance that resulted from the conditions attached to the PROGRESA cash transfers.

Finally, in the 2000s, an important effort was made to increase social protection for the uninsured by increasing financing and access to health services and medicines for this population through a non-contributory health insurance programme, the *Seguro Popular* (People's Insurance), and through a basic, non-contributory, universal pension, the *Programa de Adultos Mayores* (Programme for Senior Citizens). Both of these programmes expanded their coverage gradually and are aiming to achieve universal coverage of uninsured households and senior citizens, respectively.[20]

Despite these pro-poor reforms in social transfers, a much larger share of growth in social spending has been absorbed by transfers to the contributory pension systems in this period. A small share of these transfers represents statutory government contributions or minimum pension guarantees but most are devoted to payments of current pensions, fully financed by the government, in the transition towards defined contribution systems, as well as from unfunded

---

[17] In addition to the original research, Scott et al. (2017) draw on Komives et al. (2009), Scott (2002, 2004, 2005, 2009a, 2009b, 2014), and Scott and Hernandez (2018).

[18] For an overview of the extensive PROGRESA evaluation literature, see Parker and Todd (2017).

[19] For a detailed description of the programmes, see Scott et al. (2017).

[20] For an overview of the evolution of multi-dimensional poverty and Mexico's social programmes, see CONEVAL (2017a, 2017b), respectively.

benefits of systems yet to be reformed (such as the one associated with the state-owned oil company PEMEX). Of note is the fact that, in the context of austerity measures, between 2015 and 2017 total spending by the Ministry of Social Development (mainly the two flagship cash transfers) declined by 10 per cent while transfers to fill the financial gap of the contributory pensions system rose by 18 per cent.

It is important to note that the expansion of social spending (including the transfers to contributory pensions) was not financed through new taxes (as repeated attempted fiscal reforms failed to pass), but through a reallocation of the functional distribution of public spending, from economic to social development, in the 1990s—in terms of share of central government spending, social spending doubled from 30 to 60 per cent—and through rising but short-lived oil revenues associated with the oil boom in the 2000s. The reallocation of public spending from the economic function was mostly achieved through a significant reduction in public investment and privatization of public enterprises of lesser importance.

In order to estimate the redistributive and poverty-reducing effects, Scott et al. (2017) rely on standard fiscal incidence analysis.[21] As stated in Lustig and Higgins (2018: 15):

> Fiscal incidence analysis consists of allocating taxes (personal income tax and consumption taxes, in particular) and public spending (social spending and consumption subsidies, in particular) to households or individuals so that one can compare incomes before taxes and transfers with incomes after taxes and transfers.

That is, starting from pre-fiscal income—which here we call market income plus (contributory) pensions[22]—taxes and transfers are sequentially subtracted and added to construct three additional key income concepts: disposable income (subtracts direct personal income taxes and adds cash transfers to market income plus pensions), consumable income (subtracts indirect taxes and adds subsidies to disposable income), and final income (adds government spending on education and health to consumable income) (Figure 8.4).

---

[21] For a detailed description of the methodology, data, and caveats, see Scott et al. (2017).

[22] As discussed in Lustig and Higgins (2018: 16), 'social insurance contributory pensions are partly deferred income and therefore should have a portion of them added to Market Income (and contributions subtracted from factor income); and partly government transfer and therefore a portion of them should be included with the rest of government transfers (and contributions treated as any other direct tax). However, since at this point there is no conventional method to determine which portion should be allocated to Market Income and which to government transfers when the only information available is a cross-section household survey', one should calculate the impact of the net fiscal system under the two extreme scenarios: (1) contributory pensions are pure deferred income (also known as replacement income) and (2) contributory pensions are a pure government transfer. Here we present results for the first scenario. Results with contributory pensions as pure transfers should be requested from John Scott, lead author of Scott et al. (2017). Note that non-contributory pensions are always treated as a pure government transfer.

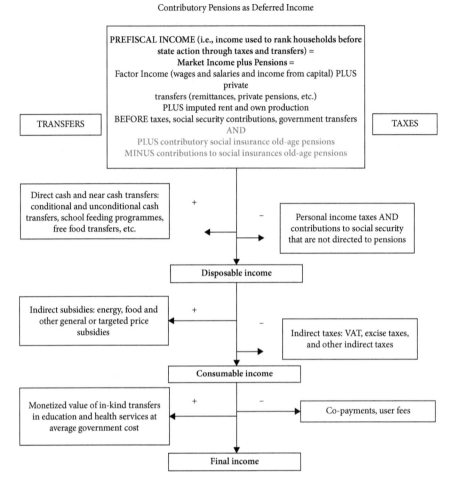

Figure 8.4 Fiscal incidence analysis, core income concepts
Source: Lustig and Higgins (2018), reproduced under CC BY-NC-ND 4.0.

4.1 Revenues and Spending: Size and Composition

As discussed in Lustig (2018b), the redistributive and poverty-reducing effects of the fiscal system depend on the size and progressivity of the various components that integrate the fiscal system. In terms of revenue collection, Mexico's fiscal capacity has been historically limited. In contrast to many middle- and high-income countries, where tax revenues expanded significantly over the century, (non-oil) tax revenues in Mexico have remained stagnant at around 10 per cent of GDP (mostly below this) over the past forty years (1974–2014).

Social spending expanded over the past two decades, reaching around 10 per cent of GDP by 2015 excluding contributory pensions, and 13 per cent including

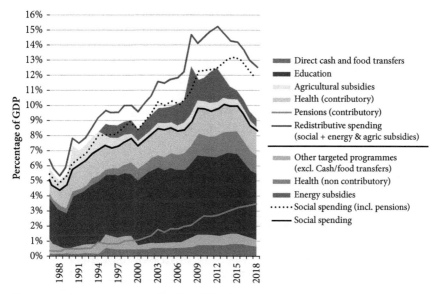

Figure 8.5 Government transfers (% of GDP), 1988–2018
Source: Based on Scott et al. (2017).

pensions (Figure 8.5). Total redistributive spending (including agricultural and energy subsidies) reached 15 per cent of GDP in 2012. Since 2015, social spending has declined to 8.3 per cent of GDP, excluding pensions (2017 and 2018 federal budgets), and redistributive spending to 12.6 per cent. Mexico's size of social spending in relation to GDP is below the average for a group of thirty low- and middle-income countries (Lustig 2018b).

4.2 Redistributive Effects of the Fiscal System: Inequality and Poverty

Figure 8.6 shows the effects of fiscal policy on the Gini coefficient for the period 1996–2014. From 1996 to 2006, the analysis includes the spending side only. From 2008 to 2014, the effects of taxes (personal and indirect) have been incorporated. The results for 2015 are produced by simulating the switch from subsidizing to taxing gasoline consumption implemented in this year on the 2014 fiscal incidence exercise. In the figure, we show the change in the Gini coefficient from market income plus pensions to the income concepts described in Figure 8.4. For the period 1996–2008, one can observe a notable increase in the equalizing effect of direct cash transfers up to 2000 followed by a reduction of this effect (shown by the line that traces the change from market income plus pensions to gross income). In contrast, the equalizing effect of education and health spending estimated at 2.6 percentage points in 1996 rose throughout.

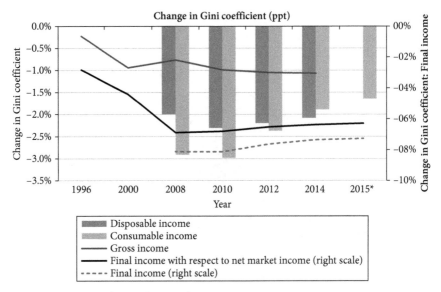

Figure 8.6 Fiscal policy and inequality, 1996–2015

Note: *The 2015 estimate considers the effect of the increase in net indirect taxes in that year, using the 2014 survey and assuming the rest of the fiscal system remains the same as in 2014. The redistributive effect for final income appears on the right-hand scale. The definition of income concepts is shown in Figure 8.4. Gross income equals market income plus pensions plus direct transfers. 'ppt' means percentage points.

Source: Based on Scott et al. (2017).

For the 2008–14 period, in which the analysis comprehends both the tax and the spending sides, the total redistributive effect is modest and declines after 2010: with respect to market income plus pensions, inequality in disposable income fell by 2.3 percentage points in 2010 and 2 percentage points in 2014, while consumable income inequality fell by 3 percentage points in 2010 and 1.9 percentage points in 2014 (1.6 in the 2015 simulation). Adding in-kind transfers such as education and health valued at average cost to the government has a larger redistributive effect. The latter was estimated at 6.9 percentage points in 2008 and declined thereafter, but it is still considerably higher than it was in 1996, as shown by the solid line for final income with respect to net market income.

The marginal contribution of direct transfers (measured by the change in gross income Gini with respect to market income plus pensions) is equalizing; it rose during the 1996–2000 period and remained unchanged for the rest of the period. In contrast to previous years, by 2014 the marginal contribution of net indirect subsidies is unequalizing: that is, the fiscally induced decline in inequality would have been higher if there were no net indirect taxes.

How does Mexico compare with other low- and middle-income countries? Lustig (2018b) shows results for a set of thirty countries from around 2010 from the Commitment to Equity (CEQ) Institute's Data Center. Mexico (2012) ranks in the top third of countries and, for the scenario with contributory pensions as deferred income, its redistributive effect is slightly above the average (blue horizontal line); it is about average for the scenario that assumes contributory pensions are a pure government transfer (red horizontal line).

It is important to stress that the effects of a fiscal system on inequality and poverty are distinct. As shown in Lustig (2018b), while fiscal systems are equalizing for a group of thirty low- and middle-income countries, they are poverty-increasing in a number of them because what the poor pay in taxes exceeds what they receive in transfers. In Mexico, the fiscal system has been both equalizing and poverty-reducing. However, as shown in Figure 8.7, the effect on poverty has been falling over time and, if the simulated results for 2015 are an accurate description of the effects of switching from subsidizing to taxing gasoline consumption, the fiscal system may have switched to a poverty-increasing one (consumable income poverty surpasses market income poverty).

The effect of direct transfers on extreme poverty increased from a reduction of less than 0.5 percentage points in 1996 to more than 2 percentage points in 2012 and 2014 (using the US$2.5 international poverty line). This represents some 2.4 million persons out of poverty as an effect of direct transfers. Once we add net indirect taxes (consumable income), however, this gain is significantly reduced, except in 2008, when gasoline subsidies reached an all-time high and net subsidies actually reduced poverty with respect to disposable income (Figure 8.7). By 2014, when gasoline subsidies had been almost completely eliminated, net indirect taxes erased the poverty effect of direct transfers and increased extreme poverty by more than 1.4 percentage points. By 2015, when gasoline subsidies

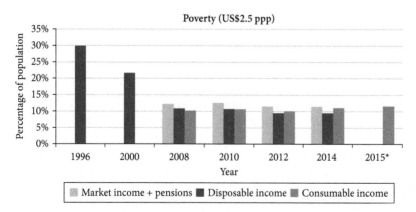

Figure 8.7 Fiscal policy and poverty, 2008–15

Note: Poverty measured by the incidence (headcount ratio). *The 2015 estimate considers the effect of the increase in net indirect taxes in that year using the 2014 survey and assuming the rest of the fiscal system is constant as in 2014.

Source: Authors' illustration based on Scott et al. (2017).

gave way to a large gasoline tax, the impoverishing effect of net indirect taxes increased by 2.5 percentage points, with some three million persons added to the extremely poor category.

5 Main Conclusions and Policy Implications

With a Gini coefficient hovering around 0.5, Mexico belongs to the group of countries in the world with high levels of income inequality. When data is corrected for under-coverage and under-reporting of top incomes using tax registries, concentration at the top becomes even more pronounced.

The evolution of income inequality during the 1989–2014 period can be summarized as follows: between 1989 and 1994, inequality increased; between 1994 and 2006, inequality declined; and between 2006 and 2014, inequality seemed to be on the rise again. The key component that underlies the 'rise–decline–rise again' pattern is the evolution of labour income inequality. Labour income inequality seems to be influenced in particular by the evolution of the skill premium. During the period 1989–94, driven by both market forces (demand for skills) and institutional factors (real minimum wage and unionization rate fell), the skill premium rose. During the period of declining labour income inequality (1994–2006), the skill premium declined. The latter was not driven by institutional factors because the real minimum wage and unionization rate remained flat. The increase in supply of workers with at least high school degrees, over and above the increase in their demand, appears to have driven the decline in returns to higher skills. Lastly, during the 2006–14 period, as we saw, inequality appeared to be on the rise again.

Given the patterns observed in the dynamics of labour income inequality, two key policy implications emerge. First, continuing the expansion of access to higher levels of education is key, as long as it is of reasonable quality. Second, minimum wages should be gradually increased towards the levels they were at before they started to decline in the 1980s. Given the large size of Mexico's informal labour market, however, care must be taken that the minimum wage increases do not exacerbate it. There are a whole set of reforms that should be undertaken in social policy to address informality, as discussed by Levy (2018).

Direct cash transfers are largely targeted at the poor. However, in spite of the expansion of targeted programmes since the second half of the 1990s, their effect remains limited because of their small scale (relative to the fiscal system and to market household income). As a result, while the combination of taxes, transfers, and spending on education and health has a significant redistributive effect on final income inequality, it has a relatively more modest one on disposable or consumable income inequality (which only captures the effect of direct cash transfers and direct and indirect taxes, not spending on education and health). Moreover, the redistributive effect has declined significantly since 2010, as transfers have become less progressive and net indirect taxes have increased.

The modest redistributive impact of Mexico's fiscal system is not due to a particularly high indirect tax burden (even after the recent increase, Mexico lags behind most countries), nor to limited revenues, but to a minimal allocation of these resources to cash transfers benefiting the poor. Even at their peak (2014), these transfers represented just 0.8 per cent of GDP, transferring 0.35 per cent of GDP to the poorest quintile (which roughly corresponds to the extreme poor). However, the expansion of net indirect taxes after 2012 has in effect cancelled out the increase in benefits to the poor associated with the expansion of direct transfers over the previous decade (2002–12).

What would be an optimal redistributive fiscal reform for Mexico in this context? An obvious reform would be to increase cash transfers through the flagship conditional cash transfer programme (*PROSPERA*), until recently the most effectively targeted transfer instrument available in Mexico, with significant coverage. Given the coverage that this programme had achieved (six million households, or a fifth of the population), and the possible economic disincentives that a significant expansion in the level of transfers per beneficiary might entail, a major expansion, which preserves its current targeting and effectiveness, may be difficult to implement. Recent efforts to introduce new components into the programme to increase the productive capacities of its beneficiaries have been frustrated by the institutional and operational difficulties of implementing such a complex component on a large scale.

Perhaps the time has come to consider more universal transfers. Based on Scott (2017), Scott et al. (2017) simulate the redistributive potential of the simplest, cheapest (in terms of targeting, administrative, and participation costs), and least distortionary transfer possible: a universal, non-targeted, non-conditional transfer. This may be interpreted as a universal basic income designed to eliminate extreme poverty or as a universal, non-contributory, social protection system designed to achieve full coverage and eliminate the gaps in social protection associated with informality. The authors find that in spite of the absence of targeting, if all the resources devoted to non-progressive transfers could be reallocated to the universal basic income scheme, this reform would be highly progressive in the context of Mexico's high market income inequality.

An alternative and bolder policy scenario would be to increase the size of the universal basic income to equal the average poverty gap in 2014 (instead of keeping it equal to the total current budget allocated to transfers divided by the population). According to Scott et al. (2017), the fiscal cost of this basic income would be 2.87 per cent of GDP. Although this would represent a significant commitment in the context of Mexico's limited tax revenues, it is still below both the recent increase in net indirect taxes and the current tax-financed transfers to the contributory pension systems. To make this change budget neutral, the authors consider two scenarios: relying on the use of oil revenues or increasing direct taxes. Under either, extreme poverty measured with consumable income would be reduced by an estimated 2 percentage points, taking approximately two million additional people out of extreme poverty. The incidence of direct personal income taxes for the top 10 per cent would have to rise from roughly 8 per cent to 13 per cent, an order of magnitude which seems reasonable given the enormous concentration of income and wealth at the top and the relatively low burden of direct personal and wealth taxes for the richest group within the top.

A more realistic and potentially effective alternative would be to combine the best of both worlds by targeting the poorest and most vulnerable as population groups—poor localities, indigenous population, senior citizens, infants, the disabled, unemployed youth—but offering transfers universally within these groups.

References

Airola, J., and C. Juhn (2005). 'Wage inequality in post-reform Mexico'. IZA Discussion Papers 1525. Bonn: Institute for the Study of Labour (IZA).

Almeida dos Reis, J., and R. Paes de Barros (1991). 'Wage Inequality and the Distribution of Education: A Study of the Evolution of Regional Differences in Inequality in Metropolitan Brazil'. *Journal of Development Economics*, 36(1): 117–43.

Alvaredo, F., S. Garriga, and F. Pinto (2017). 'Household Surveys, Administrative Records, and National Accounts in Mexico 2009–2014. Is a reconciliation possible?' Paris: Paris School of Economics. Unpublished paper.

Atkin, D. (2016). 'Endogenous Skill Acquisition and Export Manufacturing in Mexico'. *American Economic Review*, 106(8): 2046–85.

Bosch, M., and M. Manacorda (2010). 'Minimum Wages and Earnings Inequality in Urban Mexico'. *American Economic Journal: Applied Economics*, 2(4): 128–49.

Bouillon, C., A. Legovini, and N. Lustig (1999). 'Can education explain income inequality changes in Mexico?' Inter-American Development Bank Draft. Washington, DC: Inter-American Development Bank.

Bouillon, C.P. (2000a). *Inequality and Mexico's Labor Market after Trade Reform*. Inter-American Development Bank and Georgetown University Technical Report. Washington, DC: Inter-American Development Bank and Georgetown University.

Bouillon, C.P. (2000b). *Returns to Education, Sector Premiums, and Male Wage Inequality in Mexico*. Inter-American Development Bank Technical Report. Washington, DC: Inter-American Development Bank.

Bound, J., and G. Johnson (1992). 'Changes in the Structure of Wages in the 1980s: An Evaluation of Alternative Explanations'. *The American Economic Review*, 82(3): 371–92.

Bourguignon, F., F.H.G. Ferreira, and N. Lustig (2005). *The Microeconomics of Income Distribution Dynamics in East Asia and Latin America*. Washington, DC: Oxford University Press.

Campos-Vazquez, R., G. Esquivel, and N. Lustig (2014). 'The Rise and Fall of Income Inequality in Mexico, 1989–2010'. In G.A. Cornia (ed.), *Falling Inequality in Latin America: Policy Changes and Lessons*. New York: Oxford University Press.

Campos-Vazquez, R., L.F. Lopez-Calva, and N. Lustig (2016). 'Declining Wages for College-educated Workers in Mexico: Are Younger or Older Cohorts Hurt the Most?' *Revista de Economía Mundial*, 43: 93–112.

Campos-Vazquez, R., and N. Lustig (2017). 'Labour Income Inequality in Mexico: Puzzles Solved and Unsolved'. WIDER Working Paper 2017/186. Helsinki, UNU-WIDER.

Campos-Vazquez, R.M. (2013). 'Why Did Wage Inequality Decrease in Mexico after NAFTA?' *Economía Mexicana Nueva Época*, 22(2): 245–78.

CONEVAL (2017a). Evolución de las dimensiones de la pobreza 1990–2016 [Evolution of the Dimensions of Poverty, 1990–2016]. Available at: https://www.coneval.org.mx/Medicion/Paginas/Evolucion-de-las-dimensiones-de-pobreza.aspx (accessed October 2017).

CONEVAL (2017b). *Inventario CONEVAL de programas y acciones federales de desarrollo social* [CONEVAL Inventory of Federal Programmes and Actions in Social Development]. Available at: https://www.coneval.org.mx/Evaluacion/IPFE/Paginas/historico.aspx (accessed November 2017).

Cortez, W.W. (2001). 'What is Behind Increasing Wage Inequality in Mexico?' *World Development*, 29(11): 1905–22.

Cragg, M.I., and M. Epelbaum (1996). 'Why Has Wage Dispersion Grown in Mexico? Is It the Incidence of Reforms or the Growing Demand for Skills?' *Journal of Development Economics*, 51(1): 99–116.

DiNardo, J., N.M. Fortin, and T. Lemieux (1996). 'Labour Market Institutions and the Distribution of Wages, 1973–1992: A Semiparametric Approach'. *Econometrica*, 64(5): 1001–44.

Escobar Toledo, S. (2014). 'Salarios Mínimos: Desiguladad y Desarrollo'. *Economía UNAM*, 11(3): 94–109.

Esquivel, G. (2011). 'The Dynamics of Income Inequality in Mexico since NAFTA'. *Economía*, 12(1): 155–79.

Esquivel, G., N. Lustig, and J. Scott (2010). 'Mexico: A Decade of Falling Inequality: Market Forces or State Action?'. In L.F. Lopez and N. Lustig (eds), *Declining Inequality in Latin America: A Decade of Progress?* Washington, DC: Brookings Institution Press and New York: United Nations Development Programme.

Esquivel, G., and J.A. Rodríguez-Lopez (2003). 'Technology, Trade, and Wage Inequality in Mexico Before and After NAFTA'. *Journal of Development Economics*, 72(2): 543–65.

Fairris, D. (2003). 'Unions and Wage Inequality in Mexico'. *Industrial and Labour Relations Review*, 56(3): 481–97.

Fairris, D., and E. Levine (2004). 'La disminución del poder sindical en Mexico'. *El Trimestre Económico*, 71(284): 847–76.

Fairris, D., G. Popli, and E. Zepeda (2008). 'Minimum Wages and the Wage Structure in Mexico'. *Review of Social Economy*, 66(2): 181–208.

Feenstra, R., and G. Hanson (1997). 'Foreign Direct Investment and Relative Wages: Evidence from Mexico's Maquiladoras'. *Journal of International Economics*, 42(3): 371–93.

Feliciano, Z.M. (2001). 'Workers and Trade Liberalization: The Impact of Trade Reforms in Mexico on Wages and Employment'. *Industrial and Labour Relations Review*, 55(1): 95–115.

Firpo, S., N. Fortin, and T. Lemieux (2009). 'Unconditional Quantile Regressions'. *Econometrica*, 77(3): 953–73.

Gasparini, L., S. Galiani, G. Cruces, and P. Acosta (2011). 'Educational Upgrading and Returns to Skills in Latin America. Evidence from a Supply–Demand Framework'. World Bank Policy Research Working Paper 5921. Washington, DC: World Bank.

Halliday, T., D. Lederman, and R. Robertson (2016). 'Tracking wage inequality trends with prices and different trade models: evidence from Mexico'. IZA Discussion Paper 10156. Bonn: IZA.

Hanson, G.H. (2003). 'What has happened to wages in Mexico since NAFTA? Implications for hemispheric free trade'. NBER Working Paper 9563. Cambridge, MA: National Bureau of Economic Research.

Hanson, G., and A. Harrison (1999). 'Trade Liberalization and Wage Inequality in Mexico'. *ILR Review*, 52(2): 271–88.

INEGI (1989, 1992, 1994, 1996, 1998, 2000, 2002, 2004, 2006, 2008, 2010, 2012, 2014). *Encuesta Nacional de Ingresos y Gastos de los Hogares* (ENIGH) [National Survey of Household Income and Expenditure]. Mexico: Instituto Nacional de Estadística y Geografía (INEGI).

Juhn, C., K. Murphy, and B. Pierce (1993). 'Wage Inequality and the Rise in Returns to Skill'. *Journal of Political Economy*, 3(3): 410–48.

Kaplan, D.S., and F. Perez-Arce Novaro (2006). 'El Efecto de los Salarios Mínimos en los Ingresos Labourales en México'. *El Trimestre Económico*, 73(289): 139–73.

Komives, J., A. Halpern, and J. Scott (2009). 'Residential electricity subsidies in Mexico. Exploring options for reform and for enhancing the impact on the poor'. Working Paper 160/2009. Washington, DC: World Bank.

Kurokawa, Y. (2011). 'Is a Skill Intensity Reversal a Mere Theoretical Curiosum? Evidence from the US and Mexico'. *Economics Letters*, 112(2): 151–4.

Legovini, A., C. Bouillon, and N. Lustig (2005). 'Can Education Explain Changes in Income Inequality in Mexico?' In F. Bourguignon, F.H.G. Ferreira, and N. Lustig (eds), *The Microeconomics of Income Distribution Dynamics*. Washington, DC: World Bank and New York, NY: Oxford University Press.

Levy, S. (2018). *Under-rewarded Efforts. The Elusive Quest for Prosperity in Mexico*. Washington, DC: Inter-American Development Bank.

Levy, S., and L.F. Lopez-Calva (2016). 'Labour Earnings, Misallocation, and the Returns to Education in Mexico'. IDB Working Paper Series 671. Washington, DC: Inter-American Development Bank.

Lopez-Acevedo, G. (2004). 'Mexico: Evolution of Earnings Inequality and Rates of Returns to Education (1988–2002)'. *Estudios Económicos*, 38(19): 211–84.

Lopez-Acevedo, G. (2006). 'Mexico: two decades of the evolution of education and inequality'. World Bank Policy Research Working Paper 3919. Washington, DC: World Bank.

Lustig, N. (2018a). 'Measuring the Distribution of Household Income, Consumption and Wealth: State of Play and Measurement Challenges'. In M. Durand, J. Paul Fitoussi, and J.E. Stiglitz (eds), *For Good Measure: Advancing Research on Well-Being Metrics Beyond GDP*. OECD report by the High Level Expert Group on Measuring Economic Performance and Social Progress. Paris: OECD Publishing.

Lustig, N. (2018b). 'Fiscal Policy, Income Redistribution, and Poverty Reduction in Low- and Middle-Income Countries'. In N. Lustig (ed.) *Commitment to Equity Handbook: Estimating the Impact of Fiscal Policy on Inequality and Poverty*. Washington, DC: Brookings Institution Press and New Orleans, LA: CEQ Institute, Tulane University.

Lustig, N., and S. Higgins (2018). 'The CEQ Assessment: Measuring the Impact of Fiscal Policy on Inequality and Poverty'. In N. Lustig (ed.) *Commitment to Equity Handbook: Estimating the Impact of Fiscal Policy on Inequality and Poverty*. Washington, DC: Brookings Institution Press and New Orleans, LA: CEQ Institute, Tulane University.

Machado, J.A.F., and J. Mata (2005). 'Counterfactual Decomposition of Changes in Wage Distributions using Quantile Regression'. *Journal of Applied Econometrics*, 20(4): 445–65.

Meza González, L. (1999). 'Cambios en la Estructura Salarial de México en el Período 1988–1993 y el Aumento en el Rendimiento de la Educación Superior'. *El Trimestre Económico*, 66(262): 189–226.

Mishra, P. (2007). 'Emigration and Wages in Source Countries: Evidence from Mexico'. *Journal of Development Economics*, 82(1): 180–99.

Parker, S.W., and P.E. Todd (2017). 'Conditional Cash Transfers: The Case of PROGRESA/*Oportunidades*'. *Journal of Economic Literature*, 55(3): 866–915.

Popli, G.K. (2011). 'Changes in Human Capital and Wage Inequality in Mexico'. *Oxford Development Studies*, 39(3): 369–87.

Robertson, R. (2004). 'Relative Prices and Wage Inequality: Evidence from Mexico'. *Journal of International Economics*, 64(2): 387–409.

Robertson, R. (2007). 'Trade and Wages: Two Puzzles from Mexico'. *The World Economy*, 30(9): 1378–98.

Scott, J. (2002). 'High Inequality, Low Revenue: Redistributive Efficiency of Latin American Fiscal Policy in Comparative Perspective'. Paper prepared for the conference 'Fiscal Aspects of Social Programs: Studies on Poverty and Social Protection, Regional Policy Dialogue, Poverty Reduction, and Social Protection Network'. Inter-American Development Bank. Available at: https://idbdocs.iadb. org/wsdocs/getdocument.aspx?docnum=616098.

Scott, J. (2004). Eficiencia redistributiva de los programas contra la pobreza en México. [Redistributive Efficiency of Anti-Poverty Programmes in Mexico]. Working Paper 330. Mexico City: Economics Division, CIDE.

Scott, J. (2005). 'Social Security and Inequality in Mexico: From Polarization to Universality'. *Well-Being and Social Policy*, 1: 59–82.

Scott, J. (2009a). 'Gasto Público y Desarrollo Humano en México: Análisis de Incidencia y Equidad'. Working paper for Informe de Desarrollo Humano de México 2008–2009. Mexico: PNUD.

Scott, J. (2009b). 'The incidence of agricultural subsidies in Mexico'. Paper for the project 'Agricultural Trade Adjustment and Rural Poverty: Transparency, Accountability, and Compensatory Programs in Mexico'. Washington, DC: Mexico Institute, Woodrow Wilson International Center for Scholars. Available at: https:// www.wilsoncenter.org/index.cfm?fuseaction=topics.homeand%20topic_id=5949

Scott, J. (2014). 'Redistributive Impact and Efficiency of Mexico's Fiscal System'. *Public Finance Review*, 42(3): 368–90.

Scott, J. (2017). *Las posibilidades de un sistema de renta básica en México* [The Possibilities of a Basic Income System in Mexico]. A study for the Instituto Belisario Dominguez. Available at: http://bibliodigitalibd.senado.gob.mx/handle/123456789/3564 (accessed November 2017).

Scott, J., R. Aranda, and E. de la Rosa (2017). 'Inequality and fiscal redistribution in Mexico: 1992–2015'. WIDER Working Paper 2017/194. Helsinki: UNU-WIDER.

Scott, J., and C. Hernandez (2018). 'From Food Subsidies to Targeted Transfers in Mexico'. In H. Alderman, U. Gentilini, and R. Yemtsov (eds), *The 1.5 Billion People Question: Food, Vouchers, or Cash Transfers?* Washington, DC: World Bank.

9

South Africa

The Top End, Labour Markets, Fiscal Redistribution, and the Persistence of Very High Inequality

Murray Leibbrandt, Vimal Ranchhod, and Pippa Green

1 Introduction

South Africa is widely recognized as one of the most unequal countries in the world.[1] This has been the case since the advent of the post-apartheid era. Throughout, inequality has been seen as a clear indicator of a society with a long history of explicitly privileging a small minority of its population and explicitly disadvantaging the vast majority in every aspect of its socioeconomic development.

The contemporary inequality literature is unambiguous about the fact that such extremely high levels of inequality are detrimental to a country's development path and stifle a country's potential. Although much of this literature is recent, in 1994 there was an intuitive sense of the social and economic sub-optimalities of the embedded spatial inequalities and many inequalities of opportunity that history bequeathed to South Africa's new democracy. It is hardly surprising, then, that clear evidence of substantial progress in transitioning to a more equal society has served as the key metric of progress on building a new, inclusive South Africa. Given this, the post-apartheid period has seen substantial policy attention being devoted to addressing this situation and a substantial literature has developed to measure and track progress on inequality reduction.[2]

In the context of a South African economy that was mostly in a slow but steady growth phase from the mid-1990s until the late 2000s, a number of proactive policies

[1] The authors are especially grateful to UNU-WIDER for the support, and participants at a special session on the Inequality in the Giants project at the UNU-WIDER Development Conference *Think Development—Think WIDER* held in Helsinki, Finland, September 2018, for their helpful comments and insights. Murray Leibbrandt acknowledges support from the Research Chairs Initiative of the South African National Research Foundation, and from the South African Department of Science and Technology, which funds his Chair in Poverty and Inequality Research.
[2] See Leibbrandt et al. (2016) for a detailed summary of the research work, and Inchauste et al. (2015) for a detailed review of fiscal policy.

Murray Leibbrandt, Vimal Ranchhod, and Pippa Green, *South Africa: The Top End, Labour Markets, Fiscal Redistribution, and the Persistence of Very High Inequality* In: *Inequality in the Developing World*. Edited by: Carlos Gradín, Murray Leibbrandt, and Finn Tarp, Oxford University Press (2021). © United Nations University World Institute for Development Economics Research (UNU-WIDER). DOI: 10.1093/oso/9780198863960.003.0009

were put in place. As reviewed by Leibbrandt et al. (2010), cash grants were rolled out for millions of pensioners and children; housing, water, and electrification policies saw rapid improvements in access to these assets; and education policies led to levels of educational attainment increasing markedly among younger cohorts.

These policies are important prongs in any anti-inequality programme. Yet despite this, there was little or no progress in reducing income inequality. The evolution of the labour market is key to understanding this lack of success. During the growth phase, the number of net new jobs also increased significantly, but labour force participation rates increased faster than the rate at which new jobs were created. Thus the unemployment rate increased from 14 per cent in 1993 to 23 per cent in 2008 using the narrow definition.[3] At the same time, the skills composition of labour demand changed in such a way that unskilled workers saw a net decline in jobs. While unskilled workers were more likely to become unemployed, the returns to a tertiary qualification increased, which resulted in an even wider earnings distribution among those who were employed.

These dynamics had a direct bearing on rising inequality and led to a situation in which extensive policy efforts did not translate into equivalent results. Levy et al. (2014: 26) point out that 'relative to other middle-income countries, South Africa has an unusually small fraction of the population that gains directly from sustained economic growth'.

Table 9.1 shows that annual growth has slowed significantly since the global financial crisis in 2007–8. The decline in the growth rate limits the freedom for further possible expansion of progressive social spending. Coupled with the previously high levels of fiscal debt and a large fiscal deficit, these macro indicators suggest, at most, limited room for further expansion of existing fiscal policies to effect greater redistribution. In order to significantly reduce poverty, unemployment, and inequality, the National Development Plan (National Planning Commission n.d.) planned for an average annual growth rate of 5.4 per cent until 2030. It is clear from Table 9.1 that recent growth rates have fallen short of this.

Table 9.1 Real annual growth rates in South Africa since 1990

Year	Growth rate (%)	Year	Growth rate (%)
1995–9	2.59	2011	3.28
2000–4	3.61	2012	2.21
2005–7	5.41	2013	2.49
2008–10	1.56	2014	1.85

Source: Based on data in Hundenborn et al. (2018b: Table 1).

[3] This statistic masks the full extent of the unemployment problem, as discouraged workers are excluded from the official unemployment rate. Including discouraged workers in the definition of unemployment raises the 2008 statistic to about 32 per cent.

Thus, rather than making progress, the past decade has been a time of economic hardship for many South Africans. The unemployment rate increased to nearly 28 per cent in 2018, up from 22 per cent in 2007. Unemployment has affected young people disproportionately: just over half of all young people are unemployed. This is a much more unfavourable environment in which to have to ramp up a strategy to overcome inequality. Indeed, this most recent decade has seen no additional substantial interventions and even some loss of focus and progress on the matrix of policies that were put in place in the 1990s.

This is the socioeconomic context within which the studies were produced for the South African case study within the Giants project.[4] We have sought to make two major contributions through our studies for this project. First, we contribute to the descriptive literature on contemporary South African inequality by using new data in best-practice ways. Second, in our analysis we try to move from description to understanding the drivers of income and earnings inequality. This is more analytically challenging, but it is these drivers that are the key bridge into policy.[5] This chapter synthesizes findings from these studies on South African income inequality as well as other recent relevant literature on South Africa.

We start by profiling changes in household income inequality over the post-apartheid period. Static and dynamic decomposition methods show there have been a number of changes to labour demand and supply, but that these labour market dynamics continue to dominate and drive South Africa's income inequality. This would have had an even more pernicious effect had it not been for the equalizing effects of the roll-out of our social grants, although the impact of these grants has plateaued over the last decade.

By merging tax data with income and earnings data from household surveys we are able to add analysis of the upper tail of the income distribution. Analysis of this augmented income distribution makes it clear that, since the 2008 recession, people at the top end of the income distribution have experienced much higher growth rates in both real labour-market earnings and real household incomes compared with those in the middle or bottom of the income distribution. This implies a worsening of South African inequality prior to taxes and transfers. We add further detail on the drivers of this market income distribution by modelling changes in earnings inequality. The key drivers of a widening earnings distribution are seen to be increasing returns to experience combined with an increased rate of return to tertiary qualifications.

Moving to policy, the redistributive impact of the contemporary fiscal system is described through a fiscal incidence study that updates earlier studies of a

---

[4] There are four core studies: Hundenborn et al. (2018a, 2018b); Maboshe and Woolard (2018); Finn and Leibbrandt (2018).

[5] Many of these exercises are similar to those undertaken in other country studies, thus allowing for comparability of within-country inequality dynamics. See the project's page on the UNU-WIDER website: www.wider.unu.edu/project/inequality-giants.

similar nature and then probes new areas. This work confirms that the substantial system of social grants is well targeted and highly progressive. On the tax side, direct personal income taxes are seen to be highly progressive. However, our research shows that the allowance of certain tax benefits (exemptions) for health insurance and pension fund contributions is regressive in terms of their impact on inequality.

The aggregate conclusion from this systematic stock-take confirms that South Africa has not made progress over the past decade in the fight against inequality. We probe this further, drawing on research that uses nationally representative panel data to explore social mobility over this period.

In concluding, we reflect on further research and potential policy options that may undergird more successful strategies to overcome South Africa's inequality.

2 The Drivers of Post-Apartheid Income Inequality

As a useful framing of how inequality has changed over the post-apartheid period, Hundenborn et al. (2018a) use nationally representative household surveys from 1993, 2008, and 2014 to describe levels of inequality and analyse changes in inequality. The 2008 and 2014 situations are derived from National Income Dynamics Study (NIDS) data, and 1993 is described using data from the Project for Statistics on Living Standards and Development, collected at the dawn of the democracy. Both datasets collect detailed information on different income sources for both households and individuals.

Table 9.2 draws on these datasets to show that households potentially have multiple sources of income. In South Africa the predominant sources of household income are labour market income, government grants, remittances, and investment income. Of these, the single largest component (on average) by far is labour market income, followed by government grants. Comparable data for income from subsistence agriculture and rental of property are not available and these sources are omitted from this comparison and all analysis in this chapter.[6]
Labour market income is earned as salaries or from self-employment of household members. It accounts for the largest proportion of household income, and the proportion of households who earn some income in the labour market has increased since 1993, from 60.5 per cent of income to 73 per cent. Measured in 2014 real rands per capita, average labour market income in households has increased over this interval from R1,078 to R1,972.

---

[6] From periods in which we have decent data for these income sources, it seems that neither contribute substantial sources of household income. That said, it is important to note that, by rental income, we mean income from properties that have been let out for cash. The effects of imputed rental income—i.e. the implicit income derived from living in one's own property—may well be substantial. This income source is also excluded as its measurement cannot be made comparable over time.

Table 9.2 Income components in per capita terms (real 2014 prices, rand)

Variable	1993	2008	2014
Total household (HH) income			
Mean of HH income	1,328.17	2,062.68	2,398.57
Gini of HH income	0.68	0.69	0.66
Labour income			
Mean of labour income	1,078.18	1,659.86	1,971.98
Share in total HH income (%)	83.6	74.5	73.0
Proportion of HHs receiving labour income (%)	60.5	64.4	72.6
Gini of labour income	0.73	0.76	0.73
Income from government grants			
Mean of government grants	86.17	161.31	187.34
Share in total HH income (%)	3.4	15.6	16.4
Proportion of HHs receiving government grants (%)	23.5	56.3	68.0
Gini of government grants	0.92	0.78	0.76
Income from remittances			
Mean of remittance income	50.56	86.69	93.94
Share in total HH income (%)	4.6	3.6	6.1
Proportion of HHs receiving remittances (%)	22.2	13.9	38.3
Gini of remittances	0.91	0.97	0.91
Investment income			
Mean of investment income	113.28	154.81	145.31
Share in total HH income (%)	8.3%	6.3	4.5
Proportion of HHs receiving investment income (%)	3.5	5.6	23.3
Gini of investment income	0.99	0.97	0.98
N unweighted	39,180	28,225	37,965
N weighted	39,020,805	49,295,750	54,941,051

Source: Based on data in Hundenborn et al. (2018b: Table 1).

Government grants include the child support and old-age grant most notably, but also include a sickness and disability grant, a veterans' grant, and a social relief of distress grant. The proportion of households receiving grants has increased from 23.5 per cent in 1993 to 68 per cent in 2014, suggesting a substantial increase in access to grants since the end of apartheid. Moreover, grant income has increased as a proportion of total income, from 3.4 per cent in 1993 to 16.4 per cent in 2014. Investment income is a source of income for an increasing proportion of households over the period, up from 3.5 per cent of households in 1993 to 23 per cent of households in 2014. Although the average income from this source has increased since 1993, it has declined as a share of overall income. This implies that the returns to other sources of income have grown more rapidly.

Overall, remittances account for a very small share of household income. Nonetheless, the share of household income accounted for by remittances increased from 4.6 per cent to 6.1 per cent by 2014.

Table 9.3 Household composition from 1993 to 2014

Variable	1993	2008	2014
Household size	4.38	3.53	3.21
Number of adults in HH	2.81	2.70	2.59
Number of employed in HH	1.08	0.96	1.02
Share of adults in HH	0.73	0.88	0.95
Share of employed in HH	0.37	0.38	0.46

Source: Based on data in Hundenborn et al. (2018b: Table 2).

Household income is also affected by changes in household composition. Table 9.3 profiles these changes. While the number of people of working age per household has decreased, the share of working-age people in households has increased. This implies that households have become smaller, and that working-age persons account for a larger proportion within them. There has not been any significant change in the number of employed people per household, although the decrease in household size results in an increase in the share of those employed per household.

Coupled with the changes in income, where the average amount of all sources increased over the period, the changes in household composition result in even greater increases in mean household income per capita. On average, as shown in Table 9.2, mean household income per capita has grown from R1,328 to R2,399. Inequality decreased slightly between 1993 and 2014, although it remained remarkably high. Income inequality increased from 1993 to 2008, with corresponding Gini coefficients of 0.68 and 0.69. The coefficient then dropped to 0.66 by 2014.

There is a long tradition in South Africa of using static income source decomposition techniques to extend these income profiles to look at the drivers of inequality.[7] This chapter replicates this static analysis for 1993, 2008, and 2014, and affirms the standard results of this literature. From the static decompositions, we estimate that between 1993 and 2014, labour market income is highly correlated with overall inequality and accounts for 84–90 per cent of the overall Gini coefficient.[8] Labour market income was by far the most important determinant of household income inequality. This replication work was not our primary focus in this chapter. Rather, we applied some newly developed dynamic decomposition techniques that allow us to add an understanding of how the various *changes* in income sources explain the *changes* in inequality.[9] These results

---

[7] See review in Leibbrandt et al. (2012).

[8] This table is not included in this chapter. The estimates are from Hundenborn et al. (2018a: Table 3).

[9] This methodology was obtained from Azevedo et al. (2013), and essentially involves piece-wise and cumulative micro-simulations of the effects of observed changes in the various sub-categories of income on the aggregate Gini coefficient.

Table 9.4 Dynamic decompositions including household composition and re-rankings, 1993–2008

Variable	1993–2008		2008–14	
	Gini change	% change	Gini change	% change
Share of adults in HH	0.002	0.3	0.006	0.9
Share of employed in HH	−0.025	−3.7	0.007	1.0
One over employed	0.02	2.9	−0.003	−0.4
One over adults	0.007	1.0	0.004	0.6
Labour income				
Ranked by total HH income	0.045	6.6	−0.046	−6.7
Ranked by labour income	0.05	7.3	−0.046	−6.7
Government grants				
Ranked by total HH income	−0.041	−6.0	−0.006	−0.9
Ranked by government grants	−0.044	−6.5	−0.008	−1.2
Remittances				
Ranked by total HH income	0.005	0.7	−0.004	−0.6
Ranked by remittances	0.003	0.4	−0.006	−0.9
Investment				
Ranked by total HH income	−0.016	−2.3	−0.011	−.6
Ranked by investment	−0.02	−2.9	−0.002	−0.3

Source: Based on data in Hundenborn et al. (2018b: Tables 6 and 7).

are reported in Table 9.4. Given that income per capita is being used as the measure of well-being, these dynamic techniques can separate out the effects of demographic changes—driving the denominator—from the income changes—driving the numerator. While these demographic changes are not always highly influential in and of themselves, separating them from the contributions of the income sources decreases the contributions of these income sources substantially.

We turn now to the findings from the dynamic decompositions. The decompositions from 1993 to 2008 and from 2008 to 2014 are presented in Table 9.4. In the 1993–2008 period there is a very small total change in the Gini, from 0.68 to 0.69. In the 2008–14 period there is a sharper reduction in the Gini, from 0.69 to 0.655.

Despite the fact that the Gini barely changes in the first period, the dynamic decomposition shows that, on their own, labour market changes would have increased the Gini very strongly, by 6.6 per cent and even 7.3 per cent if allowance is made for the fact that improvements went to those higher up the distribution of labour incomes. After 2008, the disequalizing effect of labour-market income decreased. This does not mean that they became equalizing. Rather, the reduced impact of wages has a large role (almost half of one Gini point) to play in explaining the reduction in the Gini from 0.69 to 0.66.

Although government grants are a relatively small proportion of overall household income, they have played an important role in reducing inequality. Since 1993, the government has improved the targeting of grants and extended eligibility. These improvements in grant access were able to almost exactly offset the inequality-increasing effects of labour market income that took place between 1993 and 2008. This equalizing effect was even larger when allowance is made for the fact that the correlation of grant income with households in the bottom half of the income distribution improved between 1993 and 2008. From 2008 to 2014, grants continued to contribute to the overall decline in inequality, although their impact on further change was much smaller. Again, that this does not mean that grants are not a crucial equalizing income source. Rather, it means they did not become much more equalizing after 2008.

The effects on inequality of changes in remittance and investment income sources are found to be relatively small. Investment income contributed to inequality reductions and this effect was larger from 1993 to 2008 than it was from 2008 to 2014. Remittances are found to have the potential to reduce inequality because, in South Africa, they are an income source flowing to the bottom half of the distribution. But they have a small overall effect on changes in inequality. Between 1993 and 2008, remittance income actually increased inequality, while from 2008 to 2014 remittance income reduced inequality. This accords largely with the decrease in the share of households with remittance senders over the first period, and the reversal of this trend over the second. The average effect of the full period from 1993 to 2014 was negligible as the positive and negative effects cancelled one another out. Household composition changes also affected overall inequality. The increase in the number of adults in a household increased inequality by a small amount over the full period, while changes in the proportion of employed adults in a household were inequality-reducing from 1993 to 2008 and inequality-increasing from 2008 to 2014.

Nonetheless, the overall changes in inequality are largely driven by changes in the different income sources rather than by the demographic changes. Government grants have been shown to have been very important in dampening the increasing inequality between 1993 and 2008 and have continued to play a role in reducing inequality over the past decade. This recent role has been smaller, corresponding to the massive roll-out of the child support grants in the 2000s and their later stabilization. Both the strong inequality-reducing role of social grants and the plateauing of these are strongly affirmed in the paper by Maboshe and Woolard (2018) which we discuss later. This suggests that in addressing the intolerably high levels of inequality that remain after grants have been paid, the government will need to investigate policy alternatives beyond these existing cash transfers. As the most prominent contributor to the overall Gini coefficient, the labour market has to be a core focus of policies aiming to reduce inequality. We undertook detailed analysis of these labour market dynamics in this project and discuss this later in the chapter.

Before we shift the focus to the labour market and the distribution of earnings, we augment the discussion of household income inequality by summarizing and discussing new work that addresses the top end of the household income distribution. This is an important gap to fill in the discussion of income sources and total household income derived as the aggregation of these sources. Our analysis of these income sources has been based on survey data. Any frailties or omissions in these data are effectively embedded in the income source decompositions. There has been increasing recognition in recent years that the income sources that are particularly important to those at the top end of the income distribution—investment income being a good example—are likely to be understated by household survey data.

3 A New Focus on the Top End of the Income Distribution

Two recent studies, one produced for this project (Hundenborn et al. 2018b) and another produced alongside this project (Bassier and Woolard 2018), have added substantially to our understanding of two key dynamics: one is on the way the growth in top incomes have diverged from those of the rest of the population; the other is on the effects this particular growth path has had on inequality.

The effect of top incomes on income inequality is analysed in Hundenborn et al. (2018b), who use the same NIDS survey data that were used in earlier studies, as well as an important second source of data from the South African Revenue Services (SARS). This latter dataset comprises aggregate tax records as well as micro-files of anonymized individual records. The advantage of this second source is that the tax data are expected to measure top incomes more precisely (Alvaredo et al. 2017). Household surveys often miss or are forced to impute high earnings because many top earners either refuse to participate in the surveys, understate their incomes, or avoid the questions on income.

Figure 9.1 reflects the different details revealed by the NIDS and SARS data. In line with the international literature, we see that in 2014, for all individual incomes above R1 million per annum, NIDS underestimates incomes relative to the tax data by about 12 per cent for those over R5 million. Interestingly, it underestimates incomes consistently by about 30 per cent compared with the tax data from the 91st percentile of the income distribution upwards, though it appears to pick up a few large incomes at the top. South Africa has a relatively high mandatory filing threshold for personal income tax (PIT). Unsurprisingly, the figure shows that the PIT data do not reliably capture income below this threshold. The mandatory filing threshold in 2014 was R250,000 per year; in 2011 it was R120,000 per year. This represents the very top percentiles of income. Hundenborn et al. (2018b) write that, in 2014, the mandatory filing threshold was at the 97.5th percentile.

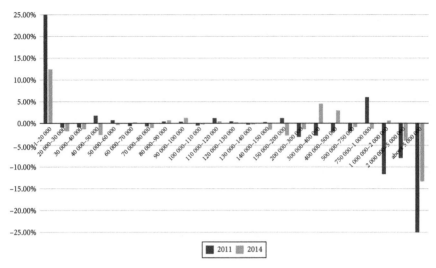

Figure 9.1 Difference in estimated mean taxable income between NIDS and PIT by income bracket

Source: Hundenborn et al. (2018b: Figure 1).

The careful work in the paper by Hundenborn et al. reveals some subtlety in the merging of the two datasets. We see that in some cases the household surveys actually overstate a particular bracket of top incomes: those between R750,000 and R1 million. Hundenborn et al. argue that this may be because NIDS is a panel survey with a high attrition rate of top earners. This results in the relatively few surviving individuals in the sample being more heavily weighted. This weighting effect will also accentuate any mismeasurement of these incomes in the surveys.

Table 9.5 reflects the impact of this data work on measured inequality using the Gini constructed from both survey data and administrative income tax data from SARS. It is important to remember that this measure only considers *taxable income*, which does not include income received as part of a government transfer (typically a payment from the government as part of a welfare programme).

The effect of combining the data on taxable income with household surveys is complex. The Gini coefficient of taxable income from household survey data fell marginally from 0.823 in 2011 to 0.813 in 2014. When these survey datasets were augmented in 2011 and 2014 to improve the statistical description of the taxable income at the top end, the augmented Gini was 0.832 in 2011 and 0.790 in 2014. The picture is very similar if the data are combined at the 99th percentile rather than at the tax threshold.

This chapter is complemented by recent work by Bassier and Woolard (2018), who drill down into the SARS data and household survey data to make two critical points. The first is that in the years between 2003 and 2015, nearly 60 per cent

Table 9.5 Gini coefficients at different thresholds

Threshold	2011	2011 data at the 2014 threshold	2014
Combining datasets at different filing thresholds			
Overall	0.832	0.826	0.790
Below filing threshold (NIDS)	0.762	0.783	0.735
Above filing threshold (PIT)	0.367	0.326	0.349
Combining datasets at the 99th percentile			
Overall	0.826	–	0.791
NIDS	0.782	–	0.742
PIT	0.328	–	0.343

Source: Based on data in Hundenborn et al. (2018b: Table 6).

of the population earned zero taxable income.[10] Over the same period, the incomes of the top 5 per cent of income earners increased by 5.1 per cent per annum. The second is that the growth in real incomes of the top 5 per cent after the 2008–9 recession was more than double the rate of growth of gross national income (GNI). In contrast, the incomes of the other 95 per cent either stagnated or, in the case of the bottom of the distribution, showed only slight growth. Between 2003 and 2016, the real incomes of the top 1 per cent almost doubled. And in the six years between 2010 and 2016, the income share of the top 1 per cent increased from 10.5 per cent to 12.6 per cent of GNI.

In addition, the top percentile in the income distribution, which starts at a taxable income of R800,000 per annum, has a much higher wealth-to-income ratio than the rest of the earnings distribution. Income from sources other than salaries increases rapidly in the top two percentiles. This is especially interesting given its salience with the argument made by Piketty (2014) that inequality increases when the rate of return to capital is greater than the rate of growth. So, the owners of capital accrue wealth faster, with the divergence growing stronger in periods of low growth. A second component of this fast, post-recession growth in top incomes is due to labour market dynamics in which high-skilled professionals at the top end of the income distribution have more bargaining power as they are not easily replaced. Also, technical changes in the economy may further favour this group.

In sum, then, the SARS data have been critical in understanding income inequality because the growth of top incomes relative to the rest of the distribution has a large but previously underexplored impact on measured inequality. The use of this database has also helped identify a greater number of top earners than was previously thought. For instance, in 2016 Credit Suisse estimated that there were about 45,000 dollar millionaires in the country, but Bassier and Woolard

---

[10] Some would have been recipients of government grants or would have been supported by other household members.

(2018) put the number at about 182,000. Hundenborn et al. (2018b) calculate that the number of people who earned over R10 million per year had more than doubled from 482 in 2011 to 1,048 in 2014.[11]

4 Earnings and the Labour Market: The Drivers of Earnings Inequality

The attention that we have given to assets and wealth at the top end of the income distribution is not meant to discount the importance of the labour market for the well-being of most of the South African population. Earlier our income decomposition analysis showed the dominance of labour market income in driving both levels of income inequality and changes in this inequality. Alongside its status as the highest income inequality country in the world, South Africa also has the highest earnings inequality. Thus, there is a clear need to understand the key factors driving this earnings inequality.

Finn and Leibbrandt (2018) start by reviewing a growing literature on earnings inequality in South Africa.[12] To add to this available literature, the chapter provides an in-depth study of the key changes in the South African earnings distribution over the period 2001–14 and then uses some modelling work to discern the impact of various factors on these changes on the inequality of earnings.

From 2001 to 2014, South Africa saw the average real earnings of workers rise from R5,740 to R7,951. Over the same period, however, wage increases went mostly to top earners, so overall inequality increased. As measured by the Gini coefficient, inequality was raised from 0.552 to 0.634, an atypically large increase. Before trying to analyse these changes, Finn and Leibbrandt (2018) flag an anomaly in the earnings data, which seem to change substantially after 2012. By Finn and Leibbrandt's measurements there is a sudden jump—of some 18 per cent—in inequality between 2011 and 2014. This is almost certainly an indication of a change in the method of data collection rather than actual forces in the labour market.

Indeed, in 2012 South African officials changed the way they measured key earnings variables, and Finn and Leibbrandt find that the earnings Gini floated in a band from 0.54 to 0.57 up to 2011, and in a much higher band between 0.63 and 0.66 after 2011. The chapter proceeds on the assumption that the trends in each of these sub-periods are correct but that the jump in inequality in 2012 is an artefact of the change in measurement. Thus, any analysis of trends in earning and earnings inequality that spans this break will overstate the change in inequality. Finn

---

[11] However, it should be borne in mind that, adjusting for inflation, R10 million in 2011 was valued at just below R8 million in 2014, which may account for some of this growth.
[12] Additional good reviews are provided by Wittenberg (2017a, 2017b, 2017c).

and Leibbrandt illustrate this point by showing that their modelling work yields notably different answers when it is allowed to span the break in the data. With due regard to this periodization, they use a re-centred influence function approach (Fortin et al. 2011) to establish which factors drive changes in the Gini coefficient of earnings between 2001 and 2014. Eight potential explanations are evaluated. These are: education, experience, unionization, informal sector, race, gender, geographic location, and sector.

Table 9.6 profiles the labour market over the relevant period. We see that mean years of education of wage earners increased by almost two full years between 2000–14, while unionization rates decreased by 5 percentage points, or by about 15 per cent. Female labour force participation increased by 15 per cent, from 40 per cent to 46 per cent, while the proportion of wage earners in urban areas increased from 0.68 to 0.77. We further see substantial decreases in the share of workers employed in mining, agriculture, manufacturing, and domestic work, which have been historically large sectors employing relatively unskilled labour. At the same time, we observe the increasing importance of the finance and services sectors, both of which reflect an increase in the share of workers of 5 percentage points. This points to important inequality-enhancing forces in an increasingly

Table 9.6 Labour market summary statistics, 2000, 2011, and 2014

	2000	2011	2014
Years of education	8.77	10.54	10.75
Potential experience	22.25	21.33	21.52
Union member	0.34	0.30	0.29
Formal employment	0.79	0.75	0.78
African	0.70	0.70	0.73
Coloured	0.12	0.12	0.12
Asian/Indian	0.03	0.03	0.02
White	0.14	0.14	0.13
Female	0.40	0.45	0.46
Urban	0.68	0.79	0.77
Sectoral shares			
Agriculture	0.10	0.05	0.06
Mining	0.07	0.03	0.03
Manufacturing	0.14	0.14	0.12
Utilities	0.01	0.01	0.01
Construction	0.06	0.07	0.07
Trade	0.15	0.18	0.17
Transport	0.05	0.06	0.06
Finance	0.08	0.13	0.13
Services	0.20	0.24	0.25
Domestic services	0.13	0.10	0.10
Earnings (rand)	5,740	7,418	7,951
Log earnings	8.06	8.31	8.18
Observations	24,276	67,235	63,845

Source: Based on Finn and Leibbrandt (2018: Table 1).

difficult labour market for relatively less skilled workers. The rest of the chapter substantiates this.

The post-2011 period saw a flattening of earnings increases for the lowest earners, which had been robust between 2001 and 2011; a decline in real earnings for middle earners; and a continuation of the trend of earnings increases for top earners—all factors that indicate that real inequality rose over this sub-period.

Most of the changes profiled in Table 9.6 are inequality-reducing for most workers, except for those at the very top of the earnings distribution. Africans increased their rate of labour force participation by 3 percentage points and saw the gap between their earnings and the earnings of whites shrink by 10 percentage points. Women increased their labour force participation rate by 6 percentage points and saw a 5 percentage point reduction in the gender wage gap. The difference between earnings of unionized and non-unionized workers also fell by 6 percentage points, alongside an overall reduction in unionization of 5 percentage points.

The statistical modelling examines two impacts on earnings inequality stemming from these changes. The first is the impact of changes on the distribution of characteristics of members of the labour force, sometimes called endowment changes. The second is the changing relative earnings values of these characteristics, sometimes called changing price effects or changes in the returns to endowments. This modelling shows that the equalizing effects of the changing characteristics of workers listed above are offset by the effects of growing compensation for both educated and more experienced South African workers that exacerbate inequality. Figure 9.2 shows that prior to 2011, the returns to experience actually reduced inequality, but after 2011 this dynamic was reversed. It also shows that the biggest driver of inequality since 2012 is educational attainment, and particularly the returns to tertiary education. This return accrues disproportionately to top earners.

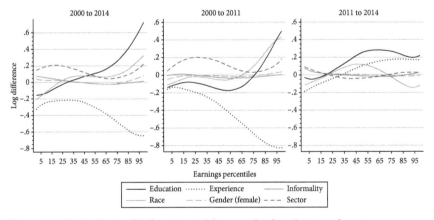

Figure 9.2 Total effects of different variables over the distribution of earnings
Source: Finn and Leibbrandt (2018: Figure 12).

Thus, on the one hand, changes in the composition of the labour force have offset inequality in South Africa, but on the other, structural factors continue to drive it. From 2000 to 2011, the net increase in the earnings Gini was 1.1 percentage points. From 2011 to 2014, the net increase was 7.13 percentage points. Overall, structural changes accounted for 7.99 of the 8.24 net percentage point increase in measured Gini from 2001 to 2014. The increase in the number and general level of education of workers resulted in increasing the Gini coefficient only slightly, by 0.42 percentage points, while increases in the earnings of tertiary-educated workers contributed to an 11.17 percentage point increase. Most of this effect was observed from 2011 to 2014, as prior to 2011 the impact on inequality had been offset by wage stagnation. Increases, when they were granted, mostly went to top earners, who are more likely to have had higher levels of education. In spite of decreasing inequality between racial groups, it is important to remember that the earnings gap between African people and white people is still large, at 57 per cent. Holding these other effects constant, racial disparity in earnings continued to drive growth in inequality of nearly 3.5 percentage points over the period.

This picture from Finn and Leibbrandt is complemented by findings from a number of other recent studies on earnings inequality. Wittenberg (2018) shows that earnings have narrowed at the bottom end of the distribution, possibly due to wage setting through collective bargaining and minimum wage determinations, but they have widened at the top end. Mean real earnings have increased but the median has not; this implies an increase in earnings inequality in the top half of the earnings distribution, while the bottom half has become more compressed. Wage earners 'stuck' at a median level of earnings—which has not moved since the end of apartheid—are especially vulnerable to forces driving the demand for labour and wage setting in the contemporary labour market. This is despite the fact that they have far higher levels of education than median earners in 1993.

Median earners are predominantly African, male, and in their thirties. Those earning below the median are most likely to be women. Median earners are also less likely to be unionized than in 1993 or even 2000. They comprise a mix of occupations including elementary, craft workers, and service and clerical posts, while the proportion of manufacturing workers at the median has dropped. Median earners are now less likely to be members of a trade union than they were in 1993, while 40 per cent of those in the top half of the earnings distribution are unionized. The average age of the median band has not changed markedly, but it has increased in the top half. This indicates that younger entrants are finding it harder to move into higher-paying jobs. Nor has it changed much in the bottom half, indicating that young people are finding it difficult to enter the labour force at all.

Kerr and Wittenberg (2017) show that the public sector, which employs about 18 per cent of all employees, reflects earnings consistently above the median. Public sector employment has increased since 2007, and then more sharply since

2010 after a slight dip around the 2008 recession. In 2014, it employed about 2.7 million people. Kerr and Wittenberg establish that from 1997 to 2007, median and mean earnings in the public sector grew by 33 per cent and 25 per cent respectively. The mean in the private sector grew by 25 per cent in the same period, while the median remained unchanged. Clearly, those working in the public sector have generally done better than those employed in the private sector. In an examination of occupationally similar positions in the private and public sectors, Kerr and Wittenberg found that at almost every rung—except at the very top of the ladder—public sector workers did better in terms of wages, especially those who were unionized. At the same time, the premium attached to union membership in the private sector has declined, suggesting a weakening of union power here.

Finally, as in the case of household income, there is important recent work using tax data to address measurement issues at the top end of the earnings distribution. Wittenberg (2017a) used two datasets, one based on four waves of 2010 Quarterly Labour Force Survey (QLFS) data and the other on 2011 PIT data. His findings are unequivocal: earnings inequality has widened since the end of apartheid. Wittenberg estimates that the Gini coefficient (for earnings), when measured by the tax data, could be 3 percentage points higher than previously thought, increasing from 0.567 to 0.599. The Gini coefficient for self-employment, measured by the QLFS, also goes up by 3 percentage points to 0.716. The widening inequality is driven mainly by a rise in top earnings. In 2014, the incomes of the top 2.5 per cent increased the Gini coefficient by 5.5 percentage points.

5 Towards Policy: Evidence from Fiscal Incidence Studies

Inequality-enhancing trends in the labour market place a substantial responsibility on the taxes and transfers of the fiscal system to serve as a counterweight. Despite the fact that post-apartheid South Africa has been one of the most unequal societies in the world, several studies have shown that the fiscal system is well designed to be strongly redistributive.[13] For this project, the fiscal incidence analysis by Maboshe and Woolard (2018) updates earlier work using 2017 data and adds new analysis of the incidence of tax benefits. The largest component of direct taxation is PIT, accounting for R353 billion in 2015 tax receipts, or 36 per cent of total revenue. As shown in Figure 9.3, direct taxes on income are progressive. In South Africa, the top 20 per cent of income earners contribute 96 per cent of all PIT. In terms of indirect taxes, such as VAT and the fuel levy, Inchauste et al.

---

[13] Inchauste et al. (2015) provide a very thorough example and also a good review of earlier fiscal incidence work.

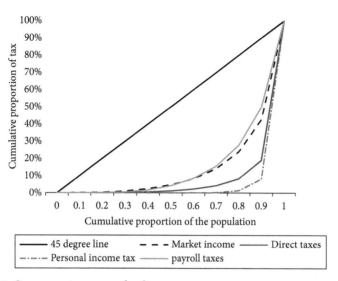

Figure 9.3 Concentration curves for direct taxes
Source: Maboshe and Woolard (2018: Figure 3).

(2015) have shown they are progressive. However, excise taxes on alcohol and tobacco are regressive.

Maboshe and Woolard also analyse tax credits, allowances, and deductions for the first time. These benefits allow taxpayers to reduce their PIT. The largest of these deductions are for interest earned on savings and investments, credits for the use of private medical services, and allowances for private pension contributions and retirement savings. Figure 9.4 shows that these policies are highly regressive in absolute terms, with 85 per cent of the total benefit accruing to the top 30 per cent. The poor lack access to private or non-subsidized medical care and do not accumulate large savings.

The racial and gender dimensions of these deductions are also clear. Whites receive 80 per cent of the total interest exemption benefits although they represent only 8 per cent of the population. They also receive the largest share of the deductions for contributions to private pensions. Expenditures for medical credits, though, benefited more black than white people in absolute terms (44 per cent of the total compared with 39 per cent), reflecting the fact that most formal sector workers have private medical aid coverage. However, this is still racially skewed in relative terms, as black people comprise 80 per cent of the population.

Maboshe and Woolard also analyse South Africa's extensive social spending, which, in South Africa, is nearly twice the median for developing economies. Spending amounts to 10.2 per cent of the annual budget or 3.1 per cent of annual gross domestic product. The number of social-grant beneficiaries has also grown from 9.4 million in 1994 to 16.5 million in 2014. The largest transfers by aggregate expenditure are the old-age pensions, at R49.4 million, and the child support

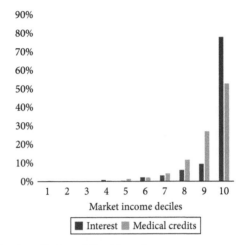

Figure 9.4 Distribution of selected fiscal benefits
Source: Maboshe and Woolard (2018: Figure 4).

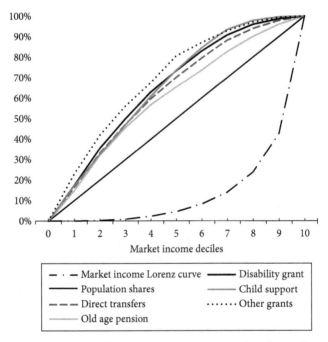

Figure 9.5 The progressivity of each of the three main social cash transfers in South Africa
Source: Maboshe and Woolard (2018: Figure 6).

and foster-care grants, at R43.4 million. The size of the benefit, per person, is much larger for the old-age pension than it is for the child support grant, meaning that 11.6 million children receive similar support to 3.07 million elderly people. Disability grants are another significant transfer.

Figure 9.5 shows that these transfers are well targeted by income group. More than 70 per cent of the direct transfers goes to the poorest half of the population, with 50 per cent of spending going to the bottom 30 per cent. Disaggregating, 74 per cent of the children's benefit, 73 per cent of the disability grant, and 65 per cent of the pension benefit go to the poorest half of the population.

Transfers are also mainly progressive when accounting for the intersection of gender, race, and class. For example, 76 per cent of transfers going to female-headed households and 64 per cent going to male-headed households go to the bottom halves of these, respectively. In sum, this study confirms that tax policy remains progressive in general and budgeted expenditures on social grants are well targeted to reach those who need them. However, the chapter also highlights the fact that some important tax benefits are sharply regressive.

6 Disappointing Outcomes: Inequality Persistence and Low Social Mobility

Despite some well-designed and well-targeted policies, South Africa's inequality has remained persistent. Indeed, new research shows that, over the past decade, progress has slowed and even stalled. An important study by Schotte et al. (2018) shows that the stable middle class in contemporary South Africa is much smaller than previously thought, and that the poor make up almost half of the population. In fact, a significant proportion of South Africans have for the past decade been in a game of 'snakes and ladders'. Schotte et al. use five waves of the NIDS to track movements into and out of poverty between 2008 and 2017, and to delineate five major socioeconomic classes in South Africa: the chronically poor, the transient poor, the vulnerable middle class, the stable middle class, and the elite.

A key finding is that the stable middle class is relatively small—only one in four people can be considered to be part of either the stable middle class or the elite. Another is that poverty, over time, is much more pervasive than a cross-sectional analysis tells us. StatsSA estimates that in 2015 55 per cent of the population lived in poverty (Statistics South Africa 2017). Schotte et al. (2018) refine this, estimating that about 49 per cent live in chronic, persistent poverty. In addition, another 11.4 per cent can be classified as 'transient poor', and about 19 per cent are part of a 'vulnerable middle class'. Both of these groups are at risk of falling back into poverty from one wave to the next. Figure 9.6 reflects this picture.

What are the triggers that propel people from one state to another? Two key triggers are either a labour-market event—losing or gaining a job—or a demographic event—gaining or losing a member of the household. Job gains accounted

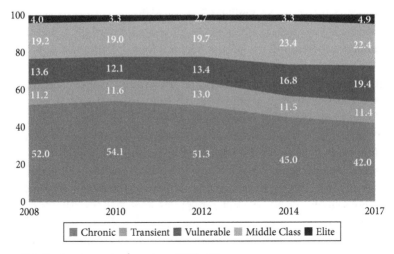

Figure 9.6 Socioeconomic class sizes, 2008–17
Source: Authors' illustration, based on data from Schotte et al. (2018).

for one-third of all exits from poverty, while a change in household size accounted for half of all poverty entries or exits. Although getting a job can be important in lifting people out of poverty, it is not sufficient. Those with unstable jobs—without contracts or union protection—are more vulnerable to falling back into poverty than those with permanent, generally formal sector employment.

Chronic poverty has clear characteristics associated with it: poor education (less than matric), larger households, female-headed households, unemployment, geographic location, and race. The legacies of apartheid, which forced many African people to live in poverty-stricken rural 'homelands' far from economic opportunities, are still deeply felt. So, for instance, only 2.5 per cent of rural households remained non-poor through all five waves from 2008 to 2017, while nearly 83 per cent were poor in four or five waves.

In contrast, about one-quarter of urban households remained stably non-poor (and 34.2 per cent were non-poor in four or five periods), and 42.7 per cent were poor in four or five periods. For the non-poor who live in an urban area, the risks of falling into poverty are less than for similar people residing in rural areas. But for the poor, the chances of escaping it are not significantly different from those of their counterparts in rural areas. In fact, the urban African population is more affected by transient poverty over the five waves of NIDS.

The other striking feature of poverty is its female, and youthful, face. Nearly 72 per cent of households that were female-headed in all five waves remained in poverty in four or five waves, compared with only 29 per cent of those in male-headed households. It is also worth noting that female-headed households are three times as likely as male-headed households to be single-parent households.

Race is another persistent legacy. Although the sample of white people was relatively small—just 274 individuals who were tracked in all five waves—the vast majority, 93.6 per cent, were observed to be consistently non-poor. By contrast, about 63 per cent of Africans were poor in four or five waves, with only about 9 per cent remaining non-poor in all five waves.

The stable middle class, comprising about 21 per cent of the population, shows characteristics that set it apart from the vulnerable middle class. One key indicator is the level of education: two-thirds of middle-class household heads are educated at matric level or higher. The other is employment: three-quarters are employed, typically as formal sector employees in more secure jobs. They also earn on average twice as much from the labour market as households in the vulnerable class (R13,127.37 compared with R5,366.17).

The elite is almost three-quarters white, predominantly urban-based, and has an expenditure level much higher than the stable middle class (R25,659 compared with R4,536, average per capita). This class earns much more from the labour market than the stable middle class—R38,223 compared with R13,127. As reported earlier in this chapter, though, its members also get a significant amount of their income from capital investments.

7 Conclusion

This synthesis chapter began with a very brief summary of the findings from the literature on income inequality that existed prior to our most recent research conducted within the Inequality in the Giants project. We then built on this to discuss some of our key findings and contributions from more recent studies, and to consider how the bigger picture has become sharper and more coherent.

Knowing that inequality has remained exceptionally high in post-apartheid South Africa, we used dynamic decomposition methods to investigate the drivers of income inequality and compare the static and dynamic decompositions. The key finding, which corroborates the existing literature, is that the labour market remains key to understanding the evolution of inequality in South Africa. A secondary finding was that while government grants played an important role in reducing inequality in earlier periods, the effects of this mitigating force have become weaker.

We then reviewed some new empirical work that incorporates tax data, which is better able to measure the incomes of high-income individuals. This provides us with potentially better estimates of the overall income distribution, as there are several reasons why survey data may not adequately capture the incomes of a small proportion of high-income people. This work highlighted two important points. First, about 60 per cent of the population earn no taxable income. Second, those at the top end of the income distribution have experienced much higher rates of real income growth than the remainder of the population. Their growth has also been higher than the growth rate of GNI, which means that this group is receiving a greater 'share of the pie' than was previously the case. This has put upward pressure on South Africa's inequality levels, which partly explains why inequality has remained so persistent.

Another methodological innovation has been to decompose the sources of changes in earnings inequality into changes in the distribution of endowments and returns to these endowments, while explicitly allowing for heterogeneity in these returns. This work required a caveat due to some implausibly large changes in the measured Gini coefficient of earnings, likely due to a change in definitions or survey methodology. Nonetheless, the method highlighted that despite the increased average education level, which would have reduced inequality by itself, there were structural changes in the economy that enhanced earnings inequality. In particular, the increased returns to education accrued primarily to those with a tertiary qualification, and this interacted with a change in the returns to experience that caused an increase in earnings inequality.

In the policy space, we reviewed some of the fiscal incidence literature in South Africa by incorporating additional information on tax exemptions. This work confirmed that while the direct tax system is progressive and social benefits well targeted, some of the tax benefits are indeed regressive. This suggests there may still be room for further fiscal policy to target inequality, although the authors are cautious in their interpretation as the benefits involve healthcare and pension contributions, which are likely valuable for welfare in direct ways over and above the implications for inequality.

We concluded our review by considering some of the most recent work on social mobility in South Africa using the country's most recent nationally representative household- and individual-level panel data. The main finding is that the stable middle class is very small in South Africa. This has implications for social and political stability, among other things. A large proportion of South Africans are vulnerable to periods in poverty. This includes a large fraction of middle-class people who remain extremely vulnerable to a negative shock that can, and frequently does, push them back into poverty.

Where does all of this leave us, either as academic researchers who work on inequality or as concerned individuals who would like to make a contribution to reducing the unacceptably high levels of inequality? As researchers, we feel inadequately answered questions remain about the roles and importance of assets and wealth in perpetuating the high levels of inequality. With our focus on the top end of the income and earnings distribution, we have shown very clearly that those at the top end have flourished even when others have struggled. They have done this by being able to draw on a far broader array of income sources and physical, financial, and human assets. But we need to know more about exactly how wealth is transferred inter-generationally and, more generally, about the drivers of social mobility.

A key question that remains unanswered, even though it has been flagged since the late 1990s, is why the South African labour market continues to display such extraordinary levels of unemployment. This would require a better grasp of the demand for labour, in conjunction with market structure and market power. Our analysis of the labour market has shown that the finance and services sectors have grown substantially faster than the more traditional sectors of mining, manufacturing, agriculture, and domestic work; it may be a useful line of enquiry to consider longer-run, historical, and holistic views of the labour market to understand our particular challenges.

At the top end of the labour market, there are questions relating to the earnings and income of the very high earners. Why do South African CEOs earn so many multiples more than the median workers relative to their counterparts in other countries? Is this a social norm in a society that has historically justified high levels of inequality? Is it a failure in corporate governance processes? Or is it due to policies that may themselves be related to a relatively well-paid public sector? These are questions that we could only make conjectures about at present.

From the policy side, there are some key lessons. All the evidence points to the importance of social grants for reducing both poverty and inequality. However, there is evidence that the ability to raise taxes further may be limited, and at the same time it may be harder to extend substantively the inequality-reducing effects of grants. This suggests two different policy approaches. First, there may be value in aiming to extract better and higher-quality service delivery from the existing budgets. An increase in such efficiency may improve welfare even if the budget constraint is binding. Second, one needs to consider policies that can positively shape the distribution of productive assets and the returns to these assets that would raise the market incomes of people who are economically vulnerable and marginalized. Such policies would include those dealing with education, and market regulations that stimulate competition between firms, encourage new players, support innovation and dynamism, and reduce the market power of the larger incumbents.

So, there are several possible ways forward. While it is not clear which subset of these is necessary to place South Africa on a more positive, transformative, dynamic trajectory, there is widespread and growing acceptance that levels of inequality such as those that prevail in South Africa are unsustainably high. They threaten the social fabric of society, they increase the risks of political and economic upheaval, and they prevent the majority of people from living up to their full potential. All of these are likely to harm the country's long-term developmental prospects. Significantly reducing inequality in South Africa warrants sustained attention and effort from all sections of society.

References

Alvaredo, F., A. Atkinson, L. Chancel, T. Piketty, E. Saez, and G. Zucman (2017). 'Distributional National Accounts (DINA) guidelines: concepts and methods used in WID.World'. WID. World Working Paper 2017/6. World Inequality Lab.

Azevedo, J.P., G. Inchaust, and V. Sanfelice (2013). 'Decomposing the recent inequality decline in Latin America'. World Bank Policy Research Working Paper 6715. Washington, DC: World Bank.

Bassier, I., and I. Woolard (2018). 'Exclusive growth: rapidly increasing top incomes amidst low national growth in South Africa'. REDI3x3 Working Paper 47. Cape Town: SALDRU, University of Cape Town.

Finn, A., and M. Leibbrandt (2018). 'The evolution and determination of earnings inequality in Post-Apartheid South Africa'. WIDER Working Paper 2018/83. Helsinki: UNU-WIDER.

Fortin, N., T. Lemieux, and S. Firpo (2011). 'Decomposition Methods in Economics'. In O. Ashenfelter and D. Card (eds), *Handbook of Labour Economics*, volume 4A. Oxford: Elsevier Science.

Hundenborn, J., M. Leibbrandt, and I. Woolard (2018a). 'Drivers of inequality in South Africa'. WIDER Working Paper 2018/162. Helsinki: UNU-WIDER.

Hundenborn, J., I. Woolard, and J. Jellema (2018b). 'The effect of top incomes on inequality in South Africa'. WIDER Working Paper 2018/90. Helsinki: UNU-WIDER.

Inchauste, G., N. Lustig, M. Maboshe, C. Purfield, and I. Woolard (2015). 'The distributional impact of fiscal policy in South Africa'. Policy Research Working Paper 7194. Washington, DC: World Bank.

Kerr, A., and M. Wittenberg (2017). 'Public sector wages and employment in South Africa'. REDI3x3 Working Paper 42. Cape Town: SALDRU, University of Cape Town.

Leibbrandt, M., A. Finn, and M. Oosthuizen (2016). 'Poverty, Inequality and Prices in Post-Apartheid South Africa'. In C. Arndt, A. McKay, and F. Tarp (eds), *Growth and Poverty in Sub-Saharan Africa*. New York: Oxford University Press.

Leibbrandt, M., A. Finn, and I. Woolard (2012). 'Describing and Decomposing Post-Apartheid Income Inequality in South Africa'. *Development Southern Africa*, 29(1): 19–34.

Leibbrandt, M., W. Ingrid, A. Finn, and J. Argent (2010). 'Trends in South African income distribution and poverty since the fall of apartheid'. OECD Social, Employment and Migration Working Paper 101. Paris: OECD.

Levy, B., A. Hirsch, and I. Woolard (2014). 'South Africa's evolving political settlement in comparative perspective'. SALDRU Working Paper 138. Cape Town: SALDRU, University of Cape Town.

Maboshe, M., and I. Woolard (2018). 'Revisiting the impact of direct taxes and transfers on poverty and inequality in South Africa'. WIDER Working Paper 2018/79. Helsinki: UNU-WIDER.

National Planning Commission (n.d.) 'National Development Plan 2030: Our Future—Make It Work'. Pretoria: National Planning Commission.

Piketty, T. (2014). *Capital in the Twenty-First Century*. Translated by Arthur Goldhammer. Cambridge, MA: The Belknap Press of Harvard University Press.

Schotte, S., R. Zizzamia, and M. Leibbrandt (2018). 'Snakes and Ladders with a Loaded Dice'. Econ3x3 Draft Paper. Cape Town: SALDRU, University of Cape Town.

Statistics South Africa (2017). 'Poverty Trends in South Africa: An Examination of Absolute Poverty Between 2006 and 2015'. Pretoria: Statistics South Africa.

Wittenberg, M. (2017a). 'Measurement of Earnings: Comparing South African Tax and Survey Data'. REDI3x3 Working Paper 41. Cape Town: SALDRU, University of Cape Town.

Wittenberg, M. (2017b). 'Wages and Wage Inequality in South Africa 1994–2011: Part 1—Wage Measurement and Trends'. *South African Journal of Economics*, 85(2): 279–97.

Wittenberg, M. (2017c). 'Wages and Wage Inequality in South Africa 1994–2011: Part 2—Inequality Measurement and Trends'. *South African Journal of Economics*, 85(2): 298–318.

Wittenberg, M. (2018). 'The Top Tail of South Africa's Earnings Distribution 1993–2014: Evidence from the Pareto Distribution'. SALDRU Working Paper 224. Cape Town: SALDRU, University of Cape Town.

PART IV
INEQUALITY IN A BROADER CONTEXT

10

Economic Inequality and Subjective Well-Being Across the World

Andrew E. Clark and Conchita D'Ambrosio

1 Introduction

There is widespread consensus that economic inequality influences individual well-being through a number of different channels.[1] Living in a society where the gap between the rich and the poor is wide has both economic and social consequences. As Van de Werfhorst and Salverda (2012) report in the introduction of the special issue they edited on the consequences of economic inequality, in unequal societies crime rates are higher, population health is worse, child bullying occurs more often, housing conditions are more disparate, social trust erodes, and political participation deteriorates. We refer the reader to the references therein, and to the excellent discussion that appears in the articles making up this special issue, for details on these findings.

Our aim here is to contribute to this literature and focus on the study of the relationship between subjective evaluations of individual living conditions and economic inequality. We aim to explore empirically whether individuals' evaluations of their present and future living conditions are influenced by the level of economic inequality pertaining in their country of residence. We do so using data for seventy-six different countries across the world, observed at a number of different points in time between 1998 and 2015. We use all of the available Barometers data, which allows us to consider a spatial analysis of this relationship for different continents to see whether our findings are universal or whether they differ by region. To the best of our knowledge, our work here is the first to offer a complete global picture of how differences in control over economic resources are reflected in individuals' subjective evaluations of their living conditions, both current and future.

There has been an upsurge of interest in subjective measures of well-being, as complements to the more traditional income- or resource-based objective

[1] We are very grateful to Anthony Lepinteur for excellent research assistance. Conchita D'Ambrosio gratefully acknowledges support from the Fonds National de la Recherche Luxembourg (Grant C18/SC/12677653).

Andrew E. Clark and Conchita D'Ambrosio, *Economic Inequality and Subjective Well-Being Across the World* In: *Inequality in the Developing World*. Edited by: Carlos Gradín, Murray Leibbrandt, and Finn Tarp, Oxford University Press (2021).
DOI: 10.1093/oso/9780198863960.003.0010

measures. For data reasons, this analysis has most often concentrated on OECD countries. However, more recent work has extended these analyses to developing countries. Some examples in this respect are presented by Akay and Martinsson (2011), Bookwalter and Dalenberg (2010), Lentz (2017), Clark and D'Ambrosio (2017), the contributions in the volume by Clark and Senik (2014), and the chapters in the recent World Happiness Reports that describe the analysis of Gallup well-being data covering every country in the world.

There are a number of reasons to expect a relationship between economic inequality and subjective well-being. Here we use the term 'economic inequality' to refer to any disparities in the command over economic resources between individuals (i.e. there is economic inequality when individuals have different levels of command over resources). As opposed to many of the other variables that have been related to individual well-being, economic inequality does not exist at the individual level and is rather measured only at an aggregate, often societal, level. The key axiom in the measurement of inequality is the Pigou–Dalton principle of transfers, according to which inequality increases whenever there is a transfer of resources from a poorer to a richer individual. Even though economic inequality as such is not an individual-level concept, any distribution of economic resources will have individual-level effects due to the way it changes the individual's own access to economic resources and her standing with respect to those who are richer or poorer.

The theoretical framework we follow here was introduced in some of our previous work (Clark and D'Ambrosio 2015). We postulate that the effects of inequality on individual well-being are both *normative* and *comparative*. The latter channel is based on the observation that individuals do not live in isolation, and when assessing their own social standing they will compare themselves to individuals in their reference group. When the individual is a member of this group, her well-being is commonly assumed to be negatively affected by those who possess more due to a sentiment of relative deprivation; in a similar vein, the comparison with those who possess less affects her well-being positively due to relative satisfaction. When the individual is not currently a member of the reference group, but aspires to be part of the group in question, comparisons with respect to richer individuals in the group may give rise to positive feelings, as the individual anticipates being as well-off as the group members once she joins the group. This idea is akin to that of the tunnel effect presented by Hirschman (1973). As is obvious from the above discussion, the measurement of deprivation and satisfaction requires individual-level data.

The *normative* channel between inequality and well-being works via the individual's disinterested evaluation of economic inequality *without* her making any comparisons to others: depending on the attitudes and social norms prevailing within a group, the individual can evaluate the income gaps in the group as being either fair or unfair. As such, the summary level of inequality in the individual's country of residence may have an independent effect on her evaluation of living conditions, in addition to that reflecting her comparisons of her own situation to better-off and worse-off individuals. For the analysis of the normative channel, aggregate inequality data are sufficient. The following section describes how we measure inequality in the various Barometer datasets.

2 Measuring Inequality

Our analysis requires information on three different types of inequality measures: (1) an aggregate overall index of differences in the command over economic resources; (2) an individual-level measure that captures the gaps between the individual and all relevant individuals who are better-off than her; and (3) an analogous individual-level measure of the gaps between the individual and those who are worse-off. The most popular type-1 inequality measure is the Gini coefficient at the country/year level. The two best sources of cross-country and over-time Gini indices available to researchers are the SWIID dataset (Standardized World Income Inequality Database; see Solt 2013) and the WIID dataset (World Income Inequality Database), which is compiled and maintained by UNU-WIDER. There is a third well-known source, the LIS (Luxembourg Income Study Database), but its coverage in terms of both countries and years is lower, which will prevent us using it in the current analysis. Jenkins (2015) and Ferreira et al. (2015), in their evaluation of cross-country inequality datasets, recommend using the WIID. We follow their recommendation and use data from WIID 3.4, released in January 2017, containing Gini indices of income inequality for all the countries and years of our sample.

For the measures of inequality of types 2 and 3 we rely on the information available in the Barometer surveys on the command over economic resources (see also D'Ambrosio and Rodrigues (2008) for a similar application to the study of deprivation in the city of São Paulo). Unfortunately, information on income is not available in many of the Barometer surveys. In order to be able to analyse as many countries and years as possible, we consider different measures of well-being in a non-income framework. These items differ by Barometer, and Table 10.A1 lists the items that we describe in what follows. In each round of the Afrobarometer in our sample, individuals are asked the following questions: 'Over the past year, how often, if ever have you or your family gone without _____?' The interviewer asks this question for each of the following four basic necessities: 'Enough food to eat', 'Enough clean water for home use', 'Medicines or medical treatment', and 'Enough fuel to cook your food'. The possible answers to this question are: 0 = never, 1 = just once or twice, 2 = several times, 3 = many times, and 4 = always. While there is information on a fifth item, 'A cash income', we decided to exclude the latter as the availability of sufficient cash income will very likely determine the answers to all of the other items: someone who does not have enough cash income will also probably not have enough food to eat, clean water for home use, medical treatment, or fuel with which to cook food, leading to an over-count of the sources of deprivation. We use the answers to these four questions to first construct an indicator of functioning failure for each individual as the sum of their scores in these four basic domains of a decent life. This indicator thus takes on values between 0, for individuals who are never deprived in any of the domains, and 16, for individuals who are always deprived in all domains. See Shenga (2010) for an alternative dummy approach using the same dataset, recoding the responses so that 0 refers to never or just once or twice, and 1 refers to several times, many times, or always.

In the Asianbarometer, individual are asked 'Do you or your family own the following?', with possible answers of *Yes* or *No*. Among the listed items, we here focus on the answers to the questions regarding the following items, which appear in all of the waves: mobile phone, electric fan/cooler, fridge, telephone, TV, cable TV, radio, and camera. The indicator of functioning failure we construct for the Asianbarometer therefore takes on values between 0, for individuals who have access to all items, and 8, for individuals who are deprived in every dimension. The questions are similar in the Latinobarometer, and the items we consider here are TV, refrigerator, computer, washing machine, telephone, car, drinking water, and sewerage system. The indicator of functioning failure in the Latinobarometer then also takes on values between 0, for individuals who have access to all items, and 8, for individuals who are always deprived (although the domains that are evaluated in the Asianbarometer and Latinobarometer are not the same—only three items appear in both lists). The same question is asked in the Eurobarometer and the list of items we include are TV, DVD player, computer, internet access, car, laptop, tablet, and smartphone. This again produces an indicator of functioning failure that takes on values between 0 and 8.

We formally define the individual indices of relative deprivation and satisfaction by introducing the following notation. Let N denote the set of all positive integers and R (R+) the set of all (all non-negative) real numbers. The distinct levels of functioning failures are collected in a vector $(q_1, \ldots, q_k)$, where $k \in N \setminus \{1\}$. Let π_j indicate the population share of individuals who have the same q_j level of functioning failures. The distribution is $(\pi, q) \equiv (\pi_1, \ldots, \pi_k; q_1, \ldots, q_k)$, $q_i \neq q_j$ for all $i, j \in \{1, \ldots, k\}$. Let Ω be the space of all distributions. Define $\bar{q}$ as the illfare-ranked permutation of the vector q, so that $\bar{q}_1 \leq \bar{q}_2 \ldots \leq \bar{q}_k$. In the second step, we calculate well-being indices over these distributions, which we describe in what follows.

The first measure we use in the analysis of individual well-being is the traditional indicator of individual command over economic resources given by the number of functioning failures, q_i (see, among many others, Alkire and Foster 2011; Bossert et al. 2013). Here, the higher the value of q_i, the more deprived is the individual. As noted previously, in the Afrobarometer this variable ranges from 0, corresponding to the situation of no deprivation (no functioning failures), to 16, the maximum possible value referring to individuals who are always deprived in all dimensions. For the other three Barometer datasets, this variable ranges between 0 (no functioning failures) and 8 (deprivation in all dimensions).

The second group of measures aims to capture the feelings of relative deprivation and satisfaction that an individual experiences from their comparisons to others. Yitzhaki (1979) was the first to introduce the measurement of income deprivation in the economics literature. Rewritten in terms of functioning failures, the index of individual relative deprivation, a function $D_i : \Omega \to \mathbf{R}_+$, is given by:

$$D_i(\pi,q) = \sum_{i=1}^{j-1} (\overline{q}_i - \overline{q}_j) \pi_j \qquad (1)$$

for all $(\pi,q) \in \Omega$. The deprivation from which individual i suffers here is defined as the sum of all functioning-failure differentials with respect to individuals who are less deprived in the society under consideration (i.e. who have fewer functioning failures). Analogously, we can measure the complement to deprivation, satisfaction $S_i : \Omega \to \mathbf{R}_+$, as:

$$S_i(\pi,q) = \sum_{j=i+1}^{k} (\overline{q}_j - \overline{q}_i) \pi_j \qquad (2)$$

for all $(\pi,q) \in \Omega$. This reflects the sum of the functioning-failure differentials with respect to individuals who are more deprived than individual i.

The second type of measure we consider with respect to comparisons aims to capture the individual sentiment due to comparisons to others who do not share the exact level of functioning failure, without any further distinction. If we sum the two indices of relative deprivation and satisfaction at the individual level, we obtain the measure of individual alienation, $A_i : \Omega \to \mathbf{R}_+$, defined as:

$$A_i(\pi,q) = \sum_{j=1}^{k} |\overline{q}_i - \overline{q}_j| \pi_j \qquad (3)$$

While deprivation and satisfaction are asymmetric measures, based on comparisons only to those who are better-off or worse-off respectively, alienation is assumed to be experienced with respect to everybody. Davies (2016), interpreting the Gini coefficient, highlights that the individual sum of differences with respect to everyone else, which corresponds to the alienation measure introduced above, A_i, is the basis for an individual inequality index. The (absolute) Gini coefficient can be interpreted as the average value of this index across the population. Davies also shows that this personal inequality index can be further decomposed into two components corresponding to the relative deprivation and satisfaction measures introduced above, D_i and S_i.

3 Data, Methods, and Results

3.1 Data

Our empirical analysis is carried out using data from four different Barometer series, which are repeated cross-section regional surveys on public attitudes towards democracy, governance, economic conditions, and related issues.[2] Tables 10.A2–A5 list the years we analyse and the size of the sample per country per wave. Our samples of individuals between the ages of 18 and 90 contain information on 43,385 Africans living in eighteen countries of the continent in Table 10.A2's Afrobarometer, 13,542 Asians from nine countries in Table 10.A3's Asianbarometer, 168,278 Latin and Central Americans from eighteen countries in Table 10.A4's Latinobarometer, and 100,379 Europeans living in thirty-one different countries in Table 10.A5's Eurobarometer. The datasets are cross-sectional, and not every country appears in every year.

Our dependent variables are self-assessed current and future living conditions, which we will denote by wb_{itc} for individual i in year t in country c. In the Afrobarometer, individuals are asked the following question about their current living conditions: 'In general, how would you describe your own present living conditions?', with the possible answers 'Very Bad', 'Fairly Bad', 'Neither Good nor Bad', 'Fairly Good', and 'Very Good'. Regarding the future, the question reads 'Looking ahead, do you expect your living conditions in twelve months' time to be better or worse?', with the possible answers 'Much Worse', 'Worse', 'Same', 'Better', and 'Much Better'. In the Asianbarometer the two analogous questions are 'As for your own family, how do you rate your economic situation today?' and 'What do you think the economic situation of your family will be a few years from now?' The possible answers to the first question are 'Very Bad', 'Bad', 'Neither Good nor Bad', 'Good', and 'Very Good', and to the second 'Much Worse', 'A Little Worse', 'About the Same', 'A Little Better', and 'Much Better'. The answers to the two questions in the Latinobarometer are exactly the same, although the wording of the questions is slightly different: 'In general, how would you describe your present economic situation and that of your family?' and 'And in the next twelve months do you think that your economic situation and that of your family will be much better, a little better, about the same, a little

[2] See www.afrobarometer.org, www.asianbarometer.org, www.latinobarometro.org, and http://ec.europa.eu/commfrontoffice/publicopinion/index.cfm (the last of these is the Eurobarometer).

worse or much worse compared to the way it is now?' Two similar questions are asked in the Eurobarometer: 'How would you judge the current financial situation of your household?' with possible answers 'Very Bad', 'Rather Bad', 'Rather Good', and 'Very Good'; and 'What are your expectations for the next twelve months: will the next twelve months be better, worse or the same, when it comes to the financial situation of your household?'

To homogenize the analysis as far as possible between different regions, we regroup the first two and last two answers on future living conditions in the Afrobarometer, Latinobarometer, and Asianbarometer to correspond to the categories in the Eurobarometer. The same procedure is not possible for the answers to the current living conditions question, as the median category 'Neither Good nor Bad' does not appear in the possible answers in the Eurobarometer. The distributions of the dependent variables averaged over all the years are shown in Figure 10.1; the distributions for each separate year are very similar and have been omitted. Current living conditions are evaluated as neither good nor bad by the majority of Asians and Central and Latin Americans, followed by around 20 per cent of the sample who answer 'Good'. A similar finding holds in Europe, where the majority answer 'Rather Good'. The African distribution is more polarized. The two most common answers are 'Fairly Bad' and 'Fairly Good'. Notably, just under one in five Africans judge their present living conditions as 'Very Bad', a figure that is far higher than that observed in any other region.

Expectations regarding future living conditions reveal a generalized level of optimism everywhere but Europe, where only around 20 per cent expect the future financial situation of the household to be better than it is today. The analogous optimism figures are at least 60 per cent in Asia and Africa, and 45 per cent in Central and Latin America. Only around 20 per cent of Africans, Central and Latin Americans, and Europeans expect the future to be worse than today, while among the more optimistic Asians this figure is closer to 10 per cent. (For a discussion on optimism and poverty in Africa, see Graham and Hoover 2007.)

3.2 Method

When we carry out our multivariate regression analyses of current and future living conditions, we will control for a number of individual-level variables so that we compare like with like. In particular, we will control for age, age-squared, gender, the highest level of education achieved (with three levels: at most primary, at most secondary, and at least post-secondary), and labour-force status (unemployed, employed, and out of the labour force). In Asian and African countries we will include an additional control for living in urban or rural areas. All regressions will include wave and country dummies, although their associated coefficients will not be reported for space reasons.

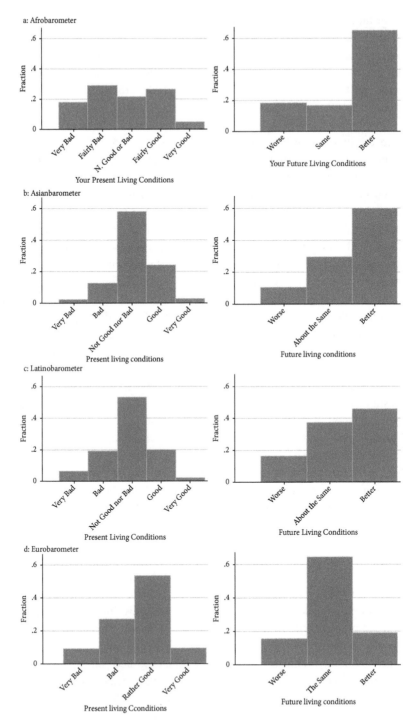

Figure 10.1 The distribution of the dependent variables

Source: Authors', based on data from the Afrobarometer, Asianbarometer, Latinobarometer, and Eurobarometer.

The descriptive statistics for the variables that appear in our sample are shown in Tables 10.1–4 for our four different Barometer surveys. The majority of the sample are of working age and employed (except in the Afrobarometer). In the Afrobarometer and Asianbarometer surveys that provide information on the area of residence, the majority live in rural areas. Regarding education, the most

Table 10.1 Descriptive statistics: Afrobarometer

	Mean	SD	Min.	Max.
Present living conditions [1–5]	2.67	1.16	1	5
Future living conditions [1–3]	2.46	0.79	1	3
No. functioning failures [0–16]	4.25	3.76	0	16
Deprivation	1.86	2.17	0	13.90
Satisfaction	1.86	1.52	0	9.29
Alienation	3.72	1.51	0	13.92
Gini	46.31	9.60	24	64.79
Age	36.98	14.43	19	89
Female	0.50	0.50	0	1
At most primary education	0.56	0.50	0	1
At most secondary education	0.34	0.47	0	1
At least post-secondary education	0.11	0.31	0	1
Employed	0.34	0.47	0	1
Unemployed	0.30	0.46	0	1
Out of the labour force	0.36	0.48	0	1
Urban	0.37	0.48	0	1

Source: Authors' illustration based on the Afrobarometer.

Table 10.2 Descriptive statistics: Asianbarometer

	Mean	SD	Min.	Max.
Present living conditions [1–5]	3.18	0.73	1	5
Future living conditions [1–3]	2.49	0.68	1	3
No. functioning failures [0–8]	3.87	2.12	0	8
Deprivation	0.90	0.84	0	6.05
Satisfaction	0.90	0.95	0	5.96
Alienation	1.81	0.70	1.02	6.05
Gini	39.88	3.79	33.44	46.05
Age	41.85	14.34	20	89
Female	0.50	0.50	0	1
At most primary education	0.40	0.49	0	1
At most secondary education	0.45	0.50	0	1
At least post-secondary education	0.15	0.36	0	1
Employed	0.69	0.46	0	1
Unemployed	0.08	0.28	0	1
Out of the labour force	0.22	0.42	0	1
Urban	0.39	0.49	0	1

Source: Authors' illustration based on the Asianbarometer.

Table 10.3 Descriptive statistics: Latinobarometer

	Mean	SD	Min.	Max.
Present living conditions [1–5]	2.91	0.85	1	5
Future living conditions [1–3]	2.29	0.73	1	3
No. functioning failures [0–8]	3.31	2.04	0	8
Deprivation	0.92	0.94	0	6.90
Satisfaction	0.92	0.90	0	6.51
Alienation	1.83	0.73	0.30	6.90
Gini	51.08	4.52	36	59.10
Age	41.00	15.67	20	90
Female	0.51	0.50	0	1
At most primary education	0.46	0.50	0	1
At most secondary education	0.36	0.48	0	1
At least post-secondary education	0.18	0.38	0	1
Employed	0.59	0.49	0	1
Unemployed	0.07	0.25	0	1
Out the labour-force	0.35	0.48	0	1

Source: Authors' illustration, based on the Latinobarometer.

Table 10.4 Descriptive statistics: Eurobarometer

	Mean	SD	Min.	Max.
Present living conditions [1–4]	2.64	0.78	1	4
Future living conditions [1–3]	2.04	0.59	1	3
No. functioning failures [0–8]	3.21	2.19	0	7
Deprivation	1.16	1.17	0	5.62
Satisfaction	1.16	0.98	0	5.05
Alienation	2.31	0.70	1.17	5.62
Gini	30.56	4.15	23.70	38.60
Age	52.37	16.70	18	90
Female	0.55	0.50	0	1
At most primary education	0.32	0.47	0	1
At most secondary education	0.42	0.49	0	1
At least post-secondary education	0.26	0.44	0	1
Employed	0.51	0.50	0	1
Unemployed	0.10	0.30	0	1
Out of the labour-force	0.39	0.49	0	1

Source: Authors' illustration, based on the Eurobarometer.

common category in Africa and Central and Latin America is having at most achieved a primary level of education, while in Asia and Europe the most common category is at least secondary level.

The general model of subjective well-being we estimate is of the following form:

$$wb_{itc} = \beta_1 + \beta_2 M_{itc} + \beta_3 Gini_{tc} + \beta_4 X_{itc} + \alpha_c + \lambda_t + \epsilon_{itc} \tag{4}$$

where q_{itc} is the count of functioning failures (which here is a measure of the absolute living standards of the individual); M_{itc} refers to one of the relative inequality measures discussed in Section 2 to assess the comparative perspective of inequality; and $Gini_{tc}$ is the Gini index, capturing individuals' normative reactions to inequality.

The specification in equation 4 allows us to estimate the absolute, comparative, and normative components of subjective well-being with respect to economic resources. For the indices in which a comparison group has to be specified, we impose that this group consists of individuals living in the same country at a given point in time. The vector X_{itc} includes individual-level control variables (age, gender, urban residence, education, and labour-force status), while α_c and λ_t are respectively the country and wave fixed effects. We present results here based on linear (OLS) estimation: the pattern of results is the same using non-linear estimation techniques such as ordered probit or ordered logit. We standardize both the dependent variable and all of the objective measures of deprivation, so that the estimated coefficients are βs, representing the effect in terms of the standard deviation of the dependent variable of a one standard deviation change in the objective measure on the right-hand side. All regressions have standard errors clustered at the country/year level.

3.3 Results

The control variables attract the following estimated coefficients (see Tables 10. A6–A9). As in the subjective well-being literature, the relationship between age and current living conditions is U-shaped, with the lowest level at around age 50. Women and those living in urban areas have a more negative evaluation of their living conditions. With respect to labour-force status, we find a negative estimated coefficient for the unemployed and a positive coefficient for the employed, as compared to our reference category of individuals who are out of the labour force. Education is very strongly correlated with current living conditions, which is to be expected if it is acting as a proxy for income. Similar results hold for the evaluation of future living conditions, even though the size of the coefficients is smaller.

Tables 10.5–8 show the estimated coefficients of our key explanatory variables (which also appear at the head of the full set of results in Tables 10.A6–A9). There are two specifications, depending on how the comparative component is specified: as two separate sums of the differences with worse-off and better-off individuals (deprivation and satisfaction in columns 1 and 3), or as a global sum of differences with respect to everybody (alienation in columns 2 and 4). The first coefficient in each regression refers to the absolute component of standards of living, the number of functioning failures, q_{itc}; the following three entries then capture the comparative effect of inequality via relative deprivation and satisfaction together,

Table 10.5 Economic conditions and inequality: OLS results in the Afrobarometer

	Present		Future	
	(1)	(2)	(3)	(4)
No. functioning failures	−0.203***	−0.231***	−0.169***	−0.144***
	(0.050)	(0.012)	(0.044)	(0.012)
Deprivation	0.017		0.053*	
	(0.034)		(0.031)	
Satisfaction	0.037*		0.017	
	(0.021)		(0.019)	
Alienation		0.028**		0.027**
		(0.012)		(0.012)
Gini	0.100	0.097	0.128*	0.130*
	(0.076)	(0.076)	(0.074)	(0.074)
No.observations	43,865	43,865	38,514	38,514
Adjusted R^2	0.140	0.140	0.135	0.135

Notes: Clustered standard errors are in parentheses. The controls include the variables in Table 10.1, and wave and country fixed effects. * $p < 0.1$, ** $p < 0.05$, *** $p < 0.01$.

Source: Authors' calculations, based on data from the Afrobarometer.

Table 10.6 Economic conditions and inequality: OLS results in the Asianbarometer

	Present		Future	
	(1)	(2)	(3)	(4)
No. functioning failures	−0.002	−0.173***	0.075	−0.053***
	(0.068)	(0.027)	(0.054)	(0.011)
Deprivation	−0.098**		−0.064**	
	(0.039)		(0.032)	
Satisfaction	0.034		0.036	
	(0.029)		(0.022)	
Alienation		−0.027		−0.012
		(0.017)		(0.015)
Gini	−0.064***	−0.067**	−0.038**	−0.040*
	(0.013)	(0.026)	(0.015)	(0.021)
No. observations	13,542	13,542	13,542	13,542
Adjusted R^2	0.110	0.110	0.240	0.240

Notes: Clustered standard errors are in parentheses. The controls include the variables in Table 10.2, and wave and country fixed effects. * $p < 0.1$, ** $p < 0.05$, *** $p < 0.01$.

Source: Authors' calculations based on data from the Asianbarometer.

Table 10.7 Economic conditions and inequality: OLS results in the Latinobarometer

	Present		Future	
	(1)	(2)	(3)	(4)
No. functioning failures	-0.144***	-0.165***	-0.082***	-0.068***
	(0.022)	(0.009)	(0.021)	(0.007)
Deprivation	0.002		0.022**	
	(0.011)		(0.009)	
Satisfaction	0.024**		0.006	
	(0.012)		(0.011)	
Alienation		0.010**		0.011***
		(0.005)		(0.004)
Gini	-0.035	-0.035	0.138***	0.137***
	(0.048)	(0.048)	(0.046)	(0.046)
No. observations	168,279	168,279	135,216	135,216
Adjusted R^2	0.135	0.135	0.077	0.077

Notes: Clustered standard errors are in parentheses. The controls include the variables in Table 10.3, and wave and country fixed effects. * $p < 0.1$, ** $p < 0.05$, *** $p < 0.01$.

Source: Authors' calculations based on data from the Latinobarometer.

Table 10.8 Economic conditions and inequality: OLS results in the Eurobarometer

	Present		Future	
	(1)	(2)	(3)	(4)
No. functioning failures	0.019	-0.202***	0.143	-0.074***
	(0.095)	(0.006)	(0.136)	(0.008)
Deprivation	-0.099*		-0.100	
	(0.052)		(0.072)	
Satisfaction	0.115***		0.110*	
	(0.041)		(0.062)	
Alienation		0.011**		0.009**
		(0.005)		(0.004)
Gini	0.035	0.020	0.061	0.048
	(0.035)	(0.034)	(0.040)	(0.036)
Observations	100,379	100,379	97,778	97,778
Adjusted R^2	0.305	0.305	0.082	0.082

Notes: Clustered standard errors are in parentheses. The controls include the variables in Table 10.4, and wave and country fixed effects. * $p < 0.1$, ** $p < 0.05$, *** $p < 0.01$.

Source: Authors' calculations based on data from the Eurobarometer.

or alienation where the gaps between the individual and the better-off and worse-off individuals are treated symmetrically; the final estimated coefficient is that on the Gini coefficient that measures the normative effect of inequality.

Functioning failures reduce the evaluation of current living standards, as might be expected: the more objectively deprived the individual is, the lower the evaluation of their current life. The effect size is large here: a one standard deviation rise in the index in question reduces the evaluation of current living conditions by around one-quarter of a standard deviation. The results for the expectations of future living conditions are similar, although the effect size is, on average, lower, and in one instance, for the Eurobarometer in the first specification, positive.

When relative comparisons are introduced in the form of deprivation and satisfaction in the evaluation of the present, they are both separately significant only in the Eurobarometer. Here, seeing oneself as better-off than others increases the evaluation of current living conditions while comparisons with the better-off have the opposite effect. In the other continents, only one of the two is significant. In Asia it is the negative effect of relative deprivation that matters, while in Africa and Central and Latin America what counts is the positive effect of satisfaction with respect to those who are worse-off. The results for expected future living conditions for Europeans and Asians are not qualitatively different from those with respect to their current living conditions, while in the Afrobarometer and Latinobarometer being more deprived now attracts a positive and significant coefficient (with the coefficient on deprivation being twice as large as that on satisfaction).

While the (positive, but not always significant) satisfaction result is to be expected, the positive effect of comparisons to the *better-off*, as measured by D_p is more commonly found in volatile socioeconomic environments, such as in the earlier stages of economic development, which can be argued to apply to many of the African and Central and Latin American countries in our sample. This positive effect of others' good fortune on the individual's own evaluation of their life is known in the literature as the 'tunnel effect' of Hirschman (1973): the presence of better-off individuals here does not produce a sentiment of relative deprivation due to social comparisons, but rather a positive signal that the individual may improve their own situation in the future (see Senik (2004) for a similar result in Russia during the 1990s, and Grosfeld and Senik (2010) for the analysis of attitudes to inequality in a growing country, Poland; see also D'Ambrosio and Frick (2012) for a dynamic version of the tunnel effect).

When relative comparisons are introduced in the form of differences to others without further distinction between the better-off and worse-off, the positive effect prevails everywhere except in Asia, which was to be expected from the previous results where only relative deprivation mattered (the satisfaction coefficient in columns 1 and 3 is insignificant). Europe is of particular interest here, where both deprivation and satisfaction had independent and significant effects: when added together, what prevails is the positive effect of satisfaction.

The normative effect of inequality is measured by the coefficient on the Gini index. This is not calculated from within the Barometer data, but is matched in as an aggregate measure of income inequality from an independent source, the WIID. The coefficient on the Gini index captures the effect of the individual's disinterested evaluation of economic inequality without making any comparisons to others. The results are very mixed across our regions of the world—arguably mirroring the wide variety of findings in the existing literature summarized by Clark and D'Ambrosio (2015).

Aggregate inequality in the country of residence attracts a positive, but insignificant, estimated coefficient in the Afrobarometer and the Eurobarometer, and a negative, but insignificant, estimated coefficient in the Latinobarometer. The only significant estimated coefficient on inequality for current living conditions is negative in the Asianbarometer. The results regarding the correlation between the Gini and future living conditions are more significant in general, but still not uniform: this correlation is positive for Africans and Central and Latin Americans, negative for Asians, and insignificant for Europeans.

4 Conclusion

We have appealed to repeated cross-section information on well-being, as captured by current and future evaluations of standards of living, from across the world in four different Barometer series. We relate these well-being measures to not only one's own economic resources but also the distribution of resources at the country–year level. With respect to the latter, we divide this distribution up into a comparative component (as measured by the gaps between those who are richer than the individual—deprivation—and the sum of gaps between those who are poorer—satisfaction) and the normative evaluation of distribution (conditional on these gaps), given by the Gini coefficient.

We find that all of the absolute, comparative, and normative components of inequality matter for individuals' evaluations of their current and future living conditions, which underlines the multi-faceted nature of the evaluation of standard of living. While the positive correlation between one's own resources and life evaluations is unsurprising, the relationship of the latter to the distribution of resources is anything bar standard across the four regions of the world that we have considered. The 'typical' pattern of a negative effect of gaps to the better-off but a positive effect of gaps to the worse-off turns out to hold only in Europe. In some other parts of the world, gaps to the better-off either have no correlation with life evaluations or, in Africa and Central and Latin America, are associated with more positive expectations of one's future life. The positive estimated coefficient on gaps to the worse-off is found more often, but is notably absent in Asia, a result that surely bears further research. Last, the Gini coefficient itself exhibits a wide variety of estimated coefficients, being negatively correlated with current life evaluation in Asia only, and attracting insignificant coefficients everywhere else. The story is somewhat more uniform regarding future life evaluations, where the Gini coefficient attracts a positive and significant estimated coefficient in Africa and Central and Latin America (in line with the positive effect of gaps to the better-off noted previously), but a negative significant coefficient in Asia. Clearly the nature of the relationship between the distribution of the resources and measures of individual well-being over time is not universal, and merits substantial separate research in different regions of the world.

References

Akay, A., and P. Martinsson (2011). 'Does Relative Income Matter for the Very Poor? Evidence from Rural Ethiopia'. *Economics Letters*, 110: 213–15.

Alkire, S. and J.E. Foster (2011). 'Counting and Multidimensional Poverty Measurement'. *Journal of Public Economics*, 95: 476–87.

Bookwalter, J., and D. Dalenberg (2010). 'Relative to What or Whom? The Importance of Norms and Relative Standing to Wellbeing in South Africa'. *World Development*, 38: 345–55.

Bossert, W., C. D'Ambrosio, and S.R. Chakravarty (2013). 'Multidimensional Poverty and Material Deprivation with Discrete Data'. *Review of Income and Wealth*, 59: 29–43.

Clark, A.E., and C. D'Ambrosio (2015). 'Attitudes to Income Inequality: Experimental and Survey Evidence'. In A. Atkinson and F. Bourguignon (eds), *Handbook of Income Distribution*, Volume 2A. Amsterdam: Elsevier.

Clark, A.E., and C. D'Ambrosio (2017). 'Living conditions and wellbeing: evidence from African countries'. WIDER Working Paper 2017/209. Helsinki: UNU-WIDER.

Clark, A.E., and C. Senik (eds) (2014). *Happiness and Economic Growth: Lessons from Developing Countries*. Oxford: Oxford University Press.

D'Ambrosio, C., and J. Frick (2012). 'Individual Wellbeing in a Dynamic Perspective'. *Economica*, 79: 284–302.

D'Ambrosio, C., and R.I. Rodrigues (2008). 'Deprivation in the São Paulo Districts: Evidence from 2000'. *World Development*, 36: 1094–112.

Davies, J.B. (2016). 'The Gini Coefficient and Personal Inequality Measurement'. Mimeo. London, Canada: University of Western Ontario.

Ferreira, F.H., N. Lustig, and D. Teles (2015). 'Appraising Cross-National Income Inequality Databases: An Introduction'. *Journal of Economic Inequality*, 13: 497–526.

Graham, C., and M. Hoover (2007). 'Optimism and Poverty in Africa: Adaptation or a Means to Survival?' Afrobarometer Working Paper 76. Accra: Afrobarometer.

Grosfeld, I., and C. Senik (2010). 'The Emerging Aversion to Inequality: Evidence from Poland 1992–2005'. *Economics of Transition*, 18: 1–26.

Hirschman, A.O. (1973). 'The Changing Tolerance for Income Inequality in the Course of Economic Development'. *Quarterly Journal of Economics*, 87: 544–66.

Jenkins, S.P. (2015). 'World Income Inequality Databases: An Assessment of WIID and SWIID'. *Journal of Economic Inequality*, 13: 629–71.

Lentz, E. (2017). 'Keeping Up with the Neighbors? Reference Groups in Ghana'. *Economic Development and Cultural Change*, 66: 91–112.

Senik, C. (2004). 'When Information Dominates Comparison: Learning from Russian Subjective Panel Data'. *Journal of Public Economics*, 88: 2099–123.

Shenga, C. (2010). 'Economic conditions, living conditions and poverty in Mozambique'. Afrobarometer Briefing Paper 87. Accra: Afrobarometer

Solt, F. (2013). 'SWIID: The Standardized World Income Inequality Database, Version 4.0'. Statistical database. Iowa City: University of Iowa.

Van de Werfhorst, H.G., and W. Salverda (2012). 'Consequences of Economic Inequality: Introduction to a Special Issue'. *Research in Social Stratification and Mobility*, 30: 377–87.

Yitzhaki, S. (1979). 'Relative Deprivation and the Gini Coefficient'. *Quarterly Journal of Economics*, 93: 321–4.

Appendix

Table 10.A1 List of items per dataset

Afrobarometer	Asianbarometer	Latinobarometer	Eurobarometer
Food	Mobile phone	TV	TV
Water	Cooler	Refrigerator	DVD player
Medical care	Fridge	Computer	Computer
Cooking fuel	Telephone	Washing machine	Internet access
	TV	Telephone	Car
	Radio	Car	Laptop
	Camera	Drinking water	Tablet
	Cable TV	Sewerage system	Smartphone

Source: Authors' illustration based on the Afrobarometer, Asianbarometer, Latinobarometer, and Eurobarometer.

Table 10.A2 Number of observations per country per wave: Afrobarometer

	2003	2004	2008	2010	Total
Botswana	1,112	0	0	1,126	2,238
Burkina Faso	0	0	1,080	0	1,080
Cape Verde	1,140	0	1,189	0	2,329
Egypt	0	0	0	1,148	1,148
Ghana	0	1,128	0	0	1,128
Kenya	0	1,209	0	0	1,209
Lesotho	1,156	0	0	0	1,156
Liberia	0	0	1,143	0	1,143
Madagascar	0	0	0	1,138	1,138
Malawi	0	1,073	1,086	2,252	4,411
Mali	1,189	0	1,171	0	2,360
Mozambique	1,044	0	1,016	0	2,060
Namibia	1,126	0	1,141	1,112	3,379
Nigeria	2,253	0	2,157	2,215	6,625
Senegal	1,045	1,101	0	0	2,146
South Africa	0	2,256	2,258	0	4,514
Tanzania	1,162	0	0	0	1,162
Uganda	0	2,294	2,345	0	4,639
Total	11,227	9,061	14,586	8,991	43,685

Source: Authors' illustration based on the Afrobarometer.

Table 10.A3 Number of observations per country per wave: Asianbarometer

	2006	2010	Total
Cambodia	716	1,098	1,814
Indonesia	0	1,286	1,286
Japan	767	1,465	2,232
Malaysia	972	1,034	2,006
Mongolia	1,086	0	1,086
Philippines	0	1,042	1,042
Singapore	0	666	666
Thailand	970	946	1,916
Total	4,819	5,825	13,542
Vietnam	1,075	419	1,494

Source: Authors' illustration based on the Asianbarometer.

Table 10.A4 Number of observations per country per wave: Latinobarometer

	1998	2000	2001	2002	2003	2004	2005	2006	2007	2008	2009	2010	Total
Argentina	1,054	1,067	1,008	1,053	1,095	1,080	1,057	0	1,076	1,097	1,084	1,110	11,781
Bolivia	539	879	934	1,088	0	1,068	1,018	1,050	1,052	1,056	1,077	0	9,761
Brazil	876	876	860	863	1,045	1,042	1,059	1,050	1,040	1,067	1,063	1,067	11,908
Chile	1,072	1,066	0	0	1,106	0	0	1,103	0	0	1,113	0	5,460
Colombia	0	1,118	1,105	1,087	1,099	1,101	1,089	0	1,094	1,112	1,066	1,108	10,970
Costa Rica	513	808	892	922	0	928	906	841	856	861	898	875	9,300
Dominican Rep.	0	0	0	0	0	925	912	805	794	856	799	905	5,996
Ecuador	0	1,081	1,051	1,087	1,111	1,106	1,078	1,114	1,100	1,108	1,108	1,103	12,044
El Salvador	782	900	899	913	940	929	926	905	828	826	826	877	10,565
Guatemala	0	788	0	876	903	911	0	808	0	0	0	893	5,179
Honduras	726	0	905	904	912	906	918	820	747	858	858	891	9,475
Mexico	1,044	0	0	1,132	0	1,047	1,061	1,103	0	1,118	0	1,128	7,633
Nicaragua	537	0	843	0	0	0	841	0	0	0	889	0	3,110
Panama	0	907	879	928	910	933	930	914	872	903	903	900	9,979
Paraguay	0	0	515	514	531	540	1,079	1,034	1,025	1,066	1,082	1,065	8,451
Peru	885	895	917	1,099	1,100	1,100	1,082	1,094	1,073	1,064	1,091	1,086	12,486
Uruguay	1,090	1,116	1,124	1,109	1,088	1,102	1,119	1,119	1,074	1,121	1,091	1,071	13,224
Venezuela	0	1,088	1,098	1,091	1,100	1,100	1,101	1,111	1,093	1,093	0	1,082	10,957
Total	9,118	12,589	13,030	14,657	12,940	15,818	16,176	14,871	13,724	15,206	14,989	15,161	168,279

Source: Authors' illustration based on the Latinobarometer.

Table 10.A5 Number of observations per country per wave: Eurobarometer

	2014 (April)	2014 (November)	2015 (April)	2015 (November)	Total
Austria	852	941	927	921	3,641
Belgium	921	949	913	929	3,718
Bulgaria	930	921	951	922	3,724
Croatia	888	889	890	894	3,561
Cyprus	455	443	447	459	1,804
Czech Republic	978	976	920	928	3,802
Denmark	927	900	932	905	3,664
Estonia	926	895	890	893	3,604
Finland	913	901	913	897	3,624
France	913	929	893	940	3,675
Germany	1,340	1,449	1,376	1,422	5,587
Greece	921	922	927	922	3,692
Hungary	930	1,009	979	986	3,904
Ireland	1,203	1,193	0	0	2,396
Italy	871	880	872	870	3,493
Latvia	890	897	894	909	3,590
Lithuania	892	892	895	906	3,585
Luxembourg	446	459	456	465	1,826
Macedonia	0	942	0	0	942
Malta	470	471	467	455	1,863
Montenegro	0	416	0	0	416
Netherlands	943	940	921	952	3,756
Poland	898	876	858	787	3,419
Portugal	857	901	908	866	3,532
Romania	906	882	877	865	3,530
Serbia	0	838	839	771	2,448
Slovakia	893	939	928	936	3,696
Slovenia	940	956	897	900	3,693
Spain	922	939	884	892	3,637
Sweden	994	950	969	957	3,870
United Kingdom	871	917	889	919	3,596
Total	24,902	27,414	24,516	24,470	100,379

Source: Authors' illustration based on the Eurobarometer.

Table 10.A6 Economic conditions and inequality: OLS results in the Afrobarometer—all controls

	Present		Future	
	(1)	(2)	(3)	(4)
No. functioning failures	−0.203***	−0.231***	−0.169***	−0.144***
	(0.050)	(0.012)	(0.044)	(0.012)
Deprivation	0.017		0.053*	
	(0.034)		(0.031)	
Satisfaction	0.037*		0.017	
	(0.021)		(0.019)	
Alienation		0.028**		0.027**
		(0.012)		(0.012)
Gini	0.100	0.097	0.128*	0.130*
	(0.076)	(0.076)	(0.074)	(0.074)
Age	−0.013***	−0.013***	−0.011***	−0.011***
	(0.002)	(0.002)	(0.002)	(0.002)
Age-squared/100	0.012***	0.012***	0.008***	0.008***
	(0.002)	(0.002)	(0.002)	(0.002)
Female	0.002	0.002	−0.004	−0.003
	(0.011)	(0.011)	(0.011)	(0.011)
At most secondary education	0.057***	0.056***	0.033*	0.034*
	(0.017)	(0.017)	(0.020)	(0.020)
At least post-secondary education	0.206***	0.206***	0.074***	0.074***
	(0.021)	(0.021)	(0.025)	(0.025)
Employed	0.040**	0.039**	0.058***	0.058***
	(0.019)	(0.019)	(0.021)	(0.021)
Unemployed	−0.108***	−0.109***	0.009	0.009
	(0.017)	(0.017)	(0.019)	(0.019)
Urban	0.019	0.015	−0.055***	−0.052***
	(0.019)	(0.018)	(0.020)	(0.019)
Observations	43,865	43,865	38,514	38,514
Adjusted R^2	0.140	0.140	0.135	0.135

Notes: Clustered standard errors are in parentheses. Wave and country fixed effects are included but the coefficients are not reported. * $p < 0.1$, ** $p < 0.05$, *** $p < 0.01$.

Source: Authors' calculations based on data from the Afrobarometer.

Table 10.A7 Economic conditions and inequality: OLS results in the Asianbarometer—all controls

	Present		Future	
	(1)	(2)	(3)	(4)
No. functioning failures	−0.002	−0.173***	0.075	−0.053***
	(0.068)	(0.027)	(0.054)	(0.012)
Deprivation	−0.098**		−0.064*	
	(0.039)		(0.032)	
Satisfaction	0.034		0.036	
	(0.029)		(0.022)	
Alienation		−0.027		−0.012
		(0.017)		(0.009)
Gini	−0.064***	−0.067**	−0.038**	−0.040
	(0.013)	(0.026)	(0.015)	(0.026)
Age	−0.029***	−0.029***	−0.018***	0.010***
	(0.006)	(0.006)	(0.004)	(0.003)
Age-squared/100	0.028***	0.028***	0.010***	−0.001
	(0.006)	(0.006)	(0.003)	(0.016)
Female	−0.004	−0.003	−0.002	−0.002
	(0.022)	(0.022)	(0.018)	(0.018)
At most secondary education	0.019	0.021	0.033	0.035
	(0.023)	(0.023)	(0.034)	(0.034)
At least post-secondary education	0.120***	0.122***	0.067*	0.069*
	(0.030)	(0.031)	(0.036)	(0.036)
Employed	0.010	0.011	0.015	0.015
	(0.033)	(0.033)	(0.019)	(0.019)
Unemployed	−0.139**	−0.137**	0.063***	0.064***
	(0.052)	(0.052)	(0.020)	(0.020)
Urban	−0.079	−0.082	−0.015	−0.018
	(0.051)	(0.051)	(0.024)	(0.024)
Observations	13,542	13,542	13,542	13,542
Adjusted R^2	0.110	0.110	0.240	0.240

Notes: Clustered standard errors are in parentheses. Wave and country fixed effects are included but the coefficients are not reported. $^*p < 0.1$, $^{**}p < 0.05$, $^{***}p < 0.01$.

Source: Authors' calculations based on data from the Asianbarometer.

Table 10.A8 Economic conditions and inequality: OLS results in the Latinobarometer—all controls

	Present		Future	
	(1)	(2)	(3)	(4)
No. functioning failures	−0.144***	−0.165***	−0.082***	−0.068***
	(0.022)	(0.009)	(0.021)	(0.007)
Deprivation	0.002		0.022**	
	(0.011)		(0.009)	
Satisfaction	0.024**		0.006	
	(0.012)		(0.011)	
Alienation		0.010**		0.011***
		(0.005)		(0.004)
Gini	−0.035	−0.035	0.138***	0.137***
	(0.048)	(0.048)	(0.046)	(0.046)
Age	−0.023***	−0.023***	−0.017***	−0.017***
	(0.001)	(0.001)	(0.001)	(0.001)
Age-squared/100	0.019***	0.019***	0.010***	0.010***
	(0.001)	(0.001)	(0.001)	(0.001)
Female	−0.031***	−0.031***	−0.006	−0.006
	(0.007)	(0.007)	(0.007)	(0.007)
At most secondary education	0.058***	0.057***	0.052***	0.053***
	(0.009)	(0.009)	(0.010)	(0.010)
At least post-secondary education	0.117***	0.117***	0.025*	0.025*
	(0.015)	(0.015)	(0.014)	(0.014)
Employed	0.012*	0.012*	0.020**	0.020**
	(0.007)	(0.007)	(0.008)	(0.008)
Unemployed	−0.204***	−0.206***	−0.010	−0.010
	(0.015)	(0.016)	(0.013)	(0.013)
Observations	168,279	168,279	135,216	135,216
Adjusted R^2	0.135	0.135	0.077	0.077

Notes: Clustered standard errors are in parentheses. Wave and country fixed effects are included but the coefficients are not reported. * $p < 0.1$, ** $p < 0.05$, *** $p < 0.01$.

Source: Authors' calculations based on data from the Latinobarometer.

Table 10.A9 Economic conditions and inequality: OLS results in the Eurobarometer—all controls

	Present		Future	
	(1)	(2)	(3)	(4)
No. functioning failures	0.019	-0.202***	0.143	-0.074***
	(0.095)	(0.006)	(0.136)	(0.008)
Deprivation	-0.099*		-0.100	
	(0.052)		(0.072)	
Satisfaction	0.115***		0.110*	
	(0.041)		(0.062)	
Alienation		0.011**		0.009**
		(0.005)		(0.004)
Gini	0.035	0.020	0.061	0.048
	(0.035)	(0.034)	(0.040)	(0.036)
Age	-0.032***	-0.032***	-0.031***	-0.031***
	(0.002)	(0.002)	(0.002)	(0.002)
Age-squared/100	0.037***	0.037***	0.022***	0.022***
	(0.001)	(0.001)	(0.001)	(0.001)
Female	-0.024***	-0.024***	-0.023***	-0.023***
	(0.006)	(0.006)	(0.007)	(0.007)
At most secondary education	0.145***	0.144***	0.046***	0.045***
	(0.009)	(0.009)	(0.008)	(0.008)
At least post-secondary education	0.263***	0.263***	0.108***	0.108***
	(0.012)	(0.012)	(0.011)	(0.011)
Employed	0.173***	0.173***	0.043***	0.043***
	(0.012)	(0.012)	(0.010)	(0.010)
Unemployed	-0.480***	-0.480***	-0.009	-0.009
	(0.019)	(0.019)	(0.020)	(0.020)
Observations	100,379	100,379	97,778	97,778
Adjusted R^2	0.305	0.305	0.082	0.082

Notes: Clustered standard errors are in parentheses. Wave and country fixed effects are included but the coefficients are not reported. * $p < 0.1$, ** $p < 0.05$, *** $p < 0.01$.

Source: Authors' calculations based on data from the Eurobarometer.

11

China and the United States

Different Economic Models But Similarly Low Levels of Socioeconomic Mobility

Roy van der Weide and Ambar Narayan

1 Introduction

The US and China are the world's largest economies, accounting for about one-third of the world's economic output.[1] The two giants are different in a multitude of ways, including in population size, political system, and level of development. The US has historically ranked among the world's richest countries in per capita terms. But China has been catching up. While output per capita is still notably lower in China, rapid economic growth sustained over multiple decades has brought China to parity with the US in terms of aggregate output (Cheremukhin et al. 2015; Song et al. 2011; Zhu 2012; Zilibotti 2017).

The unprecedented economic development in China is said to have fuelled a level of optimism in the country. A recent op-ed in the *New York Times* (Hernandez and Bui 2018) observes:

> China is still much poorer overall than the US. But the Chinese have taken a commanding lead in that most intangible but valuable of economic indicators: optimism...the Chinese are now among the most optimistic people in the world—much more so than Americans and Europeans, according to public opinion surveys. What has changed? Most of all, an economic expansion without precedent in modern history.

On the other hand, the US of course is home to the American Dream, which embodies a certain degree of optimism. The American Dream represents the

[1] The authors are most grateful to John Giles, Branko Milanovic, Finn Tarp, Colin Xu, and Li Yang for providing valuable inputs and comments. We also wish to thank Rakesh Gupta Nichanametla Ramasubbaiah for excellent research assistance. The findings, interpretations, and conclusions expressed in this paper are entirely those of the authors. They do not necessarily represent the views of the International Bank for Reconstruction and Development—World Bank and its affiliated organizations, or those of the Executive Directors of the World Bank or the governments they represent.

Roy van der Weide and Ambar Narayan, *China and the United States: Different Economic Models But Similarly Low Levels of Socioeconomic Mobility* In: *Inequality in the Developing World*. Edited by: Carlos Gradín, Murray Leibbrandt, and Finn Tarp, Oxford University Press (2021). © United Nations University World Institute for Development Economics Research (UNU-WIDER). DOI: 10.1093/oso/9780198863960.003.0011

belief that with hard work and determination anyone can achieve success and prosperity. In 1931, James Truslow Adams defined it as meaning that 'life should be better and richer for everyone, with opportunity for each according to ability and achievement' regardless of the social class one is born into (Adams 1931).

Are these two economic giants indeed lands of opportunity where individuals have the best chances of realizing their human potential? A land of opportunity is a society where an individual's chances of success depend little on the socioeconomic status of the family into which he or she is born. The extent to which this is true for a country can be measured using indicators of intergenerational mobility. A country with higher intergenerational mobility is one where an individual's chances of success are more aligned with one's innate ability and efforts than with one's family background (a circumstance that is beyond a person's control). Low mobility, on the other hand, indicates an uneven playing field, which leads to a waste of human capital when talented individuals are not given the opportunity to realize their potential, and misallocation of resources when rewards are not matched with ability. Resolving this is therefore likely to raise the stock of human capital, improve efficiency, and stimulate economic growth.

Levelling the playing field to stimulate socioeconomic mobility is costly. The large national incomes of the US and China, however, give these giants the necessary fiscal space to achieve exactly that. Yet, the existing empirical literature ranks the US as a country with a relatively low level of intergenerational mobility when compared to other high-income countries, mostly from Europe (Björklund and Jäntti 1997; Corak 2013). How does the US compare to China? And how has mobility co-evolved over time for these two giants?

First, we examine estimates of intergenerational mobility in income for the US and China along with estimates for seventy-three other countries that have recently been compiled by Equalchances (2018) and Narayan et al. (2018). Having estimates of income mobility for seventy-five countries representative of more than 80 per cent of the world's population allows us to put the difference in income mobility between the US and China in a global perspective. Second, we estimate how intergenerational mobility in the two giants has co-evolved over time by focusing on mobility in education for individuals born in the 1940s up to those born in the 1980s (the youngest cohort that would have had a chance to complete their education at the time the survey data was collected).

The data used to estimate education mobility are the Panel Study of Income Dynamics (PSID) from 2015, for the US, and the China Family Planning Survey (CFPS) from 2012. We will focus on measures of intergenerational mobility that evaluate the degree to which individual socioeconomic success is independent of the socioeconomic success of one's parents (the success of any one individual is contingent on the family background they are born into; also referred to as 'origin independence'). Our findings are summarized in the concluding remarks.

The chapter is organized as follows. Section 2 introduces the different measures of inter-generational mobility and the data we use to estimate these measures. Section 3 places the estimates of income mobility for the US and China in a global context and confirms the strong relationship between income mobility and education mobility. A study of the co-evolution over time of intergenerational mobility in education is presented in Section 4. Section 5 provides a history of policy changes and economic conditions in the US and China that will help put the observed trends in economic mobility into context. Finally, Section 6 concludes.

2 Measuring Inter-generational Mobility

2.1 Measures of Inter-generational Mobility

Socioeconomic mobility has been interpreted in the social science literature in several ways. In this chapter, we will focus on indicators that measure the degree to which one's success is contingent on the success of one's parents. Estimates for an alternative concept of intergenerational mobility, measuring the extent of progress that one generation as a whole has made in comparison to the previous generation, are presented in Van der Weide and Narayan (2019).

Let y_i^c denote the socioeconomic status of individual i. Similarly, let y_i^p denote the socioeconomic status of their parents. Examples of socioeconomic status include one's level of income, education, and occupational prestige. The inter-generational transmission of socioeconomic status is often described by the following linear model:

$$y_i^c = c + b y_i^p + u_i,$$

where u_i denotes an error term with mean zero. Empirical estimates of b generally lie between the values 0 and 1.

We consider a variety of different indicators of intergenerational mobility: (a) $1-b$, that is, one minus the regression coefficient from eq. (1); (b) $1-\rho$, that is, one minus the Pearson correlation ρ between y_i^c and y_i^p; (c) *BHQ4*, that is, the likelihood that an individual reaches the top quarter of their generation given that he/she is born to parents from the bottom half of their generation; and (d) μ_0^{50}, that is, the expected rank of a child (in the child education distribution) whose parents are in the bottom 50 per cent of the parent education rank distribution. All these measures are common choices in the literature on inter-generational mobility, and each have their own pros and cons. The last measure is one that is advocated by Asher et al. (2019).

Note that all four measures of intergenerational mobility capture the degree to which one's socioeconomic status is determined by the socioeconomic status of one's parents. The highest values of mobility are obtained when individual success is independent from the parental background one is born into, in which case $1\text{-}b$ and $1\text{-}\rho$ would both reach unity (as the regression and correlation coefficients both tend to zero) and all individuals, including those whose parents rank in the bottom half of their generation, would have a 25 per cent likelihood of reaching the top quarter of their generation with an expected rank of 50.

The different inter-generational mobility indicators capture different aspects of the relationship between parental and individual socioeconomic status. The measures $1\text{-}b$ and $1\text{-}\rho$ focus on the strength of the relationship between parental and offspring outcomes, while BHQ4 and μ_0^{50} are also sensitive to the direction of mobility from one generation to the next. Between the four measures, ρ is the only measure that is invariant to the marginal distributions, that is, it is the only measure that is not sensitive to changes in the levels of inequality in socioeconomic outcomes across generations.

2.2 Estimating Inter-generational Mobility

2.2.1 Education Mobility

y_i^c and y_i^p in this case denote the level of education of individual i and their parents, measured by years of schooling. Boys and girls are pooled. Parental education is measured by the education level of the parent with higher education. Focusing on education in the measurement of intergenerational mobility has advantages and disadvantages. One advantage is that an individual's educational attainment does not change after a certain age when all education is likely to be completed. The same is not true for income, which varies across a person's life-cycle as he/she accumulates experience.

A potential disadvantage, however, is that education data can be relatively coarse, particularly in countries where large shares of the population have little to no education. This particularly affects the estimation of BHQ4 and μ_0^{50}, which requires the identification of individuals whose parents are in the bottom half of the parent education distribution. If most parents have no education, for example, then it is not clear which parents should be considered for the bottom half. Asher et al. (2019) put forward an approach to estimate upper and lower bounds for these mobility measures using coarse parental education data. We will use the midpoint between those two bounds as our point estimate.

2.2.2 Income Mobility

Intergenerational income mobility is commonly measured by $1\text{-}b$. Recall the linear intergenerational regression:

$$y_i^c = c + by_i^p + u_i,$$

where y_i^c and y_i^p now denote log permanent income of individual i and their parents, respectively. The regression coefficient b is often referred to as the income elasticity; $b = 0.4$ indicates that 40 per cent of differences in parental incomes are transmitted to the next generation.

We use retrospective data on parental education and age to predict parental earnings, which can then be used as an instrument in the intergenerational earnings regression. This two-sample two-stage least squares (TSTSLS) approach involves the following steps (see e.g. Björklund and Jäntti 1997): (i) estimate an income equation from an older sample that is representative of the current population of parents when they were younger (a sample of 'pseudo-parents'); (ii) use the estimated model coefficients (i.e. returns to education and experience) to predict parent income earnings at reference age using the retrospective data on the age and education of the parents as predictors; and (iii) regress offspring earnings at reference age on predicted parent earnings at reference age. Further details on the estimation of the income elasticity b can be found in the Appendix of Van der Weide and Narayan (2019).

2.3 Data

Estimates of intergenerational income elasticity are obtained directly from Equalchances (2018) and GDIM (2018).[2] These sources also provide estimates of the income elasticity for seventy-three other countries (making seventy-five countries in total, including the US and China), allowing us to place the estimates for the US and China in a global context. To facilitate cross-country comparability, all estimates have been compiled using TSTSLS as outlined in Section 2.2 with parental education and occupation serving as instruments for parental income, including for countries where parental income is in fact observed in the data (the US included). This database includes one estimate of the income elasticity per country, measuring the intergenerational transmission of income between the generation born in the 1950s/1960s and their offspring born in the 1970s/1980s. These data however do not allow us to track income mobility over time. To estimate intergenerational mobility in education in China and the US, we will be using the China Family Planning Survey (CFPS) from 2012 and the US Panel Study of Income Dynamics (PSID) from 2015,

---

[2] The Global Database of Intergenerational Mobility (GDIM) was compiled by Narayan et al. (2018).

respectively. Both surveys are nationally representative and include parental education data for individuals of all ages.[3]

In both surveys, individual education is recorded in two complementary variables: years of schooling completed and grade completed.[4] In the PSID, parental education is also available as both a continuous (years of schooling) and a categorical (grade completed) variable. In the CFPS, however, parental education is only available as a categorical variable. We convert the latter to years of schooling using UNESCO sources containing country- and year-specific mappings on the duration of educational programmes.[5]

Using these data, we will track inter-generational mobility in education from those born in the 1950s to those born in the 1980s. The decade cohorts are defined as all individuals born between the first and the last day of the relevant decade; for example, individuals from the 1980s cohort are born between 1 January 1980 and 31 December 1989. The 1980s cohort denotes the youngest cohort for which all members would have had the chance to complete their education at the time of survey data collection. Note however that individuals born in the 1980s will have benefited from public policies effective in the 1990s and 2000s, which means that estimates of inter-generational mobility for the 1980s cohort provide a measure of the extent to which recent policy interventions have been able to level the playing field.

3 Income versus Education Mobility

In a 2012 speech, the Council of Economic Advisers' chairman, Alan Krueger, observed the negative relationship between income inequality and intergenerational income mobility using data from Miles Corak for a select number of mostly developed and emerging countries. This relationship has become known as the Great Gatsby Curve (GGC); see for example Corak (2013). Social democracies such as Denmark, Norway, and Finland stand out as countries with low levels of

---

[3] The sample size of individuals aged 21 or older is about 16,000 in the PSID and 33,000 in the CFPS. In the case of China, the sampling frame does not include Hong Kong, Hainan, Inner Mongolia, Macao, Ningxia, Taiwan, Tibet, Qinghai, and Xinjiang. Data on father's education is available for 85 per cent of the PSID sample and 90 per cent of the CFPS sample. Coverage of mother's education is higher still; about 90 per cent of the PSID sample and 93 per cent of the CFPS sample.

[4] While each survey distinguishes between eight different grades, the choice of grades does not correspond perfectly, most notably the higher levels. The grades used in the PSID (CFPS) are: (1) less than primary (idem), (2) primary (idem), (3) lower secondary (junior high school), (4) upper secondary (senior high school), (5) post-secondary non-tertiary (three year college), (6) short-cycle tertiary (bachelor degree), (7) bachelor (masters), and (8) masters or doctorate (doctorate).

[5] Two sources of information are used. The first source (http://uis.unesco.org/en/isced-mappings) for the most part only conveys the duration of ISCED categories in 1997 and 2011. This source is supplemented with information from UNESCO's online database (http://data.uis.unesco.org/), which outlines the length of durations of ISCED categories by year from 1970. For further details, see Narayan et al. (2018).

inequality and some of the highest levels of mobility. At the other end of the curve are Brazil and Chile, countries with some of the highest levels of inequality and lowest levels of mobility.

It should be noted that the GGC describes a correlation, not a causal relationship. Factors that may be driving both inequality and socioeconomic mobility include large differences in quality of schooling and healthcare and differential access to these elementary services depending on the socioeconomic background children are born into, discrimination in the labour market, imperfect credit markets, and so on. One could argue that a country's position on the GGC is (in part) determined by how that country ranks in terms of inequality of opportunity, fairness, and meritocracy. In a 2013 column on the GGC, *The Economist* invokes these concepts as it compares the positions of the US with that of European countries along the curve (Suleyman 2013):

> The argument over the Great Gatsby curve is an argument about whether America's economy is fair . . . whether you are rich or poor in Europe or America depends to a great extent not on your own qualities of efforts, but on where you happen to be born. America is not a meritocracy . . . not only do those born rich tend to stay rich and vice versa, just being born in one state or another makes a huge difference to your lifelong earnings.

This observation is also highlighted in a recent study by Milanovic (2015).

How does the US compare to China in terms of inequality and socioeconomic mobility? Figure 11.1 shows an updated version of the GGC that provides global coverage by expanding the number of countries to seventy-five, including

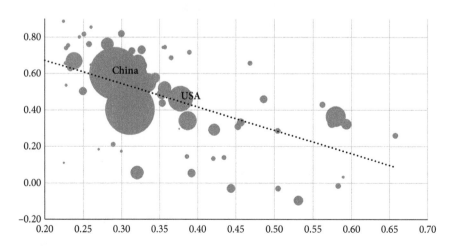

Figure 11.1 Great Gatsby curve

Source: Authors' illustration based on GDIM (2018), Equalchances (2018), and PovcalNet data.

developed, emerging, and developing countries. The size of the dots is proportional to the size of the country's economy. The US and China, standing out as the world's two largest economies, are seen to closely fit the curve, with remarkably little space between them. China is slightly more mobile and reports lower levels of inequality during parents' generation. But the differences are small when viewed from a global perspective, and inequality in China has since caught up: present generations in China and the US experience very similar levels of inequality (see e.g. Piketty et al. 2019 and Li et al. 2018).[6] The US, with income mobility comparable with selected emerging and developing countries, is notably less mobile than most high-income countries.

How has intergenerational mobility co-evolved over time? We will try to answer this question by examining intergenerational mobility in education for both countries. This allows us to estimate and compare time-trends in mobility between the two countries over an extended period of time. Education denotes an important aspect of economic well-being, and education mobility arguably has a strong association with income mobility as human capital is a key determinant of individual wage earnings.

The last statement is confirmed in Figure 11.2, which plots estimates of income mobility against estimates of education mobility for the same set of seventy-five

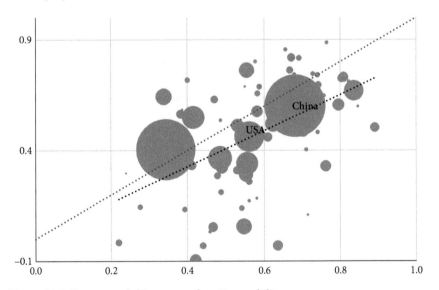

Figure 11.2 Income mobility versus education mobility

Source: Authors' illustration based on GDIM (2018), Equalchances (2018) data.

---

[6] In both the US and China, present inequality levels are high by international standards. This could negatively impact on future growth prospects (Benjamin et al. 2011; van der Weide and Milanovic 2018), particularly where high inequality reflects high inequality of opportunity and low intergenerational mobility. In the case of China, inequality at the national level has also been found to reflect significant intra-provincial inequality (Hussain et al. 1994).

countries. The two distinct measures of mobility are seen to be strongly, but not perfectly, correlated. The imperfect correlation seems intuitive. Abstracting away from estimation error(s), income mobility is also a function of whether factor markets are creating a level playing field in terms of economic opportunities (such as jobs, wages, and access to credit) in addition to reflecting differences in human capital, while education mobility solely captures the degree to which human capital accumulation is fair and efficient.

4 Intergenerational Mobility in Education over Time

A country with high relative intergenerational mobility is a country where an individual's chances of success are not contingent on the socioeconomic success of his or her parents. Governments may have several reasons for seeking to improve intergenerational mobility. In addition to arguments of fairness, there are economic arguments. When mobility is low, individuals are not operating on a level playing field. The odds of someone born to non-affluent parents will be stacked against him or her. This is not only unfair, but it also leads to a waste of human capital, as talented individuals may not be given the opportunity to reach their full potential. Reducing this inefficiency will arguably raise the stock of human capital and thereby stimulate economic growth. Since the waste of human capital tends to be concentrated toward the bottom of the distribution, the growth brought about by mobility-promoting policy interventions will more likely than not be of an inclusive nature.

Using a novel dataset for the US, Chetty et al. (2014) are able to estimate relative intergenerational mobility down to the commuting zone and county level, observing that mobility varies considerably within the country and within states.[7] Some parts of the US are found to be just as mobile as some of the most mobile countries in Europe, while in other parts of the country children face a steep uphill struggle to escape poverty when born into it. The researchers also find that the more mobile areas within the US tend to be areas that are less residentially segregated (i.e. households from different socioeconomic backgrounds and different races reside in the same neighbourhoods), have less inequality, and have higher quality public school systems, stronger social networks, and stronger family structures.

Focusing on intergenerational mobility in education, we are able to compare the time-trends in intergenerational mobility between the two giants, the US and China (see Figure 11.3). While the three different measures of mobility show slightly different trends for the US, we identify a number of conclusive

---

[7] Corak (2019) has extended this analysis to Canada.

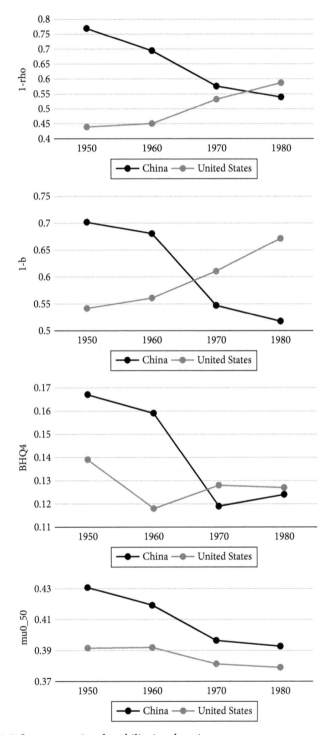

Figure 11.3 Intergenerational mobility in education

Source: Authors' illustration based on GDIM (2018) data.

observations: (1) intergenerational mobility is declining in China while it is stagnating in the US (mobility in the US is increasing by one measure (the correlation coefficient) and decreasing by another (the two measures of relative upward mobility)); (2) intergenerational mobility was historically higher in China but the two giants appear to be converging to a similar level of mobility. The stagnation in intergenerational mobility observed in the US for individuals born after 1950 is consistent with estimates obtained in the existing literature: see e.g. Hilger (2015). For perspective, Narayan et al. (2018) establish that the developing and emerging world dominate the list of countries with the lowest rates of relative upward mobility (BHQ4) for the 1980s generation. Among the bottom fifty countries, forty-six are developing or emerging countries while only four are high-income, including the US. In the median developing and emerging country, less than 15 per cent of those born into the bottom half make it to the top quarter, while more than two-thirds stay in the bottom half.

The observation that intergenerational mobility in China has steadily decreased over the past decades is consistent with the existing literature. Fan et al. (2015) study intergenerational mobility for two cohorts—individuals born between 1949 and 1970 and those born after 1970—and find that mobility is lower for the younger cohort. Using the 1990 and 2000 Chinese Population Censuses, Magnani and Zhu (2015) find that intergenerational persistence in education increased between individuals born in the period 1966–70 and individuals born in the period 1976–80. Chen et al. (2015) find that intergenerational mobility has been declining for individuals born after 1950, but that it was increasing before that (i.e. for older generations). Golley and Kong (2013) similarly observe a decline in mobility during that period, most notably for rural households.

Interestingly, the decline in intergenerational mobility in China and stagnation in the US was accompanied by large economic expansions in both countries (see Figure 11.4). This contrast is particularly obvious in China, which is one of only a few countries where mobility has declined significantly during a time of rapid economic growth (see e.g. Narayan et al. 2018). In general, a larger economic output and national income implies an increased fiscal space that would permit the funding of policy interventions that would stimulate socioeconomic mobility. It may of course be the case that the latter has not been a policy priority in either China or the US.

China underwent a massive expansion in educational attainment and achieved an unprecedented reduction in poverty over the past three to four decades (Montalvo and Ravallion 2010; Ravallion 2009; Ravallion and Chen 2007). Several explanations have been suggested as to why inter-generational mobility in education has worsened while educational attainment has increased. Chen et al. (2019) argue that the expansion of education has not sufficiently reached children from disadvantaged backgrounds. Conceivably, the expansion of higher education in particular would have primarily benefited the elites. Chen et al. (2019)

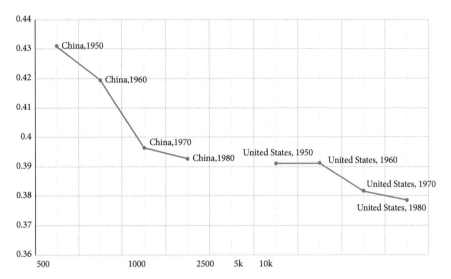

Figure 11.4 Intergenerational mobility versus GDP per capita
Source: Authors' illustration based on GDIM (2018) and Maddison Project Database data.

argue that many children did not meet the requirements for enrolment in higher education establishments.

The move from a planned to a market economy may also have played a part. It has shifted responsibility from the state to the individual and the family, which may have led to an increase in the importance of family networks impeding inter-generational mobility (Gong et al. 2012). The decline in inter-generational mobility could also be related to rising returns to higher education and rising costs of higher education. Magnani and Zhu (2015) and Fan et al. (2015) both find that returns to education have increased in recent decades, which can increase incentives for better-off parents to invest even more in children's education. Fan et al. (2015) find that tuition fees for tertiary education have increased significantly, which can make it harder for children from low-income backgrounds to access and complete higher education.

5 Policy Changes in China and the US Underlying the Trends in Socioeconomic Mobility

The objective of this section is to provide an overview of changes in policy and economic conditions in the US and China that will help put the observed trends in economic mobility into context. Li et al. (2018: Section 6) provide a comprehensive overview of the public policies China has started to put in place in an effort to moderate inequality and stimulate socioeconomic mobility, some of which are discussed in Section 5.2.

Improving socioeconomic mobility requires public policies that equalize opportunities, that is, interventions that reduce disadvantages faced by individuals because of circumstances over which they have no control, such as parental education or economic status, gender, ethnicity, or location. The success of such interventions will naturally depend on their magnitude and on how they are targeted. A growing empirical literature concludes that public interventions are more likely to increase socioeconomic mobility when: (a) public investments are sufficiently large (Iyigun 1999); (b) they are targeted to benefit disadvantaged families/neighbourhoods (Blankenau and Youderian 2015; Herrington 2015; Mayer and Lopoo 2008); (c) they focus on early childhood (Blankenau and Youderian 2015; Herrington 2015); and (d) political power is not captured by the rich unless the rich have the interests of the poor at heart (Uchida 2018).

For an inclusive review of the literature on the determinants of socioeconomic mobility and the public interventions that have been considered across the world to improve mobility, we refer the interested reader to Section 7 of Van der Weide and Narayan (2019). While most of the evidence on the drivers of mobility reviewed in what follows comes from research on the US and other developed economies, it is relevant for a middle-income country such as China, particularly as the Chinese economy rapidly approaches high-income status. Pursuing these policy objectives sits well with the growth strategy advocated by Stiglitz (2018), which underscores that future economic growth is more likely to be sustained if it is inclusive.

5.1 United States

Socioeconomic mobility in the US has historically been low relative to high-income countries with comparable levels of national income per capita, and has shown little to no progress over the past three decades. Chetty et al. (2017) also find that there has been a large decline in the rate of absolute *upward* mobility in income across successive US birth cohorts—just half of children born in 1984 were earning more than their parents, compared to 92 per cent of children born in 1940. The stagnation in mobility (and decline in absolute income mobility) has occurred along with rising income inequality. Katz and Krueger (2017), for example, link the decline in absolute mobility to the well-documented stagnant growth in real median household income and rise in income inequality beginning in the mid-1970s. Public debate on the causes of stagnating socioeconomic mobility and rising income inequality in the US has focused on several overlapping explanations—a vast body of literature that is selectively summarized in what follows, focusing on a few key explanations on which there appears to be broad consensus.

The literature suggests that interplay between an intricate set of factors related to supply and demand for human capital have contributed to rising income inequality and declining economic mobility in the US. On the supply side, Katz and Krueger (2017) highlight slower growth of human capital among children from low-income families across generations. While children born in the early 1940s had around two more years of average schooling at age 30 than their parents' generation, this advantage drops to 0.75 years of schooling for children born in the early 1980s. This decline may in part stem from the fact that the average cost of college in the US has more than doubled between 1974 and 2012, with real implications for higher education equity (Cahalan and Perna 2015). In 2012, the average net price of college less grants and aid as a percentage of average family income was 84 per cent for low-income families (bottom quartile), compared to 15 per cent for high-income families (top-quartile). Children from high-income families were on average eight times more likely to obtain a bachelors' degree by the age of 24 than children from low-income families in 2012 (77 per cent versus 9 per cent), up from four times more likely in the early 1970s (34 per cent versus 8 per cent). As a result of this trend, 'the US has gone from leading the world in educational attainment for those born in the mid-20th century to being in the middle of the pack for rich nations for those born since the 1970s' (Katz and Krueger 2017: 382).

The steep growth in wage premium to college education in the US has been identified by many researchers as the most important contributor to rising income inequality. By some estimates, roughly two-thirds of the overall rise of earnings dispersion between 1980 and 2005 in the US is 'proximately accounted for by the rising returns to schooling—primarily the growing premium to post-secondary education' (Autor 2014: 2). The wage premium for college education reflects not just returns to investment in higher education but also a fall in real earnings among non-college-educated workers, which is a cause for particular concern. While real hourly earnings of college-educated males in the US rose substantially between 1980 and 2012, real hourly earnings of males with high school or lower educational levels fell by 11–22 per cent, alongside modest growth in real earnings among females without at least some college education. The wage premium was not the only labour market driver of rising inequality. There was also a large drop in labour force participation rates among less educated males relative to males with post-secondary education between 1979 and 2007 (Autor 2014: 16–17).

From the perspective of socioeconomic mobility in the US, the rising college premium arguably denotes an important factor, in addition to the rising cost of college and the decline in higher education equity. Cross-country evidence as well as economic theory suggest that countries with higher returns to education are likely to have lower intergenerational mobility of income (Corak 2013; Narayan et al. 2018). Intuitively, the main reason for this is the link between children's educational attainment and parental education and income. Higher returns to education provide multiple advantages to children of more educated parents—with educated parents *and* more resources available for investments in education, along with higher incentives for parents to make those investments.

Earning declines for less educated workers in the US have been linked to labour-demand shifts against middle-skill jobs, which have polarized the US labour market. Increased domestic outsourcing and use of independent contractors have limited the availability of good jobs that offer a path of upward mobility (Katz and Krueger 2017). Technological change has led to machines being substituted for workers for some routine medium-skill occupations and has reduced the demand for less educated workers (Autor 2014). Globalization, particularly the rapid increase in imports from China, has led to large-scale job losses in local labour markets where the industries exposed to foreign competition are concentrated (Autor et al. 2016). A decline in unionization has reduced the bargaining power of labour unions—the share of private-sector workers belonging to unions in the US saw a decline of almost 70 per cent between 1973 and 2011 (Autor 2014). The different demand-side factors work in tandem to reinforce each other. Policy choices have also played a role in strengthening these trends, such as policies that have contributed to the decline in minimum wage in real terms and in the bargaining power of unions, and the successive declines in top federal marginal tax rates that have increased both post-tax inequality and the incentives for highly paid workers to seek still higher compensation (Autor 2014).

There is an extensive literature examining other possible drivers of rising economic inequality and stagnating social mobility in the US. Katz and Krueger (2017) associate rising US income inequality with residential economic segregation, which is likely to reduce economic mobility, given the evidence of neighbourhood effects on long-run outcomes of children (Chetty et al. 2016). Local drivers of social mobility are clearly important in the US, and there is some evidence to suggest they matter in many other parts of the world as well (see Narayan et al. 2018). For the US, at least half of the high variance in mobility across geographic areas is attributable to the causal effect of location. Neighbourhood characteristics that matter for mobility include income segregation and concentrated poverty, racial segregation, quality of schools, crime rates, and the share of two-parent families (Chetty and Hendren 2018a, 2018b). Kearney and Levine (2016) find that youth from disadvantaged socioeconomic backgrounds are more likely to drop out of school if they live in a place with a greater gap between the bottom and middle of the income distribution, suggesting that they perceive a lower rate of return to investment in their own human capital when living in a more unequal place.[8] Family structures also matter for inter-generational mobility. People raised outside stable two-parent homes are relatively likely to become low-income

---

[8] Evidence is unclear on whether there has been an increase in social (or racial) segregation of schools since the 1970s, although there is some evidence that students are more segregated by income across schools and districts today than in 1990 (Reardon and Owens 2014).

adults, and are less likely to become high-income adults than people from stable two-parent homes (Bloome 2017).

Finally, the rising prevalence of economic rents and a shift in rents away from labour to capital is likely to have contributed to rising income inequality in the US (Stiglitz 2015). Stiglitz (2016) links the rise in inequality to the growth in rents, including what he calls 'land and exploitation rents', which arise from monopoly power and political influence. People who enjoy privileged connections to rent-providing assets or jobs tend to become more well-off, which in turn reduces social mobility by increasing the incentives among parents to pass on such connections to their offspring. Furman and Orszag (2018) argue that increased income inequality in the US is also linked to increased dispersion of earnings between firms, with more and more firms enjoying super-normal returns to capital. Increasing market consolidation may be contributing to the increasing prevalence of firms with unusually high returns to capital.

A potential consequence of increased rent-seeking in the US economy could be a reduction in the overall dynamism of US labour markets, which can reduce social mobility over time. Several studies have documented that job creation and job destruction in the US fell from the late 1980s or 1990s to the late 2000s.[9] Long-distance migration, which often implies changes in employer and industry, has fallen by as much as 50 per cent since the late 1970s (Furman and Orszag 2018). Katz and Krueger (2017) argue that declining geographic mobility in the US may have contributed to reduced income mobility, since internal migration to locations with better opportunities has traditionally provided a path to upward mobility.

Given the rise in income inequality, it is interesting that educational mobility in the US, while consistently lower than comparator countries, has not declined between the generations born in the 1950s and 1980s. Autor (2014) finds that rising income inequality has not reduced intergenerational *income* mobility so far, although that may change as income among those born after 2000 is able to be observed.[10] While the stability of socioeconomic mobility can be seen as positive, it is a worrying trend when combined with rising income inequality, as it implies that 'the lifetime relative disadvantage of children born to low- versus high-income families has increased substantially...the rungs of the economic ladder have pulled farther apart but the chance of ascending the ladder has not improved' (Autor 2014: 15). The decline in absolute upward mobility in income mentioned earlier heightens this concern (Chetty et al. 2017).

---

[9] Decker et al. (2017); Davis and Haltiwanger (2014); and Hyatt and Spletzer (2013).

[10] Autor (2014: 15) cites data from Chetty et al. (2014) to conclude that there is 'no evidence that mobility in the US has appreciably changed among children born prior to the historic rise of US inequality (1971–1974) and those born afterward (1991–1993)'.

Bloome et al. (2018) offer some explanations for why intergenerational income mobility in the US did not decline in recent decades even though education-based inequalities in the labour market increased. They find that growing educational inequality by parental income and rising returns to education did reduce income mobility, as one would expect. This effect was only partly offset by the expansion of higher education that improved upward mobility among low-income children. The other key offsetting factor was parental income becoming less predictive of adult income *within* educational groups. Thus, an increase in the 'indirect effect' of parental income on adult income via education occurred alongside a decreasing 'direct effect' of parental income on adult income via pathways other than education. The latter implies a decline in the effect of parental status on the earnings of offspring through channels such as connections and networks in the labour market.

Some also argue that mobility in the US could have declined had it not been for other policy initiatives, such as expanding the Earned Income Tax Credit (EITC) for low-income workers in the 1980s and the early childhood education Head Start programme in the 1990s, and increasing federal support to college-going low-income students (Autor 2014). Narayan et al. (2018) find compelling evidence in the literature that exposure in teenage years to EITC has a positive effect on test scores, high school and college completion, being employed, and earnings as a young adult.[11] The Head Start programme—one of the largest pre-school programs in the world for low-income children—is found to have positive impacts on several long-term outcomes for children, such as high school graduation, college attendance, behaviours (self-control and self-esteem), and social outcomes (crime, teen parenthood, and health status).[12]

A decline in racial and gender discrimination in the US over the past five decades, which was at least partly aided by social policies, is also likely to have been a positive force for socioeconomic mobility. Hsieh et al. (2019) document big changes in the distribution of social groups among high-skilled occupations between 1960 and 2010, such as a fall of more than 30 per cent in the share of white men among doctors and lawyers. They interpret this to suggest that many of the innately talented black people and women in 1960 were not pursuing their comparative advantage, which amounts to a severe mis-allocation of talent for a society. The improved allocation of talent between 1960 and 2010, they estimate, explains about one-quarter of growth in aggregate output per person over this period, suggesting that improving fairness in a society produces economic benefits for the society as a whole.

---

[11] See Narayan et al. (2018: Chapter 6) citing evidence from Dahl and Lochner (2012); Chetty et al. (2011); and Bastian and Michelmore (2018).
[12] See Narayan et al. (2018: ch5) citing evidence from Bauer and Schanzenbach (2016); Carneiro and Ginja (2014); Garces et al. (2002); Deming (2009).

Katz and Krueger (2017) summarize broad priorities for policy action to improve social mobility that are consistent with the overall evidence for the US. Their overarching message, echoing Chetty et al. (2017), is that faster growth is necessary but not sufficient to restore higher intergenerational income mobility in the US. They highlight five classes of policy intervention: fostering faster productivity growth; raising investment in human capital for children born into low-income families; raising wages and employment of low-income households; updating taxes and transfers to make them more progressive; and making place-based policies to strengthen local drivers of mobility and improve geographic mobility. Bloome et al. (2018) advocate for reforms that address all stages of the education pipeline in the US, including transitions both before (graduating from high school) and after (e.g. completing graduate degrees) college, as well as progression *within* levels of education.

5.2 China

In the decades prior to the late 1970s, the first part of our period under consideration, China adopted social planning that involved collective farming, price controls, state-directed labour allocation and setting of wages, and limited labour mobility (either across occupations or geographically)—but also the provision of universal healthcare, child care, pensions, and schooling. Social planning allowed for relatively high levels of intergenerational mobility (IGM) and low levels of income inequality; IGM was notably higher and inequality notably lower than what was observed in the US. During the Maoist period, China went to extremes to eliminate the advantage of being born into a privileged family background (reflected in parental education). During the Cultural Revolution, which affected individuals born between the late 1940s and the early 1960s, admission to higher education favoured children from the poor or 'lower' social classes (considered the 'good class' backgrounds) and punished children from the rich or upper classes ('bad class' backgrounds) by restricting their access to higher education institutions and limiting their opportunities (see e.g. Giles et al. 2019). During this period, access to education in China expanded at the elementary and middle school levels, and lower classes gained preferred access to limited higher education opportunities, both of which led to positive human capital accumulation. At the same time, continued reliance on collective farming under the commune system and central planning in industry led to declining productivity.

In 1978 China initiated a transition from social planning towards a more market-oriented system. Agrarian reforms came first, moving the rural economy away from collective farming. This involved the privatization of land rights and relaxing of agricultural price controls, providing incentives by shifting responsibilities for farming to households (Li et al. 2018; Ravallion 2009; Ravallion and

Chen 2007; Zhang et al. 2005). Mid-1980s China's reform agenda addressed the non-farm sector. The first wage reform introduced in 1984 allowed firm wages to reflect firm profitability. Labour contracts were formally introduced shortly thereafter, with reforms that ended the system of permanent employment. The percentage of contract workers increased from 4 per cent of workers in the mid-1980s to almost 40 per cent ten years later. Subsequent reforms included enterprise restructuring, privatization, laying-off of state-sector workers, internal and external trade liberalization, and the liberalization of the foreign direct investment regime (Ravallion 2009; Zhang et al. 2005; Zhu 2012).[13] Milanovic (2020) observes:

> In 1978, almost 100 per cent of China's economic output came from the public sector; that figure has now dropped to less than 20 per cent. In modern China, as in the more traditionally capitalist countries of the West, the means of production are mostly in private hands, the state doesn't impose decisions about production and pricing on companies, and most workers are wage laborers.

Shortly before China initiated its economic reform agenda, it also started a campaign to reduce fertility. China formally began its one child policy (OCP) in 1979, but the campaign started in 1971 (Rosenzweig and Zhang 2009). The policy was relaxed in late 2013. The smaller number of children allowed for larger private investment per child. While this has been confirmed empirically (see also Li et al. 2008), the effect on the overall development of China's human capital has been relatively modest (Rosenzweig and Zhang 2009).

The reforms put China on a path of unprecedented economic growth as they fostered investment, more efficient allocation of resources, and technology adoption from abroad (Song et al. 2011; Zilibotti 2017). China's high growth rates primarily reflect productivity growth (Zhu 2012). With wages no longer set by the government, workers' earnings have become more aligned with workers' productivity. While human capital accumulation and the increase in labour participation also contributed to growth, their impacts are believed to have been more modest. The increase in the demand for skilled workers was seemingly large enough to offset the increase in the supply of skilled workers, leading to an increase in the returns to education that was most notable in the 1990s (Zhang et al. 2005). Economic growth and efforts to stimulate labour absorption by non-farm sectors, in addition to the growth of opportunities for migrant employment (de Brauw and Giles 2018), has lifted a large share of China's population out of poverty. Ravallion (2009) reports that headcount poverty declined from around 65 per cent in 1981 to 10 per cent in 2004. For comparison, for the

---

[13] During this period China also made large investments in infrastructure, including the construction of its national highway system (Faber 2014).

developing world excluding China, poverty declined from 30 to 20 per cent during this period.[14]

The effect of OCP on economic growth is more debatable. While it has increased average human capital, it has arguably depressed the overall stock of human capital (Wang and Zhang 2018).[15] Estimating the exact magnitude of OCP's impact is complicated in part by the fact that it coincided with China's reforms towards a more market-oriented system, which also may have impacted on fertility, to the extent that fertility is influenced by economic wellbeing (Zhang 2017). The OCP is not without costs. Its unintended consequences include rapid aging of the population and imbalanced gender ratios, and it has almost certainly increased inequality in private investment in the human capital of children.

Milanovic (2020) highlights that China's economic reforms and efforts to reduce fertility have had distributional implications:

> The flipside of China's astronomical growth has been its massive increase in inequality. During 1985–2010, the country's Gini coefficient leapt from 0.30 to around 0.50—higher than that of the US and closer to levels found in Latin America. Inequality in China has risen starkly within both rural and urban areas, and it has risen even more so in the country as a whole because of the increasing gap between those areas.

This trend is confirmed by Li et al. (2018) and Piketty et al. (2019). Key drivers of this increase in inequality include the rise in returns to education and increased wage differentials based on productivity, the emerging inequalities in schooling and health, and the geographic disparities in public investments (see e.g. Zhang et al. 2005; Ravallion 2009; Li et al. 2018).

The decline in socioeconomic mobility can similarly be rationalized by China's transition to a more market-oriented system. Socialism provided universal healthcare and schooling, and comparatively low levels of income inequality. As China departed from socialism, inequalities in access to schooling and healthcare and gaps in their quality emerged, with children from more privileged backgrounds arguably having access to higher quality education compared to children born into less privilege. Other plausible determinants of the decline in socioeconomic mobility include rising costs of education, geographic disparities in public

---

[14] China's transition entailed large urbanization and substantial growth in the export-oriented manufacturing sector. Labour absorption by non-farm sectors has been a key driver of this poverty reduction, with poverty declining faster in areas and time-periods where the manufacturing sector was labour-intensive (Lin and Liu 2008; Montalvo and Ravallion 2010; Ravallion 2009).

[15] As OCP was more strictly enforced in urban areas (where high human capital investments are comparatively high) than in rural areas, it may have negatively impacted on the overall human capital stock (Wang and Zhang 2018). Beyond this urban–rural divide, the OCP and its enforcement also exhibited notable variation over time and across provinces.

investments, increased income inequality, and reductions in fertility, which, combined with the increases in income inequality, enabled an increase in inequality in private investment in children. The high levels of mobility prior to the transition were perhaps unlikely to prevail, 'given the concentration of ownership of capital, the rising cost of education, and the importance of family connections—the intergenerational transmission of wealth and power should begin to mirror what is observed in the West' (Milanovic 2020).

Another factor that may contribute to lower socioeconomic mobility for individuals born after the 1980s is incentives created by opportunities to migrate from rural to urban areas for work (see e.g. Giles and Huang 2020 and de Brauw and Giles 2017). Some youth from less advantaged rural areas, with middle-school education, choose to pursue job opportunities in urban China over enrolling in high school. Migration of parents also has implications for education mobility, to the extent that it has negative impacts on the human capital accumulation of the children they leave behind (Meng and Yamauchi 2017). Children that migrate together with their parents will similarly be negatively impacted as they face obstacles to enrolling in urban public schools (Chen and Feng 2013). Public policy options that could help reduce these negative effects include subsidizing higher education and eliminating barriers to enrolling children of migrants in urban schools.

Low levels of IGM and equality of opportunity may slow down the accumulation of human capital when individuals are not given the opportunities needed to reach their full potential, which in turn may become an impediment to future growth. 'High inequality is a double handicap; depending on the sources of inequality—notably how much comes from inequality of opportunity—it means lower growth and that the poor share less in the gains from that growth' (Ravallion 2009). As observed in Li et al. (2018), after pursuing economic growth during the first decades of the economic reforms, China has recently shifted its development strategy to address concerns about rising inequality and declining socioeconomic mobility. Examples of these policy changes include efforts to expand rural secondary education and increase university enrolments, increasing the affordability of healthcare, cash transfers to the poor, increases in minimum wage, and extending pensions to rural China (see e.g. Li et al. 2018). This policy shift, while designed to address inequality, may ultimately also help increase the stock of human capital and future economic growth.

6 Concluding Remarks

The US and China are found to exhibit remarkably similar levels of intergenerational 'origin independence' mobility for individuals born in the 1980s, both in income and education, with mobility levels that are considered low by international standards. Before China embarked on its transition from planned to market economy, inter-generational mobility in education was relatively high—notably, higher than it was in the US at the time. Since then, inter-generational mobility has declined significantly in China and has been stagnating in the US, such that the two giants have now converged to a comparable level of both mobility and inequality.

The decline in inter-generational mobility in China and the stagnation in the US happened during a time of robust economic expansion in both countries. This contrast is particularly strong in China, which is one of only a few countries in the world where mobility underwent a significant decline during a time of rapid economic growth. Since an economy that is getting richer has access to more resources for funding policy interventions that could stimulate socioeconomic mobility, it would seem that improving mobility has not been a policy priority in either country in recent decades. This could, however, be changing, as rising inequality in both countries is increasingly drawing attention to the need to raise economic mobility as a pathway to a more fair and equitable society over time. Examples of policy changes that have been adopted in China in recent years can be found in Li et al. (2018: Section 6).

To promote economic mobility, governments can play a proactive role in 'compensating' for differences in individual and family starting points, to level the playing field in opportunities. This includes policies that aim to equalize opportunities across space, given the contribution of location to inequalities in most countries. The state also has a prominent role to play in making markets work more efficiently and equitably, since discrimination, anti-competitive behaviour, and market concentration are likely to constrain economic mobility. Fiscal policy is an important tool for realizing many of these objectives, by raising resources for investment in public goods and reducing inequality through redistribution.

Local characteristics that influence pathways to socioeconomic mobility include socioeconomic integration, the quality and availability of educational institutions, childcare, healthcare, recreational facilities, safety, and access to good jobs and opportunities. All of these are shaped by public policy. Interventions aimed at reducing the concentration of poverty and the socioeconomic segregation of neighbourhoods can be particularly beneficial for mobility. Going beyond the more traditional interventions, programmes can also attempt to bridge the deficit of role models and mentors in poor communities that constrain the aspirations of youth, possibly in partnership with the private sector and civic organizations.

A policy agenda that promotes economic mobility sits well with the growth strategy advocated by Stiglitz (2018), which underscores that future economic growth is more likely to be sustained if it is inclusive. Ignoring the timeliness of such a policy shift in the case of the US and China, and leaving inequality and lack of mobility unchecked, may end up undermining future growth. Milanovic (2020) makes a similar observation:

> What does the future hold for Western capitalist societies? The answer hinges on whether liberal meritocratic capitalism will be able to move toward a more advanced stage, what might be called 'people's capitalism', in which income from both factors of production, capital and labour, would be more equally distributed. This would require broadening meaningful capital ownership way beyond the current top ten per cent of the population and making access to top schools and the best-paying jobs independent of one's family background.[16]

Implementing public interventions that would increase socioeconomic mobility and reduce inequality naturally requires the necessary political support. This applies equally to the US and to China.

References

Adams, J.T. (1931). *The Epic of America*. 1931 Edition. Boston: Little, Brown, and Company.

Asher, S., P. Novosad, and C. Rafkin (2019). 'Getting Signal from Interval Data: Theory and Applications to Mortality and Intergenerational Mobility'. Mimeo, 1–76.

Autor, D.H. (2014). 'Skills, Education, and the Rise of Earnings Inequality among the "Other 99 Percent"'. *Science*, 344(6186): 843–51.

Autor, D.H., D. Dorn, and G.H. Hanson (2016). 'The China Shock: Learning from Labor-Market Adjustment to Large Changes in Trade'. *Annual Review of Economics*, 8(1): 205–40.

Bastian, J., and K. Michelmore (2018). 'The Long-Term Impact of the Earned Income Tax Credit on Children's Education and Employment Outcomes'. *Journal of Labor Economics*, 36(4): 1127–63.

Bauer, L., and D.W. Schanzenbach (2016). *The Long-Term Impact of the Head Start Program*. Report. Washington, DC: Brookings Institution.

Benjamin, D., L. Brandt, and J. Giles (2011). 'Did Higher Inequality Impede Growth in Rural China?'. *The Economic Journal*, 121(557): 1281–309.

Björklund, A., and M. Jäntti (1997). 'Intergenerational Income Mobility in Sweden Compared to the United States'. *American Economic Review*, 87(5): 1009–18.

---

[16] Milanovic (2020) continues: 'To achieve greater equality, countries should develop tax incentives to encourage the middle class to hold more financial assets, implement higher inheritance taxes for the very rich, improve free public education, and establish publicly funded electoral campaigns . . . this model would seek greater equality in assets, both financial and in terms of skills . . . It would require only modest redistributive policies (such as food stamps and housing benefits) because it would have already achieved a greater baseline of equality.'

Blankenau, W., and X. Youderian (2015). 'Early Childhood Education Expenditures and the Intergenerational Persistence of Income'. *Review of Economic Dynamics*, 18(2): 334–49.

Bloome, D. (2017). 'Childhood Family Structure and Intergenerational Income Mobility in the United States'. *Demography*, 54(2): 541–69.

Bloome, D., S. Dyer, and X. Zhou (2018). 'Educational Inequality, Educational Expansion, and Intergenerational Income Persistence in the United States'. *American Sociological Review*, 83(6): 1215–53.

Cahalan, M., and L. Perna (2015). *Indicators of Higher Education Equity in the United States: 45 Year Trend Report*. Washington, DC: The Pell Institute for the Study of Opportunity in Higher Education, Council for Opportunity in Education (COE): and Alliance for Higher Education and Democracy of the University of Pennsylvania (PennAHEAD).

Carneiro, P., and R. Ginja (2014). 'Long-Term Impacts of Compensatory Preschool on Health and Behavior: Evidence from Head Start'. *American Economic Journal: Economic Policy*, 6(4): 135–73.

Chen, Y., and S. Feng (2013). 'Access to Public Schools and the Education of Migrant Children in China'. *China Economic Review*, 26(1): 75–88.

Chen, Y., Y. Guo, J. Huang, and Y. Song (2019). 'Intergenerational Transmission of Education in China: New Evidence from the Chinese Cultural Revolution'. *Review of Development Economics*, 23(1): 501–27.

Chen, Y., S. Naidu, T. Yu, and N. Yuchtman (2015). 'Intergenerational Mobility and Institutional Change in 20th Century China'. *Explorations in Economic History*, 58, 44–73.

Cheremukhin, A., M. Golosov, S. Guriev, and A. Tsyvinski (2015). 'The economy of People's Republic of China from 1953'. Working Paper 21397. Cambridge: The National Bureau of Economic Research. Accessed at https://doi.org/10.3386/w21397.

Chetty, R., J.N. Friedman, and J. Rockoff (2011). *New Evidence on the Long-Term Impacts of Tax Credits*.

Chetty, R., D. Grusky, M. Hell, N. Hendren, R. Manduca, and J. Narang (2017). 'The Fading American Dream: Trends in Absolute Income Mobility since 1940'. *Science*, 356(6336): 398–406.

Chetty, R., and N. Hendren (2018a). 'The Impacts of Neighborhoods on Intergenerational Mobility I: Childhood Exposure Effects'. *Quarterly Journal of Economics*, 133(3): 1107–62.

Chetty, R., and N. Hendren (2018b). 'The Impacts of Neighborhoods on Intergenerational Mobility II: County-Level Estimates'. *Quarterly Journal of Economics*, 133(3): 1163–228.

Chetty, R., N. Hendren, and L.F. Katz (2016). 'The Effects of Exposure to Better Neighborhoods on Children: New Evidence from the Moving to Opportunity Experiment'. *American Economic Review*, 106(4): 855–902.

Chetty, R., N. Hendren, P. Kline, and E. Saez (2014). 'Where Is the Land of Opportunity? The Geography of Intergenerational Mobility in the United States'. *The Quarterly Journal of Economics*, 129(4): 1553–623.

Corak, M. (2013). 'Income Inequality, Equality of Opportunity, and Intergenerational Mobility'. *Journal of Economic Perspectives*, 27(3): 79–102.

Corak, M. (2019). 'The Canadian Geography of Intergenerational Income Mobility'. *The Economic Journal*. Accessed at https://doi.org/10.1093/ej/uez019.

Dahl, G.B., and L. Lochner (2012). 'The Impact of Family Income on Child Achievement: Evidence from the Earned Income Tax Credit'. *American Economic Review*, 102(5): 1927–56.

Davis, S.J., and J. Haltiwanger (2014). 'Labor Market Fluidity and Economic Performance'. Working Paper 20479. Cambridge: The National Bureau of Economic Research. Accessed at https://doi.org/10.3386/w20479.

de Brauw, A., and J. Giles (2017). 'Migrant Opportunity and the Educational Attainment of Youth in Rural China'. *Journal of Human Resources*, 52(1): 272–311.

de Brauw, A., and J. Giles (2018). 'Migrant Labor Markets and the Welfare of Rural Households in the Developing World: Evidence from China'. *The World Bank Economic Review*, 32(1): 1–18.

Decker, R.A., J. Haltiwanger, R.S. Jarmin, and J. Miranda (2017). 'Declining Dynamism, Allocative Efficiency, and the Productivity Slowdown'. *American Economic Review*, 107(5): 322–6.

Deming, D. (2009). 'Early Childhood Intervention and Life-Cycle Skill Development: Evidence from Head Start'. *American Economic Journal: Applied Economics*, 1(3): 111–34.

Equalchances (2018). 'International Database on Inequality of Opportunity and Social Mobility'.

Faber, B. (2014). 'Trade Integration, Market Size, and Industrialization: Evidence from China's National Trunk Highway System'. *The Review of Economic Studies*, 81(3): 1046–70.

Fan, Y., J. Yi, and J. Zhang (2015). *The Great Gatsby Curve in China: Cross-Sectional Inequality and Intergenerational Mobility*. Hong Kong.

Furman, J., and P. Orszag (2018). 'A Firm-Level Perspective on the Role of Rents in the Rise in Inequality'. In M. Guzman (ed.), *Toward a Just Society*. New York: Columbia University Press.

Garces, E., D. Thomas, and J. Currie (2002). 'Longer-Term Effects of Head Start'. *American Economic Review*, 92(4): 999–1012.

GDIM (2018). Global Database on Intergenerational Mobility.

Giles, J., and Y. Huang (2020). 'Migration and Human Capital Accumulation in China'. *IZA World of Labor*.

Giles, J., A. Park, and M. Wang (2019). 'The Great Proletarian Cultural Revolution, Disruptions to Education, and the Returns to Schooling in Urban China'. *Economic Development and Cultural Change*, 68(1): 131–64.

Golley, J., and S.T. Kong (2013). 'Inequality in Intergenerational Mobility of Education in China'. *China & World Economy*, 21(2): 15–37.

Gong, H., A. Leigh, and X. Meng (2012). 'Intergenerational Income Mobility in Urban China'. *Review of Income and Wealth*, 58(3): 481–503.

Hernandez, J.C., and Q. Bui (2018). 'The American Dream Is Alive. In China'. *The New York Times*. 18 November.

Herrington, C.M. (2015). 'Public Education Financing, Earnings Inequality, and Intergenerational Mobility'. *Review of Economic Dynamics*, 18(4): 822–42.

Hilger, N.G. (2015). 'The great escape: intergenerational mobility in the United States since 1940'. Working Paper 21217. Cambridge: The National Bureau of Economic Research. Accessed at https://doi.org/10.3386/w21217.

Hsieh, C.-T., E. Hurst, C.I. Jones, and P.J. Klenow (2019). 'The Allocation of Talent and U.S. Economic Growth'. *Econometrica*, 87(5): 1439–74.

Hussain, A., P. Lanjouw, and N. Stern (1994). 'Income Inequalities in China: Evidence from Household Survey Data'. *World Development*, 22(12): 1947–57.

Hyatt, H.R., and J.R. Spletzer (2013). 'The Recent Decline in Employment Dynamics'. *IZA Journal of Labor Economics*, 2(1). Accessed at https://doi.org/10.1186/2193-8997-2-5.

Iyigun, M.F. (1999). 'Public Education and Intergenerational Economic Mobility'. *International Economic Review*, 40(3): 697–710.

Katz, L.F., and A.B. Krueger (2017). 'Documenting Decline in U.S. Economic Mobility'. *Science*, 356(6336): 382–3.

Kearney, M.S., and P.B. Levine (2016). 'Income Inequality, Social Mobility, and the Decision to Drop Out of High School'. *Brookings Papers on Economic Activity*, 2016 (SPRING): 333–96.

Li, S., T. Sicular, and F. Tarp (2018). 'Inequality in China: development, transition, and policy'. WIDER Working Paper 174/2018, Helsinki: UNU-WIDER. Accessed at https://doi.org/10.35188/UNU-WIDER/2018/616-6.

Li, H., J. Zhang, and Y. Zhu (2008). 'The Quantity-Quality Trade-off of Children in a Developing Country: Identification Using Chinese Twins'. *Demography*, 45(1): 223–43.

Lin, J.Y., and P. Liu (2008). 'Economic Development Strategy, Openness and Rural Poverty: A Framework and China's Experiences'. In M. Nissanke and E. Thorbecke (eds), *Globalization and the Poor in Asia*. London: Palgrave Macmillan.

Magnani, E., and R. Zhu (2015). 'Social Mobility and Inequality in Urban China: Understanding the Role of Intergenerational Transmission of Education'. *Applied Economics*, 47(43): 4590–606.

Mayer, S.E., and L.M. Lopoo (2008). 'Government Spending and Intergenerational Mobility'. *Journal of Public Economics*, 92(1–2): 139–58.

Meng, X., and C. Yamauchi (2017). 'Children of Migrants: The Cumulative Impact of Parental Migration on Children's Education and Health Outcomes in China'. *Demography*, 54(5): 1677–714.

Milanovic, B. (2015). 'Global Inequality of Opportunity: How Much of Our Income Is Determined by Where We Live'. *Review of Economics and Statistics*, 97(2): 452–60.

Milanovic, B. (2020). 'How America and China Are Competing over the Future of Capitalism'. *Foreign Affairs*.

Montalvo, J.G., and M. Ravallion (2010). 'The Pattern of Growth and Poverty Reduction in China'. *Journal of Comparative Economics*, 38(1): 2–16.

Narayan, A., R. Van der Weide, A. Cojocaru, C. Lakner, S. Redaelli, D. Gerszon Mahler, R.G.N. Ramasubbaiah, and S. Thewissen (2018). 'Fair Progress?

Economic Mobility across Generations around the World'. Washington, DC: The World Bank.

Piketty, T., L. Yang, and G. Zucman (2019). 'Capital Accumulation, Private Property, and Rising Inequality in China, 1978–2015'. *American Economic Review*, 109(7): 2469–96.

Ravallion, M. (2009). 'Are There Lessons for Africa from China's Success Against Poverty'. *World Development*, 37(2): 303–13.

Ravallion, M., and S. Chen (2007). 'China's (Uneven) Progress against Poverty'. *Journal of Development Economics*, 82(1): 1–42.

Reardon, S.F., and A. Owens (2014). '60 Years After *Brown*: Trends and Consequences of School Segregation'. *Annual Review of Sociology*, 40(1): 199–218.

Rosenzweig, M.R., and J. Zhang (2009). 'Do Population Control Policies Induce More Human Capital Investment? Twins, Birth Weight and China's "One-Child" Policy'. *Review of Economic Studies*, 76(3): 1149–74.

Song, Z., K. Storesletten, and F. Zilibotti (2011). 'Growing Like China'. *American Economic Review*, 101(1): 196–233.

Stiglitz, J.E. (2015). 'The Origins of Inequality, and Policies to Contain It'. *National Tax Journal*, 68(2): 425–48.

Stiglitz, J.E. (2016). 'How to Restore Equitable and Sustainable Economic Growth in the United States'. *American Economic Review*, 106(5): 43–7.

Stiglitz, J.E. (2018). From manufacturing-led export growth to a twenty-first-century inclusive growth strategy: explaining the demise of a successful growth model and what to do about it. Working Paper 176/2018, Helsinki: UNU-WIDER. Accessed at https://doi.org/10.35188/UNU-WIDER/2018/618-0.

Suleyman, Mustafa (2013). 'The Great Gatsby Curve: Don't Worry, Old Sport'. *The Economist*.

Uchida, Y. (2018). 'Education, Social Mobility, and the Mismatch of Talents'. *Economic Theory*, 65(3): 575–607.

van der Weide, R., and B. Milanovic (2018). 'Inequality is Bad for Growth of the Poor (but Not for That of the Rich)'. *The World Bank Economic Review*, 32(3): 507–30.

Van der Weide, R., and A. Narayan (2019). 'China and the United States: different economic models but similarly low levels of socioeconomic mobility'. WIDER Working Paper 121/2019, Helsinki: UNU-WIDER. Accessed at https://doi.org/10.35188/UNU-WIDER/.

Wang, X., and J. Zhang (2018). 'Beyond the Quantity–Quality Tradeoff: Population Control Policy and Human Capital Investment'. *Journal of Development Economics*, 135: 222–34.

Zhang, J. (2017). 'The Evolution of China's One-Child Policy and Its Effects on Family Outcomes'. *Journal of Economic Perspectives*, 31(1): 141–60.

Zhang, J., Y. Zhao, A. Park, and X. Song (2005). 'Economic Returns to Schooling in Urban China, 1988 to 2001'. *Journal of Comparative Economics*, 33(4): 730–52.

Zhu, X. (2012). 'Understanding China's Growth: Past, Present, and Future'. *Journal of Economic Perspectives*, 26(4): 103–24.

Zilibotti, F. (2017). 'Growing and Slowing Down Like China'. *Journal of the European Economic Association*, 15(5): 943–88.

12

From Manufacturing-Led Export Growth to a Twenty-First Century Inclusive Growth Strategy

Explaining the Demise of a Successful Growth Model and What to Do about It

Joseph E. Stiglitz

1 Introduction

Export-led growth was the model behind the twentieth-century growth miracles.[1] There was unprecedented growth in East Asia, closing the gap in income per capita and standards of living with the advanced countries.[2] In the future that model will not work in the same way, or at least to the same extent, as it did in the past. This chapter explains why that is the case (Section 2) and what developing countries and the global community that supports development can do about it. It sets this new development strategy within the context of the broadening of the development agenda. With widespread recognition of the failures of the Washington Consensus policies, there was a need for a new 'consensus' concerning the objectives of development and how they might be achieved, as recently articulated in the Stockholm Statement (Section 3).

To formulate a new development strategy, we begin by deconstructing manufacturing export-led growth, and asking why it was so successful (Section 4). We argue in Section 5 that what is needed to replace that strategy is a multi-pronged

[1] An earlier version of this chapter was presented at the UNU-WIDER conference Think Development—Think WIDER, Helsinki, 15 September 2018. An earlier version was presented at the Economic and Social Research Foundation Annual National Conference, Dar Es Salaam, Tanzania, 2 May 2018. I am indebted to Kaushik Basu, my discussant; to Haaris Mateen for research assistance; and to Debarati Ghosh and Eamon Kircher-Allen for editorial assistance. Various parts of this chapter are based on joint work with Martin Guzman, Bruce Greenwald, and Akbar Noman, to whom I am greatly indebted: see, in particular, Noman and Stiglitz (2012a, 2012b, 2015a, 2015b); Greenwald and Stiglitz (2006, 2010, 2013, 2014); and Stiglitz and Greenwald (2010, 2014, 2015).
[2] See the World Bank's report *The East Asian Miracle*, of which I was a co-author (Birdsall et al. 1993), and Stiglitz (1996) and the references cited there for an account of the East Asian miracle.

Joseph E. Stiglitz, *From Manufacturing-Led Export Growth to a Twenty-First Century Inclusive Growth Strategy: Explaining the Demise of a Successful Growth Model and What to Do about It* In: *Inequality in the Developing World*. Edited by: Carlos Gradín, Murray Leibbrandt, and Finn Tarp, Oxford University Press (2021). © United Nations University World Institute for Development Economics Research (UNU-WIDER). DOI: 10.1093/oso/9780198863960.003.0012

strategy, entailing a combination of manufacturing, agriculture, services, and natural resources. To implement that strategy, countries will require active industrial policies (Section 6) based on a new understanding of dynamic comparative advantage (Section 7). Section 8 describes how developed countries can assist developing countries as they embark on these new strategies, and, in particular, explains how the creation of a global reserve system can help provide the finance that will be especially important if developing countries are to succeed in this twenty-first century inclusive growth strategy.

2 Explaining the End of Manufacturing-Led Growth

Manufacturing is a victim of its own success: the rate of growth of productivity (output per worker) exceeds that of demand. The result is that the share of manufacturing in GDP is declining everywhere, as Table 12.1 shows, and that in turn implies that the share of manufacturing in employment is declining even more rapidly, as we illustrate later in this chapter.[3]

Moreover, what happened to agriculture in the advanced countries is now happening globally. Productivity increases in agriculture meant that a smaller and smaller fraction of the labour force was required to produce the food that people needed and wanted; the advanced countries went from a situation in which some 70 per cent of the population was engaged in agriculture and related services to one in which a very small fraction of the workforce (in the US, less than 3 per cent)

Table 12.1 Manufacturing share of GDP (%)

	2000	2005
World	19	15
E. Asia and Pacific	25	23
Europe and Central Asia	19	16
Latin American and the Caribbean	17	14
North America	16	12
South Asia	15	16
Sub-Saharan Africa	11	11
Low income	10	8
Lower middle income	17	16
Upper middle income	24	21
High income	18	15

Source: Author's construction based on World Bank Group (2018).

---

[3] Some vertical disintegration of service components of manufacturing has given the appearance of more rapid disappearance of jobs and output than is in fact the case. Still, vertical disintegration can have real consequences (e.g. for wages and flows of knowledge).

can produce more than even an obese society can consume.[4] This means that if current trends continue unabated, a very large fraction of the labour force will have to be deployed elsewhere.

In the advanced countries, in the latter half of the nineteenth century and the first half of the twentieth, these workers were largely absorbed by manufacturing. But now, with the decline globally in manufacturing employment, this will be problematic. Even with emerging markets taking a larger share of global manufacturing jobs, and with a shift of jobs from China to Africa, new manufacturing jobs will absorb only a fraction of new entrants into the labour force in Africa.[5]

Manufacturing can, of course, still have impacts that are disproportionate to its size. And some countries may have a natural comparative advantage in some niches (or in some cases, they may even be able to create a comparative advantage). But it is unlikely that manufacturing export-led growth will have the impact that it had in China and East Asia. It cannot be the sole development strategy, or even at the heart of a country's strategy. This is especially so because the advantages of cheap labour will diminish as labour becomes of lesser importance in manufacturing itself—for example, as robots replace humans. The developing countries' advantage in low labour costs will, at least in many cases, be outweighed by locational disadvantages: an increasing fraction of production will be located near points of consumption. These are major changes that will affect development strategies going forward.

2.1 New Thinking about Development

As we think of a new strategy to replace manufacturing export-led growth, we need to incorporate the insights from earlier developmental experiences, including the global failures of the Washington Consensus policies and the successes in East Asia, and from advances in economic understandings. There are five key insights in particular that have led to a rethinking of development policies.

- What separates developing countries from developed is not just a disparity in resources, but a disparity in knowledge and institutions; see, for instance, the 1998 World Development Report (Dahlman et al. 1998).
- Development entails a structural transformation (Stiglitz 1998b).

---

[4] See Roser (2018) for historical employment in agriculture; current US data are available at the US Department of Agriculture's website, www.ers.usda.gov/data-products/ag-and-food-statistics-charting-the-essentials/ag-and-food-sectors-and-the-economy/. The economic implications of this transformation are explored in Delli Gati et al. (2012a, b).

[5] At most, some 85 million jobs could be freed up (Lin 2011), but the working-age population of Africa is expected to grow by 450 million people, or by 70 per cent, from 2015 to 2035 (World Economic Forum 2017).

- There can be growth without structural transformation—especially common in resource-dependent countries—but such growth will be neither sustainable nor equitable. All countries are, of course, in need of structural transformation—in advanced countries, in response to technology and globalization and the move from the manufacturing to the service sector; in China, from export-led growth to domestic demand-driven growth and from quantity to quality growth; in natural-resource economies, to diversify away from dependence on natural resources; and in all countries in response to the need to address problems of climate change (both mitigation and adaptation) and changing demographics. But the need for structural transformation is at the heart of development.

- Markets on their own don't manage these transformations well. There are critical impediments imposed by capital market imperfections, and important externalities and co-ordination failures. Government needs to assume an important role. How best to do this is one of the central themes of this chapter.

- Successful development and structural transformation entails a change in norms and mindsets, including the mindset that change is possible—a movement away from traditional society towards modernization. In the West, these changes are especially associated with the Enlightenment (Stiglitz and Greenwald 2014, 2015). For our purposes, the two critical ideas are (a) the mechanisms by which a society/economy learns (closing the knowledge gap to which we referred earlier) and (b) the insights about social, political, and economic organization, including the rule of law, systems of checks and balances, and the balance between the market, the state, and civil society (the subject of my 2015 WIDER Lecture, on the occasion of its thirtieth anniversary).[6]

These new understandings have led to a movement from a focus on developmental projects to policies and then to institutions, corresponding to the realization of the importance of not just physical capital, but human capital, social capital, and knowledge capital.

3 The Stockholm Statement

In an attempt to capture in a brief form these and other new understandings about development, a group of thirteen economists, including four former chief economists of the World Bank, put forward the Stockholm Statement of

---

[6] See Stiglitz (2016b). The original talk was given in September 2015.

development principles in 2016 (Alkire et al. 2016; Stiglitz 2016a), with eight key notions:

1. GDP growth is not an end in itself.
2. Development has to be inclusive.
3. Environmental sustainability is a requirement, not an option.
4. There is a need to balance market, state, and community.
5. Successful development requires providing macroeconomic stability, but this does not just mean balancing budgets or focusing exclusively on inflation.
6. One has to attend to the impact of global technology and inequality. It will be especially important to assess impacts on labour, in both developed and developing countries. Successful responses require investment in human capital, rewriting the rules of the economy to achieve a more equalitarian distribution of market income,[7] and creating new instruments of redistribution within and between countries.
7. Social norms and mindsets matter. One especially needs to bring the insights of modern behavioural economics to bear in development policies. These may provide effective ways of altering behaviour (savings, fertility, etc), and often at very low cost (Hoff and Stiglitz 2016; World Bank Group 2015).
8. Global policies have significant effects on developing countries. The international community, and especially the advanced countries, have a responsibility to ensure that global policies and international agreements are equitable and pro-development.[8] The Stockholm Statement recognized the interdependence of countries, and that the policies of the large, rich countries have large externalities on the rest of the world, which they often don't take into account (including their monetary, regulatory, trade, and migration policies). Tax havens, which the regulatory policies of the advanced countries tolerate, affect all countries, not just the developing countries. Still, the flow of money out of Africa has particularly adverse effects on Africa's growth (African Development Bank and Global Financial Integrity 2013). International agreements cover only parts of these arenas where there are global externalities, and where there are agreements (such as on climate) they often do not go far enough. And, of course, developed countries have not lived up to their commitments of 0.7 per cent of GDP in aid.

---

[7] That is, the rules of the game—including those of governing–labour relations, competition, and corporate governance—are critical in determining both the distribution of income and efficiency: see Stiglitz et al. (2015).
[8] Section 7 explains why current arrangements often stymie development.

3.1 Key Differences with the Washington Consensus

The eight principles of the Stockholm Statement represent a marked change from the Washington Consensus, with its primary emphasis on markets, its inadequate attention to market failures, its narrow view of macro-stability, and its narrow conception of the goals and instruments of development.[9]

3.1.1 Broader Goals to Reflect Challenges of the Twenty-First Century

The Washington Consensus focused on increasing GDP. But GDP is not a good measure of well-being, as the International Commission on the Measurement of Economic Performance and Social Progress has pointed out (Stiglitz et al. 2009). It takes, for instance, inadequate or no note of sustainability, whether environmental, social, political, or even economic. With climate change presenting an existential challenge to the planet, no responsible developmental strategy should ignore its impact on the environment. GDP also says nothing about how the fruits of the economy are being shared: GDP could go up even though most citizens are worse off. So another objective of a well-designed development strategy is inclusive growth. This is especially important because we have learned that trickle-down economics—which holds that if GDP goes up, the incomes of all (or most) will, too—simply doesn't work. Indeed, globalization (as it has been managed), while it may have simultaneously contributed to the increase in GDP, almost surely also contributed to the lowering of incomes of unskilled workers.

We have learned also that greater inclusivity can lead to more robust growth, especially when inequality reaches the extremes that it has in some countries (such as the US and many developing countries), and when it originates in the way it does, from rent-seeking on one hand to lack of opportunities for the poor on the other hand (Berg and Ostry 2011; Ostry et al. 2014; Stiglitz 2012, 2015). Thus, there are policies that can simultaneously increase equality and growth.

Seeing equality and growth as complements rather than substitutes is a major change in development thinking.

Employment generation is central to inclusive growth—especially where the labour force is expected to grow rapidly, as in sub-Saharan Africa (SSA). Leaving large fractions of the labour force underutilized or unutilized not only leads to large inequities, but is also inefficient. And again, growth itself does not necessarily lead to the growth of employment, especially of jobs in the formal sector. In recent years (2004–9), for instance, India has had rapid growth, but in a period in

---

[9] For an earlier discussion of the limitations of the Washington Consensus, see my 1998 WIDER Annual Lecture (Stiglitz 1998a); see also Stiglitz (2002).

which 50 million have entered the labour force, only about 1.1 million formal sector jobs were created.[10]

3.1.2 More Instruments

This new development thinking is also characterized by making use of more instruments. The Great Recession, of course, led even developed countries to embrace more instruments for monetary policy, such as quantitative easing (QE) and macroprudential regulation. But there is a need for more instruments for macrostability (now embraced in the new Institutional View of the IMF on capital controls; see IMF 2012); and more instruments for developmental transformation—including industrial policies (to be discussed in Section 6), promoting not just manufacturing but also agriculture and services; and those making use of the insights of behavioural economics.[11]

3.1.3 Clearer Distinctions between Means and Goals

One of the central failures of the Washington Consensus was the confusion between means and goals. Privatization, liberalization, deregulation, or even markets and GDP growth are not ends in themselves (see, for instance, Kanbur et al. 2018), but *may* be means to higher living standards or achieving the broader goals described earlier—or they could have just the opposite effects. The latter can especially arise because some policies that may increase static efficiency (like trade liberalization) may impede dynamic learning (Greenwald and Stiglitz 2006).

Other variables, such as inflation, budget deficits, and current account deficits, also need to be looked at through this lens. But not attending to some of these variables in a timely way may make it difficult to achieve the real goals of development.

3.1.4 Greater Participation: A Balance between Markets, Government, and Society

One of the most important differences between the Stockholm Statement and earlier articulations of development strategy involves broadening the range of participants in the development process. The narrowness of the Washington Consensus, a consensus between 15th Street (the US Treasury) and 19th Street

---

[10] According to India's National Sample Survey Office data (ICSSR Data Service 2016). A United Nations Development Programme report suggests that over a longer period of some two decades, India's employment performance, while still better than in the high-growth period, was disappointing: 'In India, the size of the working-age population increased by 300 million during the same time [1991–2013], while the number of employed people increased by only 140 million—the economy absorbed less than half the new entrants into the labour market.' See UNDP (2016).

[11] There is a large literature on industrial and LIT (learning, industrial, and technology) policies; see references, including Greenwald and Stiglitz (2006, 2013, 2014), Stiglitz (2011), Stiglitz and Greenwald (2014, 2015), and Noman and Stiglitz (2012a, b, 2015a, 2015b) for Africa. For the behavioural economics policies, see World Bank Group (2015).

(the IMF), shaped its perspectives: its focus on markets was too narrow; development entails not just markets, but government and civil society; and it is essential to understand the roles each needs to play, how each can play these roles more effectively, and how best to facilitate the appropriate interactions. For instance, all successful development has entailed government playing an important role—*the development state*. It has a multiplicity of jobs to do: providing enabling conditions for markets to work, including good physical and institutional infrastructure and an educated labour force; regulating markets—preventing negative externalities, including exploitation and excessive volatility; promoting development more directly, including through the industrial policies to which we referred earlier; understanding the 'big picture', including the problems posed by excessively rapid population growth; and co-ordinating more broadly developmental strategies among the many different participants in a country's development process.

One of the consequences of the Washington Consensus' single-minded focus on markets, with policies that restricted what the government could and should do, was that it undermined the institutional development of the state, impeding its ability to be as effective an instrument for development as it could be (Khan 2012). Even when it was finally recognized that there had to be a role for the state, it was a very circumscribed role. The state was described as *enabling the private sector*, with the real responsibility for development conferred on the private sector.[12] But for reasons I explained in my 2015 WIDER Lecture, there are many arenas, even in developed countries, in which the private sector is likely to fail to meet societal needs, and this is even more so in developing countries.

As we come to understand the importance of market failures and the need for collective action, especially in the societal transformations that are central to development, government is pivotal, so development efforts have to focus on increasing the efficiency and efficacy of government, and that includes, importantly, how to improve governance (Khan 2012; Noman et al. 2012; Stiglitz 2016b). Here, the systems of checks and balances to which we referred earlier are critical, and in this, media and civil society play a pivotal role.[13]

Critics of government action cite the numerous instances of government failure, where government fails to accomplish what is intended, or, perversely, serves the interests of the elites. Of course, 'to err is human', and all human institutions are fallible. Over the years, we have learned how to reduce the risks of failure and increase the chances of success; there have been important institutional innovations. These are part of the process of societal learning. Importantly, critics of government

---

[12] For a discussion of this point in the context of Africa, see Noman and Stiglitz (2012b) and the other papers in Noman et al. (2012).

[13] As I argue in Stiglitz (2019), there cannot be an effective *systemic* system of checks and balances in a world of excessive inequality: almost inevitably, those at the top will ensure that the political system serves their interests. Economic inequality gets translated into political inequality. See also Stiglitz (2012).

action tend to overestimate the extent of government failure, suggesting that it is inevitable, and underestimate the extent of market failure. Successes in East Asia and elsewhere show that government failure can be overcome—governments can play and have played a pivotal role in developmental transformation. By contrast, there are few if any instances of successful development where government did not play an important role.

4 Deconstructing the Success of the Manufacturing Export-Led Model

In this section we ask what made the manufacturing export-led growth model so successful, as a prelude to asking: if that model is dead, is there some other way of getting the benefits that it provided?[14]

Exports (more broadly, an open economy) allowed developing countries to avoid several of the complexities that were at the centre of earlier developmental debates. On the supply side, the problem of material balances (ensuring that internal demand for each good was equal to internal supply) did not have to be addressed—all one had to have was enough foreign exchange. When some input was needed, it could always be obtained in international markets.[15] Export-led growth generated the necessary foreign exchange. On the demand side, there was a problem of ensuring that there was adequate demand for the goods that no longer were produced. At the right exchange rate, there was unlimited demand for a country's exports, especially for small countries.

Exports also provided the basis for *learning*, so necessary for the developmental transformation discussed earlier. As we also noted earlier, what separates developed and less developed countries is a gap in knowledge, and export-led growth facilitated the transfer of that knowledge. Those engaging in trade had to interact with others, and those seeking to compete in export markets had to learn about manufacturing technology and international standards. Manufacturing is particularly well suited for learning, because it occurs in large and long-lived institutions (in contrast to, say, agriculture, where, especially in developing countries, the unit of production is a small farm). There are large economies of scale in

[14] For discussions of the East Asian manufacturing export-led growth model, see Amsden (1989), Birdsall et al. (1993), Stiglitz (1996), and Wade (1990) and the references cited there.
[15] Except for China and perhaps India, even developing countries that have large populations have a relatively small GDP. Standard trade models that assume perfect competition assume that at the right exchange rate, there is an infinite demand. Demand curves are horizontal. In practice, demand curves are downward-sloping (partly because of imperfections of competition, partly because there are large transport costs, partly because of imperfections in information).

the production and absorption of knowledge, and greater incentives for large institutions to engage in learning.[16]

Most important in the process of learning is *learning by doing*.[17] One can best (and sometimes only) learn how to increase productivity in manufacturing by manufacturing. Most relevant for development is that there are important spillovers of the learning and development in manufacturing to other industries. These spillovers include not just the direct technological spillovers (which may occur when processes in other sectors have some overlap with those in manufacturing), but also institutional spillovers (e.g. from the development of educational and financial institutions). The production of better-educated individuals and more of them, a requisite for success in manufacturing, is of benefit elsewhere in the economy. So, too, financial institutions, which may have originated to finance commerce or manufacturing, can expand their reach into other sectors of the economy. Of course, some transfer of technology could be accomplished in numerous other ways (buying technology or foreign direct investment), but these mechanisms are likely to have fewer deep learning benefits and spillovers.

Because of the importance and pervasiveness of learning and other spillovers from manufacturing exports, 'leaving it to the market' does not lead to the maximization of welfare or growth. Some form of government intervention is necessary to achieve desirable outcomes, including the industrial policies that we discuss at greater length in what follows.

Exports also provided the basis for *tax revenues*. Finance is needed for government expenditures—for the publicly provided goods that are essential for development, including infrastructure, education, and the acquisition, adaptation, and dissemination of technology. It is hard to tax the informal sector, including small farmers. That is why, traditionally, tax authorities relied heavily on taxes imposed on trade: it was easier to monitor the flow of goods that went through the limited number of ports.

Finally, the manufacturing exports generated *employment* in the urban sector, which was key in supporting structural transformation and widely shared growth. They generated jobs for new entrants into the labour force and those leaving agriculture, and the (relatively) high and increasing wages in manufacturing (resulting from ever-rising levels of productivity as an effect of learning and education) led to increasing demand for non-traded goods and higher standards of living.

Not only did manufacturing exports generate this panoply of benefits, but there were also numerous ways in which East Asian countries could promote manufacturing exports. They provided limited direct support (e.g. through

---

[16] See Stiglitz and Greenwald (2014). The next paragraph highlights that because of the importance of learning by doing, openness, when not well managed, may have adverse effects on learning and productivity increases. For an empirical discussion, see Navaretti and Tarr (2000).

[17] See Arrow (1962). Moreover, one not only learns how to do things by doing them, one learns how to learn by learning: see Stiglitz (1987). Stiglitz (2011) shows how one can use tax and subsidy policies to promote learning and development.

subsidies) but did provide access to credit at near-commercial rates to firms that were successful in exporting. This provided incentives for entrepreneurs to increase exports. And they had other instruments of industrial policy, including restrictions or taxes on competing imports and subsidies or credits for exports. Perhaps most important, though, was their provision of an enabling environment, including good infrastructure and an educated labour force.

5 A Multi-Pronged Strategy

With the limited prospects for manufacturing exports for those countries that did not take advantage of manufacturing export-led growth when it was available as the prime strategy for development, similar outcomes will require a multifaceted growth strategy, with different facets reflecting different aspects of what contributed to the success of manufacturing export-led growth. The region for which this is most true is, of course, SSA. For Africa, the last twenty-five years of the twentieth century was a lost quarter-century. Per capita income in 2000 was barely at the level of the mid-1970s. Economic decline was particularly sharp during the period 1980–95, years in which East Asia was growing rapidly under the influence of manufacturing export-led growth. Africa's decline was partially a result of a plethora of conditionalities imposed on SSA in the years after independence. At independence, of course, the colonial powers had failed to leave a legacy of either physical or human capital that would have enabled SSA to have prospered. In the currency, debt, financial, and economic crises that followed, these countries felt they had no choice but to turn to the Bretton Woods institutions for help, and in return for that help these institutions extracted a high price.

While the weakness in the agricultural sector was due largely to neglect, the fate of the industrial sector was the result of policies that were imposed on much of SSA. The share of manufacturing in GDP was once so highly correlated with per capita income that, until some fifteen or so years ago, the IMF used the term 'industrial countries' to refer to high-income countries. Reflecting the diminished importance of manufacturing, the relationship became an inverted U-shaped one some two decades or so ago, and more recently the height of the inverted U has been declining (i.e. the peak level of income at which manufacturing's share begins to shrink has been falling) (see Figure 12.1).

But under the IMF/Washington Consensus programmes, SSA began its deindustrialization in the 1980s much too prematurely and rapidly. Manufacturing as a share of value added to GDP decreased from 14.7 per cent in 1975 to 10.1 per cent in 2010 (see Table 12.2 for data from the Africa Sector Database by de Vries et al. (2015); Figure 12.2 has the corresponding numbers from the World Bank, starting from 1981).

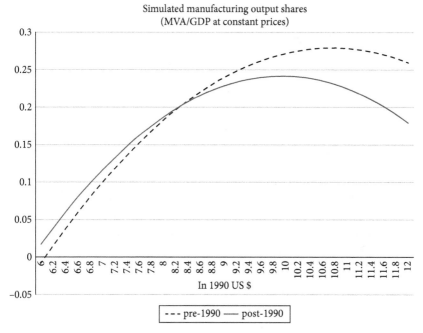

Figure 12.1 Simulated manufacturing output shares
Source: Rodrik (2015), reproduced with permission.

This history has one important implication for SSA relevant to the multi-pronged strategy that we are about to describe: this 'underindustrialization' of SSA has rightly been interpreted to mean there is more scope for 'catch-up' industrialization, notwithstanding the headwinds posed by global technological trends. There is indeed more scope for catch-up, and especially so for the kind of high-transport-cost goods that are particularly targeted at consumers and producers in the continent. Still, industrialization will, as we have already emphasized, not be able to play the role it did for East Asia.

We now turn to a more detailed look at each of the prongs of our multi-pronged strategy.

5.1 Manufacturing

Manufacturing, as we have noted, will continue to play a role, but it will be more limited and will need to be more directed, where possible taking advantage of natural advantage (such as mineral resources). (As we have also already noted, though, because of robotization and artificial intelligence, developing countries' advantage in manufacturing, arising out of cheap labour, will diminish, and even if there is some success in expanding manufacturing, in most countries this

Table 12.2 Deindustrialization in sub-Saharan Africa

Value added by sector (% of GDP)				
	1960	1975	1990	2010
Agriculture	37.6	29.2	24.9	22.4
Industry	24.3	30.0	32.6	27.8
Manufacturing	9.2	14.7	14.0	10.1
Services	38.1	40.7	42.6	49.8
Share of employment (%)				
	1960	1975	1990	2010
Agriculture	72.7	66.0	61.6	49.8
Industry	4.6	5.3	5.4	5.1
Manufacturing	4.7	7.8	8.9	8.3
Services	18.0	20.9	24.1	36.8

Source: Author's construction based on de Vries et al. (2015).

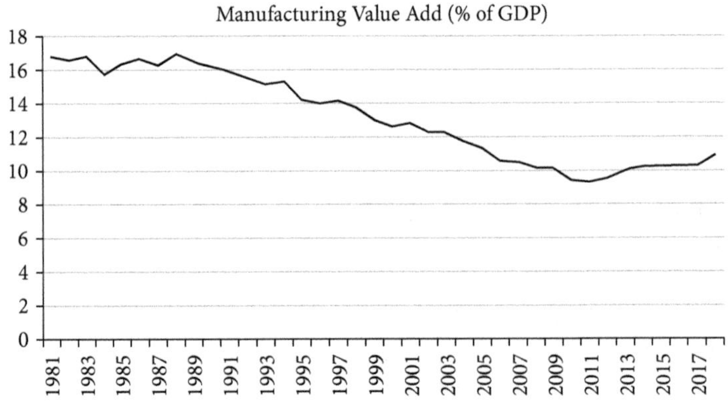

Figure 12.2 Manufacturing value added (% of GDP) in sub-Saharan Africa
Source: Author's construction based on World Bank Group (2020).

expansion will not suffice to create enough jobs for those seeking employment in the modern economy.[18])

Moreover, from now on manufacturing's ability to generate tax revenues (one of its strengths) may be hampered, as competition for low-skilled manufacturing among developing countries may result in a race to the bottom. This race would result in developing countries reaping, at most, limited benefits. The implication is that developing countries need to be careful in giving tax breaks and, more

---

[18] There is another reason why manufacturing may play a less important role in Africa's development than it did in East Asia's. The construction of global value chains has, some would argue, enabled more of the value of the economic activity occurring within a country to be extracted by the multinationals, and has structured production in ways in which there is less learning and less linkage to the rest of the economy: see Andreoni (2019).

importantly, to work together co-operatively to reach agreements that restrict the scope for this race to the bottom.[19] Instead of this race-to-the-bottom tax competition, it would be far better to have a race-to-the-top competition to provide good physical and 'institutional' infrastructure, which enhances the productivity of the economy and returns capital.

This will be especially important because of restrictions imposed by international (World Trade Organization) trade agreements. A striking feature of these agreements is that they allow agriculture subsidies (harming the developing countries, which depend heavily on agriculture), while prohibiting manufacturing subsidies. And even the structure of tariffs has traditionally been designed to inhibit developing countries from moving up the value-added chain into manufacturing (Stiglitz and Charlton 2005). Of course, in the earlier stages of advanced countries' development, they engaged in both manufacturing subsidies and protection; but now that they have succeeded, they want to 'pull up the ladder' (Chang 2002). Thus, the instruments that are at the disposal of developing countries today are more limited—and they will have to make all the use of these limited instruments that they can. Industrial policies should be at the centre of these efforts. Section 6 will discuss these policies in greater detail.

5.2 Agriculture

Agriculture will continue to provide the most important basis of employment for most developing countries, but should be restructured in ways that are more *dynamic*, with more learning and learning to learn—a kind of transformation *in situ*.

The neglect of agriculture, with its resulting lag in productivity (Block, 2016), means that, as in manufacturing, there is scope for catch-up and modernizing. (There is, in fact, a long history of development efforts being structured to the disadvantage of those in the rural sector. See Sah and Stiglitz, 1992.) Productivity is markedly lower than in East Asia, and an increase in agricultural productivity comparable to East Asia would have an enormous impact on incomes. Thus, the African Center for Economic Transformation, in its second major report released in October 2017, argued:

> Agriculture presents the easiest path to industrialization and economic transformation. Increasing productivity and output in a modern agricultural sector would, beyond improving food security and the balance of payments (through reduced food imports and increased exports), sustain agro-processing, the manufacturing of agricultural inputs, and a host of services upstream and downstream from farms, creating employment and boosting incomes across the economy.   (ACET 2017)

---

[19] The Independent Commission on Reform of International Taxation (ICRIT) has emphasized the adverse effects of this race to the bottom and has been urging an international agreement against tax competition: see ICRIT (2018).

Agriculture can have further benefits: for the many developing countries that import large amounts of foodstuffs, it can reduce the need for foreign exchange— leaving foreign exchange to be used for areas where it cannot be replaced. In some cases, there are opportunities for increasing exports of agricultural goods; the transformation should entail identifying high-value-added crops for which there is a demand elsewhere. Moreover, modern agriculture can be very 'advanced', serving as a basis of learning, with some of the skills having applicability to other areas.[20] Indeed, there are ample opportunities for non-labour-saving innov- ations—better crop mix, better fertilizers, better seeds, better planting patterns. The transformation of farming from traditional practices to modern farming can be an exemplar of general societal transformation entailing modernization.

Moreover, successful agricultural transformation will reduce the pressure arising from urban migration and the dilemmas it poses—for instance, whether to use scarce resources to build urban infrastructure, including housing. With limitations on the ability to create urban manufacturing jobs, excessive migration can be very destabilizing, giving rise to a large coterie of unemployed. And finally, the increase in productivity in agriculture will result in higher incomes, giving rise to multiplier effects and supporting an expanding non-traded service sector.

In short, the neglect of agriculture in development over the past four decades should always have been seen as a mistake. But the cost of this neglect will increase as developing countries struggle to find an alternative to manufacturing export-led growth.

5.2.1 Mechanisms for Promoting Agriculture

With small-scale production, private investments cannot provide needed advances in technology. Government will have to provide the necessary research, and transmit that research to farmers through extension services. Since agricul- tural conditions can vary greatly from one locale to another, the relevant applied research has to be done at the local level (as it was in the US, through the land- grant colleges and universities).

Education systems need to be changed. Today, to too great an extent, education is directed at enhancing the skills and knowledge required for urban jobs, rein- forcing the expectation that success entails leaving the rural sector rather than becoming more productive within it. Success in modern agriculture, by contrast, requires a better-educated labour force, and more educational resources should be directed at enhancing the productivity of the large fractions of the population that will remain within the rural sector.

One way in which the landscape has changed since the Second World War is in the growth of intellectual property rights, with large multinational giants selling

---

[20] Indeed, some aspects of modern agriculture (e.g. the growing of flowers) are, in many respects, industrial in nature: see Cramer (2019).

seeds (often genetically modified), herbicides, pesticides, and fertilizers, with often very adverse economic and social consequences. Developing countries need to be sure they adopt the right intellectual property regime—not the one foisted on them by the multinationals and Western governments (Cimoli et al. 2014a, b; Jayadev and Stiglitz 2010; Maskus and Merrill 2013).

There are also significant problems of information asymmetries in providing key inputs like seed and fertilizer to farmers. It is hard, if not impossible, to ascertain the quality at the point of purchase. In developing countries, reputation mechanisms often work imperfectly, and to the extent that they do work they can result in high degrees of imperfections of competition. When regulations fail it may be desirable to, at a minimum, have the government certify the quality of the inputs, and perhaps market them directly, because incentives and opportunities for scamming often seem just too irresistible to the private sector.[21]

Another crucial input is credit, and this is another arena in which the private sector has excelled in exploitation. Non-profit micro-credit schemes have met with enormous success in Bangladesh, but when the 'model' was taken up by for-profit lenders there was a massive failure (Haldar and Stiglitz 2013, 2016). Government should encourage these not-for-profits and co-operative lending programmes and encourage the private sector to lend (at strictly controlled rates) to agriculture, for example by requiring that a minimal fraction of loans goes to small farmers (analogous to the Community Reinvestment Act requirements for lending to minorities in the US).

Finally, in many developing countries there are serious problems in marketing, with middlemen with market power taking a disproportionately large fraction of the value. At one time, the World Bank and IMF railed against government marketing boards, which proved often inefficient and sometimes corrupt. The assumption was that with government out of the way, a competitive market would flourish, and farmers would get full value for their crops. What happened instead was the growth of monopolistic middlemen (part of the original reason for the growth of government marketing boards). They might have been more efficient; they were certainly more efficient in exploiting farmers: in some cases, what the latter received went down (Wilcox 2006; Wilcox and Abbott 2004).

5.3 Mining and Other Natural Resources

Mining and hydrocarbons will continue to be important for foreign exchange for those countries that are lucky enough to have these resources. But the development of a country's resources should be, to the extent possible, more than just a source of foreign exchange; it should be a central part of the development strategy.

---

[21] Reflecting a more general point noted by Akerlof and Shiller (2015).

The standard lessons of the resource curse[22] have not yet been learned by most countries. Countries that are rich in natural resources not only grow more slowly than one would have expected; they also have more inequality, partly as a result of the rampant rent-seeking that is so often associated with natural resources. Four central insights have emerged on how developing countries that have natural resources can best manage this prong of the multi-pronged development strategy.

- They need to maximize the revenues that they obtain from natural resources. When the resources are held by the government, this means having well-designed auctions (of the right to develop the resource) and contracts. It may be necessary to auction off different parts of the production process rather than to have a bid for an overall 'manager' of the resource. Contracts need to exhibit 'time consistency'; in particular, when the quantities of the resource or the cost of extraction turn out particularly favourably, the contract has to be designed so that the oil or mining company does not walk off with an unwarranted bonanza. When the resources are held in private hands, there should be as close as possible to a 100 per cent tax on the 'pure rents' associated with the resource. The resource should be thought of as belonging to all the people—it was part of the geography. The principle that pure rents should be taxed at 100 per cent is well established (see, for instance, George 1871). When the government has sold or leased the resource at a below-market rate (sometimes as a result of corruption, sometimes out of pure incompetence), the terms need to be renegotiated. A country is always sovereign over the resources that lie within it. Botswana's remarkable development was only possible because at the time of independence it renegotiated its diamond leases (see Stiglitz 2002).
- Contracts need to be complemented by excess profit taxes. Contracts will never be perfectly designed, so the foreign oil or mining company may well get substantial excess profits. Countries need to be careful not to sign investment agreements that circumscribe their ability to change taxes and regulations. Those that have signed such agreements should exit or renegotiate (as South Africa is doing).
- Countries need to establish sovereign wealth funds—both to manage cyclical variability and to prevent exchange-rate appreciation. Too often, the high exchange rate associated with natural resources weakens the development of other sectors of the economy, including agriculture and manufacturing.

[22] The natural resource curse is the observation that countries with more resources, by and large, do more poorly and have greater inequality than those without. Ensuring that natural resources are a blessing rather than a curse requires more than just the economics measures described below. It also requires managing the politics to prevent the kind of rent-seeking that is endemic in natural-resource economies. For a broad discussion, see Stiglitz (2007) and the other chapters in Humphreys et al. (2007).

These other sectors generate more jobs and more learning. A well-managed sovereign wealth fund can also be an important instrument for ensuring that the fruits of the country's resources (which are typically limited in amounts) are shared equitably across generations.

- Countries should look for linkages with other sectors, and industrial policies should include strategies that enhance those linkages (Jourdan 2013; Stiglitz and Greenwald 2014). Sometimes there has been a concern that fostering such linkages would entail less growth. But that is a short-run perspective. There can be long-run benefits in learning and developing a dynamic comparative advantage. There needs to be a careful appraisal of the trade-offs. Countries should also look for good partners, willing to participate in this kind of broader development strategy. While the technical knowledge associated with mining may have limited relevance to other sectors, the organizational knowledge of a foreign partner can be of broader relevance. Moreover, there can be a variety of linkages to other sectors that can be enhanced: the fact that in the past such linkages appear to have been weak may only reflect the lack of effort in developing them. It simply says that these linkages have not been developed under previous developmental strategies. At the very least, domestic firms can supply many of the required inputs, for example, construction of housing. Private mining or hydrocarbon firms, of course, may have little incentive to do so. Government intervention may be required, and the contracts with resource extraction companies have to be designed to better align private incentives with societal needs. Writing a formal contract embedding all of this may be nearly impossible, which is why, where government has the required competencies, state agencies may be preferable.

5.4 Services

Services will be the growth sector of the future, but there will be many ramifications of the move to the service sector that developing countries need to be aware of.

Production units will be smaller. For developing countries, this is a good thing: it is easier for entrepreneurs in nascent stages of development to manage small- and medium-sized enterprises. But productivity growth may be more limited. Traditionally, productivity growth in the service sector is lower than in manufacturing. While this may be partially a measurement problem, it is partially real and expected: with smaller production units, each has less incentive for investment in research and development (R&D), and the benefits of learning by doing are less widely shared. But this lower rate of productivity growth is not inevitable.[23] More to the point, there is enormous scope for developing countries to catch up to productivity levels in the service sector in the advanced countries. With the service sector comprising such a large fraction of the economy in advanced countries, disparities in productivity in the service sector are an important component of disparities in standards of living, and closing the gap in productivity should thus be an essential part of the development strategy.

As in agriculture, there is more need for co-operative and government R&D. (There are a few places around the world, such as Tuscany, where co-operative ventures have proved successful.)

The move towards a service sector economy is likely to be associated with other changes to the structure of the economy, which will require more active government intervention. The transition to a service sector economy may be associated with greater inequality, for several reasons. There will not be the kind of wage compression that typically occurs in large manufacturing enterprises (where wage differences across individuals are smaller than productivity differences). The result is that compensation is likely to be more linked to individual productivity. Moreover, there are likely to be larger productivity differences across firms (in turn, because the enterprises themselves will be less able and willing to invest in the acquisition of frontier knowledge). Finally, monopoly power may increase. The level of competition in local services is often lower than that of product competition among large international manufacturing firms, and this is especially so when there is a link between local services and the large manufacturing firms— there is likely, for instance, to be a single service provider for any car or tractor in a given locale. Indeed, many large manufacturers may generate much of their profits from these local services, precisely because there is limited competition there. Location matters. Moreover, in developing countries with high levels of unemployment, the imbalance of market power between firms and workers is likely to be even greater than in developed countries.

Again, there is an increased need for government action: to combat the increase in monopolization here, as in other areas of modern economies; to ensure that there is a greater balance of power between workers and firms (encouraging, for instance, unions among smaller enterprises and even individuals, such as taxicab drivers); to redistribute income to curb excesses of inequality and address poverty; and to promote advances in technology. There is an increased need for government to push to create a learning society, to reduce productivity differences.

Many services can be more easily inserted into the global economy through the internet, especially if there can be standard-setting, with quality certification,

---

[23] There is an important caveat: there are limits to increases in productivity in some service sectors, e.g. in the creation of works of art or in haircuts. This is sometimes referred to as *Baumol's disease* (Baumol 2013).

either through peer monitoring or certification services possibly provided by the government. Success will entail an increasing need for skills training, including languages. But the dominance of a few tech giants and the role that the advanced countries play in setting international standards may result in an uneven playing field, enabling the advanced countries to receive a disproportionate share of the value of these advances in technology and inhibiting the ability of those in developing countries to become meaningful participants in the marketplace. At the very least, developing countries will need to resist demands by the US and other developed countries to accede to international agreements reflecting the economic interests of the tech giants; and they will have to find ways to tax the revenues generated within their countries by these digital multinationals.[24]

5.4.1 The Multiple Forms of Services

The term 'services' embraces a wide range of economic activities, with quite different characteristics. Some developing countries, for instance, have successfully promoted tourism. Developing a tourist industry can promote jobs and learning and generate considerable foreign exchange. Countries such as Bhutan and Namibia have, moreover, managed the sector in ways that minimize impacts on the environment and the domestic culture.

Government plays an important role in many key service sectors (housing, education, and health), and understandably so. This means that as economies move towards a service sector economy, the role of the government should naturally increase.[25]

5.4.2 Housing Services

The process of urbanization will require large investments in housing, with a large job creation potential. Government will need to take an active role, including in planning 'livable cities' (an important part of well-being), in providing finance and local public transportation, and in ensuring that there is affordable housing for all income groups. In many cities, there is no affordable housing for low-income residents anywhere near the city centre, forcing people to travel long distances—a hidden tax. The benefits of agglomeration are often captured by those who happen to own real estate in the centre; a high tax on this real estate can recapture these windfall benefits for the public, and be used to ensure that cities are more economically integrated.

---

[24] Even European countries have become worried about the loss of tax revenues and are beginning to explore the best way to impose taxation.

The new tech giants pose serious problems not only for competition policy and taxation but also for privacy policies and democratic processes. A discussion of how these can and should be addressed would take us beyond the scope of this chapter.

[25] Earlier, we described the important role for the government in providing agricultural services, in marketing of output, in the provision of inputs (credit, seeds, and fertilizers), and in extension services, improving agricultural technology.

Private financial markets have, in many countries, done a dismal job of providing mortgages at low rates, and in forms that help individuals manage well the risks of home ownership. Governments should at least consider the possibility of providing income-contingent, long-term mortgages (when incomes fall below a certain level, payments are postponed and the mortgage is paid back over a longer period) to those who have paid income taxes for a number of years. Such a programme would encourage home ownership, reduce defaults, and have the further benefit of encouraging formality in the labour market.

5.4.3 Education

Good systems of education can both create jobs and enhance development. In many developing countries, recruitment of new enterprises is hindered by a lack of education—not just 'quantity' (average level of attainment: see Figure 12.3) but quality. Making education economically accessible through state support is an important step, but there have to be corresponding efforts to ensure quality. Otherwise there will be disappointment. Low education levels also present an increasing challenge to continued modernization, as the importance of learning grows.

5.4.4 Other Service Sectors

Many service sectors, such as telecommunications and business services, can be as modern and hi-tech as manufacturing, with learning benefits similar to those

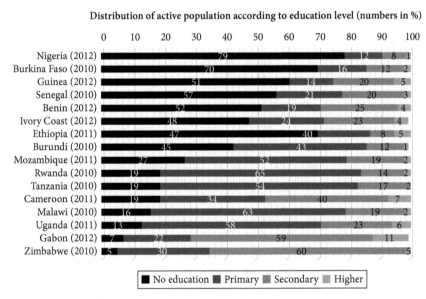

Figure 12.3 Distribution of active population according to education level
Notes: Only countries with data after 2009 are included. Numbers are in %.
Source: Chevalier and Le Goff (2014), reproduced with permission.

in manufacturing. Unfortunately, many developing countries have allowed foreign companies to develop these sectors without any focus on encouraging learning. Maximizing the development potential from foreign investment requires maximizing these learning spillovers. That may entail requiring joint ventures, as China has, or imposing local content and employment requirements.

6 Industrial Policies and Dynamic Comparative Advantage

We have already made clear that there is a need for government to take a large role in development and the associated structural transformation. Development and structural transformation are rife with market failures. It is costly to move from the 'old economy' to the new. Imperfections of capital markets become particularly evident in the process of transformation: the value of the assets of those in the 'old economy' are diminished, so firms and workers in the old economy do not have resources to make necessary investments or the collateral with which to obtain finance. Moreover, there are important learning externalities, which those making investments and production decisions do not take into account.

The need for government was made evident in the earlier transition in developed countries from agriculture to manufacturing, where the failure of government to assist in the movement of individuals out of an agrarian–rural economy to an urban manufacturing economy contributed to the Great Depression. It was only through an unintended government industrial policy—moving people to the urban sector as part of the war effort[26]—that the Great Depression was overcome and a successful transition was accomplished. But as we have already explained, the role of government in this transition to a service sector economy, through the multi-pronged approach described in the previous section, will need to be even greater, for example in closing the knowledge gap between the small production units in the service sector and the best-managed enterprises around the world, and in promoting technological advances in both the service sector and agriculture.

Industrial policy is one of the important instruments that government will need to employ. It simply entails actions that aim to alter the allocation of resources (or the choice of technology) from what the market would bring about on its own. As we noted earlier, industrial policies are not confined to industry but include policies aimed at other sectors, such as finance or IT and agriculture. Modern industrial policies might more accurately be called learning, industrial, and technology (LIT) policies. These policies are, in part, about *creating a learning society*, an essential part of modernization. Creating a learning society is more than just a matter of education; it entails trade and investment policies, labour

---

[26] Including the subsequent GI Bill, which provided education to returning veterans and helped them get housing.

policies, competition policies, and labour market policies—indeed, it touches on every aspect of a country's legal and economic framework. There is often a conflict between policies that enhance static efficiency and those that contribute to learning, and thus to long-term growth. Striking the right balance is at the core of success. One of my criticisms of the neoliberal Washington Consensus policies is that they paid no attention to learning, seemingly unaware of the potential conflict, and thus failed to strike the right balance. Allocating resources in a way that is consistent with *static* efficiency, as desirable as it may seem, may actually impede development and growth.[27]

LIT policies take many different forms. Rwanda used such policies to promote IT, Kenya to promote tea and flowers, Ethiopia to promote modern agriculture and shoes. The green revolution in South Asia was facilitated by agricultural price supports (setting a floor on output prices, thereby affecting the risk of using the new technology) as well as input subsidies, including, notably, for electricity, which enhanced the profitability of tube-well irrigation that was critical for the success of the new seeds. Industrial policies were central to almost all countries that 'caught up' (or nearly so) with the technological frontier and became developed.

These policies have, of course, played an important role even in advanced countries. As Mazzucato (2013) emphasizes in her book *The Entrepreneurial State*, government has played a central role in all of the major advances, including the internet. But the role of government in shaping the economy is pervasive. Because there is a widespread perception that without government assistance there would be an undersupply of credit to small enterprises, most advanced countries, including the US, have lending programmes directed at this 'market failure'.[28] Industrial policies arise naturally in response to the multiple market failures that characterize development and structural change, from the capital market imperfections to the learning spillovers of which we have already made note.

Greenwald and Stiglitz (2014) go further: they argue that all countries have implicit industrial policies, though citizens in some countries don't realize it. Markets do not exist in a vacuum, and the way they are structured gives advantages to some, disadvantages to others. The priority given derivatives in bankruptcy in the US encouraged derivatives; and the rule that said that student loans could not be discharged, even in bankruptcy, encourages imprudent private lending to students. Moreover, governments have to make decisions about what infrastructure to construct or how to design the educational system. These decisions about public expenditures help shape the economy. When citizens aren't aware of this, it means that the rules and patterns of expenditure are more likely to be determined

---

[27] These ideas are elaborated upon in Stiglitz and Greenwald (2014).
[28] In the US, through the Small Business Administration. For the underlying theory, see Emran and Stiglitz (2009).

by special interest groups, which are typically very aware of the consequences of these government actions. When these decisions are made in an open and transparent way, with full discussion of the implications for the country's growth strategy, the scope for this kind of rent-seeking is reduced.

Thus, we are arguing here that government must ask how the structure of its rules and regulations and expenditures can be used to promote those sectors and technologies that most enhance the country's long-run development strategy, such as promoting learning, with broad societal spillovers, and generating foreign exchange and jobs.[29]

The identification of which particular forms/subsectors of manufacturing, services, or agriculture (or which particular technologies) are most conducive to development is a broader question, beyond the scope of this chapter (see Stiglitz and Greenwald 2015). Here, we simply note that there is a growing body of research associating development with complexity: more advanced countries have the ability to produce a wide range of products, including, in particular, products entailing greater complexity (Hausmann et al. 2011; Tacchella et al. 2012). Thus, it may make sense for a country to consciously think about how it can move up the complexity scale, and how the knowledge associated with such production can be absorbed into the economy. China's strategy of joint ventures may perhaps best be thought of in this light. It was not (or not just) about stealing intellectual property, as the Trump administration has claimed. It was not about obtaining, for instance, otherwise secret blueprints. It was about learning, especially about tacit knowledge—the kind of knowledge that isn't written down, that one can't learn from a textbook. One only learns it through the process of production itself.

Some sectors are more amenable to learning, and some learning in specific sectors has more spillovers to others. The general principles of industrial policies apply in each area of the multi-pronged strategy, that is, not just to manufacturing, but to agriculture, services, and natural resources. Governments need to identify, for instance, 'learning' and 'learning spillover' service sectors and agricultural activities. These can have many of the benefits of the learning provided by manufacturing. And as we have noted, industrial policies need to exploit linkages with natural resources—one of the key comparative advantages of many African countries.

7 Reassessing Comparative Advantage

Older theories of development were based on countries exploiting their static comparative advantage. This implied, for instance, that in the 1960s, when Korea

---

[29] This paper focuses on development. Industrial policies can and should be used to promote other societal objectives, such as protecting the environment and reducing inequality. See also Cimoli, Dosi, and Stiglitz (2009a, b).

was formulating its development strategy after the Korean War, it should have focused on growing rice. But Korea realized that even were it to become the best rice grower in the world, it would still be poor, or at least poorer than the more advanced countries. To close the gap in incomes between itself and the more advanced countries, it had to close the gap in knowledge, and that entailed heavy investments in education and knowledge. It also meant, at that time, industrialization. Korea realized that a country's comparative advantage could change.

Thus, the focus of a country's development strategies must be on dynamic comparative advantage, not static comparative advantage. But assessing dynamic comparative advantage is difficult; indeed, even assessing static comparative advantage in today's global economy is not so easy. Traditionally, using the Heckscher–Ohlin model, it has been argued that developed countries have a comparative advantage in capital-intensive, high-technology (skilled labour)-intensive goods, and developing countries in unskilled labour-intensive goods. But capital is highly mobile, and many aspects of technical knowledge (especially when embedded in machines) are relatively mobile. So, too, skilled labour is relatively mobile.

What, then, is the real source of comparative advantage? It can't be based on mobile factors. It must rest on *place-based* characteristics, the immobile 'factors'— most importantly, the embedded knowledge of society, its institutions and norms, the institutional infrastructure (its political system, and its stability; its rule of law; its systems of checks and balances), its physical infrastructure, its reputation ('branding'), and the skills, health, and discipline of its workforce. All of these affect the ability to attract and retain talent and capital. Young people care about the environment—about 'meaning' in their work, and co-operation and challenge (including intellectual challenge) in the workplace.

It is hard—but essential—to change these in constructive ways. It is also essential not to change them in adverse ways: the move in many countries, in recent years, to more authoritarian governments has increased the uncertainties. It is a change that alters both long-run (dynamic) comparative and absolute advantages.

8 How Can Developed Countries Help?

Having characterized a new multi-pronged development strategy, the natural question is: how can developed countries help? There is a role that they can play in trade, finance, investment, and knowledge, in closing the resource and knowledge gaps that separate developed and developing countries. A fairer *pro-development* global trade regime would obviously help, especially in both agriculture and manufacturing. The current regime has agricultural prices depressed by massive subsidies in the developed countries, and yet inhibits the developing countries from assisting their economies in making transitions out of agriculture.[30]

The investment regime that developed countries are attempting to impose is also adverse to development. It impedes the imposition of domestic requirements, which can facilitate learning. Investment agreements also impede renegotiation that would allow developing countries to get a fair share of the value of their natural resources. They also impede the imposition of regulations that protect the environment, health, and safety and promote economic stability (Stiglitz 2018).

The global intellectual property rights (IPR) regime is also adverse to development. This was recognized in 2004, when the World International Properties Rights Organization (WIPO) called for a development-oriented intellectual property regime. But the failure to achieve this parallels the failure to get a development-oriented international trade regime. While international trade agreements typically have provisions for compulsory licences, the advanced countries have put pressure on developing countries not to exercise those rights. The developed countries need to recognize that the IPR regime that is appropriate for a developing country is different from that appropriate for an advanced country—and the intellectual property regime in the advanced countries itself, a variant of which they have tried to impose around the world, is designed not to promote innovation but to promote profits in certain politically powerful sectors. The combined effects of the international trade and intellectual property regime hurts the ability of developing countries to industrialize and to create a modern agriculture sector, and it leads to increasingly large transfers from the developing countries to the developed.[31]

Moreover, the developed countries (especially the US) refuse to recognize the valuable environmental services (biodiversity) provided by the developing countries. The result of all of this is that there is a risk either of a growing knowledge gap or of a large flow of money from developing countries to developed—rather than the other way around. At the same time, the developed countries have not done what they should to stymie the flow of corrupt funds out of developing countries—providing safe havens both in offshore secrecy havens and in onshore centres for money laundering.[32] The developed countries have, at the same time, not lived up to their commitment to provide support for developing countries,

---

[30] While the international community came together in 2001 seemingly with a commitment to promote development through what was called the development round of trade negotiations, by the end of 2015 the development-round negotiations were abandoned. The problems with the existing regime are set forth, e.g., in Stiglitz and Charlton (2005).

[31] See, e.g., Cimoli, Dosi, Nelson, and Stiglitz (2009); Cimoli et al. (2014b), including the concluding chapter summarizing the findings; and Dosi and Stiglitz (2014). See also Baker et al. (2017) and the references therein.

[32] See, for instance, Peith and Stiglitz (2016) and Global Justice Now (2017). See also African Development Bank and Global Financial Integrity (2013).

either in general assistance or in assistance targeted at climate change adaptation and mitigation.

There is a simple way of providing the resources that will, at the same time, promote global stability and growth (Greenwald and Stiglitz 2010; Stiglitz and Greenwald 2010). Every year, countries around the world put aside several hundred billions of dollars in reserves—as protection against the economic volatilities and uncertainties they face. These amounts increased significantly in the aftermath of the East Asian crisis, when developing countries saw the consequences of not having enough reserves: crisis and a loss of economic sovereignty, as the IMF imposed harsh and unreasonable conditions in return for assistance. But this money—income not spent—depresses global aggregate demand. At times, this is offset by countries spending beyond their means, but most countries have realized the dangers of doing so, so that overall there is a bias towards weak global aggregate demand.

Today, most countries hold their reserves largely in dollars (though also in gold, euros, and yen). This creates a problem known as the Triffin Paradox: as the reserve currency owes more and more money to those abroad, confidence in the country may erode (Triffin 1960). Thus, the current reserve system risks both weak aggregate demand and global macro-instability.

These problems can be easily rectified by creating a global reserve system—where countries agree to convert the global reserve currency into their own currency. The annual emissions of new global reserves can be designed to offset the amounts put into reserves, maintaining the global economy at near full employment. And the emissions can be transferred to the accounts of the developing countries, increasing their purchasing power but without subtracting from the purchasing power of those in the developed countries. The provision of these funds to developing countries should be done with minimal conditionality, for example only requiring that they not engage in actions that harm the global community, such as excessive carbon emissions or nuclear proliferation.[33]

9   Concluding Remarks: Reformulating Development Thinking

Success in development over the past sixty years was greater than anyone anticipated. Simply contrast Myrdal's predictions for Asia (he anticipated that the continent would continue to be mired in poverty, as it had been for centuries) with

---

[33] There are a variety of institutional arrangements by which this could be done, including expanding the existing system of SDRs (special drawing rights): see the report of the Commission of Experts on Reforms of the International Monetary and Financial System (2010). See also Greenwald and Stiglitz (2010), Ocampo and Stiglitz (2018), Stiglitz (2006), and Stiglitz and Greenwald (2010), and the references cited therein.

what happened (Myrdal 1968). There is an enormous gap that must be closed in both knowledge and resources. Most of the advanced countries are engaged in the service sector—in the US that sector accounts for 80 per cent or more of GDP. So if there are disparities in standards of living, they relate to productivity in these service sectors. There are huge disparities in productivity within countries, even greater between countries.

The basis of the success of growth over the past half-century was export-led growth. We have deconstructed what enabled manufacturing to provide this growth spurt, this structural transformation. It won't be able to do so in the future to anything like that extent. There has to be another strategy, one that performs some of the essential roles that manufacturing export-led development did.

Successful development policy will need to be explicitly more multi-pronged, addressing the separate 'challenges' that the manufacturing sector took on simultaneously. We have shown how a co-ordinated (agriculture, manufacturing, mining, service sector) strategy has the prospect of attaining the same success as the old manufacturing export-led strategy.

9.1 Comprehensive Development Strategy

In short, what is needed is a comprehensive development strategy[34] leading to inclusive growth with inclusive participation, including a balance between markets, government, and society, based on the new understandings of what leads to successful economic and societal transformation, responding to the particular strengths of the country, and addressing the particular challenges, including those posed by demographics and climate change. Most importantly, it must create new dynamic comparative advantages.

The challenge facing the less developing countries in the coming decades is enormous. Even when successfully implemented, the multi-pronged strategy we have outlined is unlikely to provide successes of the magnitude experienced in the East Asian miracle. And it is not an easy strategy to implement. It is far more complex than the manufacturing export-led strategy. The developed countries can provide substantial help. Helping the developing countries is a moral issue. But beyond that, there will be enormous economic and political consequences of not helping the developing countries, not the least of which will arise from the inevitable migration pressure that will result from an ever-increasing gap in income.

The central message of this chapter is one of hope: there is hope for development in a post-industrial world. It will be harder. And it will require more assistance from the developed countries, or at least that they take down some of the

---

[34] This was an idea popularized in the late 1990s by the president of the World Bank, Jim Wolfensohn; see also Stiglitz (2001).

impediments that they have placed in the way of developing countries' structural transformation. But it can be done.

References

ACET (African Center for Economic Transformation) (2017). *African Transformation Report 2017: Agriculture Powering Africa's Economic Transformation*. Available at: http://acetforafrica.org/acet/wp-content/uploads/publications/2017/10/ATR17-full-report.pdf (accessed 2 January 2019).

African Development Bank and Global Financial Integrity (2013). *Illicit Financial Flows and the Problem of Net Resource Transfers from Africa: 1980–2009*. Tunis-Belvédère: African Development Bank; Washington DC: Global Financial Integrity. Available at: https://www.gfintegrity.org/storage/gfip/documents/reports/AfricaNetResources/gfi_afdb_iffs_and_the_problem_of_net_resource_transfers_from_africa_1980-2009-web.pdf (accessed 2 January 2019).

Akerlof, G., and R.J. Shiller (2015). *Phishing for Phools*. Princeton: Princeton University Press.

Alkire, S., P. Bardhan, K. Basu, H. Bhorat, F. Bourguignon, A. Deshpande, R. Kanbur, Y. Lin, K. Moene, J.-P. Platteau, J. Saavedra, J. Stiglitz, and F. Tarp (2016). 'Stockholm Statement: Towards a Consensus on the Principles of Policymaking for the Contemporary World', statement issued November, from meeting in Stockholm, Sweden, 16–17 September 2016, hosted by Swedish International Development Cooperation Agency (Sida) and the World Bank. Available at: https://www.sida.se/globalassets/sida/eng/press/stockholm-statement.pdf (accessed 2 January 2019).

Amsden, A. (1989). *Asia's Next Giant*. New York: Oxford University Press.

Andreoni A. (2019). 'A Generalized Linkage Approach to Local Production Systems Development in the Era of Global Value Chains with Special Reference to Africa'. In R. Kanbur, A. Noman, and J.E. Stiglitz (eds) *Quality of Growth in Africa*. Oxford: Oxford University Press.

Arrow, K.J. (1962). 'The Economic Implications of Learning by Doing'. *The Review of Economic Studies*, 29(3): 155–73.

Baker, D., A. Jayadev, and J.E. Stiglitz (2017). 'Innovation, intellectual property, and development: a better set of approaches for the 21st century'. Paper in the AccessIBSA series 'Innovation & Access to Medicines in India, Brazil & South Africa'. Available at: http://cepr.net/images/stories/reports/baker-jayadev-stiglitz-innovation-ip-development-2017-07.pdf (accessed 2 January 2019).

Baumol, W.J. (2013). *The Cost Disease*. New Haven: Yale University Press.

Berg, A., and J.D. Ostry (2011). 'Inequality and unsustainable growth'. IMF Staff Discussion Note 11/08. Washington DC: IMF.

Birdsall, N.M., J.E.L. Campos, C.-S. Kim, W.M. Corden, H. Pack, J. Page, R. Sabor, and J.E. Stiglitz (1993). *The East Asian Miracle: Economic Growth and Public Policy*, ed. L. MacDonald. World Bank policy research report. New York:

Oxford University Press. Available at: http://documents.worldbank.org/curated/en/975081468244550798/Main-report (accessed 2 January 2019).

Block, S. (2016). 'The Decline and Rise of Agricultural Productivity in Sub-Saharan Africa since 1961'. In S. Edwards, S. Johnson, and D.N. Weil (eds), *African Successes, Volume IV: Sustainable Growth*. Chicago: University of Chicago Press.

Chang, H.-J. (2002). *Kicking Away the Ladder*. New York: Anthem Press.

Chevalier, A., and M. Le Goff (2014). 'Dynamiques de croissance et de population en Afrique sub-saharienne'. Panorama du CEPII 2014-A-03. Paris: CEPII.

Cimoli, M., G. Dosi, K.E. Maskus, R.L. Okediji, J.H. Reichman, and J.E. Stiglitz (eds) (2014a). *Intellectual Property Rights*. Oxford: Oxford University Press.

Cimoli, M., G. Dosi, K.E. Maskus, R.L. Okediji, J.H. Reichman, and J.E. Stiglitz (2014b). 'The Role of Intellectual Property Rights in Developing Countries: Some Conclusions'. In M. Cimoli, G. Dosi, K.E. Maskus, R.L. Okediji, J.H. Reichman, and J.E. Stiglitz (eds), *Intellectual Property Rights*. Oxford and New York: Oxford University Press.

Cimoli, M., G. Dosi, R. Nelson, and J.E. Stiglitz (2009). 'Institutions and Policies in Developing Economies'. In B.Å. Lundvall, K.J. Joseph, C. Chaminade, and J. Vang (eds), *Handbook of Innovation Systems and Developing Countries*. Cheltenham and Northampton, MA: Edward Elgar Publishing.

Cimoli, M., G. Dosi, and J.E. Stiglitz (2009a). 'The Political Economy of Capabilities Accumulation'. In M. Cimoli, G. Dosi, and J.E. Stiglitz (eds), *The Political Economy of Capabilities Accumulation*. Oxford: Oxford University Press.

Cimoli, M., G. Dosi, and J.E. Stiglitz (2009b). 'The Future of Industrial Policies in the New Millennium'. In M. Cimoli, G. Dosi, and J.E. Stiglitz (eds), *The Political Economy of Capabilities Accumulation*. Oxford: Oxford University Press.

Commission of Experts on Reforms of the International Monetary and Financial System (2010). *The Stiglitz Report: Reforming the International Monetary and Financial Systems in the Wake of the Global Crisis*. New York: The New Press.

Cramer, C. (2019). 'Oranges Are Not Only Fruit'. In R. Kanbur, A. Noman, and J.E. Stiglitz (eds), *Quality of Growth in Africa*. Oxford: Oxford University Press.

Dahlman, C., A.T. Kouame, and T. Vishwanath (1998). *World Development Report 1998/1999: Knowledge for Development*. Washington, DC: World Bank Group. Available at: http://documents.worldbank.org/curated/en/729771468328524815/World-development-report-1998-1999-knowledge-for-development (accessed 2 January 2019).

De Vries, G., M. Timmer, and K.de Vries (2015). 'Structural Transformation in Africa'. *The Journal of Developmental Studies*, 51(6): 674–88.

Delli Gatti, D., M. Gallegati, B.C. Greenwald, A. Russo, and J.E. Stiglitz (2012a). 'Mobility Constraints, Productivity Trends, and Extended Crises'. *Journal of Economic Behavior & Organization*, 83(3): 375–93.

Delli Gatti, D., M. Gallegati, B.C. Greenwald, A. Russo, and J.E. Stiglitz (2012b). 'Sectoral Imbalances and Long Run Crises'. In F. Allen, M. Aoki, J.-P. Fitoussi, N. Kiyotaki, R. Gordon, and J.E. Stiglitz (eds), *The Global Macro Economy and*

Finance. IEA Conference Volume 150-III. Basingstoke and New York: Palgrave Macmillan.

Dosi, G., and J.E. Stiglitz (2014). 'The Role of Intellectual Property Rights in the Development Process, with Some Lessons from Developed Countries: An Introduction'. In M. Cimoli, G. Dosi, K.E. Maskus, R.L. Okediji, J.H. Reichman, and J.E. Stiglitz (eds), *Intellectual Property Rights.* Oxford and New York: Oxford University Press.

Emran, M.S., and J.E. Stiglitz (2009). 'Financial liberalization, financial restraint and entrepreneurial development'. Working Paper 2009–02. Washington, DC: Institute for International Economic Policy, George Washington University.

George, H. (1871). *Our Land and Land Policy.* East Lansing: Michigan State University Press.

Global Justice Now (2017). *Honest Accounts 2017.* London: Global Justice Now. Available at: https://www.globaljustice.org.uk/sites/default/files/ files/resources/ honest_accounts_2017_web_final_updated.pdf (accessed 02 January 2019).

Greenwald, B., and J.E. Stiglitz (2006). 'Helping Infant Economies Grow'. *American Economic Review: AEA Papers and Proceedings,* 96(2): 141–6.

Greenwald, B., and J.E. Stiglitz (2010). 'A Modest Proposal for International Monetary Reform'. In S. Griffith-Jones, J.A. Ocampo, and J.E. Stiglitz (eds), *Time for a Visible Hand.* Oxford: Oxford University Press.

Greenwald, B., and J.E. Stiglitz (2013). 'Learning and Industrial Policy: Implications for Africa'. In J.E. Stiglitz, J. Yifu Lin, and E. Patel (eds), *The Industrial Policy Revolution II.* Basingstoke and New York: Palgrave Macmillan.

Greenwald, B., and J.E. Stiglitz (2014). 'Industrial Policies, the Creation of a Learning Society, and Economic Development'. In J.E. Stiglitz and J. Yifu Lin (eds), *The Industrial Policy Revolution I.* Basingstoke and New York: Palgrave Macmillan.

Haldar, A., and J.E. Stiglitz (2013). 'Analyzing Legal Formality and Informality'. In D. Kennedy and J. Stiglitz (eds), *Law and Economic Development with Chinese Characteristics.* New York and Oxford: Oxford University Press.

Haldar, A., and J.E. Stiglitz (2016). 'Group Lending, Joint Liability, and Social Capital'. *Politics & Society,* 44(4): 459–97.

Hausmann, R., C.A. Hidalgo, S. Bustos, M. Coscia, A. Simoes, and M.A. Yildirim (2011). *The Atlas of Economic Complexity.* Cambridge: MIT Press.

Hoff, K., and J.E. Stiglitz (2016). 'Striving for Balance in Economics: Towards a Theory of the Social Determination of Behavior'. *Journal of Economic Behavior & Organization,* 126(Part B): 25–57.

Humphreys, M., J. Sachs, and J.E. Stiglitz (eds) (2007). *Escaping the Resource Curse.* New York: Columbia University Press.

ICRIT (2018). 'A Fairer Future for Global Taxation'. Available at: https://static1. squarespace.com/static/5a0c602bf43b5594845abb81/t/5a78e6909140b73 efc08eab6/1517872798080/ICRICT+Unitary+Taxation+Eng+Feb2018.pdf (accessed 2 January 2019).

ICSSR Data Service (2016). 'India—Employment and Unemployment: NSS 66th Round, Schedule 10, July 2009—June 2010'. Available at: http://www.icssrdataservice. in/datarepository/index.php/catalog/89/related_materials (accessed 2 January 2019).

IMF (2012). 'The Liberalization and Management of Capital Flows: An Institutional View'. IMF Policy Paper. Washington, DC: IMF. Available at: https://www.imf.org/en/ Publications/Policy-Papers/Issues/2016/12/31/The-Liberalization-and-Management-of-Capital-Flows-An-Institutional-View-PP4720 (accessed 2 January 2019).

Jayadev, A., and J.E. Stiglitz (2010). 'Medicine for Tomorrow'. *Journal of Generic Medicines*, 7(3): 217–26.

Jourdan, P. (2013). 'Toward a Resource-Based African Industrialization Strategy'. In J.E. Stiglitz, J. Yifu Lin, and E. Patel (eds), *The Industrial Policy Revolution II*. Basingstoke and New York: Palgrave Macmillan.

Kanbur, R., E. Patel, and J.E. Stiglitz (2018). 'Sustainable Development Goals and Measurement of Economic and Social Progress'. In J.E. Stiglitz, A. Sen, and J.P. Fitoussi (2011), *Advancing Research on Well-Being Metrics beyond GDP*. Report of the Commission on the Measurement of Economic Performance and Social Progress. Paris: OECD Publishing. Available at: https://read.oecd-ilibrary.org/economics/for-good-measure/sustainable-development-goals-and-the-measurement-of-economic-and-social-progress_9789264307278-4-en#page1 (accessed 2 January 2019).

Khan, M. (2012). 'Governance and Growth Challenges in Africa'. In A. Noman, K. Botchwey, H. Stein, and J.E. Stiglitz (eds), *Good Growth and Governance in Africa*. New York: Oxford University Press.

Lin, J.Y. (2011). 'Flying Geese, Leading Dragons and Africa's Potential'. World Bank Blog. Available at: http://blogs.worldbank.org/developmenttalk/flying-geese-leading-dragons-and-africa-s-potential (accessed 2 January 2019).

Maskus, K., and S. Merrill (eds) (2013). *Patent Challenges for Standard-Setting in the Global Economy*. Washington, DC: National Academies Press.

Mazzucato, M. (2013). *The Entrepreneurial State*. New York: Anthem.

Myrdal, G. (1968). *Asian Drama: An Inquiry into the Poverty of Nations (Volumes, I, II and III)*. New York: Pantheon.

Navaretti, G.B., and D.G. Tarr (2000). 'International Knowledge Flows and Economic Performance'. *The World Bank Economic Review*, 14(1): 1–15.

Noman, A., and J.E. Stiglitz (2012a). 'African Development Prospects and Possibilities'. In E. Aryeetey, S. Devarajan, R. Kanbur, and L. Kasekende (eds) *The Oxford Companion to the Economics of Africa*. Oxford: Oxford University Press.

Noman, A., and J.E. Stiglitz (2012b). 'Strategies for African Development'. In A. Noman, K. Botchwey, H. Stein, and J.E. Stiglitz (eds), *Good Growth and Governance for Africa*. Oxford and New York: Oxford University Press.

Noman, A., and J.E. Stiglitz (2015a). 'Introduction and Overview: Economic Transformation and Learning, Industrial, and Technology Policies in Africa'. In A. Noman and J.E. Stiglitz (eds), *Industrial Policy and Economic Transformation in Africa*. New York: Columbia University Press.

Noman, A., and J.E. Stiglitz (2015b). 'Economics and Policy: Some Lessons from Africa's Experience'. In C. Monga and J. Yifu Lin (eds), *The Oxford Handbook of Africa and Economics, Volume II: Policies and Practices*. Oxford and New York: Oxford University Press.

Noman, A., K. Botchwey, H. Stein, and J.E. Stiglitz (eds) (2012). *Good Growth and Governance for Africa*. Oxford and New York: Oxford University Press.

Ocampo, J.A., and J.E. Stiglitz (eds) (2018). *The Welfare State Revisited*. New York: IPD/Columbia University Press.

Ostry, J., A. Berg, and C.G. Tsangarides (2014). 'Redistribution, Inequality, and Growth'. IMF Staff Discussion Note, February. Washington, DC: IMF. Available at: http://www.imf.org/external/pubs/ft/sdn/2014/sdn1402.pdf (accessed 2 January 2019).

Peith, M., and J.E. Stiglitz (2016). 'Overcoming the Shadow Economy'. Friedrich Ebert Stiftung International Policy Analysis Paper, November. Bonn: Friedrich-Ebert-Stiftung. Available at: https://library.fes.de/pdf-files/iez/12922.pdf (accessed 2 January 2019).

Rodrik, D. (2015). 'Premature Industrialization'. NBER Working Paper 20935. Cambridge, MA: National Bureau of Economic Research.

Roser, M. (2018). 'Employment in Agriculture'. Published online at OurWorldInData. org. Available at: https://ourworldindata.org/employment-in-agriculture (accessed 2 January 2019).

Sah, R., and J.E. Stiglitz (1992). *Peasants versus City-Dwellers: Taxation and the Burden of Economic Development*. Oxford and New York: Oxford University Press.

Stiglitz, J.E. (1987). 'Learning to Learn, Localized Learning and Technological Progress'. In P. Dasgupta and P. Stoneman (eds), *Economic Policy and Technological Performance*. New York: Cambridge University Press.

Stiglitz, J.E. (1996). 'Some Lessons from the East Asian Miracle'. *World Bank Research Observer*, 11(2): 151–77.

Stiglitz, J.E. (1998a). 'More Instruments and Broader Goals: Moving toward the Post-Washington Consensus'. WIDER Annual Lecture. Available at: https://www.wider.unu.edu/event/wider-annual-lecture-2-more-instruments-and-broader-goals-moving-toward-post-washington (accessed 2 January 2019).

Stiglitz, J.E. (1998b). 'Towards a New Paradigm for Development: Strategies, Policies and Processes'. 9th Raul Prebisch Lecture for UNCTAD delivered at the Palais des Nations, Geneva, 19 October. Also in H.-J. Chang (ed.) (2001), *The Rebel Within*. London: Wimbledon Publishing Company.

Stiglitz, J.E. (2001). 'Participation and Development: Perspectives from the Comprehensive Development Paradigm'. In F. Iqbal and Y. Jong-Il (eds), *Democracy, Market Economics & Development: An Asian Perspective*. Washington, DC: World Bank. Also in H.-J. Chang (ed.), *The Rebel Within*. London: Wimbledon Publishing Company.

Stiglitz, J.E. (2002). *Globalization and Its Discontents*. New York: W.W. Norton & Company.

Stiglitz, J.E. (2006). *Making Globalization Work*. New York: W.W. Norton & Company.

Stiglitz, J.E. (2007). 'What Is the Role of the State?' In M. Humphreys, J. Sachs, and J.E. Stiglitz (eds), *Escaping the Resource Curse*. New York: Columbia University Press.

Stiglitz, J.E. (2011). 'Learning, Growth, and Development: A Lecture in Honor of Sir Partha Dasgupta'. In S. Barret, K.-G. Maler, and E.S. Maskin (eds), *Environment & Development Economics: Essays in Honor of Sir Partha Dasgupta*. Oxford: Oxford University Press. Revised version of a paper of the same title in C. Sepúlveda, A. Harrison, and J.Y. Lin (eds) (2011), *Development Challenges in a Postcrisis World: Annual World Bank Conference on Development Economics 2011*. Washington, DC: World Bank.

Stiglitz, J.E. (2012). *The Price of Inequality*. New York: W.W. Norton.

Stiglitz, J.E. (2015). *The Great Divide: Unequal Societies and What We Can Do About Them*. New York: W.W. Norton.

Stiglitz, J.E. (2016a). 'An Agenda for Sustainable and Inclusive Growth for Emerging Markets'. *Journal of Policy Modeling*, 38: 693–710.

Stiglitz, J.E. (2016b). 'The state, the market, and development'. WIDER Working Paper 2016/1. Helsinki: UNU-WIDER. Originally presented at UNU-WIDER 30th Anniversary Conference, Helsinki, September 2015. Available at: https://www.wider.unu.edu/sites/default/files/wp2016-1.pdf (accessed 2 January 2019).

Stiglitz, J.E. (2018). 'Towards a Twenty-First Century Investment Agreement'. In L. Johnson and L. Sachs (eds), *Yearbook on International Investment Law and Policy 2015–2016*. Oxford: Oxford University Press. Available at: http://ccsi.columbia.edu/files/2014/03/YB-2015-16-Front-matter.pdf (accessed 2 January 2019).

Stiglitz, J.E. (2019). *People, Power, and Profits*. New York: W.W. Norton & Company.

Stiglitz, J.E., and A. Charlton (2005). *Fair Trade for All*. New York: Oxford University Press.

Stiglitz, J.E., and B. Greenwald (2010). 'Towards A New Global Reserve System'. *Journal of Globalization and Development*, 1(2): Article 10.

Stiglitz, J.E., and B. Greenwald (2014). *Creating a Learning Society*. New York: Columbia University Press.

Stiglitz, J.E., and B. Greenwald (2015). *Creating a Learning Society*. Readers' Edition. New York: Columbia University Press.

Stiglitz, J.E., with N. Abernathy, A. Hersh, S. Holmberg, and M. Konczal (2015). *Rewriting the Rules of the American Economy*. New York: W.W. Norton & Company.

Stiglitz, J.E., A. Sen, and J. Fitoussi (2009). Report by the commission on the measurement of economic performance and social progress. Commission on the Measurement of Economic Performance and Social Progress, Paris.

Stiglitz, J.E., A. Sen, and J.P. Fitoussi (2011). *Advancing Research on Well-Being Metrics beyond GDP*. Report of the Commission on the Measurement of Economic Performance and Social Progress. Paris: OECD.

Tacchella, A., M. Cristelli, G. Caldarelli, A. Gabrielli, and L. Pietronero (2012). 'A New Metrics for Countries' Fitness and Products' Complexity'. *Nature: Scientific Reports*, 2: article 723.

Triffin, R. (1960). *Gold and the Dollar Crisis*. Princeton: Princeton University Press.

UNDP (2016). *Shaping the Future*. New York: United Nations Development Programme. Available at: http://hdr.undp.org/sites/default/files/rhdr2016-full-report-final-version1.pdf (accessed 2 January 2019).

Wade, R. (1990). *Governing the Market*. Princeton: Princeton University Press.

Wilcox, M.D. (2006). 'Farmgate Prices and Market Power in Liberalized West African Cocoa Markets'. Unpublished PhD dissertation. West Lafayette: Purdue University.

Wilcox, M.D., and P.C. Abbott (2004). 'Market Power and Structural Adjustment: The Case of West African Cocoa Market Liberalization'. Paper presented at 2004 American Agricultural Economics Association Annual Meeting, Denver, 1–4 August. Available at: http://ageconsearch.umn.edu/record/20084/files/sp04wi05.pdf (accessed 2 January 2019).

World Bank Group (2015). *World Development Report 2015: Mind, Society, and Behavior*. Washington, DC: World Bank. Available at: https://openknowledge.worldbank.org/handle/10986/20597 (accessed 2 January 2019).

World Bank Group (2018). World Development Indicators. Dataset. Available at: https://datacatalog.worldbank.org/ dataset/world-development-indicators (accessed 2 January 2019).

World Bank Group (2020). World Development Indicators. Manufacturing, value added (% of GDP). Dataset. Available at: https://data.worldbank.org/indicator/NV.IND.MANF.ZS.

World Economic Forum (2017). 'The Africa Competitiveness Report 2017: Addressing Africa's Demographic Dividend'. Geneva: World Economic Forum. Available at: https://www.weforum.org/reports/africa-competitiveness-report-2017 (accessed 2 January 2019).

PART V

SYNTHESIS AND POLICY
IMPLICATIONS

13

Synthesis and Policy Implications

Carlos Gradín, Murray Leibbrandt, and Finn Tarp

1 Introduction

We began this volume by drawing out of the prevailing body of work a strong weight of evidence and analysis stressing that inequality is a key development challenge. It holds implications for economic growth and redistribution and translates into power asymmetries that can endanger democratization and human rights, create conflict, and embed social exclusion and chronic poverty. Inequalities of income and wealth and inequality in access to basic services undermine social cohesion and economic progress.

From this point of departure, the specialist contributors to this book proceeded to bring together an analysis of global inequalities and a new and comprehensive view of the trends and drivers of inequality in five of the world's largest developing countries—Brazil, China, India, Mexico, and South Africa—jointly accounting for more than 40 per cent of the world's population. Perspectives on global inequality set the scene for the syntheses of the five case studies that, in turn, build on a large set of background papers prepared under UNU-WIDER's Inequality in the Giants project. Following the case studies, the discussion of inequality is brought back into a broader developmental context. Throughout, the contributions gave explicit attention to the data and measurement choices that undergirded their analyses of the forces and drivers of these measured levels and trends in inequality. Now we consolidate and synthesize all of this detailed work and then conclude by briefly outlining the main implications for policy.

2 New Perspectives on Global Inequalities

The analysis of global inequality, ignoring national boundaries and treating the world as one country (or one global village), is a complex task, as was made clear by all three chapters in Part II. Assessing whether inequality has declined or increased will depend on value judgements. Relative global inequality declined over recent decades, according to many inequality indices. This decline was mainly driven by the large income growth rates experienced by the global poor

Carlos Gradín, Murray Leibbrandt, and Finn Tarp, *Synthesis and Policy Implications* In: *Inequality in the Developing World.* Edited by: Carlos Gradín, Murray Leibbrandt, and Finn Tarp, Oxford University Press (2021). © United Nations University World Institute for Development Economics Research (UNU-WIDER). DOI: 10.1093/oso/9780198863960.003.0013

and middle-income groups. These unprecedented growth rates mostly reflect the fact that emerging economies, containing large shares of the world's population, have been growing faster than the industrialized world. Therefore, declining inequality between countries constituted by far the main component of declining global inequality.

This being true, Martin Ravallion points out that additionally there are two very important trends in these same global datasets. First, they show a stagnation in incomes of the global very poor, with this floor of the global income distribution therefore showing a declining income share. Second, in the other tail of the income distribution, there have been above average growth rates of top-end incomes, leading to increasing concentration of income at the top of the income distribution. Given these two trends, any analyst with special sensitivity to changes at these two ends of the income distribution can reasonably claim that global inequality increased rather than fell, with support from well-known inequality measures that are built on exactly these value judgements. The same riding trend is measured for people thinking of inequality in absolute rather than relative terms. This is because the proportionately large increases of incomes among the global poor and middle classes are still modest, when measured in dollar terms, if compared with the more substantial gains of the global rich. In addition, people with more nationalistic views, giving more weight to within-country inequality than to inequalities between countries, could make similar claims.

This discussion makes clear how important it is to clearly identify the set of value judgements under which each analysis assesses specific trends in global inequality. Such transparency makes clearer how it is possible that such an important debate has been characterized by influential groups loudly starting out from an orthogonal set of stylized facts about what has happened to global inequality. This surfaces at the broadest level, with one of the recurring lessons from the volume: measures do not speak for themselves. The assessment of inequality and the framing of policies to overcome inequality require understanding of the processes driving the levels and changes in measured inequality.

The relationships between income and wealth lie at the heart of many of the debates on the processes of inequality generation and persistence. James Davies and Anthony Shorrocks contributed to this debate in the context of global inequality by measuring in a consistent framework the levels and trends in the global income and wealth inequality. Using the between-country and within-country frameworks, they show that the trends in both cases are dominated by the decline in inequalities between countries, the main component of global inequality, with relatively small changes in within-country inequality not being enough to revert that trend. They go on to question whether this trend is sustainable over time, given that future growth in a few populous, now emerging economies will push inequality between countries upward in the future as they become richer.

Changing the focus to building a picture of global inequality from the bottom up, Daniele Checchi, Andrej Cupak, and Teresa Munzi emphasized for us all that useful measurement of global inequalities has to be built on good comparable data across countries. They went much further to show that such harmonization of income and socioeconomic characteristics is not straightforward and raises many challenges, especially in developing countries. They discussed the solutions implemented in the context of the Luxembourg Income Study, originally collecting information from mainly rich countries but recently expanded to incorporate middle-income countries, and used the resulting data to discuss the trends across the developing giants (and Russia).

The era of strong economic growth and substantial lowering of poverty that the world has seen during the past decades is unambiguously encouraging. At the same time, in many country contexts, the associated changes in well-being have not been unambiguously good, or have not been nearly as good as they should have been. It was Francois Bourguignon who first made it clear that one needs to understand inequality to understand why this is the case, when he put forward his 'iron poverty-growth-inequality triangle' (Bourguignon 2004). The same processes that have driven rising average incomes and falling poverty rates within countries have led to increasing inequality in many of these countries.

3 Inequality in Five Developing Giants: Common Patterns?

The case studies in the volume further substantiate this point by making it clear that relative inequality trends over the past years have shown heterogeneous patterns across countries and regions, although in a context of predominantly increasing or stagnating inequality in many countries, including the most populous. Understanding the driving factors of inequalities is essential in all country contexts to identify and fully understand these trends and their progress, or the lack thereof, in making growth inclusive. This is a difficult task due to both data and analytical challenges. While most developing countries have developed a consolidated set of household surveys over time, these data also present many comparability issues both over time within a country and across countries. In addition, the lack of accurate information for tracking progress of important population sub-groups remains a difficulty, particularly at the top or at the bottom of the distribution. Furthermore, income inequality is the result of complex processes in which several driving forces may play significant roles and interact with each other. The trends in these driving forces need to be measured, too, in understanding income inequality. Accordingly, coming better to grips with the inequality issue, which is at the core of SDG 10 and its relationship to other goals—especially reducing poverty (SDG 1), achieving gender equality (SDG 5), and promoting decent work (SDG 8)—requires an effort to mobilize all available data and to combine different complementary approaches.

Part III of the present volume summarizes, as already noted, a larger UNU-WIDER project that analysed the main determinants of levels and trends in income distribution in five developing economies. In this project, we put special focus on the role of the labour market, particularly on how the evolution of the skills premium shaped the inequality of earnings. Related to these labour market dynamics, and adding to them a range of other matters, inequality issues were brought to bear in the country studies, such as social mobility, spatial inequalities, and the gender gap. Different country contexts put different degrees of emphasis on these ranges of factors in explaining both the inequality of market income and the inequality of broader national income inequality. Each study also assessed non-market income by evaluating the growing role of the public sector in middle-income countries, especially with regard to the redistributive effect of taxes and social benefits. This discussion in the volume is particularly rich because each of the case countries have been very active and, in some cases, innovative in these areas during the past decades. All of this work was only possible by making the most, not only of common living conditions and labour force surveys, but also of censuses and different administrative and reported data. These include social security, tax records, national accounts, housing prices, and lists of richest people.

We proceed to discuss some of the challenges in addressing these data issues and how they were dealt with, highlighting the strengths and the limitations of using each of these data sources in the context of developing countries. Then, with sufficient confidence in the underlying data, we discuss the heterogeneous trends seen in the five countries studied, and the main determinants identified.

4 Common Challenges in Measuring Inequality: Making the Most of Data

Investigating inequality in developing countries faces a number of challenges. The first and most obvious is that there is no specialized inequality survey implemented across countries in the same way as the World Bank Living Standard Measurements Surveys (LSMS) with regard to poverty. Consequently, much of what we say and know about inequality comes from a variety of income or expenditure household surveys that are not fully standardized in methods and concepts used across countries or over time, or that in some cases have been designed for other purposes. This means that we work with known shortcomings for which there are in many cases no clear-cut solutions. While Bourguignon's iron triangle is very helpful in thinking through the links between growth, poverty, and inequality, there are, as carefully argued by Arndt, McKay, and Tarp

(2016: chapter 2), several mechanisms which could 'break' the triangle. Thus, the challenge of assessing inequality trends is by no means a simple deduction exercise.

The UNU-WIDER project therefore used several complementary data sources and methods: for example, national accounts to analyse falling labour shares in Mexico; public accounts to analyse redistribution also in Mexico; a tax-benefit microsimulation model to analyse redistribution in Brazil; social security administrative data to investigate earnings inequality in Brazil; and census and satellite data to study spatial inequalities in India. A special case was the emerging issue of adjusting top incomes (or expenditures) to known shortcomings in household survey data. Our contributing authors addressed this, using personal income tax tabulations in Brazil, individual tax records in South Africa, super-rich lists in China, and house price public listings in Mumbai (India).

The first issue to worry about when analysing inequality using household surveys is lack of response. Our results show that correcting for zero or missing values had virtually no effect on the well-known downward trend in inequality in Brazil (Hecksher, Neri, and Silva 2018). In contrast, a similar exercise partially helped to explain the inconsistent trends observed in Mexico after 2006 in the different surveys. The declining trend in inequality according to the labour force surveys vanishes after the corrections, getting closer to the increasing trend found in income and expenditure surveys (Campos-Vazquez and Lustig 2017). High and variable levels of non-response are not the only element to consider when assessing inequality trends. Unclear methodological changes in the design of the South African labour force surveys, for example, are likely to be responsible for a sharp increase in inequality in this country case after 2012 (Finn and Leibbrandt 2018).

The use of matched employer/employee administrative data in Brazil (*Registro Anual de Informações Sociais*, RAIS) helps to more accurately represent the earnings distribution and worker characteristics at a very detailed level and over a long period of time thanks to its nature and the huge amount of observations. This is especially useful in identifying the large contribution of firm-specific effects to the fall in inequality in Brazil before the last economic recession, and in showing that this trend is compatible with an increasing share obtained by very rich workers (especially the top 1 and 0.1 per cent). It also helps to analyse the gender earnings gap throughout the life cycle for different birth cohorts, identifying the important contribution of differences in occupation, industry and establishments (Neri, Machado, and Neto 2018). The fact that a large share of the Brazilian labour force is informal, with changes in formalization rates over time, and thus not represented in the universe of this dataset poses the main limitation to its use.

The Mexican case study includes another method of complementing labour force surveys; in this case, by combining these surveys with information from national accounts on wages, employment, value added, intermediate consumption, and capital stock. These augmented data highlight the falling share of labour in national income and identify the lagging productivity of the informal non-tradable sector of the economy as the main driving force (Ibarra and Ros 2017).

The country cases emphasize the importance of taxes and social expenditure policies in tackling inequality. In analysing the redistributive impacts of taxes and benefits, case country authors employed different strategies. The South African team studied the effect of reported direct taxes and cash transfers using a national household survey, the Living Conditions Survey, matched with administrative tax and expenditure data (Maboshe and Woolard 2018). The Mexican team followed a more complex approach, imputing in-kind transfers and adjusting for income underreporting in income and expenditure surveys using information from public accounts (Scott, de la Rosa, and Aranda 2017). The Brazilian team applied a tax-benefit microsimulation model (BRAHMS/UPFE) on the expenditure survey (Neri, Siqueira, Nogueira, and Osorio 2018). In all cases, these exercises both identify the important contributions of public policies deployed in emerging countries in shaping the income distribution, and define their limits in compensating the strong forces originating in the labour market.

When it comes to dealing with the impact on inequality of the misrepresentation/underestimation of the top incomes, once again different teams followed different strategies based on combining household surveys with other sources. In Brazil, the team combined household survey (PNAD) data with personal income tax tabulations for 2007 and 2015, showing a large impact on the level and trend of inequality. Yet, this administrative dataset also shows unrealistic increases in income over time, thus making the important point that tax data have their flaws as well, and also require careful interrogation (Neri and Hecksher 2018). For South Africa, the team combined the fifth wave of the National Income Dynamics Survey (NIDS) with individual tax records, showing a surprisingly small impact on both the level and the trend of inequality. This could be the result of this wave of the survey having corrected for the attrition suffered after the first wave, by refreshing the panel with additional affluent households (Hundenborn, Woolard, and Jellema 2018). Therefore, the survey estimated the top decile fairly well. Nonetheless, the survey did less well in flagging the fact that those at the very top of the distribution (1 per cent) had done extremely well through income sources not well captured in the survey. In the case of China, due to the lack of tax information, the team followed the innovative approach of constructing for this purpose a dataset combining information for 2016 from different lists of super rich people (Li, Li, and Wan 2018). This had a large impact on inequality levels in 2016, thus indicating the extent of under-measurement at the top end in Chinese survey data. Unfortunately, the analysis could not estimate the top end trends in this way. Such lists were not available in other years. In the case of India, the team followed yet another approach: combining the national consumption survey with house price data based on public listings on the online platform Makaan in Mumbai (Rongen 2018). Surprisingly, and contrary to previous evidence from Egypt (Van der Weide, Lakner, and Ianchovichina 2018), there was no sign of underestimation of expenditure inequality in these surveys after the corrections.

Finally, given the great importance of spatial inequalities in India and the lack of geographically disaggregated data, the Indian team combined the national NSS surveys and information from the census with satellite data (weather and precipitation, forest cover, share of land under cultivation, night-time luminosity) from the World Bank's Spatial Database for South Asia (Mukhopadhyay and Garcés-Urzainqui 2018). By imputing average per capita expenditure, they estimated spatial inequality between villages and blocks, and local inequality within these spatial units (as the difference between total and spatial inequality). The main result is that the divergence observed for states and districts does not amplify at small units. That is, the increase in inequality in urban India is mostly due to rising inequality within urban blocks.

In summary, the detailed country studies underlying the country synthesis chapters reported in Part III of the book show that analysts pursue very different strategies in developing countries to make the most of existing data to improve and complement available household surveys. These are and will continue to be the basis for most analyses of inequality, assuming the global research community and its funders do not take an initiative along LSMS lines for poverty, focused explicitly on inequality issues and their associated requirements.

5 Inequality Trends and Drivers

The five developing countries in focus in this volume are, or have recently become, countries with highly unequal levels of aggregate inequality. Their characteristics also include large divides among population groups, such as differences between urban and rural areas, between most and least developed regions, by ethnicity or race, by gender, etc. They have all undergone large structural economic and political changes over the past three decades: the end of apartheid in South Africa; the opening up of the Mexican and Indian economies; China's (incomplete) transition to a market economy; and the long period during which the Workers' Party ruled Brazil. Typically, these processes accentuated tensions in already existing horizontal inequalities. In Brazil, and less so in Mexico, they contributed to reducing existing inequalities. Other than China, these developing countries have largely depended on the vagaries of the commodities cycle and have, during the last decades of strong growth, been able to expand and re-design the public sector even if it is still far from comparable to the public sectors in most developed economies.

A number of chapters in the volume make it clear that developing countries do not follow a common trend in terms of inequality. Even within the broader landscape sketched above, this is also so for the five giants considered here. Several heterogeneous patterns emerged from the analysis.

Inequality steadily increased in China until 2008, when the trend seems to have reached an inflexion point that only future research can confirm. Inequality also increased in India following the structural reforms. The opposite trend, however, occurred in Brazil, with a long and unprecedented decline in inequality since the early 1990s, following the commodities boom and expansion of social programmes, until the last economic downturn. South Africa achieved only modest progress in the twenty-five years after the end of apartheid in spite of applying a wide range of redistributive policies that put an end to institutionalized racial stratification. Mexico shows long-term persistency, with an N-shaped trend with inequality first increasing, then declining, and finally increasing again (1989–1994–2006–2014). These trends refer to disposable income (or consumption in India), which by construction ignore important in-kind components of final income with an impact on living conditions of the populations that have significantly improved in all these countries, such as access to basic services like education, health, and water.

The labour market plays the most fundamental role in driving inequality trends (up or down) in all cases. This highlights the importance of how markets generate primary income in the first place, especially in countries characterized by extreme initial inequalities in education and in the access to productive assets (e.g. land) and wealth. These inequalities feed into labour markets that are highly segmented along a number of dimensions: informal versus formal; rural migrants versus urban citizens; and by gender, race, and region.

Consistent across the country studies, the returns to skills (education and experience) are a dominant driver of earnings inequality, in a context of expanding education and increasing demand for highly educated workers as the result of globalization and technological change. Moreover, there is increasing evidence of high concentration at top incomes, indicating that this process is not exclusive of high-income countries.

In Mexico, there was an initial period characterized by a higher demand for skills, the result of the opening-up of the economy and technical change, aggravated by various institutional factors, such as the falling minimum wage and de-unionization that led to an increasing skill premium, and thus increasing earnings inequality. Another period followed in which the growing supply of skilled workers outpaced the demand, and consequently the skill premium fell. After 2006, the process is less clear, with contradictory trends between household and labour force surveys. Nonetheless, the evidence is clear that the general income of all workers fell during the Great Recession, especially for low-skilled workers.

In South Africa, sluggish economic growth was in general not pro-poor, with finance and services sectors growing faster than traditional sectors (manufacturing, mining, agriculture, and domestic help). This produced unbalanced changes in supply and demand of skilled and unskilled workers despite very large increases in average years of schooling. In Brazil, similarly sharp increases in average years of schooling resulted in an earnings decompression below the ninetieth percentile, along with higher concentration among the very rich. Wage inequality increased over time in urban China, despite important wage growth at the bottom of the distribution. In the latter case, experience was more important than education in explaining wage inequality in 1988, while education was the single largest contributor (of the much larger level) in 2013. China has also witnessed large gender gaps in earnings and employment. Changes in the wage setting mechanism, rapid increase in demand for qualified labour and large inflows of relatively unqualified rural migrants to urban areas have all contributed to this trend. After 2007, however, highly paid workers' wage growth was limited within state-owned enterprises, and new rules were introduced in 2009.

With primary income driving increasing trends in inequality, the redistributive effect of taxes and benefits becomes more important. All countries have witnessed an expansion in the scale of the public sector, as well as remarkable improvements in design. While social benefits have in general become more progressive (reducing urban bias and being more inclusive of vulnerable groups), some policies can be more regressive or weakly progressive, such as contributory Social Security or tax exemptions for health care or private pensions. Policies were well targeted, as in the outstanding case of conditional cash transfers, even if its small scale does not significantly reduce inequality.

South Africa is an example of a country implementing large-scale public policies which are quite progressive and well targeted to the poor, even if they have had a diminishing impact over time. There was a massive improvement in access to basic services such as housing, electricity, and water. A very large set of unconditional cash transfers benefited pensioners, disabled, and children. More than half of means-tested benefits accrued to the poorest 30 per cent, with an increase from 24 to 68 per cent in the share of households with government grants. This represents an increase from 3 per cent to 16 per cent in the share of total income, with the largest increase right after the end of apartheid, between 1993 and 2008, smaller in subsequent years. Direct taxes are mostly borne by the richest 30 per cent, although some regressive deductions reduce the progressivity of the system. The Gini reduced from 0.73 (market income) to 0.66 (disposable income), with an important impact in reducing horizontal inequalities as well, such as by age, location, race, or gender.

Mexico is another example, with crucial changes in fiscal policy undertaken in the 1990s which were quite progressive and pro-poor. Several well-known and effective programmes such as *Progresa, Seguro Popular, Adultos Mayores*, and *Apoyos Directos al Campo* were deployed and, as in South Africa, saw large improvements in access to basic services. Thus, social spending increased and, alongside this, progressivity improved, correcting a previous strong urban bias (based on food subsidies). This process, however, reversed after 2008/10, with a sharp decline of net indirect subsidies. As a result, the redistributive effect has declined significantly since 2010; transfers have become less progressive (recent efforts have fuelled the expanding contributory pension schemes). This situation was aggravated by increasing indirect taxes to replace oil revenues. As a result, while the fiscal system has a significant redistributive effect on final income inequality, the effect on disposable (and consumable) income inequality is more modest.

6 Conclusion and Policy Implications

The UN Sustainable Development Goals (SDGs) reflect widespread and valid academic, public, and policy concern with issues of inequality in all of its many interrelated dimensions and differing interpretations. The contemporary empirical and analytic picture supported by this volume is unequivocal in showing that the present levels of inequalities of income and wealth and inequality in access to basic services, such as health and education, are undermining socio-economic progress. There has been enormous economic progress over recent decades; yet this progress has been very uneven within and across countries, and it is reversible. To understand and deal with this situation, inequality has to be analysed and addressed. The aim of this volume was to make a significant contribution to this effort through better understanding of global inequality trends, within-country trends—focusing on five key developing countries accounting for more than 40 per cent of the world's population—and the broader setting in which inequality issues are situated. The volume details exactly such unevenness and reversibility in many contexts in very recent times. Rising and persistent inequality in many places means that improved data, better inequality analysis, and concerted policy action at global, regional, national, and local levels are needed now as never before to address the level and changes in inequality.

In spite of significant improvements over the recent past, data quality and the measurement of inequality remain critically constrained. This is especially the case in developing countries. The way that inequality is measured bounds the way it is understood and addressed. In both theory and practice, many assumptions have to be made and it is important that these assumptions are explicit. Chapters 2 to 4 set out and discussed these data problems and issues in detail. They also showed that the conflicting narratives on the trend in global inequality in the public debate are often plausible with reference to differing definitions of how to measure inequality. Value premises are far from uniform, and how the bottom and the top of the distribution are treated matter significantly for the insights derived. Chapter 2, in particular, revealed that while commonly used inequality measures suggest that global inequality has gone down for several decades this assessment is subject to challenge, especially if the focus shifts from relative to absolute measures of inequality. This is not to deny, as is made clear in Chapter 3 for both income and wealth, that for all the inequality indices considered, the degree of inequality attributable to differences in mean income and wealth across countries accounts for much, if not most, of the level of global inequality measured this way. Moreover, as regards changing inequality over time, changes in mean income and wealth and population sizes have induced a strong downward element to the trend in global inequality regardless of the inequality index selected.

Turning explicitly to within-country relative inequality, it has often gone up, but this picture is quite heterogeneous. Chapter 4 cautions that comparing inequality across countries in a way that is based on harmonized income and consumption data continues to face thorny empirical challenges. Unless these are carefully addressed, robust conclusions will be elusive. Some of these measured differences may be artefacts of data incompatibility rather than differences in inequalities. In this regard, the chapter provides strong value to the volume by showing that the within-country national trends discussed in detail in each of Brazil, China, India, Mexico, and South Africa remain in place in the harmonized data. Therefore, there is some validation in place for careful comparison across these countries from the detail that they distil. As was made clear earlier in this concluding chapter, the authors of the country syntheses in Chapters 5–9 integrate information from a number of the different UNU-WIDER background papers and draw on as many data sources as are available to understand inequality in each of the five countries. In general, triangulation of data, including new data sources, was key in producing this volume and it illustrates the importance of this practice for in-depth analysis of the level and change in inequality in any given context.

Such data triangulation leads to a more robust picture of inequality, which accentuates rather than narrows the heterogeneities that emerge in the country syntheses and in the volume as a whole. In turn, this emphasizes the awkward reality that there is not a simple 'grand' narrative that captures inequality in the same way in all of our five country cases or globally. This in no way diminishes the importance of inequality. Rather, it acknowledges that *because of* the policy imperative to address inequality, the complexities of its production and reproduction have to be reflected and respected in the analysis.

This balance is well illustrated in Chapter 10, in Part IV of the volume. Here, Andrew E. Clark and Conchita D'Ambrosio examined subjective well-being as measured by the perceptions of current and future living conditions across four large, populous regions of the world. Specific attention is given to how levels of subjective well-being are linked to both personal, subjective inequality and broader income inequality. The analysis starts by examining the role of capability levels in subjective well-being. It is clear that capabilities are positively correlated with perceptions of well-being. Perceptions of inequality or subjective inequality are measured by an individual's assessment of their position relative to those in their immediate community. Controlling for this capabilities effect, the relationship between subjective well-being and this self-assessed inequality is mixed. Being relatively better off correlates (accurately) with perceptions of higher present and future living conditions. However, being relatively worse off is either not correlated with subjective well-being or even is positively correlated, seeming to imply the presence of Hirschman's famous tunnel effect. When estimated carefully, the relationship between subjective well-being and subjective inequality is never simple and differs markedly in different regions of the world. The relationship between subjective well-being and income inequality is much clearer. The higher the aggregate level of income inequality in the country of residence, the higher the expectations of future living conditions. Clearly, inequalities have important consequences for the formation of expectations about the future. Other contributions in the volume make it clear that these expectations are often not realized for the most vulnerable and one speculates as to whether this will end up feeding discontent when expectations end up unfulfilled.

Acknowledging that the careful analyses of the volume caution against grand or simple narratives in no way implies that there are not strong commonalities and central lessons for policy to be pulled from the five country case studies and from the volume as a whole. Indeed, there are a number of such lessons.

It is clear that labour market inequalities are central as a driver of overall inequality. Above we discussed evidence from the country studies of both declining and increasing labour market inequalities and the processes through which they feed through into declining and increasing national inequalities. Consequently, the imperative to understand the functioning of labour markets stands out as an important insight derived from our five cases. There is no doubt that all of these countries have functioned in the same increasingly integrated world and that this has pulled strongly through each labour market. Nevertheless, this has not been inexorable and the case studies show both the potential and the limitations of active labour market policies in mediating these forces.

Some of these limitations arise from the role of external circumstances, whether negative, as with the Great Depression, or sometimes positive, as with the commodities cycle. It is clear from many contexts that there is strong reason to highlight the importance of globalization and technological change. In many contexts, this has increased earnings inequalities by increasing the demand for skilled labour. It has also contributed to increasing profit shares, which is a rising and important concern in both developed and developing country contexts as it reinforces concentration of income and wealth among the best off. These are the forces that have increased inequality by those at the top end, and often only the very top end, pulling away from the rest of the income distribution.

Other limitations on labour market policies arise from the local context itself. The intergenerational perspective that is pursued in our country cases brings out the importance of prevailing pre-market conditions and policies that impact on the realized capabilities that individuals in each country carry into their respective labour markets. People with differing endowments and assets in terms of family background, skills, and education (as well as wealth and assets) do not participate in the labour market on an equal footing. These inequalities feed into labour markets that are highly segmented along a number of dimensions: informal versus formal; rural migrants versus urban citizens; and by gender, race, and region. These circumstances, if left untouched by policy, dampen the income growth of those at the bottom or, worse still, marginalize them altogether.

However, in each of the country cases, these circumstances have not been left untouched and fiscal policy (including both expenditure and tax policy related to income as well as wealth) has played an important role in modifying their inequalities. The country studies provide valuable and detailed learnings from their menu of successful and unsuccessful policies and results. However, standing out as important here is that even in cases where quite ambitious redistribution programmes and policies were pursued, they have either not been sustained or are yet to make a major dent in inequality of disposable incomes and inequalities in living conditions. To reach higher levels of redistribution, much more remains to be done through the budget, and much more needs to be done beyond the budget, with a direct focus on the roles of assets and wealth.

Thus, the inequality processes and policy impacts have not been simple. As countries have engaged with the globalized world, top-end incomes have moved away from the rest of the distribution. Yet, there is more to this than a top end that is flourishing more than the rest. Not everyone has flourished. In most countries, it seems that the higher average incomes were pulled up by raising the top-end incomes and, to varying extents, raising middle and lower-end incomes. Nevertheless, in many contexts, substantial sections of society were left out of these processes. The social mobility perspective of Chapter 11 consolidates and sharpens this view. Its striking conclusion is that rapid growth is by no means a guarantee of social mobility across generations. In fact, mobility may decline to very low levels if market forces are unchecked. Roy van der Weide and Ambar Narayan arrive at this conclusion by studying social mobility in two high-growth contexts, China and the United States. China had high but rapidly falling mobility and the US had persistently low social mobility. Both had rising inequality over the study period and the authors use this to infer support for the Great Gatsby Curve, linking low inter-generational mobility to high inequality. They confirm that this relationship has applicability that is more general across the globe by examining the relationship in seventy-three additional countries. The chapter concludes that both of the world's major economic powers have converged to a low level of socioeconomic mobility where talent from disadvantaged backgrounds is excluded from opportunities, implying unrealized human potential and misallocation of resources on a large scale. These relations go to the heart of this volume's concern over inequality.

At a general level, then, our study strongly confirms that to make a dent in inequality, policies must be socially and economically inclusive and sustained. In this sense, our volume lends comprehensive and support to the Stockholm Statement about the principles of policy-making for the contemporary world, from a study that covers more than 40 per cent of the world's population. More specifically, we argue that addressing inequality is essential for future growth and development and policies must include a variety of initiatives that work through, respectively, the labour market and redistributive social policies, keeping in mind throughout the long-term goal of promoting social mobility to break intergenerational inequalities. Governments must set the rules of the game and regulate markets that do not work well, in ways that will further social inclusion and greater equality.

Clearly, overcoming inequality requires associated macroeconomic and broader development policies too. In Chapter 12 Stiglitz provides us with an excellent framework for these policy implications by reminding us that the world of the twenty-first century is quite different from the world of the twentieth century. The global economy is no longer the same and the export-led manufacturing development models that have promoted economic growth in the past are no longer viable and are becoming increasingly less inclusive.

An important driver of rising within-country wealth inequality since 2008 has been the rise in equity prices, which has raised the share of the top 1 per cent in particular. In part, that rise has been due to low interest rates. If interest rates rise towards more normal levels, stock market performance would change. These trends could stabilize and improve within-country inequality. On the other hand, the decline of between-country inequality may slow or come to a halt. Further increases in China's mean income and wealth, both now above the global means, will begin to raise between-country inequality, and we cannot expect that all the poorest countries will follow the same path considering that the initial conditions and the international context they face will be very different.

Understandably, widespread concern about rising inequality of incomes and wealth and the trends of top-end income, as detailed in this volume and elsewhere, has drawn attention to the need to consider higher taxes on top incomes and wealth. Some worry about the possible consequences for growth of progressive policies and, no doubt, there is a need for care. That said, this volume has highlighted the negative consequences for pro-growth policies if no consideration is given to these policies. There are many lessons from good and bad policymaking in this area from around the world to draw on and overlay with detailed interrogation on local inequality circumstances. Fortunately, there is another set of policies that should be able to both reduce inequality and stimulate growth. Building human capital of the poorest is an obvious policy, as is social policy to support those in need. The same can be said for efforts to further economic transformation and an economy where returns to labour equalize across sectors. Balancing macroeconomic stability with guaranteeing equal access to productive assets, and making health care and education universally accessible at all levels, for example, are also sound policies that can make ordinary people better off and increase both their income and wealth.

Within a stable macroeconomic framework, there is a need to change how the economy works for all of its citizens. Economics justifies the need to crack down on crony capitalism and rent-seeking, and break up monopolies and oligopolies. The weight of evidence in this volume affirms that this would reduce income and wealth concentration at the top and increase growth by fostering stronger competition and equal access to economic opportunities. These policies are likely to reduce within-country inequality and between-country inequality as well, since they would have their most dramatic impact in poor countries. At a global level, the policy toolbox also includes foreign aid policies designed and employed to attack between-country inequality. International trade policies have been and will continue to be key to give poor countries opportunities to develop faster, linking up with the obvious need for effective domestic and international agricultural and industrial policies, in a context of increasing concern with socially and environmentally sustainable development. As stated repeatedly in this volume, well-functioning labour markets that promote job creation, decent pay and social inclusion, removing any legal or de facto discrimination based on gender, race, ethnicity, or place of origin, providing equal access to human and physical capital, and empowering the most disadvantaged population groups, are a key driver of increased equality. On this note, we conclude.

References

Arndt, C., A. McKay, and F. Tarp (2016). *Growth and Poverty in Sub-Saharan Africa*. WIDER Studies in Development Economics. Oxford: Oxford University Press. DOI: 10.1093/acprof:oso/9780198744795.001.0001.

Bourguignon, F. (2004). 'The Poverty-Growth-Inequality Triangle'. Paper presented at the Indian Council for Research on International Economic Relations, New Delhi. 4 February.

Campos-Vazquez, R., and N. Lustig (2017). 'Labour income inequality in Mexico: puzzles solved and unsolved'. WIDER Working Paper 2017/186. Helsinki: UNU-WIDER. Available at: https://www.wider.unu.edu/publication/labour-income-inequality-mexico.

Finn, A., and M. Leibbrandt (2018). 'The evolution and determination of earnings inequality in post-apartheid South Africa'. WIDER Working Paper 2018/83. Helsinki: UNU-WIDER. Available at: https://www.wider.unu.edu/publication/evolution-and-determination-earnings-inequality-post-apartheid-south-africa.

Hecksher, M., M. Neri, and P.do Na Silva (2018). 'New imputation procedures in the measurement of inequality, growth, and poverty in Brazil'. WIDER Working Paper 2018/128. Helsinki: UNU-WIDER. Available at: https://www.wider.unu.edu/publication/new-imputation-procedures-measurement-inequality-growth-and-poverty-brazil.

Hundenborn, J., I. Woolard, and J. Jellema (2018). 'The effect of top incomes on inequality in South Africa'. WIDER Working Paper 2018/90. Helsinki: UNU-WIDER. Available at: https://www.wider.unu.edu/publication/effect-top-incomes-inequality-south-africa.

Ibarra, C., and J. Ros (2017). 'The decline of the labour share in Mexico: 1990–2015'. WIDER Working Paper 2017/183. Helsinki: UNU-WIDER. Available at: https://www.wider.unu.edu/publication/decline-labour-share-mexico.

Li, Q., S. Li, and H. Wan (2018). 'Top incomes in China: data collection and the impact on income inequality'. WIDER Working Paper 2018/183. Helsinki: UNU-WIDER. Available at: https://www.wider.unu.edu/publication/top-incomes-china.

Maboshe, M., and I. Woolard (2018). 'Revisiting the impact of direct taxes and transfers on poverty and inequality in South Africa'. WIDER Working Paper 2018/79. Helsinki: UNU-WIDER. Available at: https://www.wider.unu.edu/publication/revisiting-impact-direct-taxes-and-transfers-poverty-and-inequality-south-africa.

Mukhopadhyay, A., and D. Garcés Urzainqui (2018). 'The dynamics of spatial and local inequalities in India'. WIDER Working Paper 2018/182. Helsinki: UNU-WIDER. Available at: https://www.wider.unu.edu/publication/dynamics-spatial-and-local-inequalities-india.

Neri, M., and M. Hecksher (2018). 'Top incomes impacts on growth, inequality and social welfare: combining surveys and income tax data in Brazil'. WIDER Working Paper 137/2018. Helsinki: UNU-WIDER. Available at: https://www.wider.unu.edu/publication/top-incomes%E2%80%99-impacts-inequality-growth-and-social-welfare.

Neri, M., C. Machado, and V.P. Neto (2018). 'Earnings inequality in the Brazilian formal sector: the role of firms and top incomes between 1994 and 2015'. WIDER Working Paper 157/2018. Helsinki: UNU-WIDER. Available at: https://www.wider.unu.edu/publication/earnings-inequality-brazilian-formal-sector.

Neri, M., R. Siqueira, J.R. Nogueira, and M. Osorio (2018). 'Fiscal redistribution in Brazil: 2003–2015'. WIDER Working Paper 136/2018. Helsinki: UNU-WIDER. Available at: https://www.wider.unu.edu/publication/fiscal-redistribution-brazil.

Scott, J., R. Aranda, and E.de la Rosa (2017). 'Inequality and fiscal redistribution in Mexico: 1992–2015'. WIDER Working Paper 2017/194. Helsinki: UNU-WIDER. Available at: https://www.wider.unu.edu/publication/inequality-and-fiscal-redistribution-mexico.

Rongen, G. (2018). 'A new inequality estimate for urban India? Using house prices to estimate inequality in Mumbai'. WIDER Working Paper 2018/181. Helsinki: UNU-WIDER. Available at: https://www.wider.unu.edu/publication/new-inequality-estimate-urban-india.

Van der Weide, R., C. Lakner, and E. Ianchovichina (2018). 'Is inequality underestimated in Egypt? Evidence from house prices'. *Review of Income and Wealth*, 64: S55–79. DOI: 10.1111/roiw.12338.

Index

Note: Tables and figures are indicated by an italic 't' and 'f' following the page number. Footnote numbers are indicated by 'n.' after the page number.

1% top-end 40–1, 326
  decomposition of the share of 63
  differences between inequality trends for
    income and wealth 58
  rise of share of 33, 51, 71, 334
  rise of wealth inequality 68
  see also top-end

absolute inequality 5, 7, 18–19, 37–41, 331
  absolute inequality/absolute poverty
    trade-offs 19
  absolute inequality and growth in household
    income per capita 39f
  plot of changes in absolute poverty against
    changes in absolute inequality 40f
  rise of 42
  see also global inequality
absolute poverty
  absolute inequality/absolute poverty
    trade-offs 19
  India 157, 171–2
  plot of changes in absolute poverty against
    changes in absolute inequality 40f
  see also poverty
Adams, J.T. 258
Africa
  Afrobarometer 235–6, 237, 238, 239, 240f,
    241, 241t, 246, 247, 249t, 250t, 253t
  development strategies 5
  North Africa, low inequality 25
  poverty reduction 5
  subjective wellbeing and economic
    inequality 10, 239, 246, 247, 248
  see also SSA
agriculture
  China 136, 138–9, 141f, 149
  Great Depression 305
  green revolution, South Asia 306
  India 163, 164, 165–6, 167
  labour force 285–6
  mechanisms for promoting agriculture 298–9
  multi-pronged development strategy 297–9
  subsidies 297, 309

Akay, A. 234
Akmal, M. 50, 51
Alvaredo, F. 51, 57, 58, 74,
    75, 182
Amiel, Y. 38n.32
Anand, S. 19n.5, 25, 50–1, 55
Arndt, C. 324–5
Asher, S. 259, 260
Asia 5, 74
  Asianbarometer 236, 238, 239, 240f, 241,
    241t, 247, 249t, 250t, 254t
  green revolution, South Asia 306
  subjective wellbeing and economic
    inequality 10, 239, 246, 248
  see also East Asia
Assaad, R. 75
Atkinson, A. 20, 31, 51
Atkinson index 31, 33–4, 85, 102
  see also global inequality
Autor, D.H. 272

Banerjee, A. 161
Bassier, I. 215–16
Basu, K. 17
Beddoes, Z.M. 17
between-country inequality
  decline of 31, 322
  global inequality, between-country
    components 19f
  global inequality of wealth and income,
    'between-country' factors 59–66, 61f, 64f,
    69–70, 322
  globalization 5
  policy recommendations 71, 334, 335
Bhalla, S.S. 50
Bloome, D. 273, 274
Bookwalter, J. 234
Bosch, M. 190
Bound, J. 186, 188, 188t
Bourguignon, F. 4, 19, 20, 50–1, 186
  'iron poverty-growth-inequality triangle'
    323, 324–5
Brandolini, A. 27

Brazil 5, 109–10, 128–9
  cash transfer programmes (Family Grant) 8,
    120, 124–5, 126, 129
  decline in inequality 8, 103, 109, 113, 117–18,
    119, 125–6, 129, 327, 328
  does missing income affect distribution?
    120–2, 129
  earnings inequality 8, 109, 114, 116–18, 129
  firm effects and earnings
    inequality 116–18, 129
  Gini index 109, 121, 123, 125, 129
  growth 109, 113–14, 115
  HDI (Human Development Index) 112,
    113, 128
  high inequality 8, 134–5
  household income growth 109, 113, 115
  human development 112–13
  IBGE (Brazilian Institute of Geography and
    Statistics) 110, 120
  imputation method 121–2
  income, equality, and social
    welfare 123–4, 124t
  income distribution 109–10, 115, 129
  inequality 111t
  inter-generational inertia 8, 118, 119
  labour inequality 114
  LIS (Luxembourg Income Study) 83, 87–8,
    87f, 88f, 91f, 102, 103
  MDGs (Millennium Development
    Goals) 112, 124
  mean income 110, 111, 114, 122, 123, 124,
    125, 128
  poverty 112, 121–2, 124–5, 126, 128
  SDGs (Sustainable Development Goals) 112
  shared prosperity 114–15
  social and economic
    developments 112–15, 128–9
  social welfare 109–10, 114, 115, 125, 126, 128,
    129, 328
  taxes and distributive changes 8, 123–6
  UNU-WIDER: 'Inequality in the Giants'
    project 109n.1, 128, 325
  welfare decomposition 123–4
  see also Brazil: education; Brazilian records
    and surveys
Brazil: education 8, 111, 113, 118–20
  education as driver of changes in earnings
    distribution 117–18, 129, 329
  education inertia 119, 120, 129
  education premiums 119, 120
  see also Brazil
Brazilian records and surveys 114, 116, 325, 326
  combining surveys with PIT
    records 126–8, 129

  household surveys 110, 111, 114, 115, 116,
    118, 120, 123, 125
  PIT records (personal income tax) 111, 116,
    118, 124, 126–8, 129
  PME (Pesquisa Mensal de Emprego) 114, 120
  PNAD (Pesquisa Nacional de Amostras a
    Domicílio) 110–11, 114, 115, 116, 119,
    120–2, 123, 126–8, 326
  PNADC (Pesquisa Nacional de Amostras a
    Domicilio Contínua) 114, 120, 122
  POF (nationwide expenditure
    surveys) 120, 123
  RAIS (Registro Anual de Informações
    Sociais) 110, 116, 325
  see also Brazil
BRICS (Brazil, Russia, India, China, South Africa
    group) 8, 86, 87n.11, 90, 102
  see also Brazil; China; India; Russia;
    South Africa

Cai, M. 134, 136, 151
Campello, T. 125
Campos-Vazquez, R. 9, 180, 184, 188,
    190, 191
capitalism 18
  crony capitalism 71, 335
  meritocratic capitalism 279
the Caribbean 21
Carta, F. 27
case studies 5–6, 8–10, 321, 324–7
  inequality in five developing giants: common
    patterns? 323–4
  inequality trends and drivers 327–30
  see also Brazil; China; India; Mexico;
    South Africa
cash transfer programmes
  Brazil 8, 120, 124–5, 126, 129
  China 136–7, 141, 145, 146, 151
  Mexico 192, 193n.22, 199
  South Africa 214, 223
Chancel, L. 25, 89, 161
Checchi, D. 7–8, 323
Chen, S. 20, 22, 31
Chen, Y. 267
Chetty, R. 265, 269, 274
China 5, 75, 133, 152–3
  agriculture 136, 138–9, 141f, 149
  CHIP (China Household Income
    Project) 134–5, 139, 144, 148
  corruption 8, 133, 147, 148, 153
  decline in inequality 91, 135, 139–40, 145
  dibao programme 141, 142, 151
  distributional policies 149–52, 153
  earnings inequality 144–5, 146–7, 148

economic growth 8, 21, 63, 133, 135, 136*f*,
    137–42, 149, 153, 257, 267, 275–6, 278
education 151–2, 267–8
employment 138–9, 139*f*, 143,
    144–5, 275
fiscal spending on education, medical
    insurance, social security,
    agriculture 141–2, 141*f*
gender gap 329
Gini index 74, 88–9, 134, 134*f*, 135, 143–4,
    144*f*, 145
global income inequality and 63, 71
government efforts to moderate inequality 8,
    133, 136, 141–2, 145–6, 153, 277
government transfer programmes 136–7,
    141, 145, 146, 151
hidden income 8, 133
high inequality 264n.6, 277, 333
household income 133, 136–7, 137*f*, 143, 146,
    148, 150
hukou system 140, 146, 148, 153
'Hu–Wen New Policies' 149
income gap: regional and urban/rural
    areas 135–6, 135*t*, 138, 139–40, 142, 143,
    146, 153
income inequality 8, 133, 134–7, 148,
    152–3, 329
incomplete transition 8, 133, 140,
    147–9, 153
joint ventures 305, 307
Kuznets inverted-U curve 8, 133,
    137–42, 152–3
labour absorption 8, 133, 139, 141,
    142, 275
Lewis-type path of economic development
    138, 139, 140
LIS (Luxembourg Income Study) 83, 87*f*, 88,
    88*f*, 91, 91*f*, 102
Maoist era 141, 143, 274
market integration 8, 133
mean income 51, 71, 334
migration 138, 140, 146, 148, 277
NBS (National Bureau of Statistics)
    134, 150
non-wage income 136
one child policy 140, 275, 276
policy implications 153
population 140, 143, 146, 153
poverty reduction 8, 133, 149, 150–1,
    267, 275–6
property income 146, 148
rent-seeking 8, 133, 148, 151, 153
rising inequality 20, 74, 103, 134–6, 139–40,
    144, 149, 152–3, 276, 328, 333

rural inequality 143–4
social welfare 8, 133, 141, 142, 149–52, 153,
    274, 277
SOEs (state-owned enterprises) 144, 147, 148,
    153, 329
structural change 8, 133, 137–42
trade 142, 142*f*
transition from planned to market
    economy 8, 11, 133, 143–7, 152–3, 268,
    274–5, 276
ultra-rich population 133, 135, 148, 152,
    153, 326
UNU-WIDER: 'Inequality in the Giants'
    project 325
urban wages 144–5, 144*f*, 152
wage growth of rural–urban migrant
    workers 139, 140, 140*f*
wealth inequality 147–8
see also China: inter-generational/
    socioeconomic mobility
China: inter-generational/socioeconomic
    mobility 11, 257–8, 277–9, 333
CFPS (China Family Planning
    Survey) 258, 261–2
data 258, 261–2
declining mobility/rising inequality
    relationship 11
economic growth 257, 267, 275–6, 278
education, costs of 276–7
GGC (Great Gatsby Curve) 11, 263–4, 333
high intergenerational mobility 274, 278
human capital 274, 275, 277
income vs education mobility 263–4, 264*f*
inter-generational education
    mobility 261–2, 264
inter-generational education mobility, low
    levels of 11, 267–8, 278
inter-generational education mobility over
    time 265–8, 266*f*
inter-generational mobility vs GDP per
    capita 267, 268*f*
migration 277
optimism 257
policy implications 278–9
socioeconomic mobility, low levels of 11,
    276–7, 333
socioeconomic mobility, policy changes
    underlying the trends in 268–9, 274–7
US/China comparison 257, 263–4,
    274, 277–8
see also China; inter-generational mobility;
    US: inter-generational/socioeconomic
    mobility
Clark, A. 10, 234, 247, 331

climate change 287, 289, 310, 311
consumption 53, 78–9
    consumption floor for the developing
        world 35, 36f
    India, consumption inequality 159–60,
        159t, 169
    see also household consumption
Corak, M. 262
Cortez, W.W. 191
Covid-19 pandemic 177
Cowell, F. 25n.14, 38n.32, 85
Cowen, T. 17, 18
Cragg, M.I. 189
Credit Suisse Research Institute 52
    Credit Suisse Global Wealth Report 7, 49, 51–2
    Credit Suisse Global Wealth Databook 7,
        49, 51–2
Cupak, A. 7–8, 323

Dalenberg, D. 234
Dalton, H. 31
D'Ambrosio, C. 10, 234, 247, 331
Dang, H.-A. 8–9, 170–1
Datt–Ravallion poverty decomposition 122, 124
Davies, J.B. 7, 49, 51–2, 53, 237–8, 322
Deng Xiaoping 149
developing countries see inequality in developing
        countries
development 284
    comprehensive development strategy 311–12
    development state and successful
        development 291–2, 305, 306
    economic development and high inequality 11
    human capital, social capital, knowledge
        capital 287
    inclusive growth strategy 11, 269, 278,
        289, 311
    inequality as key development challenge 3,
        321, 330
    learning 292–3, 297, 298, 301, 303, 304–5,
        306, 307
    Lewis-type path of economic
        development 138, 139, 140
    market failure 289, 291, 292, 305, 306
    new thinking about development 286–7
    reformulating development thinking 310–12
    structural transformation 286–7, 293, 305,
        306, 311, 312
    see also export-led growth model; growth;
        multi-pronged development strategy;
        Stockholm Statement; Washington
        Consensus policies
development economics 4
Dowrick, S. 50, 51

earnings inequality 324, 332
    Brazil 8, 109, 114, 116–18, 129, 329
    China 144–5, 146–7, 148
    Mexico 9
    South Africa 9, 207, 216–20, 217t,
        218f, 225–6
    see also labour income
East Asia 21
    export-led growth model 11, 284, 286, 292,
        293–4, 310–11
education 12, 330, 335
    China 151–2, 267–8, 276–7
    distribution of active population according to
        education level 304f
    as driver of inequality 90–1, 91f, 102, 328
    India 162–3
    Mexico 9, 180, 198
    multi-pronged development strategy 304
    South Africa 9, 206, 217, 218–19, 225,
        226, 329
    see also Brazil: education; inter-generational
        mobility; China: inter-generational/
        socioeconomic mobility; US: inter-
        generational/socioeconomic mobility
Elbers, C. 163, 166–7
Elliott, D.J. 147
employment
    China 138–9, 139f, 143, 144–5, 275
    multi-pronged development strategy
        289, 297
    promoting decent work (SDG 8) 324
    South Africa, unemployment 206–7,
        224, 227
    see also labour market
Entropy indices 55
Epelbaum, M. 189
Esquivel, G. 180, 189
ethics and inequality 11–12
    concept of 'inequality' 18
    ethical aversion to extremes 31–7, 42
    wealth inequality 12
Europe
    Eurobarometer 236, 238, 239, 240f, 242t, 246,
        247, 249t, 252t, 256t
    subjective wellbeing and economic
        inequality 10, 239, 246, 247
Eurostat 4, 27
Evans, M. 75
export-led growth model 11, 284, 334
    developing countries 292
    East Asian countries 11, 284, 286, 292,
        293–4, 310–11
    industrialization 294–5
    labour absorption 286

manufacturing export-led model, end
    of 285-7
manufacturing share of GDP 285, 285*f*
replacement of 284-5, 286
success of 285, 292-4, 310-11
see also development; growth; Washington
    Consensus policies

'Fair Progress? Economic Mobility Across
    Generations Around the World' (2018
    World Bank report) 11
Fairris, D. 190
Fan, Y. 267, 268
Ferreira, F. 4, 235
Finn, A. 216-17, 219
Firpo, S. 184
Flachaire, E. 25n.14
Furman, J. 272

Garcés Urzainqui, D. 167, 168-70, 327
Gasparini, L. 74, 75
GCIP (Global Consumption and Income
    Project) 51
gender-related issues 333
    China 329
    as driver of inequality 90-1, 91*f*, 102
    gender equality (SDG 5) 323
    India 163
    South Africa 217, 219, 221, 223, 224
    US 273
GIC (growth incidence curve) 31
    absolute GIC 38, 38*f*, 43
    relative GIC 32*f*, 38, 43
Gini index 20, 22
    2008 74
    absolute Gini index 37, 39-40, 40*f*
    Brazil 109, 121, 123, 125, 129
    China 74, 88-9, 134, 134*f*, 135, 143-4, 144*f*, 145
    global inequality 32-3, 37, 39, 40*f*, 50-1
    global inequality of wealth and income 52,
        55, 56, 58, 60, 63
    income inequality 4
    India 74, 159, 159*t*, 165, 166
    intra-household inequality 25-6
    limitations of 24-5, 43
    LIS 85, 87, 87*f*, 88-9, 102
    Mexico 180, 181, 182*f*, 195, 196, 198
    PPPs 26
    relative Gini index 22*f*, 37, 39
    Russia 89
    South Africa 90, 210, 211, 212, 214, 215*t*, 216,
        219, 220, 329
    subjective wellbeing and economic
        inequality 235, 237, 246, 247-8

surveying errors 24-5
    see also inequality measurement
global financial crisis (2008) *see* Great Recession
global inequality 4, 5, 6, 10-12, 41-2, 321-2
    absolute inequality 7, 18-19, 37-41, 39*f*,
        40*f*, 42, 331
    Atkinson index 33-4
    between-/within-country components 19*f*
    concept of 'inequality' 18, 41, 42, 330-1
    consumption floor for the developing
        world 36, 36*f*
    cosmopolitan view 27
    decline of 7, 17-18, 19, 23, 30, 32-3, 41, 42,
        50, 321-2, 331
    decline of between-country inequality
        31, 322
    differing narratives on 7, 17-18
    economic integration and inequality 22
    ethical aversion to extremes in either
        tail 31-7, 42
    Gini index 33, 37, 39-40, 40*f*, 50-1
    global income inequality 7, 18, 322
    global inequality for various weights on (log)
        national mean income 30*f*, 31
    globalization and 20, 32
    literature on 50-2
    mean income 7, 20, 28, 30, 30*f*, 38, 39
    middle class 32, 40, 41, 322
    MLD (Mean Log Deviation) 20-1, 21*f*
    nationalistic approach 27-8, 42, 322
    new perspectives on 321-3
    overview of evidence on 19-23
    the poorest 32, 33, 35, 42, 322
    PPP (purchasing power parity) 26, 50, 55
    relative inequality 7, 18, 43, 321-2
    relative inequality and growth in household
        income 22-3, 22*f*
    rise of 7, 17-19, 20, 31, 41-2, 50, 322
    SIA (scale invariance axiom) 18
    Theil index 33, 34
    top-end 40, 322
    see also absolute inequality; global inequality:
        data issues; global inequality of wealth
        and income
global inequality: data issues 23-31, 321, 330-1
    intra-household inequality 25-6
    limitations of data and methodology 35-6,
        41, 43, 50-1
    nationality, role of 27-8
    sub-national prices 26
    surveying errors 24-5, 41
    testing sensitivity to allowing national income
        to matter 28-31
    see also global inequality

global inequality of wealth and income 7, 49–50,
    70–1, 322, 331
  'between-country'/'within-country'
    factors 59–66, 61f, 64f, 69–70, 322
  China and 63, 71
  counterfactual trends in income
    inequality 66–7, 67f
  counterfactual trends in wealth
    inequality 67–8, 68f
  Credit Suisse Global Wealth Databook 7,
    49, 51–2
  Credit Suisse Global Wealth Report 7, 49, 51–2
  decline of 7, 58, 66, 69–70, 331
  decomposing the inequality trend of income
    and wealth 66–70
  decomposing the level of income and wealth
    inequality 58–66, 61f, 64f
  distribution of global wealth 49, 52
  Gini index 52, 55, 56, 58, 60, 63
  global distribution of household wealth 51
  high world wealth inequality 52, 70
  mean income 51, 58–9, 60, 63, 70–1, 331
  mean/median ratio 56, 63
  micro wealth database 53
  neglect of wealth dimension of global
    inequality 52
  policy implications 71, 334, 335
  rise of 58, 66, 70, 334
  Shorrocks–Shapley decomposition 50, 60, 69
  Shorrocks–Shapley decomposition of
    changes in global income and wealth
    inequality 69–70, 70t
  Shorrocks–Shapley decomposition of global
    income inequality 61t
  Shorrocks–Shapley decomposition of global
    wealth inequality 64t
  trends in income and wealth inequality 56–8,
    56f, 57f
  WIID (World Income Inequality Database) 7,
    49, 53, 56
  see also global inequality; global inequality of
    wealth and income: data issues
global inequality of wealth and income: data
    issues 52–6
  exchange rates 54–5
  income sharing rule 54
  income/wealth definitions 53–4
  inequality index 55
  target population 54
  time period 56
  top tail adjustments 55–6
  see also global inequality of wealth
    and income
globalization 4, 5, 289, 332

elephant graph and 32
global inequality and 20, 32
middle class and 32
US 271
Golley, J. 267
Gornick, J. 75
Great Depression 305, 332
Great Recession 58, 66, 68, 207
  Mexico 181, 191, 328, 330
  monetary policy 290
  South Africa 207
Green, P. 9–10
Greenwald, B. 306
growth 323
  Brazil 109, 113–14, 115
  China 8, 21, 63, 133, 135, 136f, 137–42, 149,
    153, 257, 267, 275–6, 278
  inclusive growth strategy 11, 269, 278,
    289, 311
  India 9, 157, 175, 176, 289
  South Africa 205–7, 206t, 213, 329
  US 267, 278
  see also development; export-led growth
    model; multi-pronged development
    strategy
Gustafsson, B. 134, 148, 152

health 12, 330, 335
  India 162–3
  Mexico 192
Heckscher–Ohlin model 84, 308
Helliwell, J. 29
Hickel, J. 17, 18
Higgins, S. 193
Hilger, N.G. 267
Himanshu, P. 158, 159, 162
Hoken, H. 139
household consumption 23, 87
  India 89, 159
household income 23–4
  absolute inequality and growth in household
    income per capita 39f
  Brazil, household income growth 109,
    113, 115
  China 133, 136–7, 137f, 143, 146, 148, 150
  DHI (disposable household income) 76, 82,
    83f, 90, 94
  household membership 76–7
  Latin America, household income
    growth 109
  mean household income 22, 109, 113,
    115, 210
  relative inequality and growth in household
    income 22–3, 22f

South Africa 208–10, 209*t*
surveying errors 24–5
household inequality
  household wealth, global distribution of 51
  intra-household inequality 25–6
  South Africa 207, 213
Hsieh, C.-T. 273
Huang, J. 139
human capital 11, 287, 288, 294
  building human capital of the poorest 335
  China 274, 275, 277
  India, disparities outcomes by social
    group 160–1, 160*f*, 162–3
  India, human capital accumulation 174,
    175, 177
  inter-generational mobility 258, 264–5,
    271, 334
  US 269–70
Hundenborn, J. 208, 213–14, 216

IMF (International Monetary Fund) 290, 291,
  294, 299, 310
income, definitions
  consumption 53
  gross income 53, 81–2, 81*f*
  net income 53, 81–2
  non-monetary income 76, 79–80, 79*f*
income distribution
  Brazil 109–10, 115, 129
  data on 49
  global income distribution, literature on 52
  South Africa, top end of income
    distribution 207, 213–16, 220, 225–6
income inequality 323
  Gini index 4
  global income inequality 7, 18, 41, 322
  India 157
  mean household income/income inequality
    relation 22
  see also Brazil; China; earnings inequality;
    global inequality of wealth and income;
    labour income; LIS; Mexico; South Africa
India 5, 8–9, 75, 157–8, 175–7
  absolute poverty 157, 171–2
  agriculture 163, 164, 165–6, 167
  all-India level inequality 157, 158, 159, 169,
    169*t*, 176, 177
  bird's-eye view of inequality trends and
    dynamics 157, 158–63, 176
  caste system 157, 160*f*, 162–4, 165–6, 174
  consumption inequality 159–60, 159*t*, 169
  cross-sectional inequality 9, 170
  decline in inequality 165
  economic growth 9, 157, 175, 176, 289

gender inequality 163
Gini index 74, 159, 159*t*, 165, 166
health and education 162–3
high inequality 161
household consumption 89, 159
human capital, disparities outcomes by social
  group 160–1, 160*f*, 162–3
human capital accumulation 174, 175, 177
IHDS (India Human Development
  Surveys) 160–1, 171
income inequality 157
income mobility 170, 176
inequality measurement method 9, 161,
  176, 326–7
inequality of opportunity and economic
  growth 173–5
intra-generational income mobility 9, 158,
  170–3, 176
inter-generational mobility 166–7,
  173, 176–7
inter-generational mobility and consumption
  growth 174–5, 175*f*
inter-generational mobility in education 158,
  174, 176
lifetime inequality 9, 158, 176
LIS (Luxembourg Income Study) 83, 87*f*, 88,
  88*f*, 89, 91, 91*f*, 102
local-level inequality 9, 158, 167–70, 176
mean income, rise of 51
monetary inequality 159–61
NSS (National Sample Survey
  Organization) 159, 160–1, 168, 170–1,
  173, 327
Palanpur 158, 163–7, 165*t*, 166*t*, 167, 176–7
poverty 158, 165, 167, 176
poverty, vulnerability, and
  mobility 170–2, 173*t*
poverty reduction 9, 167, 171, 172, 175–6
the rich 161
rising inequality 9, 20, 91, 103, 157, 158,
  165–6, 176, 327, 328
spacial inequality 167–70
UNU-WIDER: 'Inequality in the Giants'
  project 157n.1, 325
village-level inequality 163–7, 168, 169*t*, 176
welfare 171, 172*t*, 173, 177
WID (World Income Distribution) 158
inequality
  concept of 18
  dysfunctionality of unequal societies 4
  economic inequality/political inequality
    link 291n.13
  ethics and 11–12
  impact of 3

inequality (*cont.*)
  as key development challenge 3, 321, 330
  literature on 3–4, 5, 50–2
  reducing inequality 3, 4, 10, 212, 278
  see also absolute inequality; between-country
    inequality; Brazil; China; global inequality;
    income inequality; India; inequality in
    developing countries; inequality drivers;
    inequality measurement; Mexico; relative
    inequality; South Africa; subjective
    wellbeing and economic inequality;
    within-country inequality
inequality in developing countries 3, 5, 21*f*
  decline and rise of inequality 20
  inequality in five developing giants: common
    patterns? 323–4
  inequality trends and drivers 327–30
  mean household income/income inequality
    relation 22
  misconception: irrelevance of inequality in
    poorer countries 3–4
  MLD (Mean Log Deviation) 20–1, 21*f*
  research on 74–5
  subjective wellbeing and economic
    inequality 234
  see also Brazil; China; India; Mexico;
    South Africa
inequality drivers 5, 6, 7, 8, 323
  economic integration 22
  education 90–1, 91*f*, 102, 328
  gender 90–1, 91*f*, 102
  labour market 328, 332
  returns to skills 328–9
  rise in equity prices 71, 334
  South Africa 208–13
inequality measurement 3, 4, 321
  challenges and limitations of 18, 36, 41, 43,
    161, 182–3, 322, 323, 324–7, 330
  China 326
  concept of 'inequality' used in 18, 41,
    42, 330–1
  cosmopolitan view 27
  cross-country data 8, 75, 235, 261, 270,
    323, 331
  data sources 6
  global income inequality 18, 41
  household surveys 6, 23, 116, 323, 324,
    325, 326
  income tax records 25, 41, 57
  India 9, 161, 176, 326–7
  inequality measures as underestimated 41
  labour force surveys 324, 325, 328
  Mexico 182–3, 325–6, 328
  nationalistic approach 27
  social welfare 31

  South Africa 325, 326
  surveys 24–5, 42, 161
  top incomes, misrepresentation/
    underestimation of 326
  triangulation 41, 331
  see also Brazilian records and surveys; GIC;
    Gini index; global inequality: data issues;
    global inequality of wealth and income:
    data issues; LIS; SWIID; Theil indices;
    WID; WIID
inter-generational mobility 11, 333
  developing/emerging countries 267
  education mobility 260, 264
  education mobility, low levels of 267
  Equalchances 258, 261
  estimating inter-generational mobility 260–1
  fairness 263, 265, 273
  GDIM (Global Database of Intergenerational
    Mobility) 261
  GGC (Great Gatsby Curve) 262–4, 263*f*
  higher inter-generational mobility 258
  higher returns to education/lower
    intergenerational mobility of income, link
    between 270–1
  human capital 258, 265, 271, 334
  income mobility 260–1
  low inter-generational mobility 258, 265
  low inter-generational mobility/high
    inequality link 333–4
  measures of 259–60
  meritocracy 263
  public policies and 269
  TSTSLS (two-sample two-stage least
    squares) 261
  see also China: inter-generational/
    socioeconomic mobility; India; US:
    inter-generational/socioeconomic mobility
IPR (intellectual property rights) 309

Johnson, G. 187, 189, 189*f*

Kaplan, D.S. 191
Katz, L.F. 269–70, 271, 272, 274
Kerr, A. 220–1
Knight, J. 140
Kong, S.T. 267
Korinek, A. 24
Krueger, A.B. 262, 269–70, 271, 272, 274
Krugman, P. 170
Kuznets, S.: inverted-U curve 4, 8, 75, 84, 137–8
  China 8, 133, 137–42, 152–3

labour income
  LIS, inequality decomposition in labour
    incomes 90–1, 91*f*

LIS, labour income availability at individual level 80, 80*f*
Mexico, labour income inequality 9, 181, 183–91, 185*f*, 198
see also earnings inequality
labour market 324
China, labour absorption 8, 133, 139, 141, 142, 275
as driver of inequality 328, 332
export-led growth model, labour absorption 286
Mexico 180, 191, 198
policies on 12, 333, 334, 335
South Africa 9, 10, 206, 211, 212–13, 216–20, 217*t*, 223–4, 225, 227
US 272, 273
see also employment
Lakner, C. 30, 31, 50–1, 55, 57, 74, 76
elephant graph of Lakner and Milanovic 32, 32*f*, 35, 40
Lambert, S. 25
Lanjouw, P. 8–9, 163, 166–7, 170–1
Latin America 74
decline in inequality 87–8
high inequality 21
household income growth 109
Latinobarometer 236, 238, 239, 240*f*, 242*t*, 246, 247, 249*t*, 251*t*, 255*t*
LIS (Luxembourg Income Study) 75, 87–8
subjective wellbeing and economic inequality 10, 239, 246, 247, 248
Leibbrandt, M. 9–10, 206, 216–17, 219
Lentz, E. 234
Lessmann, C. 26
Levine, E. 190
Levy, B. 206
Levy, S. 191, 198
Li, Q. 134, 135, 148
Li, S. 8, 134, 268, 276, 277, 278
Li, Y. 167
LIS (Luxembourg Income Study) 4, 7–8, 75–6, 102–3, 323, 331
Atkinson index 85, 102
benchmark countries 83n.6, 86
Brazil 83, 87–8, 87*f*, 88*f*, 91*f*, 102, 103
BRICS countries 8, 86, 87n.11, 90, 102
challenges of harmonizing data from middle-income countries 76–83
China 83, 87*f*, 88, 88*f*, 91, 91*f*, 102
cross-country data 8, 75, 323, 331
dataset 83
DHI (disposable household income) 76, 82, 83*f*, 90, 94
Gini index 85, 87, 87*f*, 88–9, 102
harmonized LIS data 8, 83, 331

high-income countries 4, 75, 76, 81
income inequality (Gini index) vs macroeconomic country characteristics 93, 94*f*
income shares 88*f*, 89
India 83, 87*f*, 88, 88*f*, 89, 91, 91*f*, 102
inequality decomposition in labour incomes 90–1, 91*f*
inequality measures 85–6
labour income availability at individual level 80, 80*f*
Latin American 75, 87–8
methodology 84–6
middle-income countries 4, 75–6, 83, 87*f*, 102
MLD index (Mean Log Deviation) 85, 90
non-monetary income 76, 79–80, 79*f*
regression analysis/results 83, 86, 91–102, 95*t*, 98*t*, 100*t*, 103
results, descriptive analysis 86–91
Russia 7–8, 83, 87*f*, 88*f*, 89–90, 91*f*, 102, 103
South Africa 83, 87*f*, 88*f*, 90, 91, 91*f*, 102, 103
taxes and social security contributions as part of gross income 81–2, 81*f*
trends in income inequality 87, 87*f*, 103
US 86, 87*f*, 88*f*, 91*f*
variables 84, 92*t*, 93
WID (World Inequality Database) 86, 89, 90
WIID (World Income Inequality Database) 86, 89, 90
LIT policies (learning, industrial, and technology) 290n.11, 291, 305–6
Lopez-Calva, L.F. 191
Lorenz curve 24, 33, 37, 53, 58–9, 60, 116, 222*f*
1988, 2008 Lorenz curves for global income 33*f*
LSMS (Living Standard Measurements Surveys, World Bank) 324, 327
Lu, F. 139
Luo, C. 134, 135, 146
Lustig, N. 9, 88, 184, 188, 193, 194, 196–7

Maboshe, M. 212, 220–1
McKay, A. 324–5
Magnani, E. 267, 268
Manacorda, M. 190
Martinsson, P. 234
Mazzucato, M. 306
MDGs (Millennium Development Goals) 112, 124
mean income
Brazil 110, 111, 114, 122, 123, 124, 125, 128
China 51, 71, 334
India 51

mean income (*cont.*)
  global inequality and 7, 20, 28, 30, 30*f*, 38, 39
  global inequality of wealth and income 51,
    58–9, 60, 63, 70–1, 331
  mean household income 22, 109, 113,
    115, 210
MENA (Middle East and North Africa) 74, 75
Mexico 5, 83, 180–1, 197–9
  1989–2014 income inequality
    evolution 181–3, 198
  1995 financial crisis 181, 191
  Bound and Johnson decomposition 186,
    188, 188*t*
  decline of inequality 181, 190
  education, access to higher levels of 9,
    180, 198
  ENIGH (National Survey on Households'
    Income and Expenditures) 180, 181,
    182, 190
  fiscal incidence analysis, core income
    concepts 193, 194*f*
  fiscal redistribution 9, 180, 191–9,
    196*f*, 329–30
  Gini index 180, 181, 182*f*, 195, 196, 198
  Great Recession 181, 191, 328, 330
  health 192
  high inequality 134–5, 180, 198
  income inequality: 'rise–decline–rise again'
    pattern 9, 181, 198, 328
  inequality measurement 182–3, 325–6, 328
  labour income inequality 9, 181, 183–91,
    185*f*, 198
  labour markets 180, 191, 198
  migration 191
  minimum wages, increase in 9, 198
  NAFTA (North American Free Trade
    Agreement) 190, 191
  Oaxaca–Blinder decomposition 184
  pensions, transfers, remittances 192–3, 198–9
  policy implications 198–200
  poverty 183, 197–8, 197*f*, 199–200
  Progresa programme 9, 192, 330
  PROSPERA programme 199
  relative wages: demand, supply, and
    institutions 186–91, 187*f*, 188*t*
  revenues and spending: size and
    composition 194–5
  RIF (re-centred influence function) 184,
    185*f*, 190
  rise of inequality 181, 191
  skills 9, 188–9, 190, 198, 328
  top incomes: survey-based and administrative
    data 181–3
  trade 180, 188–9, 190

unionization 183, 186–90, 198, 328
UNU-WIDER: 'Inequality in the Giants'
    project 325
welfare: social policy reforms/spending 180,
    192–3, 194–5, 195*f*, 198
Middle East 25, 161
middle class
  developing world's middle class 32n.26
  globalization and 32
  rich world's 'middle class' 40
  rich world/developing world's 'middle class'
    inequality gap 41
migration
  China 138, 140, 146, 148, 277
  Mexico 191
  US 272
Milanovic, B. 4, 20, 26, 30, 40, 50–1, 55, 56, 74,
    76, 263, 279
  on China 275, 276, 277
  elephant graph of Lakner and Milanovic 32,
    32*f*, 35, 40
Mishra, P. 191
MLD (Mean Log Deviation) 20–1, 21*f*,
    25, 85, 90
Morelli, S. 20
Morrisson, C. 50–1
Mukhopadhyay, A. 167, 168–70, 327
multi-pronged development strategy 11, 284–5,
    294–305, 311
  agriculture 297–9
  comparative advantage, reassessment
    of 307–8
  developed countries, assistance
    from 308–10, 311
  developing countries 296–7, 301, 311
  dynamic comparative advantage 305–7, 311
  education 304
  employment 289, 297
  equality and growth as complements 289
  global reserve system 11, 285, 310
  housing services 303–4
  industrial policies 11, 285, 297, 301, 305–7
  manufacturing 295–7
  mining and other natural resources 299–301
  natural resource curse 300n.22
  pro-development global trade regime 308–9
  services 301–5
  see also development; growth
Munzi, T. 7–8, 323
Murgai, R. 167
Myrdal, G. 310–11

Narayan, A. 11, 167, 173, 258, 259, 267, 269,
    273, 333

National Statistical Authorities 4
Neri, M. 8, 125
Niño-Zarazúa, M. 50, 57
Novokmet, F. 75, 89–90

OECD countries (Organisation for Economic
    Co-Operation and Development) 74, 234
Orszag, P. 272
Oxfam International 17

Pareto distribution 51, 126
Paris School of Economics, World Inequality
    Lab: *2018 World Inequality Report* 4
Perez-Arce Novaro, F. 190
Pigou–Dalton transfer axiom 33n.27, 34, 234
Piketty, T. 25, 75, 89, 161, 215, 276
PIT (personal income tax)
    Brazil, 111, 116, 118, 124, 126–8, 129
    South Africa 208, 213–14, 214f, 220–1
policies 332–5
    China, policy implications 153
    China and US: inter-generational/
        socioeconomic mobility, policy
        implications 278–9
    global inequality of wealth and income 71,
        334, 335
    inclusive and sustained policies 12, 334
    labour market 12, 333, 334, 335
    Mexico, policy implications 198–200
    South Africa, policy and fiscal incidence
        studies 207–8, 220–3, 226
    South Africa, policy implications 227
    taxes and social expenditure policies,
        importance of 326
    see also redistribution
the poorest
    1% bottom end 40
    building human capital of the poorest 335
    global inequality 32, 33, 35, 42
    as 'left behind' 35, 42
poverty
    Brazil 121–2, 124–5, 126, 128
    Datt–Ravallion poverty
        decomposition 122, 124
    India 158, 165, 167, 170–3, 172t, 176
    Mexico 183, 197, 197f, 199–200
    rural poverty 142, 149, 150, 167
    South Africa 223–4, 226
    World Bank poverty line 35
    see also absolute poverty; the poorest; poverty
        reduction
poverty reduction 4, 323
    Africa 5
    Brazil 112, 128

China 8, 133, 149, 150–1, 267, 275–6
    India 9, 167, 171, 172, 175–6
    SDG 1 323
    South Africa 9, 10, 206, 227
power asymmetries 3, 321
PPP (purchasing power parity) 26, 50, 55

Qian, N. 75

R&D (research and development) 301–2
race 333
    South Africa 219, 221, 223, 224, 225, 328
    US 273
Rama, M. 167
Ranchhod, V. 9–10
Rasch, R. 75
Ravallion, M. 275–6, 277, 322
    Atkinson index of global inequality 33–4
    Datt–Ravallion poverty
        decomposition 122, 124
    developing world's middle class 32n.26
    global inequality 7, 20, 22, 26, 36, 37, 322
redistribution 324, 333
    Brazil, taxes and distributive
        changes 8, 123–6
    China, distributional policies 149–52, 153
    Mexico, fiscal redistribution 9, 180, 191–9,
        196f, 329–30
    redistributive social policies 12, 326, 329, 334
    South Africa, fiscal redistribution 206, 207–8,
        220–3, 222f, 226, 326, 328, 329
    see also policies
relative inequality 7, 18, 37, 42, 321–2
    growth in household income and 22–3, 22f
    rise of 4–5
    SIA (scale invariance axiom) 37
    within-countries relative inequality 4–5
    see also global inequality
rent-seeking 289, 300, 307, 335
    China 8, 133, 148, 151, 153
    US 272
Robertson, R. 190
Rodríguez-Lopez, J.A. 189
Roine, J. 76, 84, 103
Rongen, G. 161
Rozelle, S. 139
Russia 75, 103
    Gini index 89
    LIS (Luxembourg Income Study) 7–8, 83, 87f,
        88f, 89–90, 91f, 102, 103

Sala-I-Martin, X. 50
Salverda, W. 233
Sato, H. 139

Schotte, S. 223
Scott, J. 9, 191, 193, 199
SDGs (Sustainable Development Goals) 36, 112, 323–4
  inequality and 3, 330
  'leave no one behind' 36
  SDG 10 3, 114, 323–4
Segal, P. 19n.5, 25, 50–1, 55
Senik, C. 234, 246
Shorrocks, A. 7, 322
SIA (scale invariance axiom) 18, 37, 42
Sicular, T. 8
Singer, P. 27
SNA (System of National Accounts) 53–4
South Africa 5, 205–8, 225–7
  decline in inequality 103
  earnings inequality 9, 207, 216
  earnings inequality, drivers of 207, 216–20, 217t, 218f, 225–6
  education 9, 206, 217, 218–19, 225, 226, 329
  fiscal redistribution 206, 207–8, 220–3, 222f, 226, 326, 328, 329
  gender-related issues 217, 219, 221, 223, 224
  Gini index 90, 210, 211, 212, 214, 215t, 216, 219, 220, 329
  government grants 10, 206, 207, 208, 209, 212, 221–2, 222f, 225
  Great Recession 207
  growth 205–7, 206t, 213, 329
  high inequality 9–10, 205, 212, 216, 220, 225, 227
  household composition 210, 210t, 212, 223–4
  household income 208–10, 219t
  household income inequality 207, 213
  inequality measurement 325, 326
  inequality persistence and low social mobility 223–5, 226
  inequality reduction 205–6, 208, 212, 218, 225, 227
  labour market 9, 206, 211, 212–13, 223–4, 225, 227
  labour market inequality 10, 212, 216–20, 217t
  LIS (Luxembourg Income Study) 83, 87f, 88f, 90, 91, 91f, 102, 103
  NIDS (National Income Dynamics Study) 208, 213, 214, 223, 224, 326
  PIT (personal income tax) 208, 213–14, 214f, 220–1
  policy and fiscal incidence studies 207–8, 220–3, 226
  policy implications 227
  post-apartheid era 9, 205, 207, 220, 225, 328

  post-apartheid income inequality, drivers of 208–13
  poverty 223–4, 226
  poverty reduction 9, 10, 206, 227
  QLFS (Quarterly Labour Force Survey) 220
  race 219, 221, 223, 224, 225, 328
  remittance income 208, 209, 212
  rising inequality 91, 206
  SARS (South African Revenue Services) 213–14, 214f, 215
  socioeconomic classes 223–5, 224f, 226
  static/dynamic decomposition methods 207, 210–11, 211t, 225
  tax system 10, 208, 221f, 227
  top end of income distribution 207, 213–16, 220, 225–6
  unemployment 206–7, 224, 227
  unionization 219, 220
  UNU-WIDER: 'Inequality in the Giants' project 207, 225, 325
SRMI (Sequential Regression Multiple Imputation) 90n.15
SSA (sub-Saharan Africa) 74, 167, 289, 294–5
  deindustrialization 294–5, 296t
  manufacturing value added 296f
  simulated manufacturing output shares 294, 295f
  see also Africa
Stiglitz, J. 11, 272, 306, 334
  inclusive growth strategy 11, 269, 278
Stockholm Statement 11, 284, 287–92, 334
  eight principles of 288, 289
  Stockholm Statement/Washington Consensus comparison 289–92
Stolper–Samuelson theorem 189
subjective wellbeing and economic inequality 10, 233–4, 247–8, 331–2
  Africa 10, 239, 246, 247, 248
  Afrobarometer 235–6, 237, 238, 239, 240f, 241, 241t, 246, 247, 249t, 250t, 253t
  Asia 10, 239, 246, 248
  Asianbarometer 236, 238, 239, 240f, 241, 241t, 247, 249t, 250t, 254t
  Barometer datasets 10, 233, 235–7, 238, 247
  comparative effects of inequality on individual well-being 234, 243, 246, 247
  current living conditions 10, 238–9, 240f, 246, 248
  data 238–9, 250t, 251t, 252t
  deprivation and satisfaction 234, 237–8, 243, 246, 247
  developing countries 234

economic conditions and inequality 243, 244*t*, 245*t*, 246
economic inequality 234
Eurobarometer 236, 238, 239, 240*f*, 242*t*, 246, 247, 249*t*, 252*t*, 256*t*
Europe 10, 239, 246, 247
future living conditions, expectations of 10, 239, 240*f*, 246, 247, 332
Gini index 235, 237, 246, 247–8
Hirschman's tunnel effect 10, 234, 246, 332
income deprivation 237
inequality measurement 235–8
Latin America 10, 239, 246, 247, 248
Latinobarometer 236, 238, 239, 240*f*, 242*t*, 246, 247, 249*t*, 251*t*, 255*t*
method 239–43
normative effects of inequality on individual well-being 234–5, 243, 247
OECD countries 234
results 243–7
subjective measures of well-being 233, 242–3
variables 238–43, 240*f*, 241*t*, 242*t*, 253*t*, 254*t*, 255*t*, 256*t*
wealth in rich country/higher levels of subjective wellbeing relationship 28
WIID (World Income Inequality Database) 10, 235, 247
SWIID (Standardized World Income Inequality Database) 235

Tarp, F. 8, 324–5
taxes 326
Brazil, taxes and distributive changes 8, 123–6
higher taxes on top incomes and wealth 334
income tax records 25, 41, 57
LIS, taxes and social security contributions as part of gross income 81–2, 81*f*
South Africa 10, 208, 221*f*, 227
see also redistribution
Theil index 19n.6, 20–1, 33, 34, 116, 169
top-end 326, 334
10% top 63, 161
Brazil 111, 129
China, ultra-rich population 133, 135, 148, 152, 153, 326
global inequality 40, 322
higher taxes on top incomes and wealth 334
income growth 10, 332–3
Mexico 181–3
South Africa 207, 213–16, 220, 225–6
top incomes, misrepresentation/underestimation of 326
see also 1% top-end

trade
China 142, 142*f*
Mexico 180, 188–9, 190
translation invariance axiom 37, 42
Triffin Paradox 310

UN (United Nations) 3
unionization
Mexico 183, 186–90, 198, 328
South Africa 219, 220
US 271
UNU-WIDER: 'Inequality in the Giants' project 5–6, 321, 324, 331
Brazil 109n.1, 128, 325
China 325
data 324, 325
India 157n.1, 325
Mexico 325
South Africa 207, 225, 325
US (United States)
globalization 271
high inequality 264n.6, 333
labour market 272, 273
LIS (Luxembourg Income Study) 86, 87*f*, 88*f*, 91*f*
migration 272
rent-seeking 272
rise of inequality 269–72, 333
unionization 271
see also US: inter-generational/socioeconomic mobility
US: inter-generational/socioeconomic mobility 11, 257–8, 277–9, 333
American Dream 257–8
data 258, 261–2
economic growth 267, 278
education, costs of 270
EITC (Earned Income Tax Credit) 273
gender and 273
GGC (Great Gatsby Curve) 263–4, 333
Head Start programme 273
human capital 269–70
income vs education mobility 263–4, 264*f*
inter-generational education mobility 261–2, 264
inter-generational education mobility, low levels of 11, 267, 278
inter-generational education mobility over time 265–8, 266*f*
inter-generational income mobility 272, 273
inter-generational mobility vs GDP per capita 267, 268*f*
optimism 257–8

US: inter-generational/socioeconomic
    mobility (*cont.*)
  policy implications 274, 278–9
  PSID (Panel Study of Income
    Dynamics) 258, 261–2
  race 273
  socioeconomic mobility, low levels of 11, 258,
    269, 333
  socioeconomic mobility, policy changes
    underlying the trends in 268–74
  stagnation in inter-generational mobility 267,
    269, 278
  US/China comparison 257, 263–4,
    274, 277–8
  wage premium for college education 270
  see also China: inter-generational/
    socioeconomic mobility; inter-
    generational mobility; US

Van der Weide, R. 11, 173–5, 259, 269, 333
Van de Werfhorst, H.G. 233
Van Zanden, J.L. 50
Vigh, M. 173–5

Wagner's Law 28
Wan, H. 134, 148, 152
Washington Consensus policies 284, 294
  criticism of 286, 289, 290–1, 306
  Stockholm Statement/Washington Consensus
    comparison 289–92
wealth, definition 53
wealth inequality
  1% top-end 68
  China 147–8
  ethics and 12
  see also global inequality of wealth
    and income
welfare 31
  Brazil 109–10, 114, 115, 123–4, 125, 126, 128,
    129, 328
  China 8, 133, 141, 142, 149–52, 153, 274, 277
  India 171, 172t, 173, 177
  Mexico 180, 192–3, 194–5, 195f, 198

wellbeing 6, 7, 323
  Gallup well-being data 234
  World Happiness Reports 234
  see also subjective wellbeing and economic
    inequality
WID (World Income Distribution) 158
WID (World Inequality Database, World
  Inequality Lab) 25, 86, 89, 90
WIID (World Income Inequality Database,
  UNU-WIDER) 4
  global inequality of wealth and income 7,
    49, 53, 56
  LIS 86, 89, 90
  subjective wellbeing and economic
    inequality 10, 235, 247
WIPO (World International Properties Rights
  Organization) 309
within-country inequality 5, 322, 331
  bias in inequality measurement 26, 41
  global inequality, within-country
    components 19f
  global inequality of wealth and income,
    'within-country' factors 59–66, 61f, 64f,
    69–70, 322
  policy recommendations 71, 334, 335
  relative inequality 4–5
  rise in equity prices 71, 334
Wittenberg, M. 219–20
Wolfensohn, Jim 311n.34
Woolard, I. 212, 214–16, 220–1
World Bank 35, 299
  PovCalnet 4
World Economic Forum 3
world income databases 51
  World Top Income Database 51
  World Wealth and Income Database 51
  see also WID; WIID
WTO (World Trade Organization) 142, 189, 297

Yitzhaki, S. 237
Yue, X. 134, 136, 151

Zhu, R. 267, 268